Canadian Churches and the First World War

McMaster Divinity College Press
McMaster General Series 4

Canadian Churches and the First World War

edited by
GORDON L. HEATH

PICKWICK *Publications* · Eugene, Oregon

CANADIAN CHURCHES AND THE FIRST WORLD WAR

McMaster Divinity College General Series 4

Copyright © 2014 Wipf and Stock Publishers. All rights reserved. Except for brief quotations in critical publications or reviews, no part of this book may be reproduced in any manner without prior written permission from the publisher. Write: Permissions, Wipf and Stock Publishers, 199 W. 8th Ave., Suite 3, Eugene, OR 97401.

McMaster Divinity College Press
1280 Main Street West
Hamilton, Ontario, Canada
L8S 4K1

Pickwick Publications
An Imprint of Wipf and Stock Publishers
199 W. 8th Ave, Suite 3
Eugene, OR 97401

www.wipfandstock.com

ISBN 13: 978-1-62564-121-2

Cataloging-in-Publication data:

Canadian churches and the first world war / edited by Gordon L. Heath.

xiv + 296 p. ; 23 cm. Includes bibliographical references and indexes.

McMaster Divinity College Press General Series 4

ISBN 13: 978-1-62564-121-2

1. History of Churches in Canada. I. Heath, Gordon L. II. Title. III. Series.

BX6251. B25 2014

Manufactured in the U.S.A.

Contents

List of Illustrations   vii

Contributors   ix

Introduction   1

1 The South African War as Prelude to the First World War
—*Gordon L. Heath*   15

2 "We are all involved in the same issue": Canada's English-Speaking Catholics and the Great War
—*Mark G. McGowan*   34

3 French-Speaking Catholics in Quebec and the First World War—*Simon Jolivet*   75

4 "Khaki has become a sacred colour": The Methodist Church and the Sanctification of World War One
—*David B. Marshall*   102

5 For Empire and God: Canadian Presbyterians and the Great War—*Stuart Macdonald*   133

6 The Anglican Church and the Great War
—*Melissa Davidson*   152

7 "O God of Battles": The Canadian Baptist Experience of the Great War—*Michael A. G. Haykin and Ian Hugh Clary*   170

8 Canadian Lutherans and the First World War
—*Norm Threinen*   197

9   Quakers and Mennonites and the Great War
    —*Robynne Rogers Healey*   218

10 Dismissed: Military Chaplains
    and Canadian Great War History—*Duff Crerar*   241

11 Paying "the price of war": Canadian Women and the Churches
    on the Home Front—*Lucille Marr*   263

Name Index   285

Subject Index   289

Scripture Index   295

Illustrations

1. First page of Rev. F. G. Scott's Sermon in *The Mitre* of November 1899. Image taken by Gordon L. Heath, of the copy in Anglican Church of Canada General Synod Archives, Toronto, Ontario.   23

2. Bishop Fallon meeting with Catholic Chaplains in France, May 1918. From Mark McGowan's collection, photographer unknown.   49

3. The Great War Plaque at Jarvis Street Baptist Church in Toronto. Photo by Chisso Wang.   171

4. A Canadian chaplain presides at the burial of an Officer, October 1916 at the Somme. Image Credit: Canada, Department of National Defence/Library and Archives Canada, copy negative PA-000652.   248

5. A Canadian chaplain visits with the wounded at a relay station behind the line. Image Credit: Canada, Department of National Defence/Library and Archives Canada, copy negative PA-001779.   251

Contributors

EDITOR AND CONTRIBUTOR

Gordon L. Heath (PhD, St. Michael's College) is Associate Professor of Christian History at McMaster Divinity College, and serves as Director of the Canadian Baptist Archives. His recent appointment to the Centenary Chair in World Christianity at the college reflects his growing interest in study of persecution leading to the elimination of Christian communities around the world. His publications include *A War with a Silver Lining: Canadian Protestant Churches and the South African War, 1899–1902* (McGill-Queen's University Press, 2009), and *Doing Church History: A User-friendly Introduction to Researching the History of Christianity* (Clements, 2008). He is co-author with Stanley E. Porter of the *The Lost Gospel of Judas: Separating Fact from Fiction* (Eerdmans, 2007). He has also recently co-edited *Canadian Baptists and Public Life* (Pickwick, 2012) and *Baptism: Historical, Theological and Pastoral Perspectives* (Pickwick, 2011).

CONTRIBUTORS

Ian Hugh Clary (ThM, Toronto Baptist Seminary) is a doctoral candidate at the Universiteit van die Vrystaat (Blomfontein) where he is writing a dissertation on the evangelical historiography of Arnold Dallimore, a twentieth-century Canadian Baptist. Ian has published two Canadian Baptist histories with Michael Haykin, and has written academic articles for *Southern Baptist Journal of Theology*, *American Theological Inquiry*, *Mid-America Journal of Theology*, *Scottish Bulletin of Evangelical Theology*, and others. Ian lectures part-time for Toronto Baptist Seminary, and teaches at Boyce College, Louisville, Kentucky. Ian and his wife Vicky have three children and live in Toronto where Ian ministers in a Baptist church.

x   *Contributors*

DUFF CRERAR completed his PhD in history at Queen's University (1989). Since then, he has published *Padres in No Man's Land: Canadian Chaplains and the Great War* (McGill-Queen's University Press, 1995), contributed a chapter on Alberta in World War One to that Province's Centennial History in 2005, and written several articles on Canadian military chaplaincy and Scottish Presbyterian migration to Canada in the nineteenth century. He also co-edited *Treaty 8 Re-visited*, a centennial history of the Canadian government's settlement with the First Nations and Métis of Northern Alberta. He is the Subject Matter Expert for the Canadian Armed Forces Chaplain General's Branch, and has taught incoming candidates and those preparing to deploy at the CF Chaplain School and Centre at Camp Borden, Ontario, since 2000.

MELISSA DAVIDSON, MA in Religious Studies (Church History) from McGill University (2013), is currently pursuing a PhD in history at the University of Ottawa. Her MA thesis is entitled "Preaching the Great War: Canadian Anglicans and the War Sermon, 1914–1918" and is a study of Anglican clerical rhetoric in Canada during the war. Her doctoral research will be an expanded exploration of clerical rhetoric in the major Canadian denominations during the Great War period.

MICHAEL A. G. HAYKIN is currently Professor of Church History and Biblical Spirituality at The Southern Baptist Theological Seminary in Louisville, Kentucky, and the Director of the Andrew Fuller Center for Baptist Studies, which operates under the auspices of The Southern Baptist Theological Seminary. Up until recently he was also Research Professor of the Irish Baptist College at Queen's University, Belfast, N. Ireland. He is the author of a number of books relating to Patristics and Baptist history, including *The Spirit of God: The Exegesis of 1 and 2 Corinthians in the Pneumatomachian Controversy of the Fourth Century* (Brill, 1994); *One Heart and One Soul: John Sutcliff of Olney, His Friends, and His Times* (Evangelical, 1994); editor of *The Life and Thought of John Gill (1697–1771): A Tercentennial Appreciation* (Brill, 1997); *The Armies of the Lamb: The Spirituality of Andrew Fuller* (Joshua, 2001); editor of *The Pure Fountain of the Word: Andrew Fuller as an Apologist* (Paternoster, 2004); editor with Kenneth J. Stewart of *The Emergence of Evangelicalism: Exploring Historical Continuities* (Apollos/InterVarsity, 2008); and *Rediscovering the Church Fathers* (Crossway, 2011).

ROBYNNE ROGERS HEALEY, PhD, is Associate Professor of History and co-director of the Gender Studies Institute at Trinity Western University in Langley, British Columbia. Her publications include *From Quaker to Upper Canada: Faith and Community among Yonge Street Friends, 1801–1850* (McGill-Queen's University Press, 2006) and a number of articles on Quakers and Quakerism. Her current research interests include the twentieth-century peace testimony, Canadian Quakerism, gender and Quakerism, and the transatlantic Quaker network in the eighteenth and nineteenth centuries.

SIMON JOLIVET is a historian. His research interests focus on the history of the Irish diaspora in Quebec and the rest of Canada and on the interactions entertained between French and Irish Canadian political and religious elites from 1890 to 1930. His book entitled *Le vert et le bleu: Identité irlandaise et identité québécoise au tournant du XXe siècle* (Les Presses de l'Université de Montréal, 2011) has recently won many academic prizes.

STUART MACDONALD is the Professor of Church and Society at Knox College, University of Toronto. He is the author of *The Witches of Fife: Witch-Hunting in a Scottish Shire, 1560–1710*. He continues to research in the field of Scottish history. The other major area of his research relates to the Presbyterian Church in Canada and the Canadian churches after the Second World War. He has written on education, ethnicity, attitudes to Vatican II, changing religious demographics (with Dr. Brian Clarke) and preaching in the First World War.

LUCILLE MARR, PhD, is adjunct professor at McGill University's Faculty of Religious Studies and course lecturer in church history there and at the Montreal School of Theology. She is a licensed clergyperson, having served as pastor at Mennonite Fellowship of Montreal as well as chaplain at Montreal's Presbyterian College. Her publications include *"I guess I won't be able to write everything I see . . .": Alice Snyder's Letters Home, 1948–1950* (Pandora, 2009) and *Transforming Power of a Century: The Evolution of Mennonite Central Committee in Ontario* (Pandora, 2003). She also has to her credit numerous articles pertaining to the history of gender and church institutions (including Mennonite Central Committee and Christian Education in the United Church of Canada) and the Brethren in Christ response to mental illness. Her current research is focused on the biographies of a father and daughter who together were the impetus for major change in the nineteenth-century American Brethren in Christ community.

DAVID B. MARSHALL (PhD, University of Toronto) is a member of the Department of History at the University of Calgary. His publications include *Secularizing the Faith: Canadian Protestant Clergy and the Crisis of Faith 1860–1940* (University of Toronto Press, 1992) and "'I thank God . . . that I am proud of my boy': Fatherhood and Religion in the Gordon Family," in E. A. Heaman et al., eds., *Essays in Honour of Michael Bliss: Figuring the Social* (University of Toronto Press, 2008). Recent essays include "Religion in Canada, 1867–1945," which appeared in the *Cambridge History of Religions in North America*, edited by Stephen J. Stein, and "Biography in the Public Square: Canadian Biography and the Canadian Identity" in *How Canadians Communicate about Politics*, edited by David Tars and Christopher Waddell. Currently he is completing a biography of the clergyman Charles W. Gordon who wrote under the pseudonym "Ralph Connor."

MARK G. MCGOWAN is a Professor of History at the University of Toronto and from 2002 to 2011 served as Principal of St. Michael's College. He is the recipient of four university teaching awards and now serves as Coordinator of the Book & Media Studies Program, and as a Special Advisor to the Vice-Provost (Students) at the University of Toronto. A specialist in the religious, migration, and educational history of Canada, he published *The Waning of the Green: Catholics, the Irish and Identity in Toronto, 1887–1922* (McGill-Queen's University Press, 1999), *Michael Power (1804–1847): The Struggle to Build the Catholic Church on the Canadian Frontier* (McGill-Queen's University Press, 2005), and *Creating Canadian Historical Memory: The Case of the Famine Migration of 1847* for the Canadian Historical Association (2006). His most recent book, *Death or Canada: The Irish Famine Migration to Toronto, 1847* (Novalis, 2009), was partnered with an Ireland-Canada co-production feature-length documentary of the same name. Currently, he is researching a history of religion and broadcasting in Canada, and writing a book on Canada's Irish Catholics and the First World War.

NORMAN J. THREINEN was born in rural Manitoba, raised in Saskatchewan, and attended Concordia College in Alberta. A clergyman of Lutheran Church–Canada since 1961, he subsequently received his theological training in St. Louis, Missouri, where he also earned his STM (1962) and ThD (1980). His dissertation was entitled "The Convergence of Canadian Lutheranism." He has served as a parish pastor, church administrator, and seminary professor. He has travelled and worked extensively in Europe and Ukraine and has been a prolific writer on Canadian Lutheranism. Included among his recent books are *A Religious-Cultural Mosaic*, *A History of Lutherans in Canada* and *They Called Him Red*. He presently lives in retirement with his wife Muriel in Summerland, British Columbia.

Introduction

GORDON L. HEATH

CANADIAN CHURCHES HAD AN influence on society unlike any other institution at the beginning of the twentieth century, and Protestant and Catholic leaders and organizations were committed to shaping national identity in the decades following Confederation.[1] There were challenges to overcome in the new nation, as well as competition between Christian communions; however, optimism best describes the overall ethos of the churches. Increased coordination and cooperation among Protestants was achieved through church unions, home mission work was expanding, immigrants were being assimilated into the nation, and the ongoing Christianizing (whether Catholic or Protestant) of Canada seemed to be proceeding apace. In 1911 there were just over seven million Canadians. There were 2,833,000 Catholics comprising 39.3 percent of the Canadian population. The Methodists, Presbyterians, Anglicans, and Baptists were the largest and most influential Protestant denominations at that time, with 1,079,000 Methodists, 1,115,000 Presbyterians, 1,043,000 Anglicans, and 382,000 Baptists for a total of 50.6 percent of the Canadian population.[2] Lutherans were just over 3 percent of the population, with numerous other Christian groups hovering around 1 percent or less.[3] The optimism of those years can be seen in the churches' publications. For instance, *Westminster*'s "Canada in the Twentieth Century" expressed the expectations and hopes of many when it sur-

---

1. For instance, see Airhart, "Ordering a Nation"; Fay, *History of Canadian Catholics*; Noll, *History of Christianity*, ch. 10; McGowan, "Rendering unto Caesar."

2. Semple, *Lord's Dominion*, 182.

3. Wright, "Protestant Tradition," 141.

mised that there could be up to seventy to eighty million Canadians by the end of the new century.[4] With similar optimism the *Canadian Epworth Era* listed the many reasons for pride in Canada: development of natural resources, population increases, cultivated prairies, prosperity, and loyal bonds with Britain. With all of these exciting developments, it concluded, "May we not reasonably expect this Dominion to become one of the greatest countries in the world? Let us seek to do all we can to make it so."[5]

There was optimism as well in regards to international relations. Developments in international arbitration that emerged from the First Hague Conference (1899) and the Second Hague Conference (1907) fueled expectations that differences between imperial powers could be resolved through nonviolent means. Growing tensions in Europe were noted in the months before the war, and were commented on in church papers, synods, presbyteries, and the like, but Canadian church leaders and congregants entered the summer of 1914 with little inkling of the unmitigated disaster looming just over the horizon, and were unprepared when they found themselves at war on 4 August 1914.

Canada's military was also unprepared for the war, its relatively small number of soldiers and officers mainly under-trained and overconfident.[6] In its previous war in 1899–1902, Canada had sent over seven thousand troops to fight alongside the British and other colonial troops against the Boers in South Africa. While the war in Africa did reveal deficiencies in Canada's military, as well as foster tensions between English and French Canadians over support for imperial wars, it did little to burden the economy of the nation as a whole. The war in Europe, on the other hand, rapidly militarized all aspects of Canadian life as "total war" became a grim reality. The Canadian Expeditionary

---

4. "Canada in the Twentieth Century," *Westminster*, 5 January 1901, 8.

5. "Dominion Day," *Canadian Epworth Era*, July 1900, 209. For similar sentiment, see Rev. W. E. Norton, "The Attitude of the Church towards the Political Life of the Country," *Canadian Baptist*, 20 December 1900, 802; "Our Canadian Future," *Westminster*, 23 June 1900, 723–24; Rev. James S. Ross, "Canada—Its Extent and Its Resources," *Pleasant Hours*, 30 June 1900, 103; "Canada since Confederation," *Onward*, 9 November 1901, 353; "Greater Canada," *Canadian Churchman*, 13 February 1902, 101; "1900," *Canadian Churchman*, 4 January 1900, 4–5; "Canada's Growth," *Westminster*, 4 January 1902, 7; "Our Country," *Onward*, 18 August 1900, 259; "Our Own Country Best," *Pleasant Hours*, 21 June 1902, 100.

6. Morton, *Military History*, 131.

Force (CEF) grew to be a potent fighting force; Canada eventually sent close to 620,000 troops (roughly 8 percent of the Canadian population) and experienced 60,000 dead and 173,000 injured.[7]

While there were a number of factors that contributed to the outbreak of war, it was the assassination of Archduke Franz Ferdinand of Austria, along with his wife Sophie, at Sarajevo, Serbia, on 28 June 1914 that set in motion the decisions that culminated in multiple declarations of war. Austria-Hungary declared war on Serbia on 28 July 1914 to punish it for its complicity in the shooting. Germany declared war on Russia on 1 August 1914 in support of its ally Austria-Hungary. Anticipating hostilities with France (a Russian ally), Germany declared war on France a few days later and invaded Belgium on the way to Paris. Britain gave Germany an ultimatum to withdraw from neutral Belgium, and when this was ignored declared war on Germany on 4 August 1914. With that declaration of war Canada was automatically at war in a conflict that belligerents optimistically believed would be over by Christmas. Major powers joined the fray in the coming years: the Ottoman Turks entered the war on the side of Germany and Austria-Hungary on 28 October 1914, Italy declared war on Germany and Austria-Hungary on 23 May 1915 as did the United States on 6 April 1917. The Central Powers of Germany, Austria-Hungary, Bulgaria, and the Ottoman Empire were at war eventually with over twenty-five nations that comprised the Entente Powers. Wracked by revolution, Russia sued for peace in 1917 and signed the Treaty of Brest-Litovsk in March 1918. However, after an exhaustive and near fatal struggle, the Entente Powers prevailed over the Central Powers by late 1918.

The war was waged in Europe, Africa, and Asia, as well as in the Atlantic, Pacific, and Indian Oceans, but for Britain and Canada the Western Front was the critical theatre of operations. Repeated attempts to break through the trenches on the Western Front in order to return to a war of mobility led to horrific casualties, and the static war of attrition became a living nightmare. Modern machine guns, artillery, poison gas, and barbed wire took a grim toll; for instance, the first day of the Battle of the Somme (1916) saw close to 20,000 British dead and 35,000 wounded. By the end of the six month battle, there were approximately one million casualties on both sides. Canadian participation in battles at Ypres, Vimy, and elsewhere led to similar shocking rates of casualties.

---

7. Clodfelter, *Warfare and Armed Conflicts*, 481.

For instance, at the Battle of Passchendaele, 1917, the CEF experienced 15,000 casualties in one month.[8] The overall cost of human life during the entire war was staggering: over eight million dead and twenty-one million wounded, out of sixty-five million mobilized.[9] The rate of deaths for the entire war was an average of 6,000 soldiers a day.[10] The war has been portrayed as the "opening of an age of catastrophe"[11] and the beginning of the "bloodiest century in modern history."[12] The implications of the war defy description in this short summary. Suffice it to say that not only did the Ottoman genocide of Armenian Christians (over one million deaths) set in motion a disturbing precedent for the treatment of minorities mimicked in subsequent conflicts, the war also directly contributed to the outbreak and spread of the Spanish Influenza (fifty to one hundred million deaths), the Second World War (sixty to eighty million deaths), the Cold War, and the post-colonial breakup of European empires.

Research on Canada and the war is extensive, with the energies of historians being expended for decades on this iconic nation-building war. Such histories have focused on domestic politics, economics and industry, battles and the performance of Canadian troops, and the impact of the war on Canada both during and after the conflagration.[13] Most accounts, however, either ignore outright or merely mention in passing the churches and the war. While this exclusion may reflect the contemporary marginalization of the churches from Canadian public life and national vision, it certainly does not do justice to the remarkable influence of the wartime churches nor to the religious identity of the young Dominion. Increasingly, scholars of religion in Canada are noting the important role religion has played in public life,[14] and this volume continues that trajectory of highlighting the churches' national vision(s) and support for the war effort, or—in the case of Mennonites, Quakers,

---

8. Copp, "Military Effort," 54.
9. Bourne, "Total War I," 137. Figures of casualties vary considerably.
10. Clodfelter, *Warfare and Armed Conflicts*, 479.
11. Stevenson, *1914–1918*, 503.
12. Ferguson, *War of the World*, xxxiv.
13. Morton and Granatstein, *Marching to Armageddon*; Morton, *Military History*; Morton, *Fight or Pay*; Morton, *Number's Up*; Mackenzie, *First World War*; Miller, *Our Glory*; Vance, *Maple Leaf Empire*; Winegard, *King and Kanata*; Cook, *At the Sharp End*; Cook, *Shock Troops*.
14. For instance, see Van Die, *Religion and Public Life*; Miedema, *For Canada's Sake*; Heath and Wilson, *Baptists and Public Life*.

French Catholics, and individual dissenters—the difficulties faced when religious convictions and ethnic identities clashed with Canadian war aims. Of course, at some time in the future there needs to be a synthesis of various denominational accounts into a unified work on the churches and the war as a whole.

The neglect of the war is striking among scholars of religion. Denominational histories pay scant attention to it.[15] Surprisingly, there has been no doctoral dissertation focused solely on the churches and the war and only one monograph on the churches and the First World War.[16] That monograph, Duff Crerar's *Padres in No Man's Land*, however, focuses exclusively on chaplains. Nonetheless, various Master's theses and journal articles document a range of issues related to the churches and war; for instance, imperial identity, support for the war, conscription, dissent, the home front, the impact of the war, and the postwar period are treated in varying depth.[17] The authors of this volume provide a detailed summary of various Christian traditions and the war, both synthesizing and furthering previous research. However, readers will quickly note that some chapters that should be included in this volume are not. Perhaps the most obvious omission is a chapter on Eastern Orthodoxy and the war. The eastern European origins of many Orthodox in Canada meant that a significant number were from regions that belonged to the Central Powers. During the war there was concern expressed that those communities could be sympathetic to the Central Powers and subversive to the Canadian war effort.[18] Other areas of interest that need to be pursued in the coming years are dissident communities or individuals, church publications for children,[19] smaller denominations or movements such as the Salvation Army and Pentecostals, and the attitudes of French Catholics outside of Quebec to the war.

---

15. For instance, see Carrington, *Anglican Church*, 252; Renfree, *Heritage and Horizon*, 210–11; Moir, *Enduring Witness*, 207–12; Fay, *History of Canadian Catholics*, 172–75. For a noteworthy exception, see Semple, *Lord's Dominion*, 395–403.

16. It should also be noted that there has been no doctoral dissertation that has focused on the churches and the Second World War. Faulkner's dissertation, "For Christian Civilization," only partly covers the Second World War years (1939–1942).

17. For a comprehensive survey of research on Canadian churches and war, see Heath, "Canadian Churches."

18. Boudreau, "Enemy Alien Problem."

19. For an example of imperialism in church children's publications during an earlier war, see Heath, "Prepared to do."

The chapters in this volume both deepen our understanding and break new ground in regards to our knowledge of the churches and the war. Gordon L. Heath situates the churches' responses to the Great War in the larger context of Canada's participation in the South African War. He demonstrates how the reactions of the churches to the Great War were a continuation of precedents established during the war in Africa, and the trajectories established during that smaller conflict were followed by the churches in the larger conflict. Studies that investigate the Canadian churches and the First World War often ignore such precedents, and for this reason, they are missing vital links with a previous war that shaped the churches' wartime conceptions and practices. In fact, Heath argues, no study of the churches and the Great War can be complete without recognizing the legacy of reactions to the South African War.

What can be lost in the discussion of Canadian Catholics and the war is the reality that the Catholic Church was much more than just its French Canadian majority. In his chapter, Mark McGowan details the struggle of English-speaking Catholics to achieve a level of respectability in Canada among their Protestant neighbors. It is well known that the Great War ripped Canada apart along linguistic, ethnic, and class lines, but little has been written on the troubled situation of English-speaking Catholics who were torn between their linguistic and cultural ties to English-speaking Protestant Canada on the one hand, and their religious ties to French Canada on the other. In the period leading up to the war, English-speaking Catholics had improved their material conditions in Canada, advanced in their political status, and had increasingly become more comfortable in identifying themselves with the patriotic aspirations of other English-speaking Canadians and the international questions relating to the British Empire. Despite ongoing Protestant prejudice and French-Catholic opposition, this identification with English Canada led to widespread support for the war among English-speaking Catholics.

Simon Jolivet demonstrates how the events of the war forced the Catholic authorities in Quebec to adapt to the new reality. After 1916, public opinion in Quebec grew increasingly suspicious of the government's decisions and the episcopate had to revise its traditional position of unreserved loyalty to the British crown and Empire. Feeling betrayed by the Canadian Government and Sir Robert Borden, Quebec Bishops, such as Cardinal Louis-Nazaire Bégin and Montreal's Archbishop Paul

Bruchési, felt they had little choice but to support their parishioners and even some of their own priests who publicly condemned the government. In 1918, some of their own influential priests, such as Canon Philippe Perrier and Canon Lionel Groulx, asked their brethren not to fill out the National Register created by Prime Minister Borden and encouraged them to oppose conscription. However, Jolivet notes that the Acadian or Franco-Ontarian episcopate did not always mirror attitudes emanating from Quebec, an indication of how the war contributed to tensions and divisions among French-speaking Catholics.

The Methodist Church of Canada's response to the First World War has received the lion's share of attention from Canadian historians, and, as David Marshall argues, there was no uniform response to the war on the part of the Methodist Church. There were no easy or straightforward answers to the complicated and urgent questions posed by wartime, such as the relationship between the Christian faith and war, the use of violence and resort to killing, the reasons for and significance of sacrifice, the meaning of death, and the nature of the afterlife. Within Methodism, there was a range of experiences and perspectives and, in many cases, religious beliefs and practices changed or were fluid depending on the particular circumstances being faced in the chaos of the war. Some Methodists questioned the existence of a loving and merciful God as a result of the terrible carnage of the war and others were critical of the Methodist Church's identification with the cause of the war. On the other hand, the Christian notion of salvation through sacrifice as a way to understand the terrible toll of the war offered a powerful note of consolation.

Stuart Macdonald focuses on the Presbyterian Church in Canada and its reaction to the war. He traces the widespread support for the nation, Britain, and Empire during the war, as well as noting an evolution in the discourse from the war being a "just war" to the war being understood as a "holy war." The war was most often portrayed as neither a political or economic contest nor a scramble for colonies or empire; rather, it was deemed to be an apocalyptic struggle between good and evil. Macdonald notes how Presbyterians raised issues with the government such as venereal disease or temperance, but never challenged the core issue of the war itself. Despite their yearly declarations of independence and a covenanting tradition that affirmed an independence from the state, Canadian Presbyterians made little distinction between their loyalty to King Jesus and their loyalty to the King of Great Britain and the Empire.

Melissa Davidson notes that by 1916 Anglicans made up roughly 40 percent of the CEF.[20] Given their pre-war population, as many as 12 to 16 percent of all Canadian Anglicans were in uniform by the fall of 1916. Davidson identifies the near universal support for the war, and argues that the war, for Anglicans, was neither a just war fought for political reasons nor a holy war fought because God had ordained it, but a righteous war fought in defence of Christian values and civilization and understood as part of Britain's imperial mission. She also details the enormous impact the war had on the denomination; Anglican families faced widespread dislocation from fathers and husbands, local churches and parishes suffered from lack of men and workers, theological colleges and seminaries were barely attended, and numerous bishops and societies also expressed difficulties caused by a lack of workers and/or funds.

The support of Baptists for the war effort, Michael Haykin and Ian Clary argue, was primarily rooted in support for the unjustly invaded nation of Belgium as well as loyalty to their "motherland," Britain. Accounts of German atrocities confirmed and reinforced their initial outrage. Haykin and Clary's examination of Baptists primarily—but not exclusively—in central Canada indicates that Baptist support was widespread, and was bolstered by the preaching of T. T. Shields, the well-known pastor of Jarvis Street Baptist Church in Toronto. They do note that while Baptist leadership officially supported conscription, there were some Baptists, such as students at McMaster University, who objected to conscription because they did not want to abandon traditional liberal principles by enforcing compulsory military service. Haykin and Clary also detail the cost of the war on the churches, such as the departure of men overseas leading to churches without pastors.

Most Lutherans in Canada were a part of ethnic churches that were self-consciously German, Icelandic, Norwegian, Swedish, Finnish, or Danish, and Norm Threinen details how, as the war progressed, these Lutherans were increasingly viewed with suspicion and treated harshly by both government and citizens. Anti-German sentiment was particularly strong in areas where there was a high concentration of Germans,

---

20. Up until 1955 what we today call the Anglican Church was called the Church of England in Canada. For simplicity and ease of identification, the modern title "Anglican" is used throughout this volume.

such as Berlin, Ontario (renamed Kitchener during the war). Threinen describes how the war forced a Canadianization of the Lutheran churches. It played a direct role in leading the Lutheran bodies in Canada to cooperate in support of certain vital ministries, and, in the process, raising their awareness of their Canadian identity. The closure of church schools during the Great War was a severe blow to German Lutheran communities in terms of their identity, but led to an increased English-Canadian content in classes. The need to make statements that disagreed with the opinions of the leadership of their church's parent body in Germany led Canadian Lutherans to become aware that they were not merely a northern branch of North American Lutheranism; they had an identity that was uniquely Canadian.

Robynne Healey demonstrates how the years preceding the First World War, as well as the war itself, were a turning point for the Religious Society of Friends. Canadian Quakers, alongside Quakers around the world, began to take an active position for peace and against war, seeking to understand and ameliorate the underlying causes of armed conflict. The war was also pivotal for Canadian Mennonites. While they remained committed to the separation of their communities from mainstream Canadian society in this period, the war brought disparate Mennonite groups together in cooperation. Representatives from a number of Mennonite groups joined together to establish the Non-Resistant Relief Organization (NRRO), and Mennonites spearheaded the founding of the Conference of Historic Peace Churches. Nevertheless, ethnic identity separated the war experience of Quakers and Mennonites. Amidst the rhetoric of patriotism, ethnic nationalism, and anti-Germanism of the First World War, pacifist Mennonites were considered dirty shirkers, potential spies, and unfit as "true" Canadians. Quakers, on the other hand, were respected as people of conscience and conviction.

Duff Crerar details the ministry that chaplains carried out under hellish conditions at the front and debilitating political intrigue in the rear. He identifies the role that Rev. John Almond played in bringing much-needed reform to the Chaplaincy Service, and argues that many Canadian Great War chaplains came home from the war with high hopes for a church-led revolution in public life, one in which they would play a leading role. Yet victory did not bring vindication. Joining up as individuals, they served together in the CEF, where their branch sought to give meaning and purpose to the brutality, chaos, and pain of war.

Coming home, Crerar asserts, they found themselves alone again, individuals left by demobilization serving congregations, alienated and divided, that were often unwilling to take on the postwar mission the chaplains envisioned overseas. They also faced many returning soldiers whose faith had been shattered by the horrors of the war.

Lucille Marr focuses on the essential role played by the churches in supporting and shaping women's contributions to the war effort from the home front, and how women's involvement in religion gave them space to fulfill and expand their roles. Two religious communities—Canadian Anglicans and Ontario Swiss (or Old) Mennonites—serve as case studies to illustrate the extremes in Canadian church women's experiences on the home front. Women were actively involved in the churches, and they provided the majority of members. As "civic cheerleaders" and "official mourners" on the one hand, and as carriers of the "banner of nonconformity" for the "pacifist few" on the other, Anglican and Mennonite women provided stability in their respective faith communities. This chapter demonstrates how they often offered parallel contributions, while at other times they came into conflict as they fostered the particular convictions of their denominations.

No aspect of Canadian life was untouched by the war, and the churches' experience was no exception. The war eventually impinged on every facet of the churches' life related to identity, ministry, and aspirations. As for identity, those who supported the war had no need to prove to anyone that they were "true" Canadians, while conscientious objectors such as Quakers and Mennonites, or those who opposed conscription such as French Catholics, faced derision, violence, or even arrest for their alleged lack of patriotism. German Lutherans encountered hostility even when they supported the war effort. As a result, the process of Canadianization was relatively seamless for some denominations, while in other cases it was contested, forced, and divisive. In regard to ministry, there was no escaping the seemingly insatiable demands of total war: the pastoral responsibilities to soldiers and their families swelled as the war dragged on and the casualty list grew longer, the shortage of men for leadership put myriad stresses on local parishes and theological schools, and the theological issues raised by a God who allowed such horrors to continue year after year gnawed at faith in a benevolent God. In regard to aspirations, the war's supporters believed the war to be fought for high ideals such as righteousness, freedom, civilization, and an end to genocide.[21] While there were excesses—such as recruitment from pulpits, the discourse of holy war, and even jingoistic support for empire—the churches' support was just as often nuanced and critical, shaped by either the classic just war paradigm of just cause (*jus ad bellum*) and just means (*jus in bello*) or pacifism's outright rejection of violence. For those church leaders imbued with the often radical ideals of the social gospel, the war was not only a defense of justice in Europe, but also an opportunity to apply a more radical approach to state control of industry—or morals, in the case of prohibition—for the Christianization of the nation. It was anticipated that the sacrifice of sons and wealth would lead to a renewed and reinvigorated Christianity and nation, and the "war to end all wars" would usher in a new world order.

The war led neither to a reinvigorated faith nor to peace. While there was no precipitous postwar decline in numbers of Sunday worshipers and the formation of Forward Movements indicates a degree of optimism among church-goers, the faith of countless soldiers had died or been crippled in the trenches. Parish life in the following decade was adversely impacted by the doubts and despair of those who had suffered trauma during the war, and leaders—some more radical than others—realized the need to adjust to the complexities of the modern world if Christianity was to remain relevant. Denominations also experienced divisions, for wartime disagreements were neither easily nor readily forgotten in the postwar years. International peace was also elusive, with civil war and military conflicts continuing unabated into the 1920s. The Treaty of Versailles (1919), a product of the victor nations at the Paris Peace Conference, was not a permanent solution, nor was the formation of the League of Nations (1919). The interwar period was marked by a reconsideration of support for war, and at the outbreak of the Second World War the churches had been sobered by their postwar experience. Consequently, naive optimism surrounding the efficacy of war had vanished and those who supported the war against Hitler did so believing it to be a "messy but necessary job."[22]

---

21. In regards to waging war to end genocide, see Heath, "Thor and Allah."
22. Wright, "The Canadian Protestant Tradition," 188.

BIBLIOGRAPHY

Primary Sources

NEWSPAPERS

Canadian Baptist
Canadian Churchman
Canadian Epworth Era
Onward
Pleasant Hours
Westminster

Secondary Sources

Airhart, Phyllis, D. "Ordering a Nation and Reordering Protestantism, 1867–1914." In *The Canadian Protestant Experience, 1760–1990*, edited by George Rawlyk, 98–138. Burlington: Welch, 1990.

Boudreau, Joseph A. "The Enemy Alien Problem in Canada, 1914–1921." PhD diss., University of California, 1965.

Bourne, John. "Total War I: The Great War." In *The Oxford History of Modern War*, edited by Charles Townshend, 117–37. Oxford: Oxford University Press, 2005.

Carrington, Philip. *The Anglican Church in Canada: A History*. Toronto: Collins, 1963.

Clodfelter, Michael. *Warfare and Armed Conflicts: A Statistical Encyclopedia of Casualty and Other Figures, 1494–2007*. Jefferson, NC: McFarland, 2008.

Cook, Tim. *At the Sharp End: Canadians Fighting the Great War 1914–1916*. Toronto: Viking, 2007.

———. *Shock Troops: Canadians Fighting the Great War, 1917–1918*. Toronto: Viking, 2008.

Copp, Terry. "The Military Effort, 1914–1918." In *Canada and the First World War: Essays in Honour of Robert Craig Brown*, edited by David Mackenzie, 35–61. Toronto: University of Toronto Press, 2005.

Faulkner, Charles Thomas Sinclair. "'For Christian Civilization': Churches and Canada's War Effort, 1939–1942." PhD diss., University of Chicago, 1975.

Fay, Terence. *A History of Canadian Catholics: Gallicanism, Romanism, and Canadianism*. Montreal and Kingston: McGill-Queen's University Press, 2002.

Ferguson, Niall. *The War of the World: History's Age of Hatred*. London: Penguin, 2007.

Heath, Gordon L. "Canadian Churches and War: An Introductory Essay and Annotated Bibliography." *MJTM* 12 (2010–2011) 61–124.

———. "'Prepared to do, prepared to die': Evangelicals, Imperialism, and Late-Victorian Canadian Children's Publications." *Perichoresis* 9 (2011) 3–27.

———. "'Thor and Allah . . . in a hideous, unholy confederacy': The Armenian Genocide in the Canadian Protestant Press." In *The Globalization of Christianity: Implications for Christian Ministry and Theology*, edited by Gordon L. Heath and Steve Studebaker. Eugene, OR: Pickwick, forthcoming.

Heath, Gordon L. and Paul R. Wilson, eds. *Baptists and Public Life in Canada*. Eugene, OR: Pickwick, 2012.

Mackenzie, David. *Canada and the First World War: Essays in Honour of Robert Craig Brown*. Toronto: University of Toronto Press, 2005.

McGowan, Mark G. "Rendering unto Caesar: Catholics, the State, and the Idea of a Christian Canada." *CSCH Historical Papers* (2011) 65–85.

Miedema, Gary. *For Canada's Sake: Public Religion, Centennial Celebrations, and the Remaking of Canada in the 1960s.* Montreal and Kingston: McGill-Queen's University Press, 2005.

Miller, Ian. *Our Glory and Our Grief: Torontonians and the Great War.* Toronto: University of Toronto Press, 2002.

Moir, John S. *Enduring Witness: A History of the Presbyterian Church in Canada.* Hamilton: Presbyterian Church in Canada, 1974.

Morton, Desmond. *Fight or Pay: Soldiers' Families in the Great War.* Vancouver: UBC Press, 2004.

———. *A Military History of Canada.* Toronto: McClelland & Stewart, 2007.

———. *When Your Number's Up: The Canadian Soldier in the First World War.* Toronto: Random House, 1993.

Morton, Desmond, and J. L. Granatstein. *Marching to Armageddon: Canada and the Great War, 1914–1919.* Toronto: Lester & Orpen Dennys, 1989.

Noll, Mark. *A History of Christianity in the United States and Canada.* Grand Rapids: Eerdmans, 1992.

Renfree, Harry A. *Heritage and Horizon: The Baptist Story in Canada.* Mississauga, ON: Canadian Baptist Federation, 1988.

Semple, Neil. *The Lord's Dominion: The History of Canadian Methodism.* Montreal and Kingston: McGill-Queen's University Press, 1996.

Stevenson, David. *1914–1918: The History of the First World War.* London: Allen Lane, 2004.

Van Die, Marguerite, ed. *Religion and Public Life in Canada: Historical and Comparative Perspectives.* Toronto: University of Toronto Press, 2001.

Vance, Jonathan F. *Maple Leaf Empire: Canada, Britain, and Two World Wars.* Oxford: Oxford University Press, 2012.

Winegard, Timothy C. *For King and Kanata: Canadian Indians and the First World War.* University of Manitoba Press, 2012.

Wright, Robert A. "The Canadian Protestant Tradition, 1914–1945." In *The Canadian Protestant Experience, 1760–1990,* edited by George Rawlyk, 139–97. Burlington, ON: Welch, 1990.

1

The South African War as Prelude to the First World War

Gordon L. Heath

Carman Miller contends that studies of the Great War should take seriously the legacy of the South African War.[1] His argument is that while recent scholarship on the First World War is welcome, extensive, and innovative in its conclusions, most contemporary research into the First World War neglects to frame the war in the larger context of the South African War. In his own words, "The most striking feature of this expanded body of research and writing on . . . Canada's Great War experience is the dearth of references to the South African War that preceded it only 15 years before."[2] Miller claims that at least two reasons are behind this omission. First, scholars fail to "absorb and explore the implications of Carl Berger's thesis that imperialism was another form of Canadian nationalism" or to appreciate the broader contours of Canada in the British world.[3] The ardent imperialism that marked Canada's reaction to the South African War, it seems, is an embarrassment to those who see it as an inferior form of nationalism compared to the less-British-more-"Canadian" identity and autonomy that allegedly began after the Great War. Second, the disparity between the wars in regards

---

1. Miller, "Framing." The South African War has also been called the Boer War, or the Second Anglo-Boer War.

2. Ibid., 4.

3. Ibid.

to cost, casualties, and consequences has led to ignoring the impact of the South African War. How could a war that only had 7,000 troops participate in Africa be of any interest to those considering a war that saw over 600,000 Canadian troops sent to Europe, and how could a war that led to 270 Canadian casualties be of any interest to those analyzing a war with a casualty roll of over 61,000 dead and 173,000 injured? Miller's argument, however, is that the relatively small war fifteen years earlier in South Africa had a pervasive influence on the ways in which Canadians conceptualized, organized, and fought the war in Europe.

This chapter narrows the focus of Miller's research to concentrate exclusively on Canadian churches, and claims that the reactions of the churches to the Great War were a continuation of precedents established during the South African War, and the trajectories established during that smaller conflict were followed by the churches in the larger conflict.[4] Perhaps not surprisingly in light of Miller's observations, investigation of the Canadian churches and the First World War often ignores precedents established in the South African War. For this reason, such studies are missing vital links with a previous war that shaped the churches' wartime conceptions and practices. Of course, there were differences in degree, and sometimes in kind, among the denominational reactions, and there is a danger that "historical realities" can be distorted by trying to make "analogies" and identify "antecedents,"[5] but what is most striking are the continuities between wars. In fact, no study of the churches and the Great War can be complete without recognizing the legacy of reactions to the South African War.

The churches were prescient during the South African War. The conflict was Canada's first war as a nascent Dominion, and church leaders realized that precedents were being established. It was believed that whatever rights or patterns they established would be followed in Canada's next war,[6] and followed they were, but on a much grander

---

4. Miller includes the churches in his analysis, but his focus is more wide-ranging. "Churches" refers to Roman Catholics and the four largest Protestant denominations: Anglican, Baptist, Methodist, and Presbyterian.

5. Miller, "Framing," 16.

6. "We are making history and establishing precedents, and every loyal Methodist should demand that our Church receive full rights, justice and recognition" ("Letter to Editor," *Wesleyan*, 28 March 1900, 5). Those concerned with precedents were quite right in their assumption that the war was a precedent-setting one. See Morton, *Military History*, 117–18.

scale. Before looking at those practical actions related to the churches' support, however, the following section will demonstrate how a number of assumptions undergirding support for the wars were strikingly similar throughout the two conflicts. While assumptions may be difficult to evaluate in terms of impact, "only the churches had the ideological resources to provide solace and comfort to the discouraged, the frightened, the despairing, and the mourning."[7] Assumptions also shaped the nature and extent of the churches' reaction to the First World War beyond just pastoral care. More specifically, assumptions related to nation, empire, and justice during the Great War were forged in Canada's first war only fifteen years earlier.

Not all assumptions were universally shared, however. For instance, while, generally speaking, English Protestants supported the wars and French Catholics were opposed, there were countless exceptions, nuances, and areas of dissent within such communions.[8] Neither Catholicism nor Protestantism was monolithic—and that reality needs to be kept in mind when examining larger patterns. That being said, even the divergence and dissonance within the two communions followed a similar pattern in 1914–1918 to that manifested earlier in the South African War.

ASSUMPTIONS

Nation-Building

By the end of the nineteenth century and into the twentieth, the Protestant churches had an influence on English-Canadian society unlike any other institution, and as Phyllis Airhart and others have shown, the English Protestant churches had taken upon themselves the identity of nation-builders.[9] The Catholic Church shared a similar influence among French-speaking citizens in and outside of Quebec, as well as among

---

7. Bliss, "Methodist Church," 219.

8. For Protestant dissent during the South African War, see Miller, "English-Canadian Opposition." Stacey argues that the French willingness to fight for the Pope in 1868 illustrates how differently Quebecers saw the world. See Stacey, *Canada*, 7. Silver claims that there was a French Canadian imperialism, except that this imperialism saw its divine mission to be the preservation and promotion of Catholicism in North America and the world, a role that France had abandoned. See Silver, "Quebec Attitudes."

9. Airhart, "Ordering," 99.

English-speaking Catholics, and it too had a unique nation-building vision and identity.[10] Both Catholics and Protestants sought to shape the nation into their own image, oftentimes leading to conflict between the two Christian communities, and sometimes, as Mark McGowan has demonstrated, even between French and English-speaking Catholics, who had opposing national visions.[11] During the South African War, commitment to nation-building meant that the churches took it upon themselves to construct national and imperial ideals and identity through their services, sermons, organizations, and literature, as well as support—or criticize—the war effort in numerous ways. In regard to their vision for the nation, and their role in it, with few exceptions the churches in the First World War acted out of the same conceptual framework that they had fifteen years earlier. Of course, the churches' nation-building activities in regard to the war effort in Europe were on an unprecedented scale. Nevertheless, commitment to nation-building during the war in South Africa set a precedent for English-speaking Catholic and Protestant support for the Great War and French-Catholic opposition to the war, and also "set the stage" for future controversy between French and English-speaking Catholics.[12]

Empire

From the declaration of war in 1914 to the announcement of peace in 1918 the Protestant churches were avid supporters of a war effort framed in no small measure to defend the Empire.[13] Zeal for defending the Empire was not new, however, for Protestant support for the Empire mirrored the imperial zeal displayed during the South African War.[14] Nevertheless, Catholic support for an imperial war in Africa was divided between most French-speaking Catholics, who were opposed, and English-speaking Catholics, who were mainly supportive.[15] Positive com-

10. Silver, *French-Canadian Idea*; Silver, "Quebec Attitudes"; Perin, "Elaborating"; Fay, *Canadian Catholics*; Noll, *History*, ch. 10.

11. McGowan, "Rendering unto Caesar," 76.

12. Ibid., 75.

13. For instance, see Richards, "Propaganda"; Angus, "Living"; Fowler, "Keeping the Faith."

14. Heath, *Silver Lining*, ch. 4. For evidence of support for the Empire before the South African War, see Heath, "Nile Expedition."

15. McGowan, "Rendering unto Caesar," 72–76; McGowan, "Rally"; Brewer, "Antigonish."

mentary on the Empire among the churches reinforces Carl Berger's thesis that late nineteenth-century imperialism was one form of Canadian nationalism,[16] and illustrates Philip Buckner's observation that popular enthusiasm for Britishness, monarchy, and empire had not diminished in any significant way by 1914.[17] What needs to be kept in mind when exploring imperial identities and the churches, however, is that French Catholics and English Protestants often had different conceptions of empire,[18] and that English-speaking (Irish) Catholics differed from their French Catholic sisters and brothers due to the Irish identification with the imperial cause—something that can be dated back to their participation in the South African War.[19] Recent scholarship has noted that the imperial idea in the periphery was far from homogeneous; rather than being uniform it was imagined, elastic, and contested, often meaning "different things to different people,"[20] and this diversity of attitudes to empire applies to perspectives in the Canadian churches. Nevertheless, the general precedents for the churches support—or not—for the British Empire had been established in the South African War.

Justice

Prime Minister Sir Wilfrid Laurier made it clear that he considered the cause to be one of justice when Canada's first contingent of 1,039 troops prepared to board the 425 foot *Sardinian* in Quebec City on Monday 30 October 1899. In the presence of the Governor General, the Premier of the province of Quebec, other civil and religious leaders, as well as 50,000 exuberant spectators, Laurier declared that "the cause for which you men of Canada are going to fight is the cause of justice, the cause of humanity, of civil rights and religious liberty. This is not a war of conquest. . . . The object is not to crush out the Dutch population, but to establish in that land . . . British sovereign law, to assure to all men of

---

16. Berger, *Sense of Power*. For other important works related to imperialism and nationalism in Canada, see Penlington, *Canada and Imperialism*; Page, "Canada"; Page, *Boer War*; Page, "Carl Berger"; Cole, "Imperialists"; Cook, "George R. Parkin."

17. Buckner, "Casting Daylight."

18. For a study of Canadian anti-imperial sentiment, see Miller, "English-Canadian Opposition"; Ostergaard, "Canadian Nationalism." For French-Canadian views of empire, see Silver, "Quebec Attitudes."

19. McGowan, "Rally," 3.

20. Bell, *Idea*, 7.

that country an equal share of liberty."[21] Protestants, as well as a number of English-speaking Catholics, echoed the Prime Minister's vision for the advancement of justice. The message in sermons, the press, church meetings, and special services was that the war was being waged for liberty and freedom for the Utlanders, for the "natives," for all of Africa, the world, and even ultimately for the Boers (although they did not appreciate it yet).[22] One gets a glimpse of this grand vision in announcements of the ending of the war. For instance, the *Christian Guardian* declared: "It will be interesting to our readers to know the general outlook for international peace. It is brighter now than at any time in the previous history of the world."[23] After initial hesitations, the English-speaking Catholic papers the *Register*, *Casket*, *Record*, and *Freeman* echoed the same conviction that the cause was just and peace would be advanced by a British victory.[24] French Catholics were not as convinced as their non-French coreligionists, and the question of the justice of the cause in Africa remained a point of tension among Catholics.

The social gospel impulse was an important component to the churches' (especially the Methodist) mandate to better the nation and the world,[25] and John Webster Grant has noted how church support for the war effort against the Central Powers in Europe was, in part, a reflection of the social gospel impulse within the churches. In fact, a victory for the Entente Powers was considered to be critical for the future peace and justice of the nations:

> Enthusiastic support for the [First World War] did not distract interest from social concerns. On the contrary, wholehearted support rested on the conviction that tremendous moral and social issues were at stake. The war provided an occasion for applying the social message of the churches both as law and as gospel. On the one hand, its prosecution demanded a total dedication of the self that fitted well with the current emphasis on national conversion, and indeed churchmen experienced some exhilaration in being able to press their calls for self-discipline on a public made responsive by crisis. On the other hand, its successful con-

---

21. As quoted in Page, *Boer War*, 13.
22. Heath, *Silver Lining*, ch. 2.
23. "The Outlook in the War against War," *Christian Guardian*, 11 June 1902, 369.
24. McGowan, "Rally," 16.
25. Allen, *Religion*.

clusion seemed to promise the age of peace and plenty to which social gospellers had long looked forward.[26]

However, the reaction of the churches to the South African War indicates that fusion of war and the social gospel agenda was made over a decade before the First World War. Such hope in the efficacy of war predates the postwar optimism of the Great War in 1918, and the language surrounding the war in South Africa was no less optimistic that the victory would bring lasting peace and the spread of justice. With such lofty expectations for the future, Protestants and various Catholics felt confident that their support for the war in South Africa had been justified, and that same confidence in the efficacy of war was carried over into the crusade against Germany.

ACTIONS

While the churches shared much in common in regards to the South African War and the First World War in the area of assumptions, there were also practical aspects to the responses of the churches in the First World War that bear remarkable resemblance to the activities of the churches during the South African War. This is not to claim that all activities were exactly the same, for there were, at times, important differences. Nevertheless, the pattern and trajectory of conduct for the First World War was most definitely shaped during the South African War.

Press

First, the denominational press was used for nation-building and supporting both war efforts. The role of newspapers in the formation of public opinion is widely recognized. For instance, the New Journalism was linked to the New Imperialism, and John A. Hobson, one of the most prominent late-Victorian opponents of imperialism, was concerned about the power of the press in promoting it.[27] John Bourinot claimed that the influence of the press played a critical role in educating the "masses" about the key issues of the day.[28] Denis Judd and other contemporary historians have also noted how influential the press was

---

26. Grant, *Canadian Era*, 114.
27. Hobson, *Imperialism*, 216–17 (page citation is from the reprint edition).
28. Bourinot, *Intellectual Development*, 83.

in swaying public opinion during wartime.[29] Paula Krebs goes so far as to argue that the press actually created the spontaneous outburst of imperial fervor during the South African War.[30] While there were limits to what influence the press could have on its readers, the press did have the power to set agendas, mobilize, stereotype, confer status, manipulate, socialize, and legitimize,[31] and that power of the press extended to the denominational newspapers. John MacKenzie has noted how in Britain there was no pressing need for government agencies to be involved in imperial propaganda, for a number of non-governmental agencies were enthusiastically doing it for them.[32] MacKenzie was not necessarily referring to Christian denominations, but the extent to which late-Victorian denominational newspapers supported and promoted imperialism is one clear example of such voluntary promotion of the Empire.

Heath has identified how the Canadian Protestant denominational press was used extensively in a nation-building role during the war years 1899–1902, and McGowan has noted a similar response of the Irish Catholic press to the war.[33] In the same way, the religious press during the Great War was active in shaping its constituency's attitudes—whether pro or con—to empire, war, national identity, and civic responsibility.

Pulpit, Property, Services, and Structures

Second, the Protestant churches during the South African War were ardent supporters of the war effort, and as the war progressed so were a number of English-speaking Catholics. Sermons extolled the virtues of the cause and celebrated victories, churches collected donations for the Patriotic Fund, governing bodies declared their loyalty, and troops were sent off or welcomed home at church social functions.

---

29. Judd and Surridge, *Boer War*, ch. 19; Harrington, "Pictorial Journalism."
30. Krebs, *Gender*, 2.
31. Rutherford, *Victorian Authority*, 7–8.
32. MacKenzie, *Propaganda*, 2–3.
33. Heath, "Forming"; Heath, *Silver Lining*, xxiv–xxv; McGowan, "Rally," 16. Research is needed on a survey of the French-language Catholic press and nation-building during the South African War.

The Mitre.

VOL. VII.   LENNOXVILLE, P. Q., NOVEMBER. 1899.   NO. 2.

BOARD OF DIRECTORS.

W. W. WADLEIGH, (Arts '00.)   EDITOR-IN-CHIEF.
N. C. DAVIES, (Arts '00.)   BUSINESS MANAGER.

ASSOCIATE EDITORS.

E. G. HENRY, (Arts '00.)   C. W. BALFOUR, B. A. (Divinity.)
J. M. BONELLI, (Arts '01.)   R. W. HIBBARD, B. A. (B. C. S.)
C. W. MITCHELL, B. A. (Divinity.)   R. MEREDITH, (B. C. S.)
J. A. GILLESPIE, (Medicine.)   Not elected (Music.)
        J. H. WURTELE, (Arts '00.) ATHLETIC EDITOR. (Arts and Divinity)

ASSISTANT BUSINESS MANAGERS.

P. CALLIS, B. A. (Divinity.)   H. S. ORR, (Arts '00.)
C. H. CLEVELAND, (B. C. S.)   Not elected (Music.)
Not elected (Medicine)   Not elected (Dentistry.)

"THE MITRE", is published monthly during the College year by the Students of Bishop's College and the Boys of Bishop's College School.
Terms, $1.00 per year in advance; single copy 15 cents.
Contributors of articles are entitled to receive three copies gratis of the number containing their articles.
Copyright will be secured on all articles sent to and accepted by the Editor-in-Chief, accompanied by a written request that they be copyrighted.
The Editor does not take upon himself responsibility for the opinions expressed by contributors and correspondents.
Address all contributions to the Editor-in-Chief, and all business correspondence to the Business Manager,

THE MITRE, BISHOP'S COLLEGE, LENNOXVILLE, QUE.   PRINTED BY GEO. GALE & SONS, WATERVILLE, QUE.

SERMON
— BY THE —
REV. F. G. SCOTT
——ON THE OCCASION OF THE——

Departure of the 2nd(special service)Battalion of the Royal Canadian Regiment

——FOR——

SOUTH AFRICA

CATHEDRAL OF THE HOLY TRINITY, QUEBEC, SUNDAY,
OCTOBER 29th, 1899.

"The Eternal God is thy refuge, and underneath are the everlasting arms, and He shall thrust out the enemy from before thee."—Deuteronomy xxxiii-27.

These words are taken from the blessing wherewith Moses blessed the children of Israel before his death. The great patriot had led the people successfully from the land of captivity and through the weary deserts of Sinai, and now on the borders of the Promised Land the call comes to him to lay

The first page of Rev. F. G. Scott's Sermon in *The Mitre* of November 1899. Image taken by Gordon L. Heath, of the copy in Anglican Church of Canada General Synod Archives, Toronto, Ontario.

The Anglican Church even promoted a Day of Humble Supplication on 11 February 1900 as a response to the dismal performance of the imperial troops in South Africa.[34] The churches' bolstering of the war effort against Germany and the Central Powers was all consuming—at least for those that supported the war effort—and the use of pulpit, property, services, and structures in support of the war effort followed the precedents established in the South African War. Methodist pulpits were deemed to be the "best recruiting stations in the first year of the war."[35] Besides support from the pulpit on Sunday morning, Protestant ministers or Catholic priests who supported the war effort preached sermons at troop sendoffs, troop returns, church meetings, and military parades. Special services were planned for the sole purpose of recruiting or fund raising. Special services were also called for repentance and supplication to God for victory, or for celebrating the end of the war. Wartime prayers were produced, printed, and circulated. Church bodies such as the Methodist Army and Navy Board took pains to get ministers to identify possible recruits in the churches,[36] and church leaders such as Catholic bishop Michael Fallon of the Diocese of London, Ontario, used their prominent positions to exhort the faithful to support the war.[37] As McGowan and Simon Jolivet indicate in chapters that follow, Catholic attitudes to the war were complex and often fragmented. However, this general description fits well with most Protestant and English-speaking Catholic experiences.

John Webster Grant claims that the churches (especially the Methodist) in the First World War "lacked a clearly defined tradition of the proper roles of church and state."[38] Grant's error is obvious when examined in light of the churches' experience in the South African War, for the response of the churches to this war provided clear precedents and traditions that informed their response to the war in 1914. Grant is partially correct in his appraisal of the churches' reaction to the Great War, however, for their participation—such as recruiting from the pulpit—evolved beyond traditional roles, penetrating every aspect of church life beyond anything experienced during the South African War.

34. Heath, *Silver Lining*, 64–69; Heath, "Sin in the Camp."
35. Bliss, "Methodist Church," 217. See also Davidson, "Preaching."
36. Bliss, "Methodist Church," 217–18.
37. Ciani, "Imperialist Irishman."
38. Grant, *Canadian Era*, 114.

It should be noted that these activities of the churches contributed to the construction of two identities. First, H. V. Nelles argues in *The Art of Nation-Building* that the commemoration of Quebec's Tercentenary in 1908 was "an act of self-invention."[39] It was an opportunity where various parties remembered the past, but also negotiated to shape the future. It was a time when a particular vision of Canada was being "made." In a similar way, through their many public services, symbols, and sermons during the two wars, the churches sought to shape a yet "unmade" Canada to fit their particular national vision. Second, while the vigorous support for both wars shown by Irish (and other) English-speaking Catholics alienated them from French-speaking Catholics, such support played an important role in demonstrating to Protestants that Catholics were loyal Canadians too.[40]

Chaplains

Third, a number of the chaplains involved in the war effort in Europe gained experience in South Africa, and lessons learned in the South African War were often drawn upon by chaplains in the Great War.[41] The selection and sending of chaplains with the contingents to South Africa failed to change the "improvised nature" of the way Canadian chaplains were appointed—that would not end until the First World War.[42] However, the churches' ardent patriotism, and active fights to make certain that chaplains traveled with the contingents, did ensure that the government took into account the churches' particular wishes when it made plans for its contingents. The churches active campaigning and participation also led to the permanent inclusion of a chaplain with every contingent, something that in previous decades had not been the government's policy.[43] Consequently, when war broke out in 1914, the expectation was that chaplains would be assigned to the contingents.

Denominational competition for chaplain postings and key leadership positions marked the opening months of the Great War (much

---

39. Nelles, *Nation-Building*, 12.
40. McGowan, "Rendering unto Caesar," 76.
41. Miller also notes this; see Miller, "Framing," 8–9.
42. Duff Crerar argues that improvisation marked the selection of Canadian chaplains from the 1860s to the First World War. See Crerar, *Padres*, 4.
43. Crerar notes that after 1900 the chaplain's office was "here to stay." See ibid., 22.

like during the South African War).[44] Clerics with South African experience were often favored in the selection of chaplains.[45] John Almond, an Anglican chaplain with the First Contingent to South Africa, served as a chaplain in the First World War and eventually became the head of the chaplains and was responsible for numerous reforms to the chaplaincy service.[46] Along with Almond were a number of chaplains who were veterans from the war in Africa "whose experience informed their subsequent war service."[47] Methods used in South Africa were deemed by some to be directly applicable to the war in Europe.[48] This assumption held true in the case of Father O'Leary, a Catholic chaplain with the first contingent to South Africa. His down-to-earth approach, lack of concern for his own safety, and living with the troops at the front led to his becoming a "living legend" and the "prototype Canadian chaplain."[49] However, there was no precedent established for the crisis of faith among soldiers generated by the despair and carnage of the trenches in Europe: Canadian chaplains in the Great War had to face an unprecedented disaster.[50]

Rhetoric

Fourth, Miller notes how much of the rhetoric and literary representations during the South African War were echoed in the First World War. Church commentary during the war in Africa idealized soldiering and inculcated imperialism even among the churches' youth.[51] The idea of a "good soldier" and "good Christian" that dated back to the Crimean War was invoked,[52] and the Christian character of the British troops emphasized. Analogies were made between good soldiers of Jesus Christ and good soldiers of the Queen.[53] Conversely, church commentary on the

---

44. For the most extensive discussion of Canada's chaplains during the Great War, see ibid.
45. Ibid., 33.
46. Ibid., ch. 3.
47. Miller, "Framing," 8.
48. Crerar, *Padres*, 31.
49. Miller, "Framing," 9.
50. Marshall, "Methodism Embattled"; Crerar, *Padres*, 146–60.
51. Heath, "Prepared."
52. Anderson, "Christian Militarism."
53. J. W. Weeks, "Soldiership," *Canadian Baptist*, 25 January 1900, 662–63.

Boers had often been venomous and virulent. They were cast as "incorrigibly ignorant" in their attack on the British Empire, "incurably perfidious" in diplomacy, "mercilessly cruel" to natives, "treacherous foes" due to their violations of the rules of warfare,[54] and were the "craftiest, most hypocritical, most dishonest, most untruthful, cruelest, most ignorant, most overbearing, most immoral, and stupidest race of white people in the world."[55] Contributing to the negative images of the Boers were accounts of their alleged atrocities, and the headlines underscored the brutality.[56] These accounts of alleged savagery were published throughout the entire course of the war, with the criticisms after 1900 noting a shift in Boer tactics to an unorthodox guerrilla campaign against British occupation.[57] While the use of such rhetoric was carried over into the churches' discourse in the First World War, the unprecedented horrors of the Great War eventually made the Boer conflict seem like a small, noble, heroic, "gentleman's war."[58]

The portrayal of the "other" in the religious press during the First World War mirrored general patterns in society at large, and was marked by rhetoric that often dehumanized and demonized the enemy. The rhetoric was initially framed in traditional "just war" language, but, as atrocity accounts surfaced and the war dragged on interminably, the language shifted to that of a crusade.[59] Canadians were angered by the actions of Germany depicted in atrocity accounts, and those accounts—oft-reiterated in the churches' press and pulpits—both contributed to

---

54. "The Boer Character," *Onward*, 31 March 1900, 97.

55. "Truth about the Boers," *Onward*, 29 March 1900, 95.

56. "Boer Atrocities," *Onward*, 16 December 1899, 405; Julian Ralph, "Treachery and Cruelty of the Boers," *Onward*, 9 June 1900, 178; "Condemned by Boer Evidence," *Canadian Baptist*, 20 February 1902, 16.

57. For instance, see "Flags of Truce," *Onward*, 21 April 1900, 128; "A Blot upon Civilization," *Onward*, 15 December 1900, 402; "De Wet's Savagery," *Onward*, 16 March 1901, 85; "Violations of the Rules of War," *Christian Guardian*, 28 March 1900, 201; "British Refugees," *Methodist Magazine and Review*, July 1900, 87; "De Wet's Savagery," *Methodist Magazine and Review*, February 1900, 190–91; "South Africa," *Westminster*, 11 January 1902, 52–53; Thos. G. Shearman, "What the Boer Government Is," *Presbyterian Witness*, 30 March 1900, 70; "Stories of the Humanity and Inhumanity of the Boers," *Canadian Baptist*, 5 April 1900, 215; "Guerrilla Warfare Unchristian," *Canadian Baptist*, 14 November 1901, 736; "Boer Brutality," *Canadian Church Magazine and Mission News*, January 1901, 3; "Barbarity of Boers," *Canadian Churchman*, 8 March 1900, 148.

58. Fuller, *Gentleman's War*, 5–6.

59. MacDonald, "Just War to Crusade."

and perpetuated negative images of Germans. For instance, in a sermon preached by Rev. J. R. H. Warren, Anglican rector of St. Matthew's Church, Toronto, the Kaiser was portrayed to be the "enemy of Christian civilization, and was himself utterly unscrupulous as to the methods he would employ to gain his ends. No means seem too foul for him to use. Devastation and destruction everywhere mark his path. Like another Attila he harries the land."[60] As for Germany's ally, the Ottoman Turks, accounts of atrocities against the Armenians in Ottoman territory went beyond describing the events to both constructing and confirming an image of the "terrible Turk" that was common in the West.[61] Turkish rule had made "no single vital contribution" to the "raising of the standard of life" in any marked way; their only "original contribution" to civilization being the "harem."[62] The end of Turkish rule, consequently, was considered to be a boon to all within and outside the borders of the Ottoman Empire.[63] While this rhetoric was indeed harsh, as Miller notes, it also had a history: "In the decade and more before the Great War the Boer War's influence on military and civilian language, perceptions, assumptions and expectations of warfare appears obvious; it constituted an arsenal of well tested notions and language that Great War leaders did not hesitate to employ to advance their claims."[64] In similar manner, the churches' creation of myths and construction of history, its idealization of war and soldiering, and its demonizing of the enemy in the First World War demonstrated striking continuities with the depiction of the previous conflict a decade and a half earlier.

While the Protestant churches in the First World War imitated much of the rhetoric occurring in English Canada, one noteworthy exception is that of the response to the conscription crisis in 1917. The political battles related to the passage of Military Service Act (MSA) on 29

60. Rev. J. R. H. Warren, "The Duty of the Hour," *Canadian Churchman*, 8 July 1915, 425–26.

61. For instance, see "The Doom of Turkey," *Presbyterian Witness*, 10 April 1915, 1; "After Three Years of War," *Montreal Churchman*, August 1917, 1; "Missionary Notes," *The Missionary Outlook*, July 1918, 146; "Missionary Notes," *The Missionary Outlook*, March 1916, 50.

62. James Endicott, "Ought the Turkish Rule in Europe to Be Ended?" *Christian Guardian*, 24 January 1917, 7.

63. For further discussion of commentary on Turkish rule, see Heath, "Thor and Allah."

64. Miller, "Framing."

August 1917, and the debates surrounding the 17 December 1917 federal election and Union Government, made "all the stops to be pulled and the flood tide of Anglo-Saxon racism to be unleashed."[65] J. L. Granatstein and J. M. Hitsman claim "no single issue has done more to muddy the political waters or to destroy the unity of the nation" than conscription, and Elizabeth Armstrong declares it "seemed that the end had come" to the unique Canadian experiment of fusing two races into one.[66] What made the matter so dangerous for the fledgling nation were the shrill denunciations of Quebec emanating from English Canada that further stoked the passions of an already enflamed populace in that province. The Protestant religious press, however, denounced harsh polemics and advocated conciliation with Catholics in Quebec.[67] Yet even this conciliatory response had its roots in the Boer War, for in that earlier conflict the Protestant churches had been faced with growing hostility on the part of English Canada over what it deemed an unpatriotic lack of support for the war among French Catholics—hostility that boiled over into violence in Montreal in 1900.[68] The religious press, however, avoided and condemned harsh polemics while warning that hostility would drive a wedge between Canada's two founding peoples and possibly even destroy the fledgling nation.[69]

CONCLUSION

What had the churches learned from the experience of the South African War? For those opposed to the war, it had been an unwelcome reminder of Canada's British imperial identity and obligations—what was there to learn, except to hope that it never happened again? For those who were supportive, the war in Africa had cost little, relatively speaking, and seemed to contribute much in the way of justice and national glory—what was there to learn, except to simply to repeat what had been done before? However, in a global conflagration that was unprecedented in scale and catastrophic in impact, those same assumptions, commitments, and activities were amplified far beyond the experience of the churches in the

---

65. Granatstein and Hitsman, *Broken Promises*, 76. For a summary of other violent reactions, or threats of violence, see Armstrong, *Crisis*, 179–81.

66. Granatstein and Hitsman, *Broken Promises*, 264; Armstrong, *Crisis*, 161.

67. Heath, "Conscription Crisis."

68. Miller, *Painting*, 443–44; Miller, "Flag Riot."

69. Heath, *Silver Lining*, 82–86.

South African War. And in the decades after the Great War the churches had difficult questions to answer about the wisdom of such unqualified and total support, or lack thereof. Such questions then needed to be asked, however, in the larger context of the precedents established during the South African War, for the assumptions and actions that directly shaped the churches' response to the war in Europe were forged during the earlier conflict in Africa. Of course, there were differences in degree, and sometimes in kind, among the denominational reactions, but what is most striking are the continuities between the wars. Even the wartime divisions between French and English-speaking Catholics, as well as between French Catholics and Protestants, were mirror images. In fact, no study of the churches and the Great War can be complete without recognizing the legacy of the churches' reactions to the South African War.

BIBLIOGRAPHY

Primary Sources

NEWSPAPERS

Canadian Baptist
Canadian Church Magazine and Mission News
Canadian Churchman
Christian Guardian
Methodist Magazine and Review
Montreal Churchman
Onward
Presbyterian Witness
The Missionary Outlook
Wesleyan
Westminster

OTHER

Bourinot, John George. *The Intellectual Development of the Canadian People: An Historical Review.* Toronto: Hunter, Rose, 1881.

Secondary Sources

Airhart, Phyllis D. "Ordering a New Nation and Reordering Protestantism, 1867-1914." In *The Canadian Protestant Experience, 1760-1990*, edited by George A. Rawlyk, 98-138. Burlington: Welch, 1990.

Allen, Richard. *Religion and Social Reform in Canada, 1914-1928*. Toronto: University of Toronto Press, 1971.

Anderson, Olive. "The Growth of Christian Militarism in Mid-Victorian Britain." *English Historical Review* 86 (1971) 46-72.

Angus, Murray E. "Living in the 'World of the Tiger': The Methodist and Presbyterian Churches in Nova Scotia and the Great War, 1914-1918." MA thesis, Dalhousie University, 1993.

Armstrong, Elizabeth. *The Crisis of Quebec, 1914-1918*. Toronto: McClelland & Stewart, 1974.

Bell, Duncan. *The Idea of Greater Britain: Empire and the Future of World Order, 1860-1900*. Princeton: Princeton University Press, 2007.

Bliss, J. M. "The Methodist Church and World War I." *Canadian Historical Review* 49 (1968) 213-33.

Brewer, Charles G. "The Diocese of Antigonish and World War 1." MA Thesis, University of New Brunswick, 1975.

Buckner, Philip. "Casting Daylight upon Magic: Deconstructing the Royal Tour of 1901 to Canada." *Journal of Imperial and Commonwealth History* 31 (2003) 158-89.

Ciani, Adriani. "'An Imperialist Irishman': Bishop Michael Fallon, the Diocese of London and the Great War." *CCHA Historical Studies* 74 (2008) 73-94.

Cole, Douglas. "Canada's 'Nationalistic' Imperialists." *Journal of Canadian Studies* 5 (1970) 44-49.

Cook, Terry. "George R. Parkin and the Concept of Britannic Idealism." *Journal of Canadian Studies* 10 (1975) 15–31.

Crerar, Duff. *Padres in No Man's Land: Canadian Chaplains and the Great War*. Montreal and Kingston: McGill-Queen's University Press, 1995.

Davidson, Melissa. "Preaching the Great War: Canadian Anglicans and the War Sermon, 1914–1918." MA thesis, McGill University, 2013.

Fay, Terence J. *A History of Canadian Catholics*. Montreal and Kingston: McGill-Queen's University Press, 2002.

Fowler, Michelle. "Keeping the Faith: The Presbyterian Press in Peace and War, 1913–1919." MA thesis, Wilfrid Laurier University, 2005.

Fuller, J. F. C. *The Last of the Gentleman's War: A Subaltern's Journal of the War in South Africa, 1899–1902*. London: Faber & Faber, 1937.

Granatstein, J. L., and J. Mackay Hitsman. *Broken Promises: A History of Conscription in Canada*. Toronto: Oxford University Press, 1977.

Grant, John Webster. *The Church in the Canadian Era: The First Century of the Canadian Era*. Toronto/Montreal: McGraw-Hill Ryerson, 1972.

Harrington, Peter. "Pictorial Journalism and the Boer War: The London Illustrated Weeklies." In *The Boer War: Direction, Experience and Image*, edited by John Gooch, 224–44. London: Frank Cass, 2000.

Heath, Gordon L. "The Canadian Protestant Press and the Conscription Crisis, 1917–1918." *Historical Studies* 78 (2012) 27–46.

———. "'Forming Sound Public Opinion': The Late-Victorian Canadian Protestant Press and Nation-Building." *Journal of the Canadian Church Historical Society* 48 (2006) 109–59.

———. "The Nile Expedition, New Imperialism and Canadian Baptists, 1884–1885." *Baptist Quarterly* 44 (2011) 171–86.

———. "'Prepared to do, prepared to die': Evangelicals, Imperialism and Late-Victorian Canadian Children's Publications." *Perichoresis* 9 (2011) 3–27.

———. "Sin in the Camp: The Day of Humble Supplication in the Anglican Church in Canada in the Early Months of the South African War." *Journal of the Canadian Church Historical Society* 44 (2002) 207–26.

———. "'Thor and Allah . . . in a hideous, unholy confederacy': The Armenian Genocide in the Canadian Protestant Press." In *The Globalization of Christianity: Implications for Christian Ministry and Theology*, edited by Steve Studebaker and Gordon L. Heath. Eugene, OR: Pickwick Publications (forthcoming).

———. *A War with a Silver Lining: Canadian Protestant Churches and the South African War, 1899–1902*. Montreal and Kingston: McGill-Queen's University Press, 2009.

Hobson, John A. *Imperialism: A Study*. London: George Allen & Unwin, 1902; reprint, Ann Arbor, MI: University of Michigan, 1967.

Judd, Denis, and Keith Surridge. *The Boer War*. New York: Palgrave Macmillan, 2002.

Krebs, Paula. *Gender, Race, and the Writing of Empire: Public Discourse and the Boer War*. Cambridge: Cambridge University Press, 1999.

MacDonald, Stuart. "From Just War to Crusade: The Wartime Sermons of the Rev. Thomas Eakin." MDiv thesis, Knox College, 1985.

MacKenzie, John M. *Propaganda and Empire: The Manipulation of British Public Opinion, 1880–1960*. Manchester: Manchester University Press, 1984.

Marshall, David. "Methodism Embattled: A Reconsideration of the Methodist Church and World War I." *Canadian Historical Review* 66 (1985) 48–64.

McGowan, Mark G. "Rendering unto Caesar: Catholics, the State, and the Idea of a Christian Canada." *CSCH Historical Papers* (2011) 65–85.

———. "To Rally the Whelps of the Lion: Canada's Irish Catholics and the South African War." Unpublished paper accessed through McGowan.

Miller, Carman. "English-Canadian Opposition to the South African War as Seen through the Press." *Canadian Historical Review* 55 (1974) 422–38.

———. "Framing Canada's Great War: A Case for Including the Boer War." *Journal of Transatlantic Studies* 6 (2008) 3–21.

———. "The Montreal Flag Riot of 1900." In *One Flag, One Queen, One Tongue: New Zealand, the British Empire and the South African War*, edited by John Crawford and Ian McGibbon, 165–79. Auckland: Auckland University Press, 2003.

———. *Painting the Map Red: Canada and the South African War, 1899-1902*. Montreal and Kingston: McGill-Queen's University Press, 1998.

Morton, Desmond. *A Military History of Canada: From Champlain to Kosovo*. Toronto: McClelland & Stewart, 1999.

Nelles, H. V. *The Art of Nation-Building: Pageantry and Spectacle at Quebec's Tercentenary*. Toronto: University of Toronto Press, 1999.

Noll, Mark A. *A History of Christianity in the United States and Canada*. Grand Rapids: Eerdmans, 1992.

Ostergaard, Karen. "Canadian Nationalism and Anti-Imperialism, 1896–1911." PhD diss., Dalhousie University, 1976.

Page, Robert. *The Boer War and Canadian Imperialism*. Ottawa: The Canadian Historical Association, 1987.

———. "Canada and the Imperial Idea in the Boer War Years." *Journal of Canadian Studies* 5 (1970) 33–49.

———. "Carl Berger and the Intellectual Origins of Canadian Imperialist Thought, 1867–1914." *Journal of Canadian Studies* 5 (1970) 39–43.

Penlington, Norman. *Canada and Imperialism, 1896*. Toronto: University of Toronto Press, 1965.

Perin, Roberto. "Elaborating a Public Culture: The Catholic Church in Nineteenth-Century Quebec." In *Religion and Public Life in Canada: Historical and Comparative Perspectives*, edited by Marguerite Van Die, 87–105. Toronto: University of Toronto Press, 2001.

Richards, Samuel J. "Ministry of Propaganda: Canadian Methodists, Empire, and Loyalty in World War I." MA thesis, Salisbury University, 2007.

Rutherford, Paul. *A Victorian Authority: The Daily Press in Late Nineteenth-Century Canada*. Toronto: University of Toronto Press, 1982.

Semple, Neil. *The Lord's Dominion: The History of Canadian Methodism*. Montreal and Kingston: McGill-Queen's University Press, 1996.

Silver, A. I. *The French-Canadian Idea of Confederation, 1864-1900*. Toronto: University of Toronto Press, 1997.

———. "Some Quebec Attitudes in an Age of Imperialism and Ideological Conflict." *Canadian Historical Review* 57 (1976) 440–60.

Stacey, C. P. *Canada and the Age of Conflict*. Vol. 1, *1867-1921*. Toronto: University of Toronto Press, 1984.

2

"We are all involved in the same issue"

Canada's English-Speaking Catholics and the Great War

MARK G. MCGOWAN

HE HAD ENOUGH AND his patience had simply run out. "Today," fumed Neil McNeil, the Roman Catholic archbishop of Toronto, "the loyalty of the Catholic soldier and of the Catholic population is absolutely essential to the continued existence of the British Empire." McNeil's effusions of patriotism and expressions of anger were directed at allegations made by the Reverend E. I. Hart of Montreal who had accused the Catholic Church of being the mastermind behind resistance to the imperial war effort in both Quebec and Ireland. Outraged at such an accusation, McNeil pointed out to the *Toronto Star* that, by 1917, "race, not creed," lay behind the opposition of many Quebeckers to the Canadian war effort. Moreover, he added, there was no difference between the loyalty to be found among Canada's English-speaking Catholics and that of the nation's Protestants because, according to the archbishop, "we are all involved in the same issue."[1]

While McNeil's pronouncements of a strong English-speaking Catholic commitment to the British Empire and the Canadian war effort could easily have been echoed by many of his episcopal colleagues in Canada as well as many leading Catholic politicians, his words vividly reveal the ongoing struggle of English-speaking Catholics to achieve a level of respectability in Canada amidst their Protestant neighbors. It

1. *Toronto Star*, 3 November 1917.

is well known that the Great War ripped Canada apart along linguistic, ethnic, and class lines, but little has been written on the troubled situation of English-speaking Catholics who were torn between their linguistic and cultural ties to English-speaking Protestant Canada, on the one hand, and their religious ties to French Canada, on the other. In the period leading up to the war, English-speaking Catholics had improved their material conditions in Canada,[2] advanced in their political status, and had increasingly become more comfortable in identifying themselves with the patriotic aspirations of other English-speaking Canadians and the international questions relating to the British Empire.[3] The historiography of the Great War and Canada's role in it tends only to discuss the role of the Catholic Church in relationship with the French Canadian Catholic resistance to conscription and the Francophone Catholic hierarchy's struggle to maintain their loyalty to the Crown and the Canadian state while not losing their position of leadership among their faithful who were less than enthusiastic about the war effort and committed to violence to resist conscription.[4] What is lost in the historical discussion is a sense that the Catholic Church was much more than just its French Canadian majority.

In every province of Canada, Anglophone bishops, priests, and laypersons, of Irish, Scottish, American, English, Aboriginal, and European descent, were ardent supporters of the imperial war effort, were recruited voluntarily in great numbers into the Canadian Expeditionary Force, and supported fundraising and war-related programs on the domestic front. Far from being dissuaded from assisting imperial Britain by their more radically nationalistic cousins in the United States, Irish Catholics in Canada, who made up the overwhelming majority of Anglophone Catholics, were conspicuous in their activities in every aspect of the war effort. Encouraged by their spiritual leaders, young Catholic men and women enlisted in locally-based battalions, the medical corps, the artillery, the navy, and even the Royal Flying Corps, often in the face of criticism from non-Catholics that their loyalties, particularly those

2. Di Matteo, "Wealth"; Baskerville, "Did Religion Matter"; McGowan, *Waning of the Green*, ch.1.

3. McGowan, "Degreening"; Harris, "Our Own Land"; Cottrell, "Political Leadership."

4. Granatstein and Hitsman, *Broken Promises*; MacKenzie, *First World War*; Rutherdale, *Hometown Horizons*; Morton, *Number's Up*. In what is otherwise a splendid examination of soldiering in the Great War, Morton offers almost no insight into the religion of the men.

of the Irish, lay elsewhere. Indeed Irish and Scottish Catholics, despite their open support of the Canadian War effort, were constantly criticized because of the behavior of Catholics elsewhere in Canada or the world: the French Canadian Catholic aversion to military service, the Ukrainian Catholic Eparch Nykyta Budka who, before the outbreak of war, had urged his flock in Canada to support Emperor Franz Josef in Austria-Hungary, the neutrality of Pope Benedict XV, the presence of allegedly pro-German Catholics in Canada, and the Irish uprising against Britain in 1916. Walking a fine line between maintaining Church unity and professing loyalty to the Crown, the Roman Catholic bishops found themselves constantly defending themselves against domestic demagogues instead of channeling all of their energies into "winning the war." By 1918, however, Canadian Catholics faced a Church that was seriously divided along linguistic lines, with Anglophone Catholics having firmly established themselves in the civic sphere as loyal, collaborative, and articulate citizens of Canada and the Empire. While there would still be tensions between Protestant and Catholic communities on certain issues (separate schools) and in specific regions, the respectability earned by their sacrifices in the Great War would accelerate English-speaking Catholic integration into the mainstream of English-Canadian society.

It is estimated that at the onset of the twentieth century, there were over one-half million (580,229) non-French-speaking Catholics in Canada's nine provinces and territories, comprising just over ten percent of Canada's people. By 1911, this number may have been as high as 690,000.[5] Most Catholics who spoke the English language were of Irish descent and, although estimates are difficult given the nature of the reporting and cross-referencing of religion and ethnicity in the Canadian Census, these Irish, at the turn of the century, may have numbered as many as 480,000.[6] Among the non-Francophone Catholic group, the Irish were joined by clusters of Scottish Highlanders from Cape Breton, Prince Edward Island, and eastern Ontario. Other tiny minorities included Catholics of English descent (converts from Protestantism),

---

5. Estimates are based on *Fourth Census of Canada, 1901*, tables I, IX, X, and XI. See also Perin, *Rome*, 11–38. *Fifth Census of Canada, 1911*, table I and table IX.

6. *Fourth Census of Canada, 1901*, based on the total Catholic population 2,229,600 in Canada. Subtract French Canadians (1,649,371); Italians (10,834); Belgians (2,994); 25% of Germans in Waterloo (7,500), 66% Austrians (12,000); PEI Scots (15, 965); Glengarry Scots (5,075); Eastern Nova Scotian Scots (44,742) for a rough estimate of the Irish Catholics. The estimate is approximate.

American and German settlers, Italians, Poles, Ukrainians, and several bands of First Nations peoples. Those of the Irish majority were bound together by an institutional church that provided spiritual, educational, and health care, as well as social services across the country. In 1900, Irish Catholics could be found in all twenty-seven Canadian dioceses and vicariates apostolic, although those Catholics living in Ontario and the Maritime provinces would be the only ones administered by bishops of either Scottish or Irish descent.[7] By 1914, Irish and Scottish Catholic leadership extended westward to the Episcopal sees of Victoria, Vancouver, Calgary, and eventually Edmonton, and the new see of Winnipeg (1915).[8] Of great interest to observers of religion in 1901, however, was the fact that Irish Catholics across Canada displayed strong rates of regular church attendance, ranging from 73 percent in Charlotte County, New Brunswick, to 85 percent in Halifax, to allegedly 99 percent in Hamilton, Ontario.[9] This strength of affiliation confirms local churches as community centers, and local Irish church leaders as significant in the lives of Canada's non-Francophone Catholic communities.

Participation in imperial wars was by no means a new activity for English-speaking Catholics when Britain declared war on Germany and her allies in August 1914. At the turn of the century, Irish and Scottish Catholics had been recruited heavily, particularly in Ontario and Nova Scotia, for the Canadian contingents in the South African War.[10] Some Catholic bishops publicly endorsed the war effort; notable was Cornelius O'Brien of Halifax, who in a pastoral letter claimed the South African engagement to be a "noble and just" cause.[11] Lay politicians such as federal solicitor-general Charles Fitzpatrick celebrated the conflict as an opportunity for Canadians to show their imperial colors:

> The British Empire is no mere geographical expression for a number of sundered and disunited provinces—the time had

---

7. McGowan, "Rethinking."

8. McGowan, "Maritime Region," and Huel, "Conflict."

9. *Census of Canada, 1901*, volume 4, table XIX, "Churches and Sunday Schools for Canada and the Provinces." Calculations are based on these figures of actual participation when compared to basic rates of profession in the same census. See also McGowan, "Irish Catholics," 751.

10. See Appendix 1.

11. *Le Soleil*, 13 November 1899. O'Brien was in the public eye numerous times in the autumn of 1899, including the highly successful consecration of the new St. Mary's Cathedral in Halifax. See *Morning Chronicle* [Halifax], 20 October 1899.

come when it was necessary for the whelps of the lion to rally to the defence of the old land. The time had come when every man must be made to understand whether on the European continent or in South Africa, that blow for blow whensoever the blow might come, must be struck back by the British, and would be struck as freely from Australasia and Canada as from the heart of the Empire itself.[12]

Other Catholic politicians, such as Chief Justice William Wilfred Sullivan of PEI or Senator Lawrence Geoffrey Power of Nova Scotia, would agree and publicly endorse recruitment.[13] Similarly, the lay editors of Catholic newspapers—the *Catholic Record* in London, *The New Freeman* Saint John, and eventually the originally neutral *The Casket* in Antigonish and the *Catholic Register* in Toronto—would all demonstrate their support of the Canadian war effort.[14] Upon reflection, a decade after the war, some Catholics would call upon this first imperial war effort in the veldts of South Africa as a precedent for continued Catholic loyalty and duty as Europe descended into war. In the Boer War, Catholics had battle-tested their first chaplains and their first infantrymen in the imperial cause, which represented foundation stones upon which they could build in the current conflict.[15]

As the geopolitical stresses of the spring and summer of 1914 erupted into open war in August, non-Francophone Catholics, like other Canadians, were jolted from the rhythms of their everyday life. Not surprisingly, given the endorsements by Catholic bishops of the British cause in previous conflicts such as the American War of Independence

---

12. *Hansard: House of Commons Debates*, 63–64 Victoria, 20 February 1900, 668–69.

13. *The Morning Guardian* (Charlottetown), 24 October 1899. See Sullivan's obvious Tory connections in Morgan, "William Wilfred Sullivan," 985. See *Halifax Herald*, 2 November 1899. Senator Richard Scott was not as impressed, considering the war to be a conspiracy of British "jingos" and their Canadian allies. See Scott, "Sir Richard Scott," 59; Clarke, "Sir Richard Scott," 915.

14. *Catholic Record*, 9 April 1898; 29 October 1898; 18 November 1899; 25 November 1899; 16 December 1899; 24 March 1900; 29 September 1900; 9 February 1901; *Catholic Register*, 14 February 1899; 21 December 1899; *The Casket*, 2 November 1899; 25 January 1900; 15 February 1900; 22 February 1900; 24 May 1900; 12 July 1900; 17 May 1901; 24 October 1901. See MacLean, *Casket: 1852–1992*, 102; *New Freeman*, 6 January 1900; 13 January 1900; 27 January 1900; 3 February 1900; 2 June 1900.

15. *New Freeman*, 31 October 1914; *Northwest Review*, 8 August 1914. See also Burke, "Irishman's Place."

and the War of 1812, Canada's Catholic episcopate was uniform in its support of the Canadian and imperial war effort. While the archbishops of the principal Francophone Catholic sees in Quebec (Montreal, Quebec City, and Ottawa) issued a joint pastoral letter in support of the British war effort in September 1914, fifteen other Catholic bishops outside of Quebec tended to issue endorsements of military action independently and repeated those affirmations of support throughout the duration of the war. Bishops James Morrison of Antigonish, Edward McCarthy of Halifax, Louis O'Leary of Chatham, Patrick Ryan of Pembroke, Michael J. Spratt of Kingston, Michael O'Brien of Peterborough, Michael Francis Fallon of London, Neil McNeil of Toronto, James T. McNally of Calgary, Alfred Sinnott of Winnipeg (by 1915), Timothy Casey of Vancouver, and Alexander "Sandy" MacDonald of Victoria, were all publicly vocal in their support of the war effort, on spiritual grounds as a fight for Christian morality and values but also in support of the Empire's defense of small nations under attack from "Prussian Militarism."[16] Bishop MacDonald of Victoria, originally a native of Cape Breton, made an impassioned plea to Catholics for their support of the war effort based upon both imperial and Christian arguments:

> Canada is a part of the British Empire. Canadians are British subjects; we are all under the manifold obligation to the Motherland; the parliament of our country has decided by unanimous vote to discharge, in some measure, our obligation. It is, I conceive, the strict duty of every citizen of Canada to respect that act of our parliament. . . . The present crisis to my mind, is emphatically one in which the words of our Blessed Lord find an appropriate application: "He that is not for me is against me, and he that gathereth not with Me scattereth."[17]

For the outspoken Bishop Michael Francis Fallon of London, Canadians had no choice in the matter: "It either means victory or the disappearance of the British Empire with its liberty and its tradition. In this peril

---

16. *New Freeman*, 21 August 1915; 19 February 1916, (re Casey); *The Casket*, 26 November 1914, (Morrison); ADA, James Morrison Papers, Pastoral, 3 March 1915; AAH, James T. McNally Papers, vol. 5, documents 761, 771, 790, 791, and 798; AAH, Edward McCarthy Papers, vol. 1, documents 80–81; ADP, Bishop Ryan Papers, Pastorals and Circulars, 1914–1919; *Northwest Review*, 25 December 1915, (re Sinnott); *Canadian Freeman*, 9 December 1914, (re O'Brien); 8 March 1916, (re Spratt).

17. *The Casket*, 12 November 1914.

there is no line of cleavage between us. We are one because we know Britain's cause is just."[18]

The bishops also elaborated a spirituality that justified the fighting. For many, the war was fought to defend Christian values and morality that were threatened by Prussian militarism, which was now responsible for the ravaging of the tiny Catholic country of Belgium. Archbishop Michael Spratt of Kingston, Ontario, regarded the enlistment of Catholic men as a selfless sacrificial act that would bring one into a virtual *imitatio Christi* and assurance of heavenly reward: "The man who from supernatural motives, leaves house or brethren ... and goes into a far off country, to offer himself a victim for immolation upon the altar of his country, in defense of the weak and in behalf of his fellow men, without doubt acquires a title to the promised hundred-fold and life everlasting. This is the supreme act of self-denial and the plentitude of the virtue of penance."[19] These ideas of linking patriotism, Christian duty, and self-sacrifice were popularized further in the Catholic press, when such papers as the *Catholic Register* reiterated that Christ would crown "the military valour" of a soldier who died in this just cause.[20]

The words of the English-speaking Catholic Bishops of Canada were quickly actualized in all of their dioceses. In addition to prayers for peace and prayers for Canadian troops, recited regularly by congregations within the context of the Mass,[21] bishops mandated Catholic support for recruitment drives, collections for the Patriotic Fund, bond drives, food rationing,[22] fundraising for the international Red Cross and the Belgian Relief Fund, and the enlistment of Catholic chaplains to the Canadian Expeditionary Force. In Toronto, Archbishop Neil McNeil became an ardent advocate of the Patriotic Fund, designed to offer financial support to the families of Canadian soldiers and sailors. To this end, he himself pledged $5000 of his personal funds and, throughout the war, called upon Catholic Canadians to donate in the same spirit of patriotic duty: "Our Catholic people have united with their fellow

18. *Catholic Record*, 12 September 1914.
19. *Canadian Freeman*, 8 March 1916.
20. *Catholic Register*, 18 March 1915.
21. *Catholic Register*, 19 November 1914, and Michael Francis Fallon Papers, Pastoral Letter, 28 August 1914 (ADL); *Catholic Record*, 12 September 1914; *Ottawa Journal*, 12 October 1914.
22. AAW, Alfred A. Sinnott Papers, Circular letter, 28 February 1918.

citizens in past efforts of this kind and I fully expect that also in the campaign now undertaken they will not be found wanting but generous in their patriotism."[23] McNeil also took to the platform to stimulate Catholic recruitment and went so far as to endorse specific battalions as they recruited local men while billeted in the archdiocese.[24] Since he set a high standard among his fellow bishops, and by merit of the importance of the See of Toronto and the respect he commanded as a scholar, former University President, and experienced bishop, McNeil was certainly one of the most influential clerics in Canada. He was unequivocal in his support of the British war effort: "When we think of the slain we make no distinctions. Christian charity prays for all. But when we come to organizations and institutions and to causes, I am prepared to defend the cause of right, the cause of Britain and Belgium, with my life."[25]

The initiatives and strong support for the war by the non-Francophone Catholic bishops had a profound effect on the responses by the Catholic clergy and laity across the country, including parts of Quebec such as Montreal or the primarily Anglophone region including Pontiac County in the upper Ottawa Valley. Like their bishops, many priests used their pulpits to advocate for the war effort, the Patriotic Fund, the Red Cross, and recruitment of young men into the Canadian Expeditionary Force. In the Archdiocese of Toronto, McNeil had requested that his pastors, as a test of their "professions of patriotism," give $40 every six months to the Patriotic Fund.[26] In Whitby, in the extreme east of the archdiocese, Father William J. Ryan went a step further by joining local military officials and Protestant ministers in his support of the Patriotic Fund by serving on its Finance Committee.[27] Imitating the work of their bishops, many priests across the county spoke passionately at recruiting rallies. In Saint John, New Brunswick, for example, Father Miles Pius Howland pointed out to audiences the sense of urgency in recruitment: "I want to impress upon the men of military age who are in the audience tonight the terrible necessity for you offering your services to your King

23. *Catholic Register*, 25 January 1917; and ARCAT, Neil McNeil Papers, 1914 Patriotic Fund Campaign, Pledge Card# 924.

24. ARCAT, McNeil Papers, FWGC 01.103, War Box, "Catholic Young Men 'SHUN.'" See also his speech to troops printed in the *Catholic Register*, 27 August 1914.

25. *The Casket*, 7 January 1915.

26. ARCAT, McNeil Papers, PC01.02, Pastoral, 25 August 1914.

27. *Whitby Gazette*, 27 May 1915.

and country. I think you cannot realize the awfulness of this universal catastrophe."[28] In a similar spirit, but in Assiniboia, Manitoba, Father A. Sammut held special "patriotic services" to reaffirm "our boundless loyalty and sincere fidelity to our King."[29] In the Diocese of Hamilton, at the Cape Croker First Nations reserve on Georgian Bay, Jesuit missionaries took a strong hand in recruiting young Ojibwe men to such infantry units as the 160th Bruce County Battalion.[30] Not far away in Walkerton, in the same Diocese, amidst a congregation of mixed Irish and German Catholics, Father J. P. Cummings took to the recruiting platform, asserting that all the men present ought to act as true Canadian citizens and British subjects and enlist: "Everything we have we owe to the British Empire. No other people enjoys the same freedoms and same justices. We have everything to live for, everything to work for, and everything to die for. Our fate is at stake."[31] Several miles away, in the German-Catholic farming area near Formosa, Cummings's colleague Father George Brohman toasted "King and Country" at a fundraising and recruiting dinner held among the Irish and German families in the parish. It is not surprising, then, that the sailing lists of at least three battalions and the war memorials in churches and public parks in Bruce County, Ontario, German-Catholic surnames like Haas, Siegfried, Eckensweiler, Zettel, and Ernewein are conspicuous, intermixed among the Ryans, McNabs, Sullivans, and Hanleys.[32]

Catholic newspapers were also prominent in their unqualified support of the war effort in the early stages of the war through recruitment drives, and even during the challenges posed by the imposition of conscription by the Federal Government. Canada's most easterly Catholic

28. *New Freeman*, 23 October 1915.

29. *Northwest Review*, 14 August 1915.

30. AJUCP, Cape Croker Mission Diary, 1914–1918; LAC, RG 9, B 3, vol. 80, Sailing Lists, CEF, Sailing List of the 160th Battalion, Canadian Expeditionary Force.

31. *Walkerton Telescope*, 10 February 1916.

32. *Walkerton Telescope*, 2 November 1916. See also *Walkerton Telescope*, 2 September 1915; 9 September 1915; 16 September 1915; 23 September 1915; 20 January 1916; 27 April 1916. The 16 February 1916 issue of the paper specifically praised the loyalty and work of German Catholics in the county, and on 20 January 1916 the paper singled out the war efforts and recruitment of the Irish-Catholic community near the farming hamlet of Vesta in Brant Township. The tiny farming parish of St. Michael's had offered nine volunteers for the CEF. The conspicuousness of German Catholic recruits can be seen in the sailing lists of the 34th, 71st, and 160th Battalions: LAC, RG 9 II B 3, vol. 80, Sailing Lists, CEF.

newspaper, the *Casket*, published in Antigonish, reflected much of the sentiment expressed by English-language Catholic editors, both clerical and lay, across Canada. In the early stages of the war, editor William Donovan of the *Casket* was clear about Canadian and Catholic duty:

> We are at war; that is the short plain awful truth. In the fate of Great Britain, the fate of the Empire is involved. Canada is in an unprotected position and it seems unlikely that many British ships, if any, can be spared in our defense. On the other hand we may not need much protection. We hope not. The first thought of Canadians will be to do what we can, and as far as necessary to guard our own dear Canada; but besides that, unless the war proves to be a short one and favourable at once to the British Crown, there will doubtless be many thousands of brave young Canadians ere long, standing shoulder to shoulder with Englishmen, Irishmen and Scotchmen, in Belgium or wherever else the flag may be unfurled as a battle standard for the integrity of the Empire.[33]

A columnist, "Columba," in the *Catholic Record* (London) was even more singular in pointing out where Catholic loyalties lay: "Yes, Catholics are just as loyal as anyone else. We will suffer no aspersions on our allegiance to the flag. No man dare forbid us 'God bless the Pope,' but because of that 'God Save the King' loses none of its significance when uttered by Catholic lips."[34] Father Alfred E. Burke, the openly Conservative[35] and imperialist editor of the *Catholic Register* in Toronto, was second to none in his loyalty when he exclaimed in his paper: "We are as British as we always have been, and we will, praise God, always be."[36] Similarly, the *Canadian Freeman* in Kingston was unequivocal: "It is because precisely that Catholics are so loyal to the Church that they are invariably loyal to the state. A good Catholic must necessarily be a good citizen. Catholicity presupposes loyalty."[37] The *Northwest Review* (Winnipeg), and the *New Freeman* (Saint John), differed little from the editorial pronouncements of their sister papers.[38]

33. *The Casket*, 13 August 1914.
34. *Catholic Record*, 22 August 1914.
35. *Globe*, 14 June 1912.
36. *Catholic Register*, 20 October 1914.
37. *Canadian Freeman*, 20 April 1916.
38. *Northwest Review*, 29 August 1914.

Lay organizations in local parishes and Catholic fraternal benevolent organizations joined with the clergy, editors, and Catholic politicians in their endorsement of the war against Germany. Local parishes held sock drives for the troops, ladies auxiliaries created knitting circles and prepared packages for CEF troops overseas. Dinners and soirees were held to raise money for the Patriotic Fund, the Red Cross, Belgian Relief, or recruitment.[39] In her diaries, Ethel Chadwick, a parishioner at St. Joseph's Parish in the Sandy Hill district of Ottawa, reflected upon a "soldier's supper" held at St. Patrick's Hall. Organized principally by her parish to support the troops at Rockliffe Park military base, the evening as Chadwick described it was filled with speeches from the local priest and Catholic politicians, including Minister of Justice C. J. Doherty and Chief Justice Charles Fitzpatrick, and ended with the soldiers' calamitous cheer for the ladies who had "given the treat."[40] Similarly, national organizations such as the Knights of Columbus claimed the war effort as one of its priority projects. Encouraged by their Ontario State Chaplain,[41] Bishop Fallon, the Knights engaged in recruitment efforts across the province, and even claimed they would honor insurance claims made by the families of any member who served and died in the conflict.[42] Similarly, at the State Conventions of the Knights in Manitoba and Saskatchewan that was held in Brandon in 1915, the members resolved to "make every sacrifice until the glorious day arrives when the armies of the allies shall be victorious and the brutal and savage foes that have cast aside all considerations of Christian conduct and civilization are taught such a lesson that they will never attempt or even be in a position to threaten or to disturb the liberties of the free peoples of the earth."[43] Comparable

---

39. Examples of such activities can be found in *Catholic Register*, 20 July 1916; *Pickering News*, 24 March 1916; *Pickering News*, 16 July 1916; *St. Joseph's Lilies*, vol. 4 (March 1916); and ARCAT, War Box, Essays of Children from St. Cecilia's Parish, 1917.

40. LAC, Ethel Chadwick Fonds, MG 30 D 258, vol. 3, Tuesday, June 8, 1915.

41. The Knights of Columbus are a Catholic fraternal benevolent society founded in 1882 in New Haven, Connecticut, by parish priest Father Michael J. McGivney (now declared Venerable by Pope Benedict XVI). The structure was American as were many of its rituals. Organizationally councils reported to districts, which in turn reported to State Councils. In Canada, provinces were deemed "states" by the KofC. Membership of the order was restricted to male Catholics over the age of eighteen who were in communion with the Holy See. Kaufman, *Faith and Fraternalism*.

42. *Catholic Record*, 14 November 1914; 8 April 1916; *Globe*, 13 October 1914.

43. *Northwest Review*, 15 May 1915.

support was publicized by the State Convention of Knights in Ontario and by Knights in New Brunswick.[44] The Knights of Columbus were not alone in their support of the war effort; the Catholic Order of Foresters, the Ancient Order of Hibernians (of which Fallon was also chaplain), and the Italian National Club of Toronto all committed themselves to winning the war.[45] Catholic businesses, such as O'Keefe Breweries in Toronto, also made financial contributions to such fundraising drives as the Patriotic Fund.[46] Even Catholic universities contributed to the war effort, with St. Francis Xavier University creating its own field hospital (#9 Stationary Hospital) for the Canadian Expeditionary Force.[47]

One of the most significant indicators of English-speaking Catholic engagement in the war effort was the level of voluntary enlistment in the Canadian Expeditionary Force. The process of analyzing the size, cultural profile, and the social composition of Catholic recruitment in Canada during the Great War is a methodological and interpretive minefield. Religious statistics offered by the Department of the Militia and Defense are incomplete when they are included in unit files and reports at all. Because religious, linguistic, and ethnic categories are rarely employed at the same time in tables and reports, it is extremely difficult to pinpoint a definitive number of the non-Francophone Catholics who voluntarily enlisted in the CEF. What is known with some certainty is that by June 1917, essentially the end of the several phases of voluntary enlistment, approximately 51,426 Roman Catholics were enlisted in the CEF, constituting about 14 percent of the total number of recruits.[48] Military analysts and Protestant extremists like the members of the Loyal Orange Lodge, regarded this percentage of Catholic recruits as ample evidence that the Roman Catholic Church, which constituted about 40 percent of the entire Canadian population, had certainly not pulled its weight in the war effort in a capacity where it really could make a difference.[49] Reports from the Roman Catholic chaplains serving with the CEF, however, cast

---

44. *New Freeman*, 24 June 1916; *Canadian Freeman*, 26 May 1915.

45. *Globe*, 14 September 1914; *Canadian Freeman*, 16 June 1915; *Catholic Record*, 8 April 1916.

46. *Globe*, 28 August 1914.

47. *Diocese of Antigonish*, 55–56.

48. LAC, Department of Militia and Defense, RG 9 III, vol. 4673, Memoranda, Religious Statistics, 1917. See Appendix 2.

49. For Catholic population figures, see Choquette, "English-French Relations," 5.

a more discerning light on the nature of Catholic volunteers and suggest that English-speaking Catholics recruited at levels consistent with their numbers in the Canadian population in general. In 1917, Father John J. O'Gorman of Ottawa reported to his superiors in the Canadian Chaplains Service that 36,512 of the Catholic recruits were English-speaking, making them the single largest Catholic linguistic grouping in the CEF, and second only to the Anglicans in terms of the rate of recruitment, relative to their numbers in the general population. O'Gorman, who was convalescing from serious wounds received at the front, had plenty of time to crunch numbers and try to prove the anti-Catholic voices in Canada wrong. He suggested that French Canadian recruitment was about 13,000 or only little over a third of the entire Catholic total of volunteers, thus making the Irish, Scots, and other Catholic recruits a much more significant proportion of the army population than it had appeared at first glance.[50]

It would appear that the endorsements of the episcopacy, clergy, and lay leaders of the Catholic community in Anglophone Canada had a strong influence on Catholic recruitment in all regions of the country. In the West, where the non-Francophone population was small in comparison to the general population, and where most Catholics were Ukrainian, Polish, Hungarian, and German immigrants, the Anglophone Catholic recruitment was about 7 to 10 percent of volunteers. In Ontario, by the end of 1916, Catholic volunteers, most of whom were of Irish or Scottish descent, constituted about 14 percent of the total volunteers.[51] There were pockets of undeniably strong recruitment: nine English-speaking Catholic parishes in Toronto contributed more than 10 percent of their parish populations translating into 3,500 recruits, or nearly one fifth of Ontario's entire group of Catholic volunteers. St. Patrick's parish in Ottawa boasted that one quarter of all its men of military age had enlisted in the CEF, and Bishop "Sandy" MacDonald of Victoria took great pride in the heavy recruitment from his Cathedral parish of St.

---

50. LAC, Militia and Defense, RG 9 III vol. 4636, O'Gorman Memorandum to the Archbishops and Bishops of Ontario, October 1917, 10–11; also vol. 4673, Religious Statistics and RG 24, vol. 1249, HQ-593-1-77, 22 August 1916. Similar numbers appear in Armstrong, *Crisis*, 247. Her evidence is drawn from Sessional Paper 143-B.

51. LAC, Militia and Defence, RG 9 III, vol. 4652, Enlistments /6, 31 December 1916. The *Catholic Register* also included updated figures, see *Catholic Register*, 8 November 1917; 28 July 1918.

Andrew's.⁵² By far the largest group of Catholic recruits proportionally came from the Maritime provinces, particularly Nova Scotia, where Catholics constituted 47 percent of recruits. At the end of 1916, Military District 6, headquartered at Halifax and consisting of the three Maritime provinces, had the highest number of Catholic recruits for all districts at approximately 27 percent of the District's fighting force. While perhaps as many as 14 percent of the 8,825 Catholic volunteers were Acadian, some of whom would form a distinctive Acadian battalion, most of the Catholic recruits were of Irish and Scottish descent. In the Diocese of Antigonish alone (consisting of Eastern Nova Scotia and Cape Breton Island), 4,500 Catholics enlisted in the CEF, the American Expeditionary Force and the Imperial Navy.⁵³ As early as 1915, English-speaking Catholic recruitment was significant enough to warrant more permanent positions for a Catholic chaplain in at least sixteen infantry battalions in which Anglophone Catholics constituted more than 100 men each, particularly in units from the Maritimes, Eastern and Central Ontario, and Alberta.⁵⁴ By 1916, Catholics gained an unprecedented second chaplain for the 5th Brigade so that Francophone and Anglophone Catholics could have a priest exclusive to each linguistic group.

While clerical and lay leadership might account in some measure for Catholic recruitment, there were other causes. Such factors as effective recruitment efforts by militia units during the second and third phases of voluntary recruitment in 1915 and 1916, regional economic pressures and unemployment, peer pressure, the personal desire for adventure, and the lure of specialty battalions and Scottish and Irish units,

---

52. McGowan, *Waning of the Green*, appendix; *Ontario Catholic Yearbook*, 96; *The Casket*, 25 November 1915. The honor roll in St. Andrew's Cathedral holds the names of seventeen parishioners who were killed during the war. Charles Murphy, the Liberal MP for Russell, claimed that St. Theresa's Parish in center town in Ottawa had 700 recruits, but this seems unlikely given the territory of the parish sandwiched amid St. Patrick's, St. Joseph's, and Blessed Sacrament parishes. LAC, Charles Murphy Papers, vol. 49, undated speech, 22178–79.

53. *Diocese of Antigonish*, 67–158. The author calculates that about 14.6 percent of these Catholics were Syrian, Acadian, or Italian.

54. LAC, Defence, RG 24 vol. 1249, HQ-593-1-77, 30 August 1915. These units included 33rd (London), 37th (Northern Ontario), 58th (Central Ontario), 76th (Barrie, Orillia, Collingwood), 83rd (Toronto), 59th (Eastern Ontario), 77th (Ottawa), 8th Canadian Mounted Rifles (Ontario), 40th (Nova Scotia), 55th (New Brunswick), 60th (Montreal—one company of Irish Rangers), 64th (PEI, NS, NB), 54th (British Columbia), 51st (Edmonton), 63rd (Alberta), and 66th (Edmonton).

all had a role in bringing non-Francophone Catholic men to the recruiting office.[55] In Montreal, for instance, the 199th Irish Canadian Rangers drew a half to two-thirds of their strength from men of Irish Catholic descent or birth.[56] Similarly, Scottish and Irish Catholic youths in Nova Scotia were drawn to the 85th Battalion and later the 185th Battalion, Cape Breton Highlanders; in eastern Ontario and western Quebec, the 42nd Battalion and 130th Battalion, Lanark and Renfrew Highlanders, drew young Catholic men from the farms, villages, and towns on both sides of the Ottawa River. When military authorities in England began to break up these speciality battalions in order to supplement the ranks of active battalions that had been decimated at the front, both the troops and the Catholics at home who had sponsored such units were livid.[57] The appeal of such ethnically-based units, however, was not universal to Catholic men across the country. In Toronto, and in other places across the Dominion, Catholic men joined battalions raised in their neighborhoods, or units derived from known militia units where they had previously served, or they followed the lead of a father, brother, cousin, or even parish priest into the service.[58]

The most visible role for priests in the war effort was when they donned khaki themselves. Following the example of the celebrated Father Peter O'Leary,[59] who served as the only Catholic Chaplain in the South African war, Catholic priests were needed to attend directly to the spiritual needs of the Catholic troops enlisting in the CEF. Early in the war the serious lack of English-speaking priests for the first two contingents of the CEF was a result of a severe shortage of Anglophone priests in Canada, a lack of a recruitment plan by the Canadian bishops, and suspicions that the Minister of the Militia, Sam Hughes (a vocal member of the Orange Order) and his Director of the Chaplain Service, Anglican Minister Colonel R. H. Steacy, harbored an anti-Catholic bias.

---

55. An excellent discussion of recruitment patterns can be found in Brown and Loveridge, "Unrequited Faith," 56–63.

56. Burns, "Montreal Irish," and LAC, Militia and Defense, RG 9 III vol. 4650, 15th Brigade, Canadian Infantry, 21 April 1917.

57. MacIntyre, "Highlanders"; *The Casket*, 23 March 1916; 14 December 1916. See also Burns, "Montreal Irish," 75–81.

58. For examples of family-centered recruitment see McGowan, "Burdens of the Empire"; also *Diocese of Antigonish*, 158; ARCAT, Parish Boxes, St. Helen's Parish, Honour Roll, 4 April 1917; Cornwall, Ontario, St. Columban's Parish, Honour Roll.

59. Crerar, *Padres*, 21.

Bishop Michael Fallon meets with Canadian Catholic Chaplains in France, May 3, 1918. Fallon is seated in the center of the first row, without military uniform. Major J. J. O'Gorman is seated second from the right. From the author's collection, photographer unknown.

By 1915, reports reached Canada that English-speaking Catholic soldiers were rarely visited by a Catholic chaplain and when they were, the priest could not administer the sacraments in the English language with fluency. Father Alfred Burke, who had left the editorship of the *Catholic Register* and joined the Chaplaincy Service, denied the allegations, but his words were treated with suspicion since his Conservative party connections tied him closely to Hughes and Steacy.[60] As more English-speaking Catholics arrived in the CEF by mid 1916, Catholic Bishops scrambled to send more priests and by war's end over one hundred priests were in the CCS, most of whom were English-speaking. Several won the Military Cross for valor, and Father J. J. O'Gorman single-handedly brought about the complete overhaul of the administrative structure of

60. ASV, Apostolic Delegate's Correspondence (DAC), vol. 130.1, folio 1, Burke to Archbishop Pellegrino Stagni, 4 November 1915 and folio 2, R. Steacy to Father J. J. O'Gorman, 20 June 1916; and 130 ½, O'Gorman to Stagni, 21 July 1916.

the service, placing Protestant and Catholic chaplains on a more equal footing and ridding the CEF of both Steacy and Burke.[61] Until the appointment of Bishop Joseph Emard of Valleyfield as *episcopus castrensis* of the military, in late 1918, none other than Bishop Fallon of London supervised the appointment of Catholic chaplains.

Whether clerical or lay, and whatever the reasons for their enlistment, Catholic recruits differed from many of the Protestant volunteers in terms of their place of birth. During the first two phases of recruitment in 1914 and 1915, battalions in the CEF were dominated by Anglicans and Presbyterians who had been born in Scotland, England, Ireland, and Wales and were eager to return "home" and defend the Empire. It was not until the later stages of recruitment in mid 1915 and early 1916 that Canadian-born men came to dominate those who filled out their attestation papers. From the beginning of the voluntary phases of recruitment, however, Catholics were overwhelmingly Canadian-born. At least 70 percent of Irish Catholic troops, who dominated the English-speaking Catholic members of the CEF, were born in Canada.[62] The figures vary little whether the samples are extracted from parish honor rolls and lists (75.5 percent Canadian), selected battalions (71.1 percent Canadian), or the three specialty Irish battalions (68.6 percent).[63] The dominance of Canadian-born volunteers is even more evident among a sample of eighty-two Catholic nursing sisters, 89 percent of whom were born in Canada.[64] Moreover, in certain regions of the country, particularly rural areas where there had been lower levels of immigration, the "Canadianness" of the Catholic troops was remarkable, even when compared to a greater number of indigenous Protestant recruits. In the Diocese of Pembroke, which straddles the Ottawa River and encompasses farms, villages, and towns in both Ontario and Quebec, levels of Canadian-born recruits were only marginally different between Catholics and Protestants, likely because each group had deep-set

61. Crerar, "Bellicose Priests"; Crerar, *Padres,* 235–47 (Nominal List).

62. See Appendix 3.

63. These speciality battalions included the 199th (Montreal), 208th (Toronto) and the 121st (Vancouver). Parish samples were taken in Sydney and Halifax, Nova Scotia, Montreal, Ottawa, Toronto, Winnipeg, Calgary, and Victoria. Battalion samples included the 25th and 85th (Nova Scotia), the 105th (PEI), the 26th and 132nd (New Brunswick), the 38th, 75th, 77th, 160th, and 240th (Ontario), 100th (Manitoba), and the 68th (Saskatchewan).

64. See Appendix 5.

generational roots in this rural region of Canada. In the case of both Catholics and Presbyterians, 94 percent of the recruits and conscripts were Canadian born, compared to 83 percent of Anglicans, which as a denomination had far lower levels of native-born recruits at the national level.[65] Nevertheless, in 1915, the *Catholic Register* was not far from the mark when it reported that there was a distinct difference between Catholic and Protestant recruits: "Last month at Niagara-on-the-Lake there were twelve thousand Canadian soldiers. Of these ten percent were Catholics, and when we take into account that more than half of all the other soldiers were natives of European Protestant countries, and that nearly all of the Catholics were native Canadians, we can safely infer that the Catholics of Ontario are 'doing their bit' as well as any."[66]

With the empirical evidence of Catholic support for the war so clear from both the words and deeds of non-Francophone Catholic leaders, lay Catholics, clergy, and voluntary recruits, what can account for the continued questioning of the Catholic war effort, particularly from certain elements in the Protestant population? Writing in October 1916, Norman Murray, publisher of the *Sentinel* (the official organ of the Loyal Orange Lodges in British North America), took aim squarely at Catholic disloyalty:

> Another great surprise in store [during this war] was the indifference and apathy of the Roman Catholic part of the population of the British Empire. The situation in the Catholic portion of Ireland and in Quebec is almost identical, with a little to the good in favour of Catholic Ireland in the matter of recruiting to the British Army.... While the Canadian hierarchy is said to have advised its people to do their part like their fellow countrymen by enlisting in the imperial army this advice seems to have no effect whatever.... It has been suggested that the Church is playing a double game and that, while it openly proclaims its loyalty, it is secretly working the other way through the confessional and otherwise.[67]

Murray continued by presenting the recruitment of Irish Catholics in Montreal as an abject failure and his paper made repeated attacks on

---

65. See Appendix 4.

66. *Catholic Register*, 28 October 1915. *The Casket* gives similar findings in 9 December 1915.

67. *The Sentinel*, 26 October 1916.

the allegedly pro-German papacy, disloyal Irish nationalists, French-Canadian shirkers, and the "pro-Austrian" Ukrainian Catholic Eparch of Canada.[68] Attacks on Catholicism and the Papacy by the Orange Order were neither new nor surprising, but when similar arguments began to appear in the secular daily press, and came from the mouths of politicians like former Mayor Horatio Hocken of Toronto, or Liberal politician Newton Wesley Rowell,[69] or from Protestant Ministers such as E. I. Hart, English-speaking Catholic leaders knew their denomination would not be credited with the loyalty they had professed or the blood spilled by young Catholic soldiers and nurses.

There were two nagging problems that continually dogged the English-speaking Catholic leadership, neither of which were within their control to change. First, Nykyta Budka, the first Ukrainian Catholic Eparch (bishop) of Canada, had delivered a pastoral to his flock in early August 1914 urging them as former citizens of the Austro-Hungarian Empire to return home and defend their Emperor Franz-Josef from those powers (Russia and Serbia) that threatened his empire.[70] The appeal to Ukrainian immigrants was poorly timed since, within a week, Great Britain and Canada were at war with Germany and her ally, Austria-Hungary, and now Budka, although having withdrawn his comments, appeared to be a Catholic traitor.[71] Anti-clerical Ukrainians used the opportunity to distance themselves and attack Budka, while some Anglo-Canadians entertained legal action to restrain the bishop. The English-speaking Catholic bishops and their Catholic Church Extension Society had supported Budka and the Ukrainian home missions since 1908 and now, as fellow Catholics, appeared guilty by association. Although by the end of the war Budka was acquitted of all fourteen counts of sedition, the possibility of Catholic disloyalty among new Canadians hung like a stench across the Canadian Church.

The accusations made against Pope Benedict also became a problem jarring the English-speaking Catholic Church and its leadership. Officially neutral during the war, while trying to affect peace between groups of combatants with sizeable Catholic populations on both side of

68. *The Sentinel*, 20 August 1914; 24 June 1915; 20 September 1917; 4 July 1918; 25 July 1918.
69. *Canadian Freeman*, 28 March 1918.
70. Hryniuk, "Pioneer Bishop," 34–40.
71. *Renfrew Mercury*, 11 September 1914.

the trenches, Benedict XV was pilloried by both the Entente and Central Powers. French papers called him the *Bosche* Pope,[72] while the Germans referred to him as *Maledict XV*, among other names. In Canada, the Methodist *Christian Guardian* suggested he might be pro-Austrian,[73] while the *Sentinel* was relentless in its repeated accusations that the Pope and the Kaiser were in league with one another. Making all the faulty hypotheses and "leapt-to" conclusions imaginable, the paper spread the theory of the Pope's sinister aims and helped explain to Orange readership why Quebec, Ireland, Australia, and Catholics in America were either disloyal to the British Empire, or in the case of the Americans, entertained its demise.[74] When secular papers like the *Globe* suggested that the Pope could not be neutral, Neil McNeil swung into action. In February 1918 he published a pamphlet, *The Pope and the War*, which was widely distributed and sold out of its first print run. McNeil carefully analysed the Pope's position in the conflict, explored the historical interests of Catholics among the combatants, and concluded that neutrality was the Pope's only reasonable option under the circumstances. The pamphlet won praise from within and outside the Catholic community and was even significant in switching the position formerly taken by the *Globe*.[75] Instinctively, the *Sentinel* and its readers were unmoved, and the attacks continued, but now were not unanswered.[76]

A more substantial problem for the English-speaking Catholic Church in Canada during the war was the seriously deteriorating situation in Ireland, the sentimental touchstone nation for the majority of Canada's Anglophone Catholics. In 1912, the British Liberal Government of Prime Minister Herbert Asquith, with the support of John Redmond's Irish Nationalist Party, attempted a third Home Rule Bill, which would effectively establish a devolved Parliament in Dublin, federated with the United Kingdom.[77] The Bill passed in 1914 but not without the arming of Protestant and Catholic militias in Ireland, the former determined to keep the Province of Ulster under the direct rule of the Westminster

---

72. *Bosche* was a French slang insult for (1) a German (2) an obstinate person, and could imply both.
73. *Christian Guardian*, 1 January 1919.
74. *The Sentinel*, 12 April 1917; 19 July 1917; 4 October 1917; 4 July 1918.
75. *Catholic Register*, 7 March 1918.
76. *The Sentinel*, 1 March 1918.
77. *Globe*, 12 April 1912.

parliament, and the latter force to ensure Ireland its autonomy. When the war broke out in August 1914, Asquith managed to convince Irish Nationalist leader and Wexford MP, John Redmond, that the Home Rule act would be suspended until the war was finished, and hopefully won. The armed militias in Ulster and the Irish Volunteers elsewhere became excellent sources of recruits for the British Expeditionary Force. Irish Catholics recruited strongly, including family members of Redmond, who endorsed the war effort wholeheartedly.[78] On Easter Monday, 1916, however, radical elements including the Irish Republican Brotherhood staged a bloody but unsuccessful uprising in Dublin, which quickly became perceived by Ireland's detractors as a stab in the back to Britain while she was at war. Although condemned by the Catholic Church, and Irish Catholics in the diaspora,[79] the revolutionary Irish movement increased in force, particularly after the British Forces, under Sir John Maxwell, summarily executed the leaders of the "Rising."[80] As civil strife took hold of Ireland and a conscription crisis loomed, Canadian pundits, politicians, and Protestant advocates questioned English-speaking Catholic Canadian loyalties, particularly the Church's commitment to winning the war.

While there were Irish Catholic Canadians who opposed the war effort as early as 1914, they were a tiny minority and had no prominent spokesperson, either clerical or lay. While there were rumors of pro-German priests serving in the Archdiocese of Vancouver,[81] and potential plots to blow up the Welland Canal by "Fenians,"[82] these stories were more the work of fabrication than fact. During the course of the war the Irish Catholic majority among English-speaking Catholics, though not uncritical of some of the British policies in Ireland, kept their resolve to win the war. The largest Irish Catholic benevolent association, the Ancient Order of Hibernians, took exception to the *American Hibernian*, a newspaper of the American parent organization, and insisted that the Canadian Government stop its distribution at the border

78. Jeffery, *Ireland*, 20–40.

79. *Northwest Review*, 6 May 1916.

80. Stewart, *Shape*, 167; Townshend, *Easter*, 269–323; McGowan, *Waning of the Green*, 184–217.

81. LAC, Militia and Defense, RG 9 III vol. 4665, Chaplains Reports, Father Thomas Cooney File, Cooney to Lt. Colonel Sylvestre, ADCS, 20 December 1918.

82. Morton, "Supporting Soldiers' Families," 210.

on grounds that it was "anti-British" and seditious. Many branches of the AOH lobbied to separate from the American parent organization, with affirmations of loyalty such as, "We feel as Irishmen and descendants of Irishmen domiciled in this Dominion of Canada an integral part of that great Empire . . . fully conscious that participation of all British subjects in this very unfortunate European war is in the best interests of civilization."[83] Father C. J. McLaughlin of New Brunswick, a former editor of the *New Freeman* and chaplain to the AOH, ventured to the annual convention of the Order in Boston in July 1916. Addressing the convention, a full three months after the Easter Rising, he laid the issue of loyalty squarely on the table:

> Hibernian that I am, I am also a British subject. Britain's flag is our Talisman. The Roman citizen of old gloried in the title of Roman citizenship. Let me sir, assure you today that the Canadian delegates here assembled, glory in the title of Canadian-British citizenship, and indeed sirs, it would be unworthy of the race and the land from which I came if I were to sit here this morning and offer no protest to some of the remarks that I have heard here. . . . Let me answer it here by telling you that the hearts of Canadian Irish beat true and that Canadians of all classes, Irish included, are prepared to stand by Britain in this crisis to the last man and the last dollar.[84]

While not all the members of the Canadian AOH branches may have agreed with McLaughlin, the priest stood his ground representing a vast number of colleagues who remained steadfast in their determination to win the war first and make certain justice for Ireland was accomplished in good time.

This idea of double duty was perhaps best articulated by the nearly ubiquitous Father J. J. O'Gorman of Ottawa. A native of Ottawa, scion of English-speaking rights in the local separate schools in his hometown, founding pastor of Blessed Sacrament in the Glebe neighborhood, and one of four O'Gormans (priest cousins) to serve in the Chaplaincy Service, O'Gorman was also an amateur scholar of Irish history and a devotee of the memory of slain politician Thomas D'Arcy McGee. He was

---

83. Archives of Ontario, C. J. Foy papers, box 3, file 14, "To the National Board of the Ancient Order of Hibernians in America from the County Board of Carleton County," undated, unanimously adopted.

84. *New Freeman*, 29 July 1916.

well known to politicians, bishops, and high ranking military officials and was quoted frequently in Canada's English-language Catholic newspapers.[85] As the Irish situation deteriorated badly in 1917, O'Gorman addressed the issue of "double duty" to his co-religionists. His words carved a pathway for Irish Catholics who wanted to win the war, but were adamant that one of the principles for which it was being fought—the right of small nations to be free—would apply as much to Catholic Ireland as it did to Catholic Belgium or Catholic Poland:

> Though we were born in Canada, though our parents were born in Canada . . . the lifeblood that is in our veins [is Irish]. . . . He who strikes Ireland, strikes us. We will scorn the policy of sulk and continue the policy of self-sacrifice. . . . The interests of Canada as a nation, as an autonomous part of the British Empire, and as a member of the world's family of nations, demanded that we enter this war against the Turco-Teutons, and that having entered it, we should prosecute it till we finish it or it finishes us. The few voices that are raised here and there, asking that we should halt until Ireland gets Home Rule, have rightly been disregarded by the vast majority of Irish Canadians. We do not intend to do wrong that good might come.[86]

Having eloquently expressed what he believed his countrymen thought, he re-enlisted in the CEF after recovering from his wounds, and led the Catholic Army Huts program, an initiative sponsored by the Knights of Columbus to build recreation facilities for all Canadian troops, regardless of religious beliefs. In his new role, he conducted a nationwide ecumenical fundraising initiative that netted over one million dollars for the construction of the Huts in England.[87]

On the ground, the Irish rising did not appear to be a major obstacle in the recruitment of English-speaking Catholics to the CEF. Although there have been arguments made that the "Rising" provided sufficient reason to deter Irish Catholic men from enlisting, the empirical evidence derived from routinely generated records suggests other-

---

85. See McGowan, "John J. O'Gorman"; AAO, John O'Gorman Files; LAC, MG 30-D20, John J. O'Gorman Papers and RG9 III C15, vol. 4636, Chaplains Files, File C-0-3, John J. O'Gorman.

86. *Canadian Freeman*, 29 March 1917.

87. ARCAT, War Box, Catholic Army Huts, Financial Standing, 1 April 1919 and J. L. Murray to Neil McNeil, 28 April 1919. Murray cites a figure of $1,165,490.58 raised for Army Huts.

wise.[88] First, it should be noted that in mid-1916 the levels of voluntary recruitment, mostly by specialty battalions and militia units, began to dry up because of an upswing in the economy that served as a disincentive for men to leave well-paying jobs.[89] Thus, any speculation about why men chose to stay home should be mindful of the socio-economic conditions evident in Canada at the time. In random samples taken from Irish Canadian battalions that recruited during the period of the "Dublin Uprising," however, attestation papers reveal that over half of the 199th Irish Canadian Rangers enlisted after 1 May 1916 and that just under half of the 208th Toronto Irish Battalion recruited after the incident (Appendix 3). If the "Uprising" was so significant in determining Irish Catholic Canadian behavior, one must ask why the young Catholic men continued to sign up to fight the Germans instead of sitting at home in protest, stewing about what was transpiring in Dublin. Similarly, if the sample of 497 men recruited from parishes is any indication,[90] it would appear that one quarter of these men elected to enlist after the "Rising." Moreover, in a random sample of eighty-two English-speaking Catholic nurses of Irish birth or descent, 56 percent attested after the "Rising." While there are almost no studies of Irish Canadian women in the period, and their political and religious culture, these figures suggest that many educated Irish Catholic women in Canada were not driven to action or inaction based on the Irish Question.

Perhaps the issue that plagued English-speaking Catholic Canadian leadership more than any other and certainly made them appear guilty of "disloyalty" by association was the conscription question. Despite an initial flurry of patriotism in Quebec, the endorsement of the Quebec bishops for the British war effort, and the creation of several distinctive Quebec battalions including the famous Royal 22nd or "Vandoos," recruitment in French Canada was a spectacular failure.[91] Nationalist politician Henri Bourassa and his supporters were unconvinced of the necessity to take up arms when Canadian soil was not directly threatened. The war contributions could be made through growing crops

88. Contrary positions, without empirical data, are put forward in Burns, "Montreal Irish," and Jolivet, *"Le vert et le bleu,"* 169–211.

89. Brown and Loveridge, "Unrequited Faith," 60; *Labour Gazette*, 15 (July to December 1915), 1271–84; 16 (January-December 1916), 1531–44.

90. See Appendix 3.

91. Gagnon, *Le 22e bataillon*, 139–87.

and increasing industrial goods to be placed at the service of the allies. But the disinclination of many French Canadian Catholics to serve ran deeper and might have included such reasons as a huge farming population that was reluctant to leave the land, higher rates of marriage at younger ages among men,[92] and less of a sentimental attachment to France, a country that, to many clergy, had abandoned the Catholic faith and persecuted the Church since 1905 under its *laïcité* program and the Combes laws. Moreover, the Department of Militia and Defense had mishandled recruiting in Quebec and created disincentives prior to the war by dissolving some militia units and barring religious symbols from militia parades.[93] During the war, Hughes was slow to endorse the formation of Francophone units, there were few French-speaking officers, recruiting was focused in the cities, and the chief recruiter, for a time, was a Methodist minister![94] It is no surprise that few French Canadians were drawn to a military complex that was perceived to be English from the top down as well as Protestant. Bourassa, from his perch at *Le Devoir*, was able to point out the hypocrisy of fighting for liberty in Europe while depriving Franco-Ontarians at home of the right to be educated in their own language. As one his colleagues remarked, "The Prussians are next door." Even though the Catholic hierarchy continued to support the war effort, including the national registration of manpower, in 1916–1917 they begged Sir Robert Borden not to invoke conscription.[95] When conscription was implemented in late 1917 on the heels of the election of a Union Government that included no Francophone members from Quebec, French Canadian Catholics were isolated and the objects of scorn from many corners of English Canada.

Once again, the English-speaking Catholic Church was placed in a difficult position. Archbishop Mannix of Melbourne was leading the Catholic Australians against conscription, and it seemed that Ireland would be cast into civil chaos if it was introduced there. At home, the Quebec Church did not endorse the Union Government's mandate to

92. Granatstein and Hitsman, *Broken Promises*, 28–31; Dutil, "Against Isolationism," 115–16.

93. Rutherdale, *Hometown Horizons*, 11–14.

94. Granatstein and Hitsman, *Broken Promises*, 28–31.

95. LAC, Borden Papers, vol. 219, Archbishop Bruchesi to Borden, 27 May 1917, 123403–6, and 2 June 1917, 123412–13.

enact conscription and by March 1918 there was rioting in Quebec City.[96] English-speaking Catholics were not united on the issue, although the majority of its leaders appeared to acquiesce to the Military Service Act. Most of the Roman Catholic hierarchy supported conscription in principle as a means of winning the war.[97] No stranger to public controversy, Bishop Fallon openly endorsed the Union Government on the eve of the election in December 1917.[98] The *Catholic Register* and one of its leading columnists, Henry Somerville, supported conscription.[99] Both the *Catholic Record* (which had strong Liberal ties and was generally supportive of Wilfrid Laurier, the Leader of the Opposition) and the *Casket* took a more neutral path, acknowledging Parliament's right to enact the legislation, but remaining critical of some of the "firebreathing" advocates of conscription and their harsh comments about anyone who opposed compulsory military service.[100] The Catholic Mutual Benefit Association, the Catholic Truth Society, individual priests, and Professor A. B. O'Neill, President of St. Joseph's College in New Brunswick, and Catholic MP A. C. Macdonell (South Toronto), all endorsed conscription.[101] Finally, C. J. Doherty, the Minister of Justice in the Union Government and an Irish Catholic MP from Montreal, actually wrote the legislation.[102]

Yet a small group of English-speaking Catholics remained opposed to conscription including the editors of the *Canadian Freeman* and the *Northwest Review*, the former of whom questioned whether national unity should be sacrificed in this way.[103] Several priests were decidedly

---

96. *New Freeman*, 6 April 1918. This New Brunswick Catholic paper denounced the violence as "monumental folly."

97. Hopkins, *Canada at War*, 263, 331; *Northwest Review*, 26 May 1917.

98. ADL, Fallon Papers, Speeches, "Statement of Bishop Fallon in Favour of Union Government," 6 December 1917.

99. *Catholic Register*, 21 June 1917; 28 June 1917; 24 July 1917; 2 August 1917; 23 August, 1917.

100. *Catholic Record*, 30 June 1917; 7 July 1917; 28 July 1917; *The Casket*, 21 June 1917; 19 July 1917.

101. ARCAT, McNeil papers, AS07.03, J. S. McGinnis to McNeil, 15 April 1918; *The Canadian* 26 (June 1918) . *Hansard: House of Commons Debates*, 7th Session, 12th Parliament, vol. 3, 29 June 1917, 2847–54.

102. *Ottawa Journal*, 18 December 1917.

103. *Canadian Freeman*, 12 July 1917; *Canadian Freeman*, 27 December 1917; *Northwest Review*, 26 May 1917.

opposed, including the bombastic Father Matthew Whelan,[104] who had already witnessed the loss of so many of his parishioners from St. Patrick's parish in Ottawa, and Father Lewis Drummond of Edmonton, who had already acquired a reputation for being anti-British.[105] There were at least two notable Irish Catholic politicians, both Liberals and loyal to Laurier, who opposed the Union Government: Charles Murphy, the MP from Russell, Ontario,[106] and Charles "Chubby" Power, the MP from Quebec City East. Power was a veteran of the CEF who had been wounded, demobilized, and immediately threw his support behind Laurier. Power would remain a Liberal stalwart, eventually serving in William Lyon Mackenzie King's cabinet during the Second World War.[107] Despite their opposition, however, they were overshadowed in the public sphere by Fallon, Doherty, McNeil, and others who advocated calm with regards to the Quebec situation and commitment from the Catholic Church to the war effort. Thus when McNeil lashed out at Reverend Hart, it was critical in McNeil's mind not to confuse French Canadian motivations for action, based on their distinctive history and culture, with those of the Catholic Church in Canada generally.

Nevertheless, the label of disloyalty continued to dog English-speaking Catholics across Canada, particularly during the general election in December 1917. Clearly, given the passionate rhetoric of some politicians on the campaign trail, Catholic sensibilities were hurt and feelings were damaged. "Can we expect that every Catholic voter in Canada," asked the *Catholic Register*, "will be of such heroic and Christian mould that he will turn the other cheek when he is smitten? Do politicians think they can conduct 'a vile and indefensible anti-Catholic propaganda' and alienate no Catholics?"[108] Perhaps Father Arthur O'Leary, pastor of St. Joseph's Parish in Leslieville, Toronto, summed up the anxiety of many Catholics when he wrote about the incredibility of the attacks on the Catholic Church when "the Archbishop and clergy of Toronto have been

104. *Catholic Record*, 12 January 1918.

105. ARCAT, War Box, FW WE 07.02, M. J. Ryan to Neil McNeil, 1918. *Canadian Annual Review* (1917), 412–14; LAC, MG 27 III B-8, Charles Murphy Papers, vol. 14, C. W. Kerr to Murphy, 22 December 1917, and vol. 16, A. M. Latchford to Murphy, 24 May 1917.

106. LAC, Murphy Papers, vol. 49. Notes for undated speech, 22178–85.

107. QUA, Charles Gavan Power Papers, 2150, Box 78, File B, 1a, Campaign literature, "To the Electors of Quebec South, 11 December 1917."

108. *Catholic Register*, 13 September 1917.

second to none in our sincere loyalty," and our Churches have emptied themselves of young men for overseas."[109] An addition to the Catholic sense of betrayal came in 1918, when members of the local Protestant ministerial association in Guelph prodded the military authorities to raid the St. Stanislaus Novitiate of the Society of Jesus on the outskirts of the town. Under cover of darkness a detachment of military police, led by Captain A. C. Macaulay, raided the novitiate in search of young men who were allegedly "shirking" their duty under the Military Service Act. The event was farcical, given that Catholic postulants to religious orders were exempt under the general exceptions for clergy and that the raiders were met by Major William Hingston, SJ, in full uniform, who had just been demobilized as a chaplain in the CEF. Worse still for the raiders, a young postulant, Marcus Doherty, was allowed to make a phone call. He called his father, Charles Doherty, the Minister of Justice, and the one who had crafted the provisions of the Military Service Act. Although the Jesuits were eventually left alone, the military brass apologized for the incident, the perpetrators were censured for their actions, and a House of Commons inquiry outlasted the war itself, the Guelph raid may very well have confirmed in some English-speaking Catholic minds that, no matter what they did to contribute to the war effort, they would always be under suspicion.[110]

While there was bitterness left among the English-speaking Catholic leadership, they continued a program to help win the war and were visible in the Knights of Columbus Catholic Army Hut Campaign in the summer and autumn of 1918,[111] just as the tide of the war had turned and victory appeared to be within the allies' grasp. The Army Huts campaign was designed to provide recreational buildings for Canadian soldiers of all denominations at the base camps in England and France and in the training camps in Canada. The effort was sponsored by the Knights, but the day-to-day operations were managed by the Catholic branch of the Canadian Chaplains Service, in particular ADCS Father Wolston Workman and recently minted Reverend Major John J. O'Gorman. The fundraising drive for the huts was an ecumenical

---

109. LAC, Murphy Papers, vol. 23, O'Leary to Murphy, 20 March 1918.

110. Rutherdale, *Hometown Horizons*, 178–90; Hogan, "Novitiate Raid." *Hansard: House of Commons Debates*, Session 1919, vol. 2, 7 April 1919, 1218–59. The incident made news across Canada; see *New Freeman*, 29 June 1918.

111. Daniel and Casey, *For God and Country*, 15–21.

effort including Catholics, notable Protestants, the Great War Veterans Association, and major service clubs (Kiwanis, Rotary, Masons) united in a common cause to support their troops. Using the print media and public meetings, the fundraisers spread out across the country in 1917 and 1918 and raised over one million dollars. By October 1918 in Toronto, the joint fundraising effort had raised $210,000, approximately one fifth of the national total. Such fraternity and unity of purpose between denominations betrayed the city's reputation as the "Belfast of Canada" and provided sharp contrast to the stormy election campaign of December 1917 when all Catholics had been tarred with the brush of disloyalty.[112] Colonel W. S. Dinnick, chair of the Army Huts Fund Drive, and himself a Protestant, commented, "This campaign is going to go down in history as most unique. Perhaps as the turning point in the bringing together of the people no matter what religion or creed they profess."[113] For the Knights' State Deputy, Joseph L. Murray, from Pembroke, Ontario, however, the campaign marked a coming of age for Catholics among their neighbors and the promise of "a people who will be one in their Canadianism, a people who will be justly proud of their freedom, proud of their civilization, aye, proud of their Christianity ... who will ever have as their motto those golden, glorious words—'For God and Country.'"[114] Murray himself had known loss during the war; his brother Edward, a Boer War veteran, was killed in action in August 1918 during the Canadians' final push to the German frontier.[115]

When the war ended, English-speaking Catholics, like their Protestant neighbors, cheered in the streets, offered prayers of thanksgiving, mourned their lost sons, daughters, fathers, and brothers, erected memorials in their churches to the dead, and planned to celebrate the armistice annually with their fellow citizens across the Dominion. Encouraged by Bishop Morrison, the Catholics of Antigonish compiled a volume containing names and stories of all the Catholics who had served in the conflict as a memorial to their patriotism.[116] In the parishes and small missions from St. Mary's Cathedral in Halifax to St. Andrew's

---

112. *Ontario Catholic Yearbook*, 25.

113. ARCAT, Knights of Columbus Papers, Colonel Dinnick's Speech for the Catholic Army Huts Campaign, 29 September 1918.

114. Daniel and Casey, *For God and Country*, 203–4.

115. *Renfrew Mercury*, 30 August 1918.

116. *Diocese of Antigonish*.

Cathedral in Victoria, honor rolls to the dead in brass, wood, and calligraphy on parchment appeared in the foyers and near the confessionals at the back of these sacred spaces. Despite his opposition to some elements of the war effort, Father Matthew Whelan at St. Patrick's parish in Ottawa oversaw the hanging of a massive painting of a war scene at the entrance of the church, and with it a hand-painted list of the fifty-nine men from his flock who gave their lives in the conflict.[117] Farther north, in the upper Ottawa Valley at Quyon, Quebec, Catholics, Protestants, and the IODE erected a stone cenotaph on which were inscribed the names of all who served, one third of whom were English-speaking Catholics. In similar stone monuments across the country, the names of the dead and those who served were inscribed without reference or deference to their creed or culture. Finally, on 18 June 1921, the parishioners of St. Paul's Parish, Toronto, gathered with their archbishop, Neil McNeil, local MPP John O'Neill, and Mayor Tommy Church on the steps of the church to unveil a marble statue of the angel of victory and a brass plaque honouring the parish's eighty-one dead. At least 762 parishioners enlisted, the largest number from any congregation in the city. Mayor Church, a devoted Orangeman, paid tribute to the parish and all "classes and creeds" who had contributed to the victory. The separate school choir sang *O Canada*, *The Minstrel Boy*, and *Men of the North*.[118] In this one symbolic moment, it became possible to imagine that Catholics and Protestants, despite their many differences, could say as McNeil had: "They were involved in the same issue."

---

117. McEvoy et al., *Enduring Faith*, 142–59.
118. Kelly, *St. Paul's*, 171–75.

APPENDIX 1

Canada's Irish Catholic Recruits by Birth
South African War, 1898–1902

Birth Place	Irish Catholic (N=165)		SA Contingent		Census of 1901
Canada	127	77.0%	3710	63.7%	86.9%
Nova Scotia	35	21.2	435	7.5	
New Brunswick	16	9.7	353	6.1	
PEI	13	7.9	139	2.4	
Quebec	21	12.7	484	8.3	
Ontario	39	23.6	2110	36.2	
Manitoba/NWT	3	1.8	147	2.5	
BC	0	0.0	42	0.7	
British Empire	33	20.0	1710	29.4	7.8
Other	5	3.0	159	2.7	5.1

Source: Carman Miller, "A Preliminary Analysis of the Socio-economic Composition of Canada's South African War Contingents," *Histoire sociale-Social History* 8 (novembre/November 1975), 221. The Contingents' numbers reflect 5579 of 5825 (95.8%) in which nativity is identified. The random sample of 165 Irish Catholic troops was drawn from the attestation papers of solders from the South African War, selected from thirteen reels of microfilm in the RG 38 series (Reels T2069, 2079, 2080-4) found at Library and Archives Canada. Files of 234 non-francophone Catholics were discovered among the 2496 files scanned. The sample was analyzed by surname, given name, religion, place of birth, address, and next of kin to determine Irish origin. Of the 234: Irish 165 (70.5%); Scots 49 (20.9%); English & Welsh 13 (5.6%); Other 7 (3.0%).

APPENDIX 2

Voluntary Recruitment in the Canadian Expeditionary Force by Religious Denomination to 1 June 1917.

Denomination	Volunteers	Pecentage of CEF	General Population
Anglican	165,145	46.79	1,043,017
Presbyterian	70,671	19.71	1,115,324
Roman Catholic	51,426	14.20	2,833,041
Methodist	35,908	10.11	1,079,892
Baptist	18,458	5.20	382,666
Jewish	851	0.24	74,564
Other	12,409	3.75	na

APPENDIX 3

Comparison—All Units

Recruitment and Social Analysis

	Parish Recruitment	Irish Regiments	Selected Battalions	Total	National Figures*
Sample	497	102	356	955	92,529
Attested Pre April 30, 1916	347 69.8%	60 58.8%	340** 95.5%	747 78.2%	
Attested After May 1, 1916	123 24.8%	42 41.2%	12 3.4%	177 18.5%	
Conscripts (MSA)	22 4.4%	0	4 1.1%	26 2.7%	
Unknown	5 1.0%	0	0	5 0.5%	
Birth					
Canada	375 75.5%	70 68.6%	253# 71.1%	698 73.1%	36,408 39.4%
Ireland	43 8.7%	15 14.7	49 13.8%	107 11.2%	3,660 4.0%
Britain	50 10.1%	9 8.8%	43 12.1%	102 10.7%	47,455 51.3%
United States	18 3.6%	5 4.9%	3 0.8%	26 2.7%	2,163 2.3%
Other	11	3	8	22	2,841
Occupation					
Professional	38	2	14	54	2,462
Business	18	7	8	33	1610
Clerical/ Supervisory	128	19	53	200 20.9%	12,607 13.6%
Skilled Worker	109	19	55	183	

	Parish Recruitment	Irish Regiments	Selected Battalions	Total	National Figures*
Semi-Skilled	70	13	45	128	
Unskilled	106	35	132	273	
Total Blue Collar	[285]	[67]	[232]	584　　61.1%	63368　　68.5%
Agriculture/ Forestry	18	7	49	74	1,120
Unknown	10			10	
Other Features					
Married	108	20	40	168	
Students					1,362
Officers	36	2	10	48	
Previous Service	180	57	143	380	

*Library and Archives Canada, RG24, vol.1249, Occupation and Place of Birth by Infantry Battalions 18th to 85th [c. April 1915]. When the students and professionals are combined, a figure of 3,824 results. My units included students as professionals. All manual laborers are combined regardless of skill level. Total recruits to that date amounted to 92,529.

**All sample battalions were recruited before April 1916.

#Early CEF recruitment included higher proportions of British- and Irish-born volunteers.

APPENDIX 4

Sample Study

Catholics in Context—The Ottawa Valley

Group	Irish Catholic	French Catholic	Other Catholic	Church of England	Presbyterian	Methodist	Baptist	Other	No Record	Total
Birth-CDA	75	43	22	57	112	51	8	1	6	375
—Britain	4	0	0	10	8	2	1	0	0	25
—USA	0	0	0	0	0	0	0	0	1	1
—Ireland	1	0	0	2	0	0	0	0	0	3
—Other	0	0	1	0	0	0	0	0	0	1
Totals for Birth	80	43	23	69	120	53	9	1	7	405
Married	6	5	0	5	6	5	1	1	2	31
MSA	15	10	4	10	18	10	0	0	0	67
MSA Farm-Forest	7	2	2	7	14	8	0	0	0	40
Previous Service	14	3	4	7	34	12	5	1	2	82
No Record	0	0	0	0	0	0	0	0	0	0
Pre May 1, 1916	45	na	na	na	na	na	na	na	na	na

Group	Irish Catholic	French Catholic	Other Catholic	Church of England	Presbyterian	Methodist	Baptist	Other	No Record	Total
Farmer	14	4	5	13	33	19	2	0	2	92
Forester	6	4	2	1	4	3	1	0	0	21
Unskilled	23	20	12	16	13	7	1	0	1	93
Semi-Skilled	17	4	1	7	8	6	0	0	0	43
Skilled	11	8	3	9	17	9	0	0	0	57
Clerical	5	2	0	13	26	4	2	1	1	54
Business	1	0	0	4	5	0	0	0	2	12
Professional	3	0	0	5	12	5	3	0	0	28
Other	0	0	0	0	0	0	0	0	0	0
No Record	0	1	0	1	2	0	0	0	1	5
Total	80	43	23	69	120	53	9	1	7	405

APPENDIX 5

Irish Catholic Canadian Nurses
Recruitment and Social Analysis 1914–1918

	Number	Percent
Sample	82	100.0
Attestation pre 30 April 1916	36	43.9
Attestation post 1 May 1916	46	56.1
Birth		
—Canada	73	89.1
—Ireland	6	7.3
—Britain	1	1.2
—United States	1	1.2
—Other	1	1.2
—Married	0	0.0
Occupation		
—Nurse	82	100.0
—Other	0	0.0
Province of Birth		
—Nova Scotia	15	20.6
—New Brunswick	10	13.7
—PEI	1	1.4
—Quebec	3	4.1
—Ontario	44	60.3
—Manitoba	0	0.0
—Saskatchewan	0	0.0
—Alberta	0	0.0
—British Columbia	0	0.0
Previous Service	48	58.5

BIBLIOGRAPHY

Primary Sources

ARCHIVES

AAH – Archives of the Archdiocese of Halifax
AAO – Archives of the Archdiocese of Ottawa
AAW – Archives of the Archdiocese of Winnipeg
ADA – Archives of the Diocese of Antigonish
ADL – Archives of the Diocese of London
ADP – Archives of the Diocese of Pembroke
AJUCP – Archives of the Society of Jesus Upper Canada Province
AO – Archives of Ontario
ARCAT – Archives of the Roman Catholic Archdiocese of Toronto
ASV – Archivio Segreto Vaticano (Secret Vatican Archives)
LAC – Library and Archives Canada
QUA – Queen's University Archives

NEWSPAPERS

The Canadian
Canadian Freeman
Catholic Record
Catholic Register
Christian Guardian
Globe
Halifax Herald
Labour Gazette
Morning Chronicle (Halifax)
New Freeman
Northwest Review
Ottawa Journal
Pickering News
 Renfrew Mercury
Le Soleil
St. Joseph's Lilies
The Casket
The Morning Guardian (Charlottetown)
The Sentinel
Toronto Star
Walkerton Telescope
Whitby Gazette

OTHER

Canadian Annual Review of Public Affairs, 1917. Edited by J. Castell Hopkins. Toronto: Canadian Annual Review Ltd., 1918.
Catholics of the Diocese of Antigonish, Nova Scotia, and The War, 1914–1919 with Nominal Enlistment Rolls by Parishes. Antigonish: St. Francis Xavier University Press, 1919.

Fourth Census of Canada, 1901. Vol. 1, "Population," Ottawa: S. E. Dawson, Printer to the King's Most Excellent Majesty, 1902.
Fifth Census of Canada, 1911. Vol. 1. Ottawa: King's Printer, 1911.
Hansard: House of Commons Debates. Ottawa, Canada.
Harris, William Richard. "Our Own Land." Speech, "Old Boys" meeting at Beamsville, Ontario, 3 September 1900.
Morgan, Henry James. "Hon William Wilfred Sullivan." In *The Canadian Men and Women of the Time*, 985–86. Toronto: William Briggs, 1898.
Ontario Catholic Yearbook. Toronto: Newman Club, 1920.

Secondary Sources

Armstrong, Elizabeth. *The Crisis of Quebec*. Carleton Library Series. Toronto: McClelland & Stewart, 1974.
Baskerville, Peter. "Did Religion Matter? Religion and Wealth in Urban Canada at the Turn of the Twentieth Century: An Exploratory Study." *Histoire sociale–Social History* 34 (2001) 61–95.
Brown, Robert Craig, and Donald Loveridge. "Unrequited Faith: Recruiting the CEF, 1914–1918." *Révue internationale d'histoire militaire* 51 (1982) 53–79.
Burke, Alfred E. "The Irishman's Place in the Empire." In *Empire Club Speeches, 1909–1910*, edited by J. Castell Hopkins, 225–32. Toronto: Warwick & Bros & Rutter, 1910.
Burns, Robin B. "The Montreal Irish and the Great War." *CCHA Historical Studies* 52 (1985) 67–81.
Choquette, Robert. "English-French Relations in the Canadian Catholic Community." In *Creed and Culture: The Place of English-Speaking Catholics in Canada*, edited by Terrence Murphy and Gerald Stortz, 3–24. Montreal and Kingston: McGill-Queen's University Press, 1993.
Clarke, Brian P. "Sir Richard Scott." In *Dictionary of Canadian Biography*, 14:913–16. Toronto: University of Toronto Press, 1998.
Cottrell, Michael. "Irish Catholic Political Leadership in Toronto, 1855–1882." PhD diss., University of Saskatchewan, 1988.
Crerar, Duff. "Bellicose Priests: The Wars of the Canadian Catholic Chaplains, 1914–1919." *CCHA Historical Studies* 58 (1991) 21–39.
———. *Padres in No Man's Land: Canadian Chaplains and the Great War*. Montreal and Kingston: McGill-Queen's University Press, 1995.
Daniel, I. J. E., and D. A. Casey. *For God and Country: A History of the Knights of Columbus Catholic Army Huts*. Toronto: n.p., 1922.
Di Matteo, Livio. "The Wealth of the Irish in Nineteenth Century Ontario." *Social Science History* 20 (1996) 209–34.
Dutil, Patrice A. "Against Isolationism: Napoleon Belcourt, French Canada, and 'La grande guerre.'" In *Canada and the First World War*, edited by David MacKenzie, 96–137. Toronto: University of Toronto Press, 2005.
Gagnon, Jean-Pierre. *Le 22e bataillon (canadien-français) 1914–1919: Étude socio-militaire*. Quebec: Les presses de l'université Laval, 1986.
Granatstein, J. L., and J. M. Hitsman. *Broken Promises: A History of Conscription in Canada*. Toronto: Copp Clark Pitman, 1985.

Hogan, Brian F. "The Guelph Novitiate Raid: Conscription, Censorship and Bigotry during the Great War." *CCHA Study Sessions* 45 (1978) 57–80.
Hopkins, J. Castell. *Canada at War: A Record of Heroism and Achievement, 1914–1918.* Toronto: The Canadian Annual Review, 1919.
Hryniuk, Stella. "Pioneer Bishop, Pioneer Times: Nykyta Budka in Canada." *CCHA Historical Studies* 55 (1988) 21–41.
Huel, Raymond. "The Irish-French Conflict in Catholic Episcopal Nominations: The Western Sees and the Struggle for Domination within the Church." *CCHA Study Sessions* 42 (1975) 51–70.
Jeffery, Keith. *Ireland and the Great War.* Cambridge: Cambridge University Press, 2000.
Jolivet, Simon. *Le vert et le bleu: Identité québécoise et identité irlandaise au tournant du xxieme siècle.* Montreal: Les Presses de l'Université de Montréal, 2011.
Kaufman, Christopher J. *Faith and Fraternalism: A History of the Knights of Columbus, 1882–1982.* New York: Harper & Row, 1982.
Kelly, Edward. *The Story of St. Paul's Parish, Toronto.* Toronto: n.p., 1922.
MacIntyre, Leo. "The Cape Breton Highlanders." In *More Essays in Cape Breton History*, edited by R. J. Morgan, 50–61. Windsor: Lancelot, 1977.
MacKenzie, David, ed. *Canada and the First World War: Essays in Honour of Robert Craig Brown.* Toronto: University of Toronto Press, 2005.
MacLean, Ray A. *The Casket, 1852–1992: From Gutenberg to Internet: The Story of a Small-Town Weekly.* Antigonish: The Casket, 1995.
McEvoy, Fred, Cecil Chabot, Joan McEvoy Rooney, and James Scheer. *Enduring Faith: A History of St. Patrick's Basilica Parish, Ottawa, 1855–2005.* Ottawa: St. Patrick's Basilica, 2006.
McGowan, Mark G. "Irish Catholics." In *Encyclopedia of Canada's Peoples*, edited by Paul Robert Magosci, 734–83. Toronto: University of Toronto Press, 1999.
———. "John J. O'Gorman." In *The Dictionary of Canadian Biography*, 16, forthcoming.
———. *The Waning of the Green: Catholics, the Irish and Identity in Toronto, 1887–1922.* Montreal and Kingston: McGill-Queen's University Press, 1999.
———. "The Degreening of the Irish: Toronto's Irish Catholic Press, Imperialism, and the Forging of a New Identity, 1887–1914." *Canadian Historical Association Historical Papers* (1989) 118–45
———. "The Maritime Region and the Building of the Canadian Church: The Case of the Diocese of Antigonish after Confederation." *CCHA Historical Studies* 70 (2004) 48–70.
———. "Rethinking Catholic-Protestant Relations in Canada: The Episcopal Reports of 1900–1901." *CCHA Historical Studies* 59 (1992) 11–32.
———. "To Share the Burdens of the Empire: Toronto's Catholics and the Great War, 1914–1918." In *Catholics at the Gathering Place: Historical Essays on the Archdiocese of Toronto, 1841–1991*, edited by Mark G. McGowan and Brian P. Clarke, 177–207. Toronto: CCHA and Dundurn Press, 1993.
Morton, Desmond. "Supporting Soldier's Families: Separation Allowance, Assigned Pay, and the Unexpected." In *Canada and the First World War*, edited by David MacKenzie, 194–229. Toronto: University of Toronto Press, 2005.
———. *When Your Number's Up: The Canadian Solder in the First World War.* Toronto: Random House, 1993.
Perin, Roberto. *Rome in Canada: The Vatican and Canadian Affairs in the Late Victorian Age.* Toronto: University of Toronto Press, 1990.

Rutherdale, Robert. *Hometown Horizons: Local Responses to Canada's Great War*. Vancouver: University of British Columbia Press, 2004.

Scott, W. L. "Sir Richard Scott, K.C." *CCHA Report* 4 (1936–1937) 46–71.

Stewart, A. T. Q. *The Shape of Irish History*. Montreal and Kingston: McGill-Queen's University Press, 2001.

Townshend, Charles. *Easter 1916: The Irish Rebellion*. London: Penguin, 2005.

3

French-Speaking Catholics in Quebec and the First World War

SIMON JOLIVET

IT IS CUSTOMARY TO say that the First World War enabled Canada to elevate itself to the status of nationhood. The battles of the European front and the politics of the Borden government seem to have marked the emergence of a new country by the end of the conflict: "For Canadians, Vimy Ridge was a nation-building experience. For some, then and later, it symbolized the fact that the Great War was also Canada's war of independence even if it was fought at Britain's side."[1] However, the majority of French-Canadian Catholics did not share this experience. Anemic recruitment among French-Canadian Catholics in Quebec, ethno-religious divisions, and the political crisis of conscription signaled a rift. The fracture between Francophone Catholics and Anglophone Protestants is well documented, but divisions at the very heart of the French-Canadian nation, which at that time included the territories of Quebec, maritime Acadia, Ontario, New England, and Louisiana, remain relatively unknown.[2]

---

1. Morton, *Military History*, 145.

2. Due to lack of space, this chapter will not examine the important communities of Franco-Americans in New England and of Cadiens in Louisiana. The focus is on the French living solely in Canada. This being said, it would be very interesting to assess the level of implication in the First World War of the Franco-Americans and Cadiens in comparison to the French in Canada.

In Quebec, the events of the war forced the Catholic authorities to adapt to the new reality. After 1916, public opinion in Quebec grew increasingly suspicious of the government's decisions. The episcopate had to revise its traditional position of unreserved loyalty to the British Crown and Empire. Quebec bishops, like Cardinal Louis-Nazaire Bégin and Montreal's Archbishop Paul Bruchési, could not remain idle during the conscription crisis of 1917–1918. Feeling betrayed by the Canadian government and Sir Robert Borden who had previously assured them that no conscription would be adopted, Bégin and Bruchési had very little choice but to support their parishioners and even some of their own priests who publicly condemned the government. In 1918, the Quebec hierarchy faced a situation that had no parallels in the Canadian *francophonie*: some of their own influent priests, such as Canon Philippe Perrier or Canon Lionel Groulx, asked their brethren not to fill out the National Register created by Prime Minister Borden and encouraged them to oppose conscription. The Acadian and Franco-Ontarian episcopates would not have to deal with such an intense crisis.

This marked the beginning of a major transformation for the French-Canadian nation that had been created after the Act of Union of 1840. With the failure of the *Patriotes*' Rebellions of 1837–1838 and the British government's attempt to assimilate the French-Canadian minority, notably through a ban on the use of French in the new parliament, political and religious elites organized in solidarity. The Catholic authorities (missionaries, priests, and bishops) were at the heart of that project as they imagined and concretized the idea of a French-Canadian nation in North America, one distinct from the English majority through its language, religion, schools, associations, conservatism, and culture.[3] Interestingly enough, this was simultaneously the period of *la survivance* and of French Catholic *messianisme*.[4] Deprived of political power, the religious elites imagined a cultural and religious nation that went beyond the borders of Quebec and included all Francophones, who, at the same time, were migrating towards Ontario, the West, and New England.

Historians generally agree on the factors that led to the creation of Catholic French Canada after 1840. Most of them also trace its disap-

---

3. See Bock, "Tradition." See also Gervais, *Le passage*, 227; Warren, "L'invention."
4. Martel, *Le Canada français*, 35.

pearance to the moment of Quebec's Quiet Revolution in the 1960s.[5] This chapter demonstrates how the Great War was a factor of disunity rather than one of national unity for French Canadians. It appears that Quebec, as a result of the war experience, began to leave the axis of French Canada. The conflict marked the first signs of Quebec's autonomy within the French-speaking world. This would become even more apparent in the 1920s following Quebec's wartime political isolation of 1917–1918.

The focal point of this chapter revolves around the vision and actions of the Quebec French Catholic political and religious leaders in promoting or restraining the Canadian war effort. To be sure, Quebec's French Canadians had been less inclined than their Anglophone counterparts to volunteer and were more vehemently opposed to conscription between 1914 and 1918. The political leaders reflected their opinions. The clergy (higher and lower) were more divided on these issues, however. Despite low volunteer recruitment, thirteen battalions (including the 165th in Acadia) were authorized by federal authorities as a means of recruiting French Canadians. Only Quebec's 22nd French Canadian Battalion, however, would go on to fight at the front as a unit. All other battalions failed to attain the required number of soldiers and were disbanded.

This chapter confirms those recognized facts. In spite of the Quebec episcopate's repeated requests for enrollment on a voluntary basis, French Canadians from that province provided only about 2 percent of the volunteers and conscripts for the CEF. The involvement of Quebecois differed from the rest of Canada, but also from the rest of French Canada. An analysis of original sources concerning the involvement of New Brunswick and Ontario elites, however, has yet to be done. In fact, the current historiography still reveals little about the French-Canadian war effort outside of Quebec, even though "*hors-Québec* French Canada," despite its smaller population, provided a proportionally greater number of volunteers than the whole of Quebec during the war. Of the 35,000 French Canadians who took part in the Canadian Expeditionary Force, only about 15,000 came from Quebec. At that time, 1,600,000 French Canadians lived in Quebec and close to 300,000 French Canadians were spread elsewhere in Ontario and the Maritimes.[6]

---

5. Frenette, "L'évolution." See also Frenette, *Brève histoire*, 211; Martel, "Le débat."

6. Gagnon, "Les soldats," 84. See also Roy, "Démographie," 174; Gervais, "L'Ontario français," 97.

The first part of this chapter discusses the outbreak of war, recruitment efforts, and French Canadian support for the war. The second part highlights the extent of divisions that ruptured the initial accord of August 1914, an agreement that had seemingly prevailed between Francophone and Anglophone populations as well as among Franco-Catholics themselves. It does not attempt to write the history of military exploits; rather, it seeks mainly to understand how the political and military experience of Quebec's French Canadians came to weaken the initial unanimity of August 1914 and to challenge the views held until then by the Catholic bishops of the province.

THE JUST CAUSE AND THE POLITICAL-MILITARY EFFORT

In 1914, the Catholic episcopate wished to show that yesterday's enemies, Catholics and Protestants, could get along so as to fight the new German foe of today. However, the war lasted fifty-one long months. It tested the union sworn between Canada's Franco-Catholics and Anglo-Protestants, not to mention the disagreements between the Anglophone and Francophone Catholics of Ontario that arose in its wake. Although more difficult to demonstrate, it also seems that French Canadians themselves were subject to the aftershocks of world conflict in terms of their identity and nation. The world conflict and its impact on Canada signaled the first fissures within French Canadians, who would later come to change their names and refer to themselves as Québécois, Franco-Ontariens, or Franco-Américains.[7] "French Canada emerged fragmented from the war," as Patrick Dutil pertinently notes.[8]

At the start of the twentieth century, the majority of French Canadians, both within Quebec and outside its borders, did not accept the idea of an increased expansion and centralization of the British Empire. They were nevertheless obliged to pay some attention to this issue since Canadian domestic and foreign policy decisions were still made in Westminster. The Canadian army did not exist and Canada

---

7. It should be noted, however, that the Acadians, since the English conquest and the Treaty of Utrecht of 1713, have always maintained a strong national identity. In Canada, it is the Acadians who first adopted, in the 1880s, an official flag and a national hymn, and promoted a national day. However, being French and Catholic, they have always been part of the larger French Canadian nation in sharing the same religious, associational, and cultural institutions.

8. Dutil, "Against Isolationism," 129.

did not yet rely on an autonomous system of diplomacy. Paying heed to the Empire did not mean, however, the approval of all decisions taken by British and Canadian opinion leaders such as Joseph Chamberlain or George Robert Parkin. Since the Act of Union of 1840, the French Canadian episcopate admittedly supported the British colonial authorities, showing an unwavering support for the Crown and the Empire. However, the rise of a young generation of Quebec anti-imperialist activists by the 1900s challenged their hold on public opinion. It was in fact in 1899, upon the outbreak of an imperial war—the Boer War—that the ultramontane journalist and politician, Henri Bourassa, stated most plainly the French Canadian anti-imperialist and nationalistic doctrine.

The Boer War marked the beginning of a well-organized nationalistic wave in French Canada that would unfold during the First World War.[9] Henri Bourassa often articulated its policy: "French Canadians are exclusively *Canadians*. They have no other country than Canada."[10] On 6 August 1914, Sir Robert Borden and his advisors almost appeared to agree with Bourassa as they prepared an official statement attesting to Canada's national interest in this new war. It was imperative "to establish why Canada should follow the British lead. Canada did not participate in the war simply because when Britain was at war Canada was at war."[11] Whatever the justifications and subtleties, however, it was henceforth officially time to get into "war effort" mode. Generally speaking, French Canadians seemed to welcome the situation quite well. In spite of the ambient anti-imperialism in the province of Quebec, opinions were unanimous; it was necessary to fight. Entry into the war was all the more appropriate given that Catholic Belgium was subjected to the onslaught of the German Empire.

All French Canadian political leaders in Quebec and elsewhere supported the government, including *Franco-Ontarian* leader Napoléon-Antoine Belcourt; *Acadian* Senator Pascal Poirier; celebrated *Acadian* judge Pierre-Amand Landry; the leader of the Liberal opposition at the House of Commons, Wilfrid Laurier; Montreal Archbishop Paul Bruchési; powerful Quebec Cardinal Louis-Nazaire Bégin; and also Le Devoir. The *Conseil des métiers et du travail* followed suit, and

---

9. Jolivet, *Le vert et le bleu*, 85–86.

10. *Le Devoir*, 1 June 1917, 1: "Les Canadiens-français sont exclusivement *Canadiens*. Ils n'ont pas d'autre patrie que le Canada."

11. Brown, "Anglo-Canadian Relations," 203.

"the whole Montreal union movement engaged with the war effort."[12] Following the federal parliament's unanimous decision to take part in the war and taking into account the fact that France and England were reluctantly dragged into the conflict, Henri Bourassa highlighted that "it is therefore [the] national duty [of Canada] to contribute, according to its forces and by its own means of action, to the triumph and especially to the endurance of the combined efforts of France and England."[13] In September 1914, even Henri Bourassa, the anti-imperialist leader and "tireless defender of the linguistic and religious rights of all French Canadians throughout the country,"[14] accepted the idea that Canada should come to the aid of the Allies and of Belgium occupied by German forces. Bourassa's opinions would vary after 1915 and notably after the political turmoil that shook other regions of the British Empire, including Ireland.[15] For the time being, however, he aligned himself with general opinion and saw eye to eye with the Catholic episcopate.

On 23 September 1914, Quebec bishops signed a pastoral letter for the war, which was to be read "in all churches on Sunday 11 October and would be followed by a collection from which 50 percent of the takings would go to the Patriotic Fund."[16] Montreal Archbishop Bruchési himself even gave $1,000 to the Patriotic Fund, highlighting the fact that "England has protected our liberties and our faith. Under her flag we have found peace, and now in appreciation of what England has done, you go as French Canadians to do your utmost to keep the Union Jack flying in honor of the breeze."[17] The Church stated clearly that, given the care that England had taken to protect the religious and linguistic rights of Francophones since the Quebec Act of 1774, French Canada had to

12. "L'ensemble du mouvement syndical montréalais emboîte le pas à l'effort de guerre" (Dansereau, "Montréal," 135).

13. Durocher, "Bourassa," 252, quoting *Le Devoir* of 8 September 1914: "C'est donc [le] devoir national [du Canada] de contribuer, dans la mesure de ses forces et par les moyens d'action qui lui sont propres, au triomphe et surtout à l'endurance des efforts combinés de la France et de l'Angleterre." See also Armstrong, *Crisis*, 109; Lacombe, *La rencontre*, 107.

14. Durocher, "Bourassa," 248: "Le défenseur acharné des droits linguistiques et religieux de tous les Canadiens français à travers le pays."

15. Jolivet, *Le vert et le bleu*, 294.

16. "[D]ans toutes les églises, le dimanche 11 octobre et qui sera accompagné d'une quête dont cinquante pour cent des recettes iront au 'Fonds Patriotique'" (Durocher, "Bourassa," 254).

17. Armstrong, *Crisis*, 58.

come to her aid. The bishops of the Ecclesiastical Provinces of Quebec, Montreal, and Ottawa expressed the general opinion of the time: "We cannot close our eyes to the fact that this conflict, one of the most awful yet seen by the world, will make its recoil felt in our country. England is engaged in this war, and who does not see that the destiny of every part of the Empire is bound up with the fate of her armies? She counts very rightly on our co-operation."[18]

At Montreal's Sohmer Park on 15 October 1914, Wilfrid Laurier was also in the limelight at a large pro-war gathering. According to *La Presse*, the most influential French-Canadian daily in North America with a circulation of more than 140,000 per day, this was "the most grandiose demonstration ever known in Montreal."[19] All of the most influential French-Canadian politicians of the time—names such as Belcourt, Dandurand, Casgrain, Gouin, and Laurier—called for mobilization. What would be the response by men of volunteering age?

In 1912, only 27 of the 254 officers in the Canadian militia were French Canadians.[20] Structural reasons explain the absence of a French Canadian military tradition, notably the fact that the Canadian militia had long been perceived as Anglo-Protestant and associated with the Orange Order.[21] The fact that a French military tradition had long since disappeared might explain French Canadians' lack of enthusiasm for the Canadian militia. Furthermore, battles led against the Francophone Métis of Louis Riel in 1869–1870 and in 1885 did little towards making this tradition more attractive to French Catholics.[22]

The most important French-Canadian mobilization effort began in Montreal, initiated by Arthur Mignault, a pharmacist who made his fortune selling his "little red pills." Mignault granted $50,000 of his own money and the Francophone elites of the Liberal Party worked behind the scenes to convince Conservative Prime Minister Robert Borden and his

18. *The Quebec Chronicle*, 12 October 1914, 10.

19. "La plus grandiose manifestation que nous ayons jamais connue à Montréal" (*La Presse*, 16 October 1914).

20. Dutil, "Against Isolationism," 117.

21. Gagnon, *Le 22e bataillon*, 51.

22. Historians generally agree on the fact that English-Canadian officers did not show much sympathy to the French Canadian military needs, as Desmond Morton has noted: "Since Confederation, successive ministers and generals had simply ignored the special emotional and linguistic needs of a militia for French Canada" (Morton, *Military History*, 152).

Minister of Militia and Defence, Sam Hughes, to authorize the creation of an exclusively Francophone unit. The absence of French battalions in the first Canadian contingent, which had begun training at Valcartier, Quebec in August 1914, incited the economic, religious, and political elites to demand the creation of a unit composed only of Francophones. The first expeditionary contingent consisted of seventeen battalions but none had been dedicated to French Canadians.[23]

According to Jean-Pierre Gagnon, a historian specializing in the 22nd (French Canadian) Battalion, the lack of French Canadian recruits in the first expeditionary contingent—1,245 French Catholic volunteers out of a total of 36,267—led the French Canadian elites to believe that an exclusively French Canadian battalion might attract more volunteers.[24] This instinct turned out to be quite correct in the case of the "22nd Battalion that would remain the only French-speaking unit at the front."[25] However, it turned out to be quite false when the time came to fill the ranks of other Francophone battalions. In any event, the fact that less than 4 percent of recruits in the first contingent were French Canadians must not have comforted French Catholic elites who repeatedly called for mobilization.[26]

It is hardly surprising that the Montreal newspaper, *The Beck's Weekly*, was one of the first to accuse French Canadian nationalists, starting with "Boo-rassa," of cowardice.[27] On 19 September 1914, only a few weeks after the outbreak of world conflict, *The Beck's Weekly* posed the question "Why Doesn't Jean Baptiste Enlist?"[28] The mistrust exacerbated by the Boer War did not take long to resurface. The mobilization of the 22nd Battalion nevertheless served to reassure Catholic elites a little. The appeal of the Catholic Bishops to the effect that French Canadians should "offer their hearts and their lives to the defence of the British Empire"[29] seemed to have worked. Although the public response was not as quick as anticipated by the regiment's promoters, by November 1914,

23. Gagnon, "Les soldats," 84.
24. Ibid., 83.
25. Granatstein, "Conscription," 69.
26. Gagnon, "Les soldats," 84.
27. *The Beck's Weekly*, 26 September 1914, 25.
28. *The Beck's Weekly*, 19 September 1914, 10.
29. *La Patrie*, 28 September 1914, 4.

more than 900 men had nevertheless brigaded.[30] From 1915 to 1918, the total number of soldiers and officers—volunteers or conscripts—who at one point or another operated within the 22nd Battalion came to 5,584 men.[31] More than 88 percent of them had close friends in Quebec, as Jean-Pierre Gagnon notes.[32] Historians thus considered the 22nd Battalion to be mainly a Quebec regiment.

On 20 May 1915, the 22nd Battalion left the port of Halifax for Great Britain, with a total force of 1,178 men, of which forty-seven were Franco-American, eighteen Belgian, and fourteen French.[33] There is but little historiographic discussion concerning the battles of the sole French Canadian battalion at the Front.[34] Nevertheless, the Battle of Flers-Courcelette, in September 1916, made the headlines of all the important dailies of the time. The 19 September 1916 issue of *La Presse* did not fail to announce that the 22nd Battalion had distinguished itself during an important offensive, taking the German village of Courcelette.[35] For some military historians, the Battle of Courcelette was the "Vimy" of Quebec French Canadians.[36]

Other French Canadian battalions were authorized by the federal government between 1915 and 1918. Following the outbreak of conflict, the Acadian elite and Liberal and Conservative newspapers all supported the participation of Acadians in the war. It was not until December 1915 that Ottawa granted authorization to create an entirely French-Canadian battalion in the Maritimes. The religious and political elites then relied on the creation of the 165th Acadian Overseas Battalion to recruit more young people. Archbishop LeBlanc and Abbé Jean V. Gaudet actively supported the Battalion, the latter becoming its Catholic

30. Gagnon, *Le 22e bataillon*, 55–57.
31. Ibid., Appendice I, 407.
32. Gagnon, "Les soldats," 93.
33. Vennat, *Les «Poilus»*, 1:162.
34. Pierre Vennat wishes historians would discuss other things than the ethnic divisions and the Conscription Crisis of 1917–18 when dealing with the French Canadians during the Great War: "Pas un livre d'histoire qui n'omet de parler de la lutte des nôtres contre la conscription, que cela soit au cours du premier ou du deuxième grand conflit mondial. Mais nombreux sont ceux qui oublient de mentionner que, parallèlement, des milliers de volontaires canadiens-français participèrent à ces guerres sanglantes sur le front européen et s'y illustrèrent" (ibid., 1:11).
35. Labayle, "Vimy," 159. See also *La Presse*, 19 September 1916.
36. Vennat, *Les «Poilus»*, 2:69.

chaplain in January 1916. Some had already enrolled in the 22nd, the 26th New Brunswick, and the 25th Nova Scotia Battalions. According to the figures of the time, by 1916 more than 1,200 Acadian soldiers were enrolled in the 132nd and 165th Battalions and more than 3,000 others had joined the ranks of other Maritime regiments.[37] It is still difficult today to determine precisely the number of Acadian recruits enrolled during the First World War. As Andrew Theobald notes: "Acadian enlistment was substantial in Lieutenant-Colonel G. W. Mersereau's 132nd (North Shore) Battalion . . . and in the 145th (Kent-Westmorland) Battalion. However, since no questions were asked about race, ethnicity, or mother tongue on Canadian Expeditionary Force attestation papers, there is no definitive way to determine how many Acadians served in Great War military units."[38]

The 165th Acadian Battalion, commanded by Lieutenant-Colonel Louis-Cyriaque D'Aigle, did not leave for Europe until a year and a half later, in March 1917, with a reduced force of less than 700 men. Due to difficulties with filling its ranks, the 165th Battalion, bearing the official seal of the "Ave Maris Stella," was disbanded in England in May of that same year. Despite this, historian Claude Léger notes that the battalion "seems to have been the product of a national will: one of many demonstrations among Acadians, of the desire to mark themselves as a distinct people by founding their own institutions."[39]

Certain French Ontario elites also requested the creation of an exclusively Francophone Battalion, though it is still very difficult to know more on this subject. Patrice Dutil asserts that the creation of a Franco-Ontarian battalion in Eastern Ontario was authorized in the winter of 1916, but that it was immediately dismantled upon arrival in England.[40] The 38th Canadian Battalion was also authorized in January 1915 and recruited in Ottawa and the surrounding areas. In this unit, Franco-Ontarians mixed with Ontario Anglophones. On 25 November 1916, Montreal's *La Presse* highlighted that since 1914 nearly 3,000 to 4,000 Acadians and French Canadians of Ontario had volunteered in

37. Forbes and Muise, *Atlantic Provinces*, 221.

38. Theobald, "Une loi extraordinaire," 83.

39. Léger, "Le 165e bataillon": "[Le bataillon] semble avoir été une œuvre de volonté nationale: une manifestation parmi tant d'autres chez les Acadiens, du désir de se marquer comme peuple distinct en fondant leurs propres institutions."

40. Dutil, "Against Isolationism," 118.

the West, notably in the 233rd Battalion (*Canadiens-Français du Nord-Ouest*). These numbers are very difficult to validate, but we can indeed note that French Canadians outside of Quebec enlisted well, proportionally speaking: of the 14,000 French Canadian soldiers accounted for in France in April 1917, only 8,200 came from Quebec. Thus, more than 40% of French Catholic volunteers were not Quebecois.[41]

Other volunteers from Ottawa, Sudbury and Sturgeon Falls joined the controversial 163th French Canadian Battalion led by Henri DesRosiers and Olivar Asselin of Quebec.[42] Here again, however, the lack of any exhaustive work on this question makes precise analysis difficult. Nevertheless, one must not lose sight of the fact that in 1911 there were more than 1,600,000 people of Francophone origin in Quebec while Franco-Ontarians numbered 202,442 (or 8 percent of the total population of Ontario)[43] and the number of Acadians reached a maximum of 151,000 people.[44] One thing is thus apparent: recruitment in French-speaking Quebec was undeniably anemic.

In 1917, some of the most conservative and ultramontane papers in Quebec, such as *L'Idéal Catholique*, congratulated the French Canadians for not enrolling: "La participation du Canada à la guerre est énorme. . . . Mais, ce qui me console, c'est que peu de Canadiens français sont allés verser leur sang sur les champs impurs de l'Europe. Dieu a voulu nous épargner tout particulièrement."[45] This is certainly not the sort of assertion that Quebec's episcopate expected from a "good" Catholic journal. Before the announcement of Conscription in May 1917, the Catholic hierarchy repeatedly asked their *ouailles* to conform to the government's wishes. Throughout the first years of the war, Cardinal Bégin, Archbishop Bruchési, and most of the higher clergy showed their open support for recruiting and for Borden's decisions.[46] However, as became clear during the conscription crisis of 1917–1918, the lower clergy's attitude towards the war was far from supportive: "The country clergy were in closer touch with the people and less affected by outside influences than the hierarchy and city clergy. . . . The depth of their anti-war feel-

41. Ibid., 122. See also Durflinger, "Le recrutement."
42. Gagnon, *Le 22e bataillon*, 168.
43. Gervais, "L'Ontario français," 97.
44. Roy, "Démographie," 174.
45. *L'Idéal catholique*, January 1917, 1.
46. Wade, *French Canadians*, 710.

ing may be judged by the fact that they dared to oppose their superiors' views, despite the strict discipline of the Church."[47]

The lower clergy immediately reflected the populace's lack of enthusiasm for recruiting. There was indeed a recruitment problem in Quebec and certain indicators speak to this very eloquently. On 14 June 1916, for example, a car was raffled off in Quebec City to promote recruitment to the 167th French Canadian Battalion, but even this did not enable initial objectives to be reached.[48] This battalion, as with the nine other French Canadian battalions authorized in Quebec before 1917, did not manage to recruit enough volunteers. The same problems occurred outside of Quebec. Even Acadian and Franco-Ontarian battalions were not able to completely fill their ranks. As Serge Durflinger states: "Thirteen of the 258 infantry battalions raised during the war came from French Canada, and all of them had difficulty attracting and keeping recruits. These incomplete French-speaking battalions that went overseas after 1915 were all broken up so as to reinforce the 22nd and other infantry units needing reinforcement."[49]

The conclusion is clear: French Canada did not enable the ranks of the Canadian forces to be filled and the higher clergy did not succeed in convincing its brethren to volunteer. What is more, the problems were more acute in Quebec than anywhere else. Canada, with a population of around eight million people in 1914, supplied 619,000 men for the war. More than 60,000 of them died and at least 60,000 more returned wounded.[50] A maximum of 35,000 French Canadian men enlisted or were conscripted during that same conflict. This very low recruitment (despite the enlistment of conscripts in 1918) is explained partly by the great divisions that shook the country after 1915.

Federal leaders' prejudices, starting with Sam Hughes, Arthur Meighen, and Robert Borden, did not do much to help recruitment. Several historians have noted Hughes and Borden's lack of understand-

---

47. Ibid., 746–47.

48. Gagnon, *Le 22e bataillon*, 171.

49. Durflinger, "Le recrutement": "Treize des 258 bataillons d'infanterie levés durant la guerre le sont au Canada français, et tous éprouvent des difficultés à attirer des recrues et à les garder. Ces bataillons de langue française incomplets qui passent outre-mer après 1915 sont tous démembrés afin de renforcer le 22e et d'autres unités d'infanterie en mal de renforts."

50. Morton, "La guerre," 11.

ing for the French and Catholic element in Canada.[51] Sam Hughes, Minister of Militia until 1916, and described as "Anglophone and Protestant, of the Orange kind, that is to say, hardcore anti-Catholic and anti-Francophone,"[52] was often seen as the perfect scapegoat to explain the Quebecois attitude. Despite the experience of certain officers, the status of Francophones in the first contingent of 1914 was very modest. Notorious prejudices against French Canadians, links with the Orange Order, and the occasional refusal to let French Canadian recruits take part in religious processions certainly contributed to the awakening of suspicions regarding the Minister of Militia.[53] Even after 1914, some people, such as Major Olivar Asselin's brother, did not hesitate to blame the Federal Government: "What is certain is that the Barrés, Desrosiers, Piuzes, Prices and all our *French*[54] will be nothing but stopgaps, despite what they were promised when they were serving to recruit their fellow countrymen."[55]

DIVISION AND DISCORD

Indubitably, it was in Quebec that anti-imperialist and anti-conscription forces were fiercest. Perhaps because of their minority status in provinces with Anglophone majorities, Franco-Catholics in Ontario and New Brunswick did not react in exactly the same way as did Quebecois. Acadians enlisted as much as their Anglo-Protestant counterparts.[56] Also, Acadian Senators Pascal Poirier and Thomas-Jean Bourque and MP Ferdinand J. Robidoux all "urged their Quebec colleagues to emulate

51. In his memoirs, Sir Robert Borden was not always considerate towards the French Canadians, since he saw them as too parochial: "To leave them for military service beyond the seas, to cross the ocean in unknown adventure made no appeal and seemed undesirable and indeed desperate. Naturally his [the French Canadian's] vision was not very wide and sometimes it did not extend far beyond the boundaries of his parish." Borden, *Memoirs*, 612–13.

52. "Anglophone et protestant, de la variante orangiste, c'est-à-dire, pur, dur, anti-catholique et antifrancophone." See Bernier, "L'historiographie," 13.

53. Girard, *Canada*, 113. See also Granatstein and Hitsman, *Broken Promises*, 24–25.

54. In English in the original source.

55. AVM, Fonds Olivar Asselin, VMBM55S2D23, Raoul Asselin to Olivar Asselin, 7 February 1917: "Ce qui est certain, c'est que . . . les Barré, les Desrosiers, les Piuze, les Price et tous nos French ne seront que des bouche-trous, malgré ce qu'on leur avait promis lorsqu'ils servaient à l'embauchage de leurs compatriotes."

56. Theobald, "Une loi extraordinaire," 85.

the Acadian example" and to support recruiting as well as conscription: "Assuredly, many of New Brunswick's Acadian elites wholeheartedly supported conscription. Kent MP F. J. Robidoux, senators Thomas Bourque and Pascal Poirier, Bishop of Saint John Édouard LeBlanc, the majority of the Acadian clergy and the newspaper *Le Moniteur Acadien* (edited by Robidoux's father) all supported the *Military Service Act*."[57]

If Acadians voted for Liberal candidates in the 1917 Federal Elections (fought on the issue of conscription), the general attitude in Acadia was nonetheless different from that of Quebec due to their minority status. Conscription was not opposed by the majority of the Acadian elites. In Quebec, however, even the Catholic hierarchy had been forced to oppose it since the nationalist politicians and *curés* had succeeded in convincing the population.

What is certain is that pre-war attitudes and the strength of the anti-imperialist argument solidified everywhere in Quebec after 1915. Very low recruitment in Quebec raised passions from coast to coast. The anti-Catholic prejudices of the country's Orangemen and, among others, of *The Orange Sentinel* illustrate the extent of the damage to the nation caused by the war. If Henri Bourassa and his paper, *Le Devoir*, was the public enemy in English Canada and even in Anglophone Catholic circles in Ontario, the Conservative Party was the public enemy as far as Quebecois were concerned. The "priest-ridden Province of Quebec" did not do its share during the first three years of the war and voluntary recruitment gave no signs of hope to the most ardent English Canadian imperialists and Orangemen. Divisions were so strong in 1917 and 1918 that there were calls in Ontario for the Federal Government to imprison Bourassa and suppress the publication of the influential *Le Devoir*. Even the controversial Catholic Bishop of London, Ontario and his Ottawa protégés such as John James O'Gorman and Matthew Whelan became impatient with *Le Devoir*'s rhetoric.[58] By 1915, it was obvious that Bourassa regretted his September 1914 editorial in which he had supported the war.[59] By the beginning of 1915, Bourassa claimed that it was not the duty of Canada to defend Great Britain, but rather that of Great Britain to defend Canada.[60]

57. Ibid.
58. See Cardinal and Jolivet, "Nationalisme."
59. Durocher, "Bourassa," 252.
60. Bourassa, *Duty of Canada*, 39.

Aside from the question of recruitment and conscription, another issue inflamed public opinion in Canada and revealed the gap between French Canadian and English Canadian (Protestant and Catholic) visions: Regulation 17. It was adopted by the Ontario Government in June 1912 and stipulated that "English-language teaching must begin from the moment a child enters school, the use of French for instruction and communication . . . must in no case continue beyond the first class (1st and 2nd grade)."[61] In sum, from 1912 on, Franco-Ontarian children could no longer expect teaching *of* and *in* French in the province's Catholic separate schools. From that point on, a civil disobedience movement, led by political leaders who were nevertheless in favor of the war effort, including Napoléon-Antoine Belcourt and Philippe Landry, undertook to break the decision of the Ontario Government. During the entire war and even up until 1927, the struggle against Regulation 17, which the historian Gaétan Gervais describes as the founding act of Franco-Ontarian identity,[62] filled the pages of Catholic newspapers in Ontario and Quebec. Oblates and French priests who were on good terms with Montreal's *Le Devoir* and Ottawa's *Le Droit*, two vociferous opponents to Regulation 17, opposed the actions of the English-speaking Catholic hierarchy.

Charles Charlebois, a Quebec-born Oblate living in Ottawa, was one of the most powerful French Canadian opponents to the Catholic Anglophone authorities in Ontario. In 1916, in the midst of the crisis, he wrote angrily to the Ontario MP for Russell, Charles Murphy. The Russell constituency was then formed of a majority of French Canadians:

> You will find here the card that you sent me for the New Year. I am afraid, Sir, that I can't accept your wishes. These must mean something, or nothing. If they mean that you wish me to enjoy the next year to come, can you tell me why you have not yet spoken publicly . . . taking up the cause of the sacred rights of your voters? . . . What have you done to fix this wrong? Your wishes do not mean anything and they don't deserve to be accepted."[63]

61. "L'enseignement en anglais devra commencer dès l'entrée d'un enfant à l'école, l'usage du français d'instruction et de communication . . . ne devant en aucun cas se poursuivre au-delà de la première classe (1ère et 2e années)." See Lamonde, *Histoire sociale*, 59.

62. Gervais, "Règlement XVII," 123.

63. AOO, Fonds Charles Charlebois, HEB 2477.C47L13, Charles Charlebois to Charles Murphy, 5 January 1916.

Many in Quebec saw a link between the actions of the Ontario Government—actions vigorously supported by the Anglo-Catholic hierarchy led by Bishops Michael Francis Fallon, Neil McNeil, and David Joseph Scollard—and the actions of the Imperial Government.[64] The argument was simple, as was often highlighted by Armand Lavergne, a Quebec Nationalist Member of Parliament, who argued that when Ontario showed respect for the linguistic, religious, and educational rights of French Canadians, French Canadians would gladly enlist in the name of liberty, not before. The Francophone press deemed that it was Ontario's Regulation 17 that was the primary cause of French Canadian apathy regarding the war. Why fight in the name of this country and of this Anglo-Protestant Empire, exclaimed French Canadian journalists and politicians in Ontario and Quebec, when Anglo-Protestant authorities in Ontario undermined the most fundamental rights of French Canadians?

In their struggle, Franco-Ontarians could count on the support of certain members of the religious and political elites in Quebec, such as Prime Minister Lomer Gouin, Major Olivar Asselin, and Cardinal Louis-Nazaire Bégin.[65] The "casualties of Ontario" on this Ontarian battlefield were indeed helped by Quebecois. The Montreal *Société Saint-Jean-Baptiste* initiated the "sou de la pensée française" to finance the Ontario school boards and the Legislative Assembly of Quebec voted in favor of a motion against Regulation 17. These supporters from Quebec, however, were not involved in the day-to-day struggle.

Additionally, some were not afraid to assert that Quebecois were too indifferent to, if not ignorant of, what was happening in Ontario.[66] In 1912, Armand Lavergne pointed this out to the president of the *Association Canadienne-Française de l'Éducation de l'Ontario*, the main organization acting against Regulation 17: "Quebec has long been selfish and indifferent to your noble efforts. I offer you my own humble support. Should you have no need for it, all the better for you and for your cause; if this is so, my letter has no other aim than to tell you that I admire you, that I suffer with you and that I will rejoice in your victories."[67] French-

64. Choquette, *Langue et religion*, 187–98.
65. BANQ, P65/C2/4, L-N Bégin to Henri Bourassa, 25 May 1915.
66. Gervais, "Règlement XVII," 147–48.
67. ACRCCF, Fonds l'ACFO, C2/185/5, Armand Lavergne to C. S. O. Boudreault, 10 October 1912: "Quebec a été longtemps égoïste et indifférent à vos nobles efforts. Je

speaking Ontario, even aided by Quebec elites, reached maturity during this provincial conflict coinciding with the First World War.

Regulation 17 was one thing, but conscription was another for Quebecois in general. It was mainly the latter which greatly preoccupied their minds after 1915. Anti-conscription protests and editorials increased in Quebec even before the announcement by Borden's Conservative government, in December 1916, to proceed with an "inventory . . . made by the Post Office authorities, of every male between the ages of sixteen and sixty-five, residing in Canada."[68] The Government was suspected in Francophone nationalist circles of preparing for conscription. Paul Bruchési, Archbishop of Montreal and ardent promoter of the war, supported the initiative. However, he took the necessary steps to arrange a meeting in December 1916 with Minister of Justice, Irish-Montrealer Charles Joseph Doherty, and Prime Minister Borden himself to make sure this measure would not lead to conscription.[69] With the announcement of the Borden Government's intention to adopt compulsory military service in May 1917, Bruchési, like several other members of the Quebec episcopate, felt betrayed.[70] As early as 1915, certain members of the Quebec lower clergy had already sided against their bishops by favoring the anti-imperialist stance of Bourassa instead.[71] Canon Lionel Groulx, who succeeded Bourassa as the most powerful advocate of Quebec nationalism in the 1920s, underlined the fact that many Montreal priests were decidedly against voluntary enrollment. They gathered at the Mile End presbytery where they frequently met with anti-imperialist politicians:

> Le Curé [Perrier de la paroisse du Mile End] . . . est de tout coeur et d'esprit avec le groupe d'hommes, disons même l'école qui s'applique alors, au Canada français, à un relèvement national. Et il se trouve que les principaux chefs de l'école habitent presque tous la paroisse du Curé . . . Henri Bourassa est paroissien de la "Mâlaine" [Mile End] . . . Y fréquentent non moins assidûment

vous offre ma faible part, si elle vous est inutile, tant mieux pour vous et votre cause; dans ce cas ma lettre n'a d'autre objet que de vous dire que je vous admire, que je souffre avec vous et que je me réjouirai de vos triomphes."

68. *The Quebec Telegraph*, 23 December 1916, 9.
69. Durocher, "Bourassa," 265.
70. Ibid., 268.
71. Armstrong, *Crisis*, 163.

les prêtres, les religieux, et voire les personnages épiscopaux en communion plus ou moins étroite avec le credo nationaliste."[72]

In August 1917, Mgr Bruchési wrote to the Governor-General of Canada, following the adoption of the law on military service at the House of Commons: "Conscription has been voted in today. My feeling hasn't changed. I dread the consequences of this law if it is put into effect immediately. Many think as I do. The worst disturbances are possible."[73] The higher clergy had to adapt its views due notably to the lower clergy's (and the nationalists') opposition the Military Service Act. As Mason Wade has noted: "An article (published in the ultramontane paper *La Vérité* on July 7, 1917) by one 'Louis Romain,' thought to be Mgr Paquet, the rector of Laval University... demonstrated that the bishop's pastoral of 1914 had not made participation an absolute obligation. This utterance by an unofficial spokesman of the hierarchy reflected the shift in the higher clergy's attitude."[74] To Henri Bourassa, who had nonetheless often bickered with the Montreal Archbishop since 1914, Bruchési expressed his thoughts on the matter: "A few passages in your recent articles have saddened me. You know which ones. But the tone of your article this evening [28 May 1917] has my complete approval. On the issue of Conscription, I think exactly as you do. And I don't believe I am lacking in logic because I welcomed Canada's participation in the current war. I wrote two strong letters to Sir Robert Borden. They haven't stopped him from presenting his bill."[75]

Until 1916 Archbishop Bruchési had continued to urge Quebec Catholics to show "à la Grande-Bretagne une loyauté qui doit aller jusqu'à

---

72. Groulx, *Mes mémoires*, 2:275–76.

73. ACRCCF, Fonds Jean-Bruchési, P30/2/7, Paul Bruchési to Duke of Devonshire, 10 August 1917: "La conscription est aujourd'hui votée. Mon sentiment n'a pas changé. Je redoute les conséquences de cette loi si elle est mise en force immédiatement. Beaucoup pensent comme moi. Les pires désordres sont possibles."

74. Wade, *French Canadians*, 746.

75. ACRCCF, Fonds Jean-Bruchési, P30/2/8, Paul Bruchési to Henri Bourassa, Montréal, 28 May 1917: "Quelques passages de vos récents articles m'avaient fait de la peine. Vous savez lesquels. Mais votre article de ce soir [28 mai 1917] est dans une note qui a mon approbation entière. Sur la conscription je pense absolument comme vous. Et je ne crois pas manquer de logique parce que j'ai admis la participation du Canada à la guerre actuelle. J'ai écrit deux fortes lettres à Sir Robert Borden. Elles ne l'empêchent pas de présenter son projet de loi. Mais n'importe."

répandre notre sang pour elle."[76] The huge protests against conscription in all the small villages of the province in the summer of 1917 surely posed important challenges to Bruchési and the Catholic hierarchy. Anti-conscription meetings were held in Lanaudière, Bas-du-Fleuve, Saguenay, Lac Saint-Jean, Mauricie, and Montégérie—in short, in all the regions of Quebec.[77] During a meeting on the subject of conscription, held in Montreal on Saturday 26 May 1917, one speaker raised the ire of the crowd by supporting the project. He was rebuked ironically: "Mr. Guy Morey asked the crowd if it was prepared to abandon Belgium and France. Cries of 'Yes, yes,' were then heard."[78] On 22 May 1917, 10,000 people gathered in Quebec City, voting in an anti-conscription resolution and calling for a referendum. The next day 10,000 people gathered in Montreal's Parc LaFontaine.[79]

On 28 May, again in Montreal, 4,000 protestors gathered at the city's Saint-Jean-Baptiste market to applaud a speech by the president of the session, Élie Lalumière, when he spoke of the two great French Canadian leaders, Wilfrid Laurier and Henri Bourassa: "And one must hope that the two great French Canadian leaders will find a way of coming closer together, of reaching out and of making peace for the greater good of the French Canadian race."[80] Protests and petitions increased. The *Société Saint-Jean-Baptiste* (SSJB), the *Fédération nationale Saint-Jean-Baptiste* (a women's association linked to the SSJB), and even the Conservative Member of Parliament for Montreal's Jacques-Cartier riding, J. A. Descarries, signed resolutions against conscription.[81] For Quebecois, compulsory military service was unacceptable. Rejecting successive accusations that they had not sufficiently enlisted and that they now had to do their "fair share"[82] of the war effort, French Canadians and the usual

---

76. *L'Événement*, 10 January 1916, 4.

77. *La Patrie*, 14 June 1917, 5. See also *La Presse*, 31 May 1917, 10; *Le Devoir*, 28 May 1917, 5.

78. "M. Guy Morey, demanda à la foule si elle était prête à abandonner la Belgique et la France. Des cris de 'Oui, oui,' se firent alors entendre" (*La Patrie*, 31 May 1917, 5).

79. *Le Devoir*, 24 May 1917, 4.

80. "Et il faut espérer que les deux grands chefs canadiens-français trouveront le moyen de se rapprocher, de se donner la main et de vivre ensemble pour le plus grand bien de la race canadienne-française" (*Le Devoir*, 29 May 1917, 1).

81. *La Patrie*, 28 May 1917, 3.

82. Cook, *Canada*, 37.

nationalist networks[83] protested vigorously against this measure. The Catholic hierarchy was put in a difficult situation: either they continued to disapprove of the anti-conscription and nationalistic rhetoric or they sided with the majority of their brethren in criticizing the Canadian government. They decided to follow the actions taken by Sir Wilfrid Laurier and Henri Bourassa and opposed conscription.

For *La Patrie*, a conservative newspaper, the imposition of conscription seemed legitimate, insofar as the cause remained just and laudable. As the only French-language newspaper of Montreal that approved conscription, however, several of its articles in 1917 reflected certain unease. The daily indicated the social benefits that the announcement of a federal election could bring about: "That is why *La Patrie*, understanding the formidable opposition against compulsory military service that exists in the province of Quebec and in other areas, has already emphasized this accommodation (a call to the people) before putting such an important law into effect."[84]

The division was absolute. Politically, Quebecois sided overwhelmingly with Bourassa and Laurier. Wilfrid Laurier rejected conscription and demanded a referendum on the question. He refused to participate in the coalition government put in place by Robert Borden in June 1917. Ironically, several of his own English-Canadian Members of Parliament dropped him to enter into the coalition, many saying that the real political leader of Quebec was now the unelected Henri Bourassa. "Today in Quebec Bourassa is King," indicated dispatches from Ottawa to the British Minister of Canadian origins Max Aitken (Lord Beaverbrook) during the electoral campaign of December 1917.[85] The election results demonstrate the rift between the mostly Anglo-Protestant population in English Canada and the French Catholic majority in Quebec. Of the eighty-two Liberal Members of Parliament elected in Canada, sixty-two came from Quebec. In fact, sixty-two of the sixty-five members from Quebec were Liberals. The majority votes against Unionist-Conservative

83. BANQ, "Montreal, Fonds" SSJBM, P/82/1-3, Victor Morin to Governor-General of Canada, 11 August 1917.

84. "C'est pourquoi la *Patrie*, comprenant l'opposition formidable qui existe dans la province de Quebec et dans d'autres milieux, contre le service militaire obligatoire, a déjà indiqué cet accommodement (appel au peuple) avant de mettre en vigueur une loi aussi importante" (*La Patrie*, 12 July 1917).

85. HLR, Fonds Lord Beaverbrook, BBK/E/1/34-5, Canada General Election, 1917.

candidates in Quebec were staggering. In the Témiscouata riding, the Liberal candidate obtained 6,301 votes against 624 for his Conservative opponent; in Kamouraska, the Liberal candidate received 3,501 votes against 185 for his Conservative opponent.[86]

CONCLUSION

Historian Andrew Theobald notes that most of the Acadian political and religious elites supported conscription.[87] All the same, generally speaking, the Acadian response—as well as, to a lesser degree, that of Franco-Ontarians—regarding the war effort, recruitment, and conscription was somewhat different from that of Quebecois: "In spite of pronounced opposition to conscription in Acadian newspapers, within the Liberal party and among Acadians generally, no accusations were made against the war effort itself. This was in stark contrast to the oft-examined response of French Quebec, where conscription, the war, and the British Empire were all regularly denounced in colourful terms."[88] Perhaps this had something to do with the Franco-Catholics being reduced to minority status in New Brunswick and Ontario. Moreover, French-Catholic Quebecois turned out to be the least inclined to enrolment and the most violent agitators against recruitment and conscription. Dynamite placed at the Montreal home of wealthy Anglo-Protestant businessman, Hugh Graham (Lord Atholstan), and riots such as those of Easter 1918 in Quebec City—which caused the death of five civilians and marked the province's Francophone *imaginaire*—were not events repeated in other parts of French Canada.[89]

Martin Auger illustrates how the Quebec clergy did not defend the Quebec Easter Riot: "Indeed, the French-Canadian elite and the Roman Catholic Church had condemned the use of violence in Quebec City and had refused to give the rioters the slightest support. Federal and pro-

---

86. *Le Saint-Laurent*, 20 December 1917, 1.

87. Theobald, "Une loi extraordinaire," 85.

88. Ibid., 94.

89. "In early August 1917, the residence of Lord Atholstan, the owner of the proconscription *Montreal Star*, was bombed by a group of young men known as the dynamitards. A dozen French Canadians were arrested in connection with the attack. Canadian authorities then learned that the dynamitards planned to bomb other targets, including the Canadian Parliament, and to assassinate Prime Minister Borden and top Government officials supporting conscription." See Auger, "Civil War," 507.

vincial French-speaking politicians, such as Sir Wilfrid Laurier, Liberal party leader in Ottawa, and Sir Lomer Gouin, premier of Quebec, had appealed for calm, as did influential nationalist leaders like Armand Lavergne and Henri Bourassa. Cardinal L. N. Bégin, archbishop of Quebec City, had even published a letter in several Quebec newspapers during the riots commanding the faithful to obey the law and requesting local priests to use their influence to induce parishioners to cease rioting."[90] It must be emphasized that the Catholic authorities in Quebec were faced with an internal crisis that none of the other French-speaking Catholic authorities outside of Quebec ever faced during the war.

It was perhaps only in Quebec, the historical heartland of French Canada since seventeenth-century French colonization, that one could publicly show one's disagreement. Quebec, after all, was the only Canadian province with a French Catholic majority. The famous separatist motion submitted by the Provincial Liberal Member of Parliament Joseph-Napoléon Francoeur could not have been submitted elsewhere in another Canadian legislature. For the first time in the history of Quebec since 1867, separation was being proposed—albeit in a passive way: "That this House is of opinion that the Province of Quebec would be disposed to agree to breaking the Federation Compact of 1867 if the other provinces consider that it is an obstacle to the unity, progress and development of Canada."[91] Contrary to what some have written, the Francoeur motion was never rejected by the Legislative Assembly of Quebec.[92] Francoeur himself withdrew it on 23 January 1918 after inflamed debates in Parliament and in the newspapers. He stated, with the agreement of his chief, Quebec Prime Minister Lomer Gouin, that his objective had been reached: he had hoped to demonstrate that Quebec held rights that needed to be respected by all the Canadian provinces. Several MPs and Quebec newspapers concretely supported the motion nonetheless, including Hector Laferté, MP for Drummond, and the newspapers *Le Canada*, *Le Soleil*, *Le Progrès du Saguenay*, and *Le Franc-Parleur*.[93]

Previous works have often stated that the First World War divided French Canadians and English Canadians. In a way, this assertion

90. Ibid., 539.
91. NAGB, CO/722/3, *8th Year Statistical Year-Book*, Quebec, 1921.
92. English, "Political Leadership," 92.
93. Castonguay, "Un bluff politique," 22–24.

serves to veil internal divisions of an ethnic, historic, and cultural order that had existed for a long time in Canada. For instance, can the large Irish-Catholic community of Quebec or of Ontario be blended into the English-Canadian mainstream? Works by Mark McGowan, Terrence Murphy, and Gerald Stortz have shown that this trap should be avoided.[94] Similarly, French Canadians did not constitute a monolithic and homogenous group of people.

In the final evaluation, issues concerning the First World War were experienced differently in the different French Canadian regions of Canada: Acadia, Ontario and Quebec. Though all approved Canada's entry into the war in August 1914, recruitment problems in French Canada did occur early and did not unfold the same way. The only French Canadian Battalion fighting in Europe was the Quebec 22nd Regiment. For a province constituting 27 percent of the Canadian population in 1911, the establishment of only one complete regiment denotes Quebecois lack of enthusiasm for the war.

The Great War did not completely destroy national cohesion in French Canada. To pretend as much would be inappropriate. Displays of solidarity continued between Quebec and the "outposts" of French Canada that were French Ontario and Acadia. The organization of the celebrated *Congrès de la langue française* in Canada during the twentieth century, the founding of the anti-Irish *Ordre de Jacques Cartier* in Quebec and in Ontario in the 1920s, and the moral and financial support of the Quebec elites to Franco-Ontarians in their struggle against Regulation 17 up until 1927 are all proof of solidarity among the country's French Catholics.[95] The fact remains that Quebec's more vigorous national self-assertion during the war was carried out to the detriment of its analogues in other areas of French Canada. For many leaders and organizations entering the public domain during the war, including Canon Lionel Groulx, the new journal *L'Action française*, and the first Quebec separatist newspapers such as *Le Bas-Canada* and *L'Idéal catholique*, the dream of a bicultural country like the one imagined by the Fathers of Confederation in 1867 was no longer possible.[96] This also

---

94. McGowan, *Waning of the Green*, 414. See also Murphy and Stortz, *Creed and Culture*, 245.

95. Martel, *Le Canada français*, 11–15.

96. Separatist newspapers such as *Le Bas-Canada* and *L'Idéal catholique* were first published during the Great War.

contributed to challenge the long-time loyalty to the Crown and the Empire expressed by Quebec's Catholic episcopate since the eighteenth-century British conquest.

The first fissures that appeared after 1914 between members of the same French-Canadian nation represent collateral damage resulting from the ethnic and religious rift between French-Catholic Quebec and Anglo-Protestant Canada during the Great War. With Quebec claiming its distinct place at the heart of Canada more insistently, the French-Canadian Catholic "outposts" would begin to slowly but surely bear the repercussions.

BIBLIOGRAPHY

Primary Sources

Archives

ACRCCF – Archives du Centre de recherche en civilisation canadienne-française, 1917.
AVM – Archives de la ville de Montréal, 1917.
BANQ – Bibliothèque et archives nationales du Québec, 1917.
HLR – House of Lords Record Office, 1917.
NAGB – The National Archives of Great Britain, 1921.

Newspapers

Le Devoir
La Patrie
La Presse
Le Saint-Laurent
L'Événement
L'Idéal catholique
The Beck's Weekly
The Quebec Chronicle
The Quebec Telegraph

Other

Bourassa, Henri. *The Duty of Canada at the Present Hour: An Address Meant to be Delivered at Ottawa, in November and December, 1914, but Twice Suppressed in the Name of "Loyalty and Patriotism."* Montreal: L'Imprimerie du Devoir, 1914.

Secondary Sources

Armstrong, Elizabeth. *The Crisis of Quebec, 1914–1918.* New ed. Toronto: McLelland & Stewart, 1974.
Auger, Martin F. "On the Brink of Civil War: The Canadian Government and the Suppression of the 1918 Quebec Easter Riots." *Canadian Historical Review* 89 (2008) 503–40.
Bernier, Serge. "L'historiographie militaire canadienne entre 1975 et 1988." *Guerres mondiales et conflits contemporains* 157 (1990) 5–24.
Bock, Michel. "Tradition et territoire dans le projet national canadien-français." In *Balises et references: Acadies, francophonies*, edited by Martin Pâquet and Stéphane Savard, 57–78. Quebec: Les Presses de l'Université Laval, 2007.
Borden, Robert Laird. *His Memoirs.* Toronto: Macmillan, 1938.
Brown, R. C. "Sir Robert Borden, the Great War, and Anglo-Canadian Relations." In *Character and Circumstance: Essays in Honour of Donald Grant Creighton*, edited by John S. Moir, 201–24. Toronto: Macmillan, 1970.
Cardinal, Linda, and Simon Jolivet. "Nationalisme, langue et éducation: Les relations entre Irlandais catholiques et Canadiens français du Québec et de l'Ontario aux 19e et 20e siècles." In *Le Québec et l'Irlande aux 19e et 20e siècles: Culture, histoire,*

identité, edited by Linda Cardinal, Simon Jolivet, and Isabelle Matte. Quebec: Les éditions du Septentrion, forthcoming.

Castonguay, René. "Un bluff politique 1917: La motion Francoeur." *Cap-aux-Diamants* 53 (1998) 22–24.

Choquette, Robert. *Langue et religion: Histoire des conflits anglo-français en Ontario.* Ottawa: Les Presses de l'Université d'Ottawa, 1980.

Cook, Ramsay. *Canada and the French-Canadian Question.* Toronto: Macmillan, 1966.

Dansereau, Bernard. "Montréal, le mouvement ouvrier et la Première Guerre mondiale." *Bulletin d'histoire politique* 8 (2000) 134–49.

Durocher, René. "Henri Bourassa, les évêques et la guerre, 1914–1918." *Historical Papers/Communications historiques* 6 (1971) 248–75.

Durflinger, Surge. "Le recrutement au Canada français durant la Première Guerre mondiale." No pages. Online: http://www.museedelaguerre.ca/education/ressources-pedagogiques-en-ligne/depeches/le-recrutement-au-canada-francais-durant-la-premiere-guerre-mondiale/.

Dutil, Patrice. "Against Isolationism: Napoléon Belcourt, French Canada, and 'La grande guerre.'" In *Canada and the First World War: Essays in Honour of Robert Craig Brown*, edited by David Mackenzie, 96–137. Toronto: University of Toronto Press, 2005.

English, John. "Political Leadership in the First World War." In *Canada and the First World War: Essays in Honour of Robert Craig Brown*, edited by David Mackenzie, 76–95. Toronto, University of Toronto Press, 2005.

Forbes, E. R., and D. A. Muise. *The Atlantic Provinces in Confederation.* Toronto: University of Toronto Press, 2001.

Frenette, Yves. *Brève histoire des Canadiens français.* Montreal: Boréal, 1998.

———. "L'évolution des francophonies canadiennes: Éléments d'une problématique." In *Aspects de la nouvelle francophonie canadienne*, edited by Simon Langlois and Jocelyn Létourneau, 3–18. Quebec: Les Presses de l'Université Laval, 2004.

Gagnon, Jean-Pierre. "Les soldats francophones du premier contingent expéditionnaire du Canada en Europe." *Guerres mondiales et conflits contemporains* 157 (1990) 83–101.

———. *Le 22e bataillon (canadien-français) 1914–1919: Étude socio-militaire.* Quebec: Les Presses de l'Université Laval, 1986.

Gervais, Gaétan. *Des gens de résolution: Le passage du "Canada français" à "l'Ontario français."* Sudbury: Prise de Parole, 2003.

———. "L'Ontario français (1821–1910)." In *Les Franco-Ontariens*, edited by Cornelius Jaenen, 49–124. Ottawa: Les Presses de L'Université d'Ottawa, 1993.

———. "Le Règlement XVII (1912–1927)." *Revue du Nouvel-Ontario* 18 (1996) 123–92.

Girard, Camil. *Canada, a Country Divided: The Times of London and Canada, 1908–1922.* Quebec: Les éditions JCL, 2001.

Granatstein, J. L. "Conscription and the Great War." In *Canada and the First World War: Essays in Honour of Robert Craig Brown*, edited by David Mackenzie, 62–75. Toronto: University of Toronto Press, 2005.

Granatstein J. L., and J. M. Hitsman. *Broken Promises: A History of Conscription in Canada.* Toronto: University of Toronto Press, 1977.

Groulx, Lionel. *Mes mémoires.* 3 vols. Montreal: Fides, 1970–1974.

Jolivet, Simon. *Le vert et le bleu: Identité québécoise et identité irlandaise au début du XXe siècle.* Montreal: Les Presses de l'Université de Montréal, 2011.

Labayle, Éric. "La bataille de Vimy: De l'histoire à la mémoire." *Bulletin d'histoire politique* 17 (2009) 141–62.
Lacombe, Sylvie. *La rencontre de deux peuples élus: Comparaison des ambitions nationale et impériale au Canada entre 1896 et 1920*. Quebec: Les Presses de l'Université Laval, 2002.
Lamonde, Yvan. *Histoire sociale des idées au Québec, 1896–1929*. Montreal: Fides, 2004.
Léger, Claude. "Le 165e bataillon d'infanterie d'outremer." No pages. Online: http://wwi.lib.byu.edu/index.php/Le_165e_Bataillon_d%27Infanterie_d%27Outremer.
Martel, Marcel. *Le Canada français: Récit de sa formulation et de son éclatement, 1850–1967*. Ottawa: Société historique du Canada, 1998.
———. "Le débat autour de l'existence et de la disparition du Canada français: État des lieux." In *Aspects de la nouvelle francophonie canadienne*, edited by Simon Langlois and Jocelyn Létourneau, 131–45. Quebec: Les Presses de l'Université Laval, 2004.
McGowan, Mark. *The Waning of the Green: Catholics, the Irish, and Identity in Toronto*. Montreal and Kingston: McGill-Queen's University Press, 1999.
Morton, Desmond. "La guerre d'indépendance du Canada: Une perspective anglophone." In *La Première Guerre mondiale et le Canada: Contributions sociomilitaires québécoises*, edited by Jean Lamarre and Roch Legault, 11–34. Montreal: Méridien, 1999.
———. *A Military History of Canada*. Edmonton: Hurtig, 1985.
Murphy, Terrence, and Gerald Stortz. *Creed and Culture: The Place of English-speaking Catholics in Canadian Society, 1750–1930*. Montreal and Kingston: McGill-Queen's University Press, 1993.
Roy, Muriel K. "Démographie et démolinguistique en Acadie, 1871–1991." In *L'Acadie des Maritimes: Études thématiques des débuts à nos jours*, edited by Jean Daigle, 141–206. Moncton: Chaire d'études acadiennes, 1993.
Theobald, Andrew. "Une loi extraordinaire: New Brunswick Acadians and the Conscription Crisis of the First World War." *Acadiensis* 34 (2004) 80–95.
Vennat, Pierre. *Les «Poilus» québécois de 1914–1918: Histoire des militaires canadiens-français de la Première Guerre mondiale*. 2 vols. Montreal: Les éditions du Méridien, 1999–2000.
Wade, Mason. *The French Canadians, 1760–1945*. Toronto: Macmillan, 1956.
Warren, Jean-Philippe. "L'invention du Canada français: Le rôle de l'église catholique." In *Balises et références: Acadies, francophonies*, edited by Martin Pâquet and Stéphane Savard, 21–56. Quebec: Les Presses de l'Université Laval, 2007.

4

"Khaki has become a sacred colour"

The Methodist Church and the Sanctification of World War One

David B. Marshall

No church's response and activities during the First World War have received more attention from Canadian historians than those of the Methodist Church of Canada. Michael Bliss's classic study in 1968 outlined the main themes of the church's militant idealism.[1] The church's belief that the war was redemptive fuelled its drive for recruits, made it intolerant of pacifist dissent, and informed its passion for social reform. Some twenty years later, I reconsidered the story of the Methodist Church and the war.[2] Whereas Bliss's focus was primarily on the domestic front, I followed Methodist chaplains, as well as some probationers and ordained ministers, who served as soldiers overseas at the front. For Bliss, the war's end was marked by the Methodist Church's stunning and radical declaration of the social gospel. By contrast, I emphasized the growing disillusionment of many of the chaplains and soldiers and pointed to the large number of ministers and probationers who simply disappeared from the active ranks of the Methodist ministry after the war.[3] Those chaplains who remained active in the church strenuously

---

1. Bliss, "Methodist Church."
2. Marshall, "Methodism Embattled."
3. To criticize my article, it is clear that it was overly influenced by the modern-

argued that the Methodist Church had to find a new gospel that was in touch with the more realistic outlook of the returned soldier. These contrasting interpretations can be summarized by quoting the Rev. S. D. Chown, Superintendent of the Methodist Church. Near the war's beginning he declared that "khaki has become a sacred colour" and, by war's end, he had concluded in a repentant fashion that the Methodist Church could never again be caught "painting roses on the lid of hell."[4] Chown's proclamations can be regarded as bookends of the Methodist wartime experience; however, this narrative of militant idealism followed by ever deepening disillusionment—although certainly valid—masks a great deal of the complexity of the Methodist experience during the Great War.[5]

There was no single response to the war on the part of the Methodist Church. There could be no easy or straightforward answers to the complicated and urgent questions posed by wartime, such as the relationship between the Christian faith and war, the use of violence and the resort to killing, the reasons for and significance of sacrifice, the meaning of death, and the nature of the after-life. Within Methodism, there was a range of experiences and perspectives and, in many cases, religious beliefs and practices changed or were fluid depending on the particular circumstances being faced in the chaos of the war.[6] Some Methodists questioned the existence of a loving and merciful God as a result of the terrible carnage of the war. Others, as Chown's agonizing postwar musings suggest, were critical of the Methodist Church's identification with the cause of the war. On the other hand, the Christian notion of salvation through sacrifice as a way to understand the terrible toll of the war offered a powerful note of consolation. For many, the powerful image of

---

ist perspective—following the classic writings of Fussell, *The Great War*, and Leed, *No Man's Land*—that insists the Great War was a major event in the undermining of religious faith and secularization of society. A similar interpretation, although published later, is Eksteins, *Rites of Spring*.

4. UCA, S. D. Chown Papers, file 486, "War Sermon," 1915, and file 616, "The Abolition of War," n.d., ca. 1919–21.

5. A good synthesis of the contrasting points of view is offered in Semple, *The Lord's Dominion*, 395–415. Many biographical studies have also explored the thought and activities of prominent Methodists during the war. See especially McNaught, *Prophet in Politics*; Prang, *Rowell*; Bliss, *Canadian Millionaire*; and English, *Shadow of Heaven*.

6. See Robbins, *Christian Church*, 156.

the crucified Christ, as a symbol of sacrifice and life everlasting, was one way to endure the unthinkable suffering and cope with the loss of loved ones at the front.[7]

The Methodist Church was gravely concerned about the moral impact of the war upon the soldiers. In joining the Canadian Expeditionary Force, Methodist recruits were suddenly torn away from the uplifting surroundings of home, family, and church. The influence of military life and the brutalities of warfare seemed to undermine the morality of the young men who had volunteered. For many Methodists, a decline in moral standards was a sign of a deeper loss of faith; this equation of morality with piety was very strong. For the battle-hardened soldier, moral transgressions—such as swearing, drinking, and gambling, or even sexual promiscuity—did not indicate that they had abandoned their faith in Christianity or rejected God. The soldiers' disillusionment was often rooted in their resentment toward the Methodist Church's insistence that the soldier submit to a strict moral code with respect to swearing, gambling, drinking, and sexual activity in particular. As a result of the soldiers' changing moral standards, the Methodist Church no longer had a meaningful message for many of them, but these soldiers had not abandoned their belief in God and many of them held a keen sense of the meaning and importance of Christ's sacrifice. The soldiers' rejection of the Methodist Church's insistence on upholding a traditional moral code was a more common problem than any wholesale loss of faith.[8] As one Methodist chaplain pointed out to the Methodist Church's Army and Navy Board, he did not "find any great outpouring of deep religious desire such as it was said the war was producing"; but he did not witness any outright rejection of belief in Christianity.[9] The impact of the war on the Methodist Church of Canada was neither revival nor a shattering loss of faith, but a drift away from the church.

---

7. See Vance, *Death So Noble*, esp. 35–72, and Crerar, *Padres*, 161–93.

8. A similar argument is made by Snape, *God and the British Soldier*, 187, 196–99.

9. ANB, Box 8, file 219, A. C. Farrell to Moore, 28 December 1916. Farrell's view has been echoed by many recent historians. See especially Schweitzer, *Cross and the Trenches*, 263. Schweitzer suggests that neither extreme (religious revival or utter disillusionment) is a satisfactory description. Such responses existed, but more common was a range or "spectrum" of religious responses between these two polar opposites. See also Brown, *Religion and Society*, 101.

OPENING MONTHS: THE CALL TO DUTY AND SACRIFICE

In the early months of 1914, W. B. Creighton, the editor of the Methodist Church's official denominational weekly paper, the *Christian Guardian*, was in a somber mood. With the prospect of war looming, he outlined his commitment to the principles of Christian internationalism and proclaimed that if the churches spoke out against the "brutal appeal to arms" then war could be averted.[10] Creighton was not confident that this would occur, however, for in his view there was a serious lack of knowledge about God's word in contemporary society. His pessimism was based on his observation that attendance at class and prayer meetings, activity in Sunday schools, the appeal of the ministry as a calling, and "even the willingness to speak of one's personal experience of faith" had "decidedly declined."[11]

When the First World War broke out in August of 1914, Creighton admitted to being startled and being forced to re-consider his beliefs.[12] However, rather than turning to despair, he saw hope in the war itself. Although Creighton discerned the hand of God somewhere in the cataclysm of the war, he still shuddered at its inevitably terrible and tragic cost. Creighton's attitude is best described as deeply ambivalent. He believed that the war would lead to a better world, but at the same time he could not refrain from acknowledging its inevitable horrors and especially the losses that would be suffered by many families. Similarly, the General Superintendents of the Methodist Church of Canada, the octogenarian Albert Carman and the much younger and more progressive Chown, issued a "call to prayer" asking their "father in heaven . . . to restrain the carnage and bloodshed that must ensue upon the preparation of this terrible hour."[13] Their prayer was not an enthusiastic call to arms but rather a plea to bring the war to a quick resolution so that the hostilities and destruction would be of short duration. There was no

10. "The Wicked Waste of War, Is There a Way Out?" *Christian Guardian*, 28 January 1914.

11. "Where Are We Spiritually Today?" *Christian Guardian*, 8 April 1914.

12. See, for instance, the following editorials: "Is It Coming?" *Christian Guardian*, 19 August 1914; "Warfare and the Ten Commandments," *Christian Guardian*, 2 September 1914; "War and Prayer," *Christian Guardian*, 9 September 1914; "Thanksgiving and Wartime," *Christian Guardian*, 7 October 1914; "After the War: Gains and Losses," *Christian Guardian*, 18 November 1914.

13. "A Call to Prayer in View of Present Conditions in Europe," *Christian Guardian*, 12 August 1914, 6.

celebration or jubilation, for as it was clearly understood, "War is hell. . . . War is crime. In this day of progress and enlargement toward Christian ideals, war is a hideous crime against civilization and every uplifting aspiration and hope of the human race."[14]

Methodists struggled with what the church's position should be. Many had recently developed an anti-war outlook. The strains of liberal-pacifism were heard in some quarters of the Methodist Church including in the pages of the *Christian Guardian*. However, as Michael Bliss observed, these "ripples from the world tide of peace sentiment" in Canadian Methodism "did not produce a serious re-examination of the ethics of war,"[15] and as Thomas Socknat concluded, "Most pacifists grew passive in the opening months of the war. They were silenced by the rising tide of militant Christian patriotism."[16] The Methodist Church was vulnerable to charges that it had abandoned its anti-war principles in favor of a shallow patriotic militarism. One of Chown's numerous addresses outlining Methodist policy toward the war provoked much controversy.[17] Chown was a colorful orator and quite adept at using powerful imagery to make his message dramatic and memorable. In "A Message to Our Soldiers," preached at Massey Hall on 13 December 1914, he gave reasons why he had abandoned his commitment to pacifism and peace organizations. "The shock of battle," he declared, "has convinced us that we cannot build heaven on the mouth of hell." He was unequivocal in his understanding that the only way to establish peace was to end militarism, and the only way to defeat militarism was through militarism.[18] This militant position led to vigorous commentary in the daily press. Charges were leveled against Chown for being in apostasy to the peace movement while the Methodist Church was accused of joining "the ranks of the militarists."[19] In the pages of the *Christian Guardian*, Creighton denied the validity of such criticism by refuting

14. "To the God of Battles," *Christian Guardian*, 12 August 1914, 5.
15. Bliss, "Methodist Church," 214.
16. Socknat, *Witness*, 48.
17. The challenges the war posed for the church convinced the elder Carman to resign from the office of General Superintendent, leaving the younger and more dynamic S. D. Chown as the sole occupant of the office and spokesman for the church. See A. Carman, "Some Personal Explanations," *Christian Guardian*, 28 October 1914, 2.
18. "A Message to Soldiers," *Christian Guardian*, 16 December 1914, 7, 19.
19. See "Not a Militarist," *Christian Guardian*, 23 December 1914, 6.

the pacifist argument that since Jesus would not fight in the trenches or lead a bayonet charge then war was always unjustified and clearly unchristian. Jesus, he claimed, did not teach "a hard-and-fast doctrine of non-resistance." Instead Jesus's method of teaching was through the use of paradox. His own life, and especially his crucifixion on the cross, demonstrated that Christians must stand up and fight against injustice and make whatever sacrifice was necessary to insure that righteousness prevailed. Christians were now facing a similar predicament. They had to sacrifice their belief in peace and brotherhood in order to defeat the use of brute force and military aggression.[20] In these early wartime editorials, Creighton equated the war with the major drama of Christianity. Those who volunteered to fight were taking a stance similar to that of Christ. The official position of the Methodist Church was that the war was a defensive one to defeat militarism and protect Christian civilization and, as a result, it was a just war.[21]

In September 1914, General Superintendents Carman and Chown called upon Methodists, "Enlist in the Canadian army, unless you feel you can serve the Dominion and the Empire better at home in peaceful avocations than in the thickest of the fight." They assumed that those who stayed at home would soon give way to the higher calling of being combatants in battle and said, "When that conviction gives way, go to the front bravely as one who hears the call of God."[22]

Methodists did not enlist to nearly the same extent as Anglicans or Presbyterians in this early stage of the war, but, for many who did, the idea of Christian duty and sacrifice was paramount in their decision. Typical was F. G. Brown, a probationer from the Nova Scotia Conference, who said, "I felt it was in accordance with Divine Will that I should proceed to France as a Private and as a combatant."[23] He recognized that his decision to volunteer certainly involved risking his own life, for his enlistment had been prompted by the death of his brother at

20. "The Ethics of War," *Christian Guardian*, 27 January 1915, 5–6. See the responses in the *Christian Guardian*, 3 March 1915, 2–3.

21. "Christian Duty under War Conditions," *Christian Guardian*, 19 August 1914, 8–9; "Shall the War Redeem the Nations?" *Christian Guardian*, 16 September 1914, 10–11. Ernest Thomas wrote under the pseudonym Edward Trelawney in the *Christian Guardian*.

22. "Manifesto on the War Situation," q.v. "Dr. Chown on the War Situation," *Christian Guardian*, 16 September 1914, 2.

23. ANB, file 346, F. G. Brown, War Service Record.

the front. He explained, "[It is] the imperative call of Duty ... that I must do a bit to help complete the noble task that he laid his life down for." By invoking this image of dying in battle for a greater cause, the Methodist Church was drawing on a set of beliefs and values that were deeply rooted in Christianity. "Soldiering for the Lord" was a phrase commonly used to describe missionary work, and it was easily transferred to apply to military duty in the war.

The call to military duty, however, went beyond these religious considerations. While sailing on a troop ship for England, the Rev. George O. Fallis of the British Columbia Conference wrote: "I thought of Wolfe, and imagined I could hear him say, 'the paths of glory lead but to the grave.' I feel differently going to the great European struggle. My thoughts are 'The paths of glory lead to immortality.' Duty done brings heaven, and death is but a step in the great process."[24] The figure of the heroic and noble warrior making sacrifices for country and empire was a common theme in the fiction, poetry, and hagiography of the times, and much of this literature found its way into the sermons, newspapers, and school curriculum.[25] Furthermore, these ideals of heroism, courage, sacrifice, duty, and determination to act also informed the "muscular Christianity" espoused by many Methodists and promoted by organizations such as the YMCA, Boy Scouts, and the cadet movement that were supported by the Methodist Church.[26] This gospel of masculinity insisted that action, as opposed to prayer or contemplation, was essential to Christian character.[27] In many respects the soldier could be considered the epitome of the muscular Christian, for it was thought that he clearly possessed the virtues of bravery, vigor, discipline, strength, determination, dedication, and wisdom that he was calling up in the service of fighting for Christian civilization.

24. G. O. Fallis, "Extracts from a Chaplain's Diary," *Christian Guardian*, 27 October 1915. For the role of Wolfe in Canadian popular culture, see the essays in Buckner and Reid, *Remembering*, especially Coutu and McAleer, "Immortal Wolfe?"

25. See Moss, *Manliness*, passim; Berger, *Sense of Power*, 217–58; and more broadly, Mackenzie, "Heroic Myths."

26. For Methodist support of the cadet movement, see Wood, *Militia Myths*, 177.

27. Canadian historiography awaits a full-scale study of muscular Christianity, but see Mott, "Pioneers"; Lindsay and Howell, "Social Gospel." The links between muscular Christianity and fighting in the First World War are explored in Putney, *Muscular Christianity*, 162–94.

METHODISTS OVERSEAS

The first Methodist chaplain to accompany the Canadian Expeditionary Force overseas was Captain Harry A. Frost. Initially, he was stationed at Valcartier Camp, which had been hailed as an ideal military setting by the Methodist Church because it was a "dry camp."[28] The only liquor that infiltrated the camp was the small amount that was smuggled in. There was practically no drunkenness and scarcely any "scrapping" or violent altercation. Morale at the camp was high as a consequence, according to the *Christian Guardian*.[29] On 30 September 1914, Frost left Valcartier and glided out into the St. Lawrence River bound for England, where the Canadian soldiers continued their training. However, there was one difference in the military camps overseas that presented incalculable problems, in Frost's estimation. In the British Army, the wet canteen was part of a time-honored military tradition.[30] The "rum ration" was regarded as a due privilege for the hard-working, dedicated soldier and something that was necessary for maintaining morale. The Methodist Church of Canada, however, was terribly concerned about access to alcohol in the armed forces and was alarmed that it was sanctioned by the British Army, even if there were strict limits on the daily ration distributed to the soldiers. Chown, who had trained in the Kingston Military School and served briefly in the Prince of Wales Own Rifles as a young man, explained that the Methodist opposition to the wet canteen was not only a matter of upholding the morality of the men, but also of insuring the utmost efficiency and effectiveness of the troops.[31] The Rev. Dr. T. Albert Moore, Secretary of the General Conference and head of the Department of Evangelism and Social Reform, indicated that the practice of the daily rum ration and presence of the wet canteen likely endangered the willingness of loyal, devout Methodist families to offer their boys for military service.[32]

---

28. For a discussion of temperance and the Canadian soldier during the war, see Cook, "Wet Canteens."

29. See J. R. Patterson, "A Week at Valcartier," *Christian Guardian*, 14 October 1914, 8–9.

30. See Cook, "Beverage."

31. S. D. Chown, "The Soldier and the Wet Canteen," *Christian Guardian*, 28 October 1914.

32. See T. Albert Moore, "The Church and the Soldier," *Christian Guardian*, 3 February 1915, 2.

To bolster the confidence of Methodists at home, Frost reported that most soldiers were living the Christian life and attended religious worship, including services in song, biblical readings, and study, as well as evangelistic talks. They also visited him on occasion for more intimate spiritual guidance. The most important message that Frost conveyed to Methodists at home was that, despite the presence of the wet canteen, army life was not undermining the soldier's faith or moral character. To provide further reassurance, Frost offered to make a personal visit to any Methodist soldier should their loved ones at home make such a request. In this way, Frost pointed out, he could minister not only to the soldier but also to the "anxious ones in the homeland."[33] At this early stage of the war, even before any Canadian soldier was involved in any of the fighting, the major concern seemed to be whether young Methodists were being corrupted by the presence of alcohol.[34]

It was not until April 1915 at the second battle of Ypres that the Canadians saw action. Only a few chaplains were allowed to accompany the troops to the front lines. Frost remained behind in England at the camp at Shorncliffe. He informed his readers that he had organized a sacramental service for the officers and men just before they left for France because it was the last opportunity for them to worship together as a unit before seeing action. There was "the ever-present uncertainty of further opportunities of worship." Frost thought the most fitting message for the men preparing to go to the battlefront was to emphasize the correspondence between Christian sacrifice and fighting for Canada and the Empire. He pointed to the "place of the cross in the flag and the essential part which the religion of Jesus Christ must ever take in our life and great undertakings" as the most fitting message for the men preparing for battle.[35]

Most of Frost's work was now in the hospitals. Therefore, for readers of his Diary entries printed in the *Christian Guardian*, glimpses of the reality of the war were faint and distant. Of course, Frost gained a better impression of just how brutal the fighting was when he saw the maimed and war-torn men who were returned to the hospitals in England, but

33. Captain H. A. Frost, "Notes from a Chaplain's Diary," *Christian Guardian*, 13 January 1915, 11–12.

34. "Message from the General Superintendent to the Ministers and Members of the Methodist Church," *Christian Guardian*, 2 December 1914, 6.

35. H. A. Frost, "Notes from a Chaplain's Diary," *Christian Guardian*, 19 May 1915.

he dared not discuss the sheer carnage that the men had endured. In this first instance of significant Canadian casualties, he emphasized the nobility of the sacrifices, a theme that would become a constant refrain of the Methodist Church throughout the remainder of the war.[36] Frost quickly understood that his role was to console those at home as well as minister to the soldiers. Nobility of sacrifice was the only message—no matter how much it may have sanitized the awful reality of the war—that made sense to what was still a deeply Christian society. Anything else, Frost realized, would rob people of any comfort that they might receive in coping with, and making some sense of, the tragic news.[37]

Nevertheless, careful readers of the *Christian Guardian* got a fairly clear picture of the battlefield conditions from the diary extracts of Major George O. Fallis, who was assigned to an advanced dressing station just behind the front lines. He was able to convey the horrors of the battlefield simply by mentioning the shocking numbers of casualties the CEF suffered.[38] As Fallis explained in the *Christian Guardian*, he had noted in his diary that he could hear the "awful roar of the guns. It never ceased and was like a distant thunder."[39] He was under steady shellfire and experienced "a feeling of absolute helplessness" and a "torturing anxiety as to when the next one will come and where it will go."[40] These stark passages left a clear impression of the frightening circumstances the men faced during battle.

In those chaotic and frightening conditions, Fallis's emotions and thoughts were torn apart. His faith was thrown into confusion. During one burial service, he recalled that, as he listened to his Anglican colleague preach on the theme of "God is love," he was struck by the incongruity of that central Christian message with the awful reality of the war.

---

36. Ibid.

37. This chapter dissents from the historiographical convention that the idealistic rhetoric of heroic Christ-like sacrifice on the battlefront was a "delusional form of comfort and consolation." In Canada, this view is most vigorously advanced by Mackay and Swift, *Warrior Nation*, 68–83. For a fuller statement of the dissenting view, see Watson and Porter, "Bereaved."

38. G. O. Fallis, "Leaves from a Chaplain's Diary," *Christian Guardian*, 9 February 1916.

39. G. O. Fallis, "Extracts from a Chaplains Diary," *Christian Guardian*, 3 November 1915.

40. G. O. Fallis, "Leaves from a Chaplain's Diary," *Christian Guardian*, 16 May 1916.

The "screaming battery declared in its voice of deadly thunder that man is not love but man is still moth and rust and mildew, the pestilence that walketh in darkness, the destruction that wasteth at noonday."[41] In such circumstances, it was difficult to reconcile the carnage with thoughts of a Christian crusade.[42] Such emotions demonstrated how the angry, wrathful God of the Old Testament, largely forgotten in optimistic pre-war Canada, could resurface in the terribly stressful and frightening conditions of the front.[43] The carnage of the battles certainly challenged many of the idealistic and Christian notions of the true character of war. However, the prevailing notion of the nobility and Christ-like character of the sacrifices made at the front persisted throughout the war because, as Frost's diary writing indicates, it helped many to cope with the brutality of the battlefield, the horrible surroundings, and the indignities of trench life to which the soldier was exposed.

The war was also a severe test for the church and the ministry at home. People had to be reminded constantly of God's "quiet strength and unchanging love,"[44] for only that message of God's abiding presence was deemed to be able to save people from indifference and despair. The historiography of Methodism has emphasized the fact that Methodist pulpits were used as recruiting stations and local ministers were "recruiting sergeants," but just as important was the fact that during many worship services, local clergy read the names of casualties from the pulpit as a way to recognize their Christ-like sacrifice, to acknowledge the sacrifice made by the family in the congregation, and to comfort those in the community who were grieving. These very public and sobering reminders of the horrific and endless toll of the war did not lead to questions about the war and its senseless casualties, but rather to a more

41. G. O. Fallis, "Diary, 10 October 1915," *Christian Guardian*, 26 April 1916.

42. G. O. Fallis, "Diary, 6 October 1915," *Christian Guardian*, 5 April 1916. For similar rhetoric referring to an angry wrathful God of the Old Testament that had resurfaced on certain occasions in Methodism, see *Christian Guardian*, 28 July 1915, 8–9.

43. On the liberalism of pre-war Methodism in Canada, which had repudiated the idea of a vengeful condemnatory punishing God, see especially Airhart, *Serving the Present Age*; Van Die, *Evangelical Mind*.

44. George Warburton, "Will the Church Fail?" *Christian Guardian*, 16 September 1914, 12. Similar sentiments were expressed by S. D. Chown at the 1914 General Conference of the Methodist Church of Canada. See "The Vitality of Religion," Official Sermon Preached before the General Conference in Dominion Methodist Church, Ottawa, Sunday September 28th," *Christian Guardian*, 7 October 1914, 12–13. See also Byron Stauffer, "Sermons Killed by the War," *Christian Guardian*, 2 December 1914, 10.

determined and steadfast resolve to win the war so that the sacrifices made by the soldiers and their families would not be in vain.

The extent and nature of the sacrifices being made became clearer to those at home when the wounded soldiers were returned for convalescence. By the summer of 1915, the *Guardian* was struck by the tragic contrast between the men who left Canada, full of vigor and health and accompanied by lusty cheers, and those who had quietly returned to rest and recuperate and whose "fighting days, and perchance even working days, [were] over."[45] The *Guardian* did not provide any detail about the wounds, mental anguish, or emotional turmoil that many of the returned soldiers were suffering. Instead, hope was expressed that their condition would serve as further inspiration for those at home to consecrate themselves to the war effort as a meaningful and earnest way to acknowledge and honor their sacrifices. Herein lay the horrendous and relentless logic of war: to give up, or bring about a hasty peace before the war's noble objectives were realized would render the terrible sacrifices of war somehow meaningless or futile. The pastoral letters from Chown to the ministers and members of the Methodist Church became less tolerant of those who refused to enlist. By the summer of 1915, he was arguing that "every Canadian of military age, and in mental and physical health, if he is not already enlisted, must give an account to himself, to society, and to God as to why he wears civilian clothes."[46] The brutal irony of the war was that the worse its carnage became and the more its sacrifices mounted, the greater became the devotion to the war effort and the idea that it was redemptive.

RECRUITMENT, ENLISTING, AND CONSCRIPTION

Methodists were vulnerable to charges that they were insufficiently patriotic and lacking in commitment to the war as their rate of recruitment was not in line with their numbers in Canada. According to the 1911 census, there were virtually the same numbers affiliated with the Methodist Church as there were with the Anglicans and the Presbyterian Church in Canada. Department of Militia figures indicated, however, that the number of Methodists volunteering for the CEF was signifi-

---

45. "The Men Who Are Coming Back," *Christian Guardian*, 11 August 1915, 2.

46. S. D. Chown, "To Ministers Members and Adherents of the Methodist Church in Canada," *Christian Guardian*, 14 July 1915.

cantly lower than the number of Anglicans and Presbyterians.[47] Chown admitted in an open pastoral letter that Methodists had "not yet risen to the full measure of their responsibility in respect to recruiting and securing recruits for the Canadian army." He thought the Methodist Church was "caught unprepared to take full part in the military programme" as a result of Methodism's "dissenting heritage."[48] To deal with the recruitment question, the Methodist Church created an Army and Navy Board in November 1915, with a mandate to encourage the recruitment of Methodist volunteers. The secretary of the Army and Navy Board was the tireless Rev. T. A. Moore, who had worked closely with Chown before the war on social reform issues. By early 1917, the number of Methodist recruits seemed more respectable at around 36,000 men.[49]

However, while these Methodist figures may have looked more encouraging in the aftermath of the particularly bloody and long Battle of the Somme, it was clear that enthusiasm to enlist was beginning to wane; therefore, the Methodist Church became more strident in its support for the war.[50] During this period, in what for him was a momentous decision, Chown announced his conversion to the principle of conscription. Not surprisingly, this decision was challenged within Methodist circles. One correspondent from New Brunswick outlined the case against conscription on the basis of the liberal and Methodist principle of personal freedom.[51] In response, Chown made an argument that was strikingly different from the calls for equality of sacrifice that were being voiced so vehemently across the country: conscription would absolve the soldiers

---

47. The figures released by the Department of the Militia for September 1916 indicated that while only 18,000 Methodists had volunteered, over 124,000 Anglicans and over 63,000 Presbyterians had. See Semple, *The Lord's Dominion*, 398.

48. "Chown to the Ministers of the Methodist Church in Canada," *Christian Guardian*, 16 November 1915. Methodist officials were also convinced that the number of Methodist recruits had been seriously under-reported because the Department of Militia Attestation Papers utilized the word "Wesleyan," not commonly used or broadly understood in Canada, as opposed to Methodist.

49. ANB, Box 2, file 15, *First Annual Report of the Army and Navy Board*, 21. Methodist recruitment was still below the standard of the Presbyterians at 70,000 recruits and the Anglicans at 165,000 recruits. For Moore's reports to the Church on recruitment, see "Religious Affiliations of Soldiers," *Christian Guardian*, 2 and 9 May 1917.

50. "The Recruiting Problem," *Christian Guardian*, 4 October 1916.

51. UCA, S. D. Chown Papers, Box 1, file 13, Correspondence regarding World War I, 1915–1916, Kenneth Kingston to S. D. Chown, 25 November 1916.

of any responsibility for their decision to fight and for their wartime actions. It was preferable that the state imposed conscription, for then soldiers could better deal with the terrible moral dilemmas that fighting a war posed.[52]

Chown became more committed to the idea of conscription as a result of his overseas tour of the camps, hospitals, and battlefront during the summer of 1917.[53] In a fashion strikingly similar to Prime Minister Borden's 1917 visit to the troops overseas, Chown's encounters with the troops convinced him that reinforcements had to be found no matter what the cost.[54] When he returned to Canada, he immediately placed a letter in the "Forum" section of the *Christian Guardian*. His appeal was reminiscent of *In Flanders Fields* in its reference to the plea of the fallen soldiers: "From the grave of every Canadian soldier who has perished on the field of honour, a voice cries to each of us, saying: 'I suffered this for you. Oh do not let me die in vain.'"[55] The vanquished soldier still spoke: "While they 'push the daisies' their brave spirits hold in pity and contempt the 'crocks' and 'duds' that make babel in Canada to-day. They tell us that selfishness is disgraceful, and challenge us to emulate their spirit in every walk of life."[56] Anything less would be nothing short of abandoning the men at the front and signal an appalling lack of resolve to win the war.

Criticism of the Methodist Church for its militancy and support for conscription by radical social gospel ministers, such as the pacifist J. S. Woodsworth, is well known. Less known is the serious criticism of Methodist Church policies that came from some Methodist soldiers.[57] E. E. Graham had served during the Boer War in South Africa and as a chaplain during the First World War at the No. 7 Canadian General Hospital in France. His dissatisfaction with the management of Chaplaincy affairs led to his decision to make an application for a trans-

52. Ibid., Chown to Kingston, 30 November 1916.

53. The primary purpose of this tour was to investigate moral conditions at the front; it will be discussed below.

54. For Borden's 1917 overseas visit, see Brown, *Borden*, 75–84.

55. *Christian Guardian*, 12 September 1917.

56. S. D. Chown, "The Challenge of Our Heroes," *Christian Guardian*, 12 September 1917.

57. S. D. Chown, "An Open Letter on the Duty of the Hour," 6 December 1917, reprinted in the *Christian Guardian*, 12 December 1917.

fer to combatant rank in the infantry.[58] However, Graham did not want his decision to be construed as acceptance of the bellicose doctrines of the Methodist Church.[59] The horror of the battle certainly undermined some of the more idealistic or crusade-like notions about the war, as Graham's fervent dissent indicates, but on the other hand, the persistence of the image of the noble sacrifices made by the fallen, immortal soldier, referred to in Chown's appeal, indicated just how important that ideal was to an on-going commitment to the war.

MORAL AND SPIRITUAL CONDITIONS AT THE FRONT

The primary reason why Chown had gone overseas was to investigate the moral conditions of army life that troubled Methodists at home, for there was concern that reports of lax morality overseas were undermining willingness to enlist. Why would any church-going, God fearing Methodist family encourage their son to enlist if a "fall from grace" would likely result? The Methodist Church was determined to do everything possible to protect the moral standards of the young men that it so enthusiastically encouraged to volunteer. The Rev. W. B. Caswell, pastor of Broadway Methodist Church in Winnipeg, was one of many Methodist clergy concerned about the moral conditions among the soldiers. Along with prominent laymen from the prairies, he decided to raise a Methodist battalion in western Canada that was designated a "dry" battalion. Caswell was appointed chaplain with the rank of Captain. He devoted much of his effort in the early months of 1916 to enlisting men into this dry battalion.[60] By the end of May, it was almost at full strength with over 1,100 recruits.[61] At Camp Hughes, Caswell reported respectful attention on the part of the men from the Methodist dry battalion to the religious services he held, which included a mid-week service, Bible study, and a Sunday song service on top of the regular Sunday Church Parade. However, he was distressed by the more general disregard of Sabbath among the men from the other battalions: "It is true that after church parade on Sabbath a.m. that the camp is wide

---

58. ANB, Box 4, file 82, Graham to Moore, 10 November 1917.

59. Ibid., Graham to Moore, 3 January 1918.

60. ANB, Box 7, file 190, W. B. Caswell to Moore, 23 February 1916 and 16 March 1916. See also *Christian Guardian*, 15 March, 1916.

61. ANB, Box 7, file 190, Caswell to Moore, 4 July 1916.

open. It has always been so here, Canteens & Picture shows—athletic games etc. are the order of the day."⁶²

In reporting these conditions in the camps, chaplains were intent on making it clear that they were not simply shocked at being thrust into a rugged male culture after years in the pristine surroundings of the local parish. For instance, in reporting the "deplorable moral conditions" at the front, H. E. Thomas of the New Brunswick Conference felt the need to explain that his dismay about his "daily contact with immorality" was not the result of some naïve or innocent notions of the human condition:

> I feel that I have seen enough of life not to expect military affairs to be conducted as is a Methodist Sunday School, and I have known enough about the prevalence of social vice, everywhere, not to be startled at the ordinary signs of its presence; but I have to confess that moral conditions on the whole, and especially as they obtain in England, have given greater depression of spirits to me and concerned me more than anything that has taken place in France or Belgium. This war will save England from many things, but to imagine that by it the Empire will be saved with an intelligent Christian salvation, with a salvation that gives purity of heart and life, is utter folly.⁶³

The incidents of alcohol and sexual promiscuity leading to cases of venereal disease, were, Thomas said, "making an Evangelist of me where I never was one before." He revealed, "Every night I read my Bible and I pray" even though there was always "plenty of cursing around."⁶⁴ Although there was little dispute about the existence of the problems relating to drink and venereal disease, there was debate among the chaplains about how serious these moral conditions were.⁶⁵

A. D. Robb was particularly concerned about the furor in Methodist circles in Canada concerning the discovery of playing cards in parcels sent overseas. For Robb, this outburst of moral panic was misplaced. He, of course, witnessed the card-playing and the more scandalous gambling at poker. "I am the last man to deprive the lonely lads of Canada of their cards," he wrote to the Methodist Church. "Civilian life and soldier

---

62. Ibid., Caswell to Chown, 25 August 1916.
63. ANB, Box 4, file 91, H. E. Thomas to Moore, 5 January 1916.
64. Ibid., H. E. Thomas to Moore, n.d., received 22 March 1916.
65. NAC, Chaplaincy Service Papers, Fallis to Moore, file 15-7-2, 17 May 1917.

life are in two separate categories. The ethics of the Army are perhaps too broad. I fear the ethics of the Civilian is sometimes too narrow."[66] This incident was of concern to Robb because he thought that it reflected an underlying source of serious misunderstanding between the home front and the soldier. If the church insisted on judging the men overseas by such moral transgressions as card playing, Robb feared, then that puritanical and condemnatory stance would only invite ridicule of the church among the officers and the men.

With these concerns in mind, the Army and Navy Board charged S. D. Chown with investigating moral conditions overseas. As well as visiting numerous camps and hospitals in England, Chown was taken to Vimy Ridge, the Somme, and Ypres during his eight week tour in the summer of 1917. Before returning to Canada, he reported to Sir George Perley, the Overseas Minister of the Militia Forces of Canada, that his report would "dissipate many fears which have been expressed at home, concerning the morality of our soldiers and bring comfort and assurance to our people."[67] His fact finding indicated that the incidence of immoral behavior compared favorably with that of any civilian community.[68] In other words, army life was not particularly morally dangerous and it did not necessarily undermine morality. There was, nevertheless, cause for some concern, he thought. The temptations that the men were exposed to in London and in some of the camps were much greater than what should be permitted. In his typically colorful prose, he reported that "in some parts of London the streets appear to be shambles for the slaughter of souls." He continued, "It also appears clear that our Canadian boys, by having more money at command are set upon with more determination by the huzzies and decoys of the streets."[69] He criticized the military practice of "giving a preventative outfit to the men on leave and in many cases virtually forcing it upon them," arguing that it reduced "the ethics of the sexual relation to moral chaos and undermines the morals of the

---

66. ANB, Box 6, file 165, A. D. Robb to Doctor Moore, 20 November 1917.

67. ANB, Box 2, file 41, Report of S. D. Chown on the Overseas Commission, "Report to Lt. Col. John Almond, D.C.S. Canadian Overseas Forces," 15–16, and Chown to Perley, 2 August 1917.

68. On the issue of venereal disease in Canadian society and the military during World War I, see Cassel, *Secret Plague*, 122–75.

69. ANB, Box 2, file 41, "Report of S.D. Chown on the Overseas Commission," 15–16.

men."[70] He was also critical of the Canadian Army and Government for not more vigorously protesting against the wet canteen but insisting instead on a similar Canadian practice.

In his report to the Methodist Church, Chown had to balance his criticisms of the moral laxity at the front with reassurance that the morality of the men was not being seriously compromised. Echoing many of the chaplains, he suggested that there were understandable reasons for some of the troubling behavior that concerned Methodists. His interviews with soldiers helped him understand them with empathy as opposed to condemning them for breaching the Methodist Code of Discipline. Chown understood that the soldiers' sexual licentiousness was likely rooted in the frightening battlefront conditions they faced as opposed to any flaw in their moral character. "One might suppose," he wrote, that "the Tommy, by reason of his exposure to danger and daily living in apprehension that each day might be his last . . . would, thereby, be hardened, but this is not the case. [Instead,] he is full of a gushing human feeling. He loves everybody, particularly women. He loves them indiscriminately." He explained that while on leave, they were desperately lonely and homesickness came over them and they could not be considered to be living in their normal state: "Some are shattered in nerves, some in body and others experience weakness of will in the presence of the abounding temptations to which they are exposed. The very spirit of brotherhood that has been developed through comradeship and suffering may be turned into an easy path towards degradation."[71] His report, more than anything else, was a defense of the character of the Canadian men overseas. As far as he was concerned, many of the charges about the lax behavior and immoral character of the Canadian soldier were "slanderous. And showed absolutely no understanding of the challenges the men faced." In no small measure his report was designed to acknowledge the "excellent qualities of the Canadian soldier."[72] His explanation of whatever moral transgressions took place among the soldiers was, in essence, a plea for greater understanding and compassion for the soldier.

For many of the chaplains, the best defense against the problem of moral decline rested in evangelism. During the Christmas season of 1915, H. W. Burnett, from the Montreal Conference, who was attached

70. Ibid., 10.
71. Ibid., 27–28.
72. Ibid., 23–26.

to the 102nd battalion at Bramshott Camp, attempted "to get the men . . . to take a definite stand for Christ."[73] However, he found that sustained evangelistic effort was difficult to carry out. He visited the men in their recreation huts in the evening but, when he managed to get some of them together for an impromptu service, he found that it was impossible to hold it for a suitably long duration: "The movements of the troops are very uncertain, perhaps when you have made arrangements you will find that the men had received an unexpected order to go up to the trenches as a working party, to repair trenches destroyed by a sudden bombardment; so that you have to take the men whenever you can get them, that of course makes the work more difficult."[74] There was growing concern among the chaplains that this sporadic worship would have a negative impact on the habit of attending regular worship when the men returned home. On the other hand, these informal services were far more effective than the formal services of the Church Parade to which the men so strenuously objected.[75]

Despite the challenges of holding worship and prayer at the front, H. W. Burnett often managed to organize informal gatherings characterized by "the inspiring singing of the old hymns, in which all heartily joined, the fervent prayers of the men, and the remarkable spiritual influence pervading the services, [which] made them seasons of great spiritual uplift." He usually "closed each service with the Lord's Supper, simply and spiritually conducted, in which the larger number of the men present most earnestly participated." Throughout these services Burnett's "constant theme . . . was the great importance of definite decision for Christ."[76] Over five hundred men decided for Christ during evangelistic efforts extending from 10 December to New Year's Eve. Burnett's calculations were based on the number of men who sealed their decision by Communion. Burnett was determined to secure these decisions for Christ made at the front so that the men's religious commitment would become permanent. In the aftermath of these services, the names of those soldiers who had made their commitment to Christ were forwarded "to the different ministers of their home churches in

73. ANB Box 4, file 95, H. W. Burnett to T. A. Moore, 2 January 1916.

74. Ibid., H. W. Burnett to the Editor of the *Christian Guardian*, n.d.

75. ANB, Box 7, file 191, Chambers to Moore, "Report of Work in Segregation Camp Seaforth, July–August 1918," 8 August 1918.

76. ANB, Box 4, file 95, H. W. Burnett to T. A. Moore, 2 January 1916.

Canada, asking them to enroll them as members" of the local Methodist Church.[77] This letter-writing campaign was designed, in part, to help consolidate the soldier's commitment to the Church, but it was also designed to assure congregations at home that the faith and morality of the boys overseas was certainly intact, or even growing stronger.

In April of 1916, Burnett accompanied the troops to the front lines. Here, close to the fighting, he noticed that when he spoke on "immortality every eye was upon [him], for the proximity to death to any one of them at last made the subject a very vital one to them." During these services, Burnett "pleaded for the reception of the resurrected Christ." He related, "I was sure from the evident responsiveness of the large body of men present that my appeal was not in vain. I asked them to tarry for Communion at the close and a large number stayed and as I passed around the elements I could hear the murmurings of the men engaged in earnest prayer to the God of battles for deliverance from sin and for strength to face the great struggle in which they were engaged."[78] During this same time, around Easter, Burnett gave many short addresses urging the men to accept Christ as their Savior from sin and as the only refuge when they were facing danger and death. Burnett claimed:

> The men were greatly moved and when I asked for decisions for Christ, hands went up all over the field and there must have been at least one hundred decisions for Christ. I asked as many as possible to stay for an after service and very few went away. We had prayer and then entered one of the most inspiring Communion services I ever attended, the men led the singing, and after I led the Communion service and was passing the elements around in some cases to men who would never take it again.[79]

According to Burnett's calculations, around two hundred men from one battalion had attended the Communion service. Burnett was one of many chaplains who thought a religious revival was occurring at the front. He believed that the large number of decisions for Christ was a consequence of the men "being in the presence death and always in danger." In many instances, Burnett received news of the death of those men to whom he had recently served Communion. Rather than being overcome by the futility of his evangelistic efforts, he believed that

77. Ibid., H. W. Burnett to the Editor of the *Christian Guardian*, n.d.
78. Ibid., H. W. Burnett to T. A. Moore, 27 April 1916.
79. Ibid.

those men who had been killed shortly after receiving Communion at least "were fully prepared for the end."[80] Accounts of wartime religiosity suggest that it was just before and after battle, in particular, that the soldiers seemed to become the most observant. During the Battle of the Somme, Fallis recalled being approached by a soldier asking if he would administer Holy Communion, for, as he said, "We may never come out alive."[81] Before battle, Communion was regarded as a preparation, asking God for his guidance and protection, while after battle it was regarded as an opportunity for thanksgiving. However, the appeal of Communion services seemed to fade as the war was prolonged and the toll of lost lives continued to mount. Other chaplains noted that as the war dragged on fewer men partook in the Lord's Supper since some became superstitious, worrying that Communion was a preparation for death, while others rejected the idea of approaching the Lord's table, feeling too unworthy.[82]

As the men continued to witness an ever growing number of their fellow combatants being killed or maimed, they began to doubt whether their prayers were being heard. Even though the appeal of formal church services and the draw of Communion seemed to trail off as the war went on, the idea that the soldier was making a Christ-like sacrifice did not diminish. As A. D. Robb explained from his dug-out in June of 1918, Christ was with the fallen soldiers: "I have seen these boys die; I have seen them bleed; I have seen them suffer and they have given me a view of Calvary. I believe my Christ looks after these men in the field and the unnamed graves."[83] From the pen of a Methodist soldier, Private George Turpin of British Columbia, comes a similar understanding of life everlasting gained through the soldiers' sacrifice during battle: "By the way of the cross men marched to duty and danger and some found in the trenches the gateway of eternal life open for them, with Christ waiting to welcome them."[84]

---

80. ANB, Box 4, file 95, H. W. Burnett to T. A. Moore, 23 August 1916.

81. Fallis, "Diary, 11 October 1915," *Christian Guardian*, 26 April 1916.

82. UCA Pamphlet Collection, "A Message from the Chaplains of the Overseas Military Forces of Canada to the Churches at Home," 1918.

83. ANB, Box 10, file 256-57, A. D. Robb to Moore, 25 June 1918.

84. Private George Turpin, "By Way of the Cross," *Christian Guardian*, 17 July 1918.

Suggestions that there was a religious revival at the front were probably exaggerated, but on the other hand, neither was there a massive or dramatic rejection of religion. A. C. Farrell offered one of the more balanced and sober assessments of the religious conditions among the men at the front. He asserted that there was a general disregard or indifference to the "usually appointed [Church Parade] service unless that service was . . . camouflaged with some special attraction."[85] However, the soldiers' religious faith—as distinct from their attitude toward religious institution and formalized worship—was a different matter, he thought. To demonstrate the difficulty in understanding the religion of the soldier he recounted an experience that illustrated the dilemma facing the Methodist Church in its attempts to reach the battle-torn soldiers. Upon overhearing a member of his battalion talking to a friend while they were waiting for the order to go up to the line, Farrell recalled being "stunned and revolted by their loud, filthy, profane language." His first instinct was to turn away and leave, but instead he talked to the men. Very soon the soldier who had moments ago been indulging in the use of foul, profane language was showing Farrell a picture of his wife and children. He told him that he had been overseas for a long time and had many close calls and narrow escapes with death, including one where three of his friends were hit and killed by an exploding shell that narrowly missed him. Then, Farrell recalled, this soldier confessed: "I knew the power that saved me and was watching over me and I did not forget to thank Him either." Farrell emphasized that this soldier's faith in a higher benevolent spirit was from a man who only a few moments before had been "so offensively profane." To Farrell this incongruity was perplexing. He admitted that he did not fully understand and was not able to fully explain the apparent contradiction he discovered in many soldiers who indulged in clearly immoral behavior on the one hand, but on the other espoused a clear faith in God. The most important distinction that Farrell made was to point out that, while the soldier's religiosity—although somehow hardened by the war—was intact, the soldier seemed not to have much regard for the church.

---

85. ANB, Box 8, file 219, A. C. Farrell to Moore, 28 December 1916.

WAR'S END

Precisely this dilemma of the alienated soldier was dealt with by Farrell's colleague, A. D. Robb, near the end of the war: "Our experiences over here are epochal and have done for us what no Conference, no College, no Congregation could ever do for us. . . . The men at home can never understand the soldier. The people at home can never understand what the war has meant to the soldier."[86] Robb explained that he had spent over two years in close proximity to the soldiers and concluded, "They have taught me a deeper religion, a bigger brotherhood, a broader charity, than I ever knew before." Robb believed that the men represented a new spirit of bravery and brotherhood that would have to be embraced by a renewed and more tolerant church. If the Methodist Church continued to preach a narrow morality that was also bereft of a broader compassion and understanding, it would fail to hold the men, Robb warned.

Another chaplain, A. E. Lavell, also admitted that he did not realize until he had returned to Canada that "over here and over there are two different worlds."[87] Lavell did not claim to speak for all returned soldiers, or even chaplains, but in a series of articles in the *Christian Guardian* he suggested that there were some things that he felt certain were widely shared with respect to religion. The men had returned to Canada with a much clearer and more basic understanding of what the essentials of Christianity were. According to Lavell, the experiences soldiers encountered at the battlefront shook any confident dogmatism they might have held. "Reality is stripped . . . the treasured convictions and custom; the pomp, precedents, and traditions; the burdensome clothing which has hid ghastly wrong . . . have been rent into shreds and whirled away by the hurricane of the shells and storm of this most frightful war." Many old doctrines seemed to them "neither vital nor real." As Lavell explained, "They seem hollow and vain, or having nothing whatever to do with the salvation of man and the establishment of the Kingdom of our Lord." He continued,

> The religion of Jesus is not at all well stated in most of the current accepted creeds, theologies, ecclesiastical institutions, and practices. . . . When you live in the presence of immediate danger and death; when you are called to continuous and strenuous action;

---

86. ANB, Box 10, file 256. A. D. Robb to Moore, 25 June 1918.

87. A. E. Lavell, "The Returning Soldier and the Church," Part II "He May Be Right," *Christian Guardian*, 24 April 1918.

and take sacrifice for granted as once you did comfort and ease you learn the difference between religion and its frills and accretions. Your creed becomes very simple. The Apostle's Creed itself has irrelevant matter. "I believe in Jesus" will do for most of us.[88]

By 1918, enough men had returned home permanently that veterans had clearly emerged as an identifiable group in Canadian society.[89] The early commentators on the returned soldier were from the veteran ranks themselves and it took them little time to articulate their experiences and expectations. One anonymous Private, in an open letter in the *Christian Guardian*, criticized the Methodist Church and its chaplains for poor spiritual advice and inadequate counseling with respect to the soldiers' bitter feelings concerning their actions in battle.[90] To indicate how serious the disillusionment was, this correspondent suggested that some probationers did not expect to return to the work of the ministry after they were demobilized. T. A. Wilson raised similar concerns, informing the Army and Navy Board that there prevailed "an idea that many of [the] probationers will not want to return to the ministry."[91]

The Methodist Church actively tried to reintegrate its veterans back into congregational life and regular worship. Overseas in the camps, a "Citizenship Campaign," under the motto "A clean life for a clean country," was initiated by Methodist chaplains to help the soldier re-acquaint himself with civilian life. In a fashion remarkably like a nineteenth-century temperance meeting, the men attending the meetings were asked to sign "pledge cards" indicating that they would dedicate their lives to clean living and abandon battlefront habits such as swearing, drinking, gambling at cards and other games of chance once they returned to Canada.[92] In Canada, trainloads of returning men were met by Methodist chaplains who forwarded letters to local ministers so that the soldiers could quickly become re-established in their local churches. The Methodist chaplains also held information sessions to inform the re-

88. Ibid. See also C. Wellesley Whitaker (102nd battalion), "When the Boys Return," *Christian Guardian*, 6 February 1918.

89. For a full discussion of the First World War veteran in Canadian society, see Morton and Wright, *Winning*.

90. "Tom, Dick or Harry: A Private's S.O.S. to a Chaplain," *Christian Guardian*, 17 July 1918, 8–9.

91. ANB, Box 8, file 229, T. A. Wilson to Moore, 4 October 1918.

92. ANB, Box 7, file 191, Chambers to Moore, November 1918.

turned soldiers of the upcoming referenda to continue Prohibition that were being held in many provinces. These programs seemed to indicate to the men that the Methodist Church was neither changing its ways nor listening to the soldiers' demands for a religious faith unencumbered with complicated theology or demanding moral codes. The old reliance on morality, in particular, remained prominent in Methodist teaching and activities.

The most damning critique of the Methodist Church's wartime activities came from Private C. T. Watterson of the Canadian Army Medical Corps. Watterson attended Wesley College, Winnipeg, between 1913 and 1916 and when his studies were completed he enlisted in the CEF and was attached to the 11th Field Ambulance. He saw action at Ypres, the Somme, Vimy Ridge, Lens, Passchendaele, and Amiens. On 30 December 1918, he wrote to T. A. Moore of the Army and Navy Board advising that the Methodist Church's focus on and criticism of the morality of the soldier was the source of great misunderstanding between the men and the church. He advised that the Methodist Church would have to meet the problem of the "lax morals of the returning soldiers" with more than harkening back to the "Thou shall nots" of the old Methodist Discipline. Indeed, the church had to take some responsibility for the moral condition of the soldier and simply calling for "Prohibition" would be greeted with disdain: "We as a Church advised our youth to join the army. In that organization their spiritual and moral ideals have suffered a great change."[93] Watterson charged, however, that the Church was unable to deal with the moral dilemmas faced by the soldiers. Speaking as a soldier, he explained: "We can never be morally or spiritually the same as we once were. Our experiences have fashioned us so that many platitudes have forever lost their appeal. Old methods must be scrapped." In trying to shake up Methodism's traditional morality, he suggested that the men who were most often venerated at the front were the "rough, hard swearing lads" for they were the ones who "did great things because they had a fearlessness of consequences, an indifference to responsibility, and the gamblers' recklessness." He was suggesting that these men, whose rough character was not associated with piety in Methodist circles, were indeed representative of the new activist spirit of sacrifice that the church had to embrace. "I grieve," Watterson lamented, "at the deplorable attempt our Church . . . has made at outlining a

---

93. ANB, Box 23, file 459. C. T. Watterson to T. A. Moore, 30 December 1918.

message of sufficient vitality and courage to grip the spiritual nature of our troops overseas."

In the same lengthy and thoughtful letter, Watterson was also sharply critical of the Methodist Church's recent history of being "on the side of authority." He had particular disdain for those chaplains whose preaching was for the Union Government and the cause of conscription. Many editorials in the *Christian Guardian*, he pointed out, were "political propaganda." He also criticized Chown's report after his overseas visit, for he thought that Chown had not fully grasped moral conditions among the soldiers because he never got sufficiently close to them. Instead he was surrounded by military and church officials who "never mix[ed] with the men in their unrestrained moments of actual army life."[94] He concluded, in a fashion similar to many other chaplains and Methodist soldiers, that the majority of men in the ranks would "openly state that they have done with the church."[95]

CONCLUSION

In the aftermath of the war, in his typically colorful and perhaps overly dramatic way, Chown proclaimed that in "many minds the war shook with the violence of a moral and intellectual earthquake the foundations of Christian faith. It shattered many structures of belief which [sic] devout people found refuge from the storms of life . . . In deep perplexity, many silently drifted into a sheer atheism which denied the very existence of the Almighty."[96] Perhaps, but W. B. Creighton had identified a number of problems with religious faith and the church prior to the war and, in some respects, they were only persisting. Maybe what Chown discerned was not so much a sharp break from the past but rather a continuation of the drift away from the church that many Methodist clergy had long been worried about, especially among young men. No doubt the reasons for this drift were now also rooted in wartime disillusionment. However, the war did not strike a shattering blow to the Methodist Church from which it never recovered; there was no precipitous decline in attendance at worship, weekly financial offerings, mis-

---

94. Ibid.

95. Ibid. See also, Lieut. Frank Crighton, "The Returning Soldier," *Christian Guardian*, 12 March 1919.

96. UCA, S. D. Chown Papers, file 1276, "The Need of Advancing Religion in a Progressive World," n.d.

sion activity, or participation in the rites of passage. The prewar initiative of church union was picked up after the war, but with greater urgency and a new rationale based on wartime experiences at the front.[97] Also, as Robert Wright so capably demonstrates, there was not so much a crisis in Christian missions within the Methodist Church after the war, but rather a re-consideration.[98]

Perhaps the key word in Chown's sermon on postwar religious conditions was "drift." In particular, there was drift away from the church by de-mobilized men. Despite the vigorous efforts of the Methodist Church to link the returning men to their churches at home and to engage them in the upcoming temperance referendums, it was clear that many veterans were not seeking to re-establish contact with the local church of their youth.[99] The most stunning indication of this was the high number of probationers and ministers who had served in the CEF who simply allowed their contact with the church to slip away. They did not make any dramatic declarations of their opposition or rejection of the Methodist Church. Instead, they simply did not seek a new pastorate or decided against resuming their studies at theological college.[100] Recruiting young men for the ministry proved to be one of the more difficult challenges facing the Methodist Church after the war.[101] As we have seen, some of this disillusionment rested in the difficulties involved in maintaining faith in a loving and caring God. In the terrible toll of the war, both soldiers at the front and people at home sought some consolation through evidence of a God who intervened to ease pain and suffering; however, as the war dragged on and on they struggled to discover such a God. As we have seen, however, from what many of the chaplains wrote and the returned soldiers indicated to the church, the drift away from the church was more evidently a revolt against the authority of the Methodist Church, whether in the form of regular attendance at

---

97. On the prewar roots of church union see Semple, *The Lord's Dominion*, 417–32; Vipond, "National Consciousness."

98. See in particular Methodist E. W. Wallace's comments quoted in Wright, *World Mission*, 166–68.

99. For example, see "Reports to the Army and Navy Board from H. W. Burnett throughout the First Six Months of 1919" in ANB, Box 4, file 95.

100. Marshall, "Methodism Embattled," 59.

101. Marshall, *Secularizing*, 184–85. The columns of the *Christian Guardian* were full of correspondence from Methodist clergy and probationers who had served in the CEF, outlining the reasons for their difficulties with the church.

church for Sunday worship or to the moral standards of the Methodist Discipline.[102] The war changed things for the Methodist Church but the drift away from the church was not a deep rejection of the Christian faith itself. As Private George Turpin, who was a probationer in British Columbia Conference and did not abandon his studies, suggested after the war, "The religion of Jesus will not be confined within the walls of a church, nor the pages of a family Bible, but it will be alive in the hearts of men"—men who would carry out their commitment to Christianity as they did during the war by their devotion to others and willingness to make sacrifices for the hungry, needy, lonely, and abandoned in society.[103]

---

102. See also Brown, *Religion and Society*, 112, and Ebel, "Great War," both of whom argue that a major source of the soldiers' rebellion against church authority was its strict moralism.

103. George Turpin, "After the War," *Christian Guardian*, 29 August 1917.

BIBLIOGRAPHY

Primary Sources

NEWSPAPER
Christian Guardian

ARCHIVES
UCA: United Church Archives
ANB: Army and Navy Board Papers (part of UCA)
NCA: National Archives of Canada

Secondary Sources

Airhart, Phyllis. *Serving the Present Age: Revivalism, Progressivism, and the Methodist Tradition in Canada.* Montreal and Kingston: McGill-Queen's University Press, 1992.

Berger, Carl. *The Sense of Power: Studies in the Ideas of Canadian Imperialism, 1867–1914.* Toronto: University of Toronto Press, 1970.

Bliss, Michael. *A Canadian Millionaire: The Life and Business Times of Sir Joseph Flavelle, Bart. 1858–1939.* Toronto: University of Toronto Press, 1978.

———. "The Methodist Church and World War I." *Canadian Historical Review* 49 (1968) 213–33.

Brown, Callum. *Religion and Society in Twentieth-Century Britain.* London: Pearson Longman, 2006.

Brown, Robert Craig. *Robert Laird Borden: A Biography.* Vol. 2, *1914–37.* Toronto: Macmillan, 1980.

Buckner, Philip, and John C. Reid, eds. *Remembering 1759: The Conquest of Canada in Historical Memory.* Toronto: University of Toronto Press, 2012.

Cassel, Jay. *The Secret Plague: Venereal Disease in Canada, 1838–1939.* Toronto: University of Toronto Press, 1987.

Cook, Tim. "'More a Medicine than a Beverage': 'Demon Rum' and the Canadian Trench Soldier of the First World War." *Canadian Military History* 9 (2000) 6–22.

———. "Wet Canteens and Worrying Mothers: Alcohol, Soldiers, and Temperance Groups in the Great War." *Histoire Sociale/Social History* 35 (2002) 311–30.

Coutu, Joan, and John McAleer. "The Immortal Wolfe? Monuments, Memory, and the Battle of Quebec." In *Remembering 1759: The Conquest of Canada in Historical Memory*, edited by Phillip Buckner and John C. Reid, 29–57. Toronto: University of Toronto Press, 2012.

Crerar, Duff. *Padres in No Man's Land: Canadian Chaplains and the Great War.* Montreal and Kingston, McGill-Queen's University Press, 1995.

Ebel, Jonathan. "The Great War, Religious Authority, and the American Fighting Man." *Church History* 78 (2009) 99–133.

Eksteins, Mosdris. *Rites of Spring: The Great War and the Birth of the Modern Age.* New York: Doubleday, 1989.

English, John. *Shadow of Heaven: 1897–1948.* Vol. 1 of *The Life of Lester Pearson.* Toronto: Lester & Orpen Dennys, 1989.

Fussell, Paul. *The Great War and Modern Memory*. New York: Oxford University Press, 1975.
Leed, Eric J. *No Man's Land: Combat and Identity in World War I*. New York: Cambridge University Press, 1979.
Lindsay, Peter, and David Howell. "Social Gospel and the Young Boy Problem, 1895–1925." *Canadian Journal of the History of Sport* 17 (1986) 75–87.
Mackay, Ian, and Jamie Swift. *Warrior Nation: Rebranding Canada in the Age of Anxiety*. Toronto: Between the Lines, 2012.
Mackenzie, John. "Heroic Myths of the Empire." In *Popular Imperialism and the Military, 1850–1950*, edited by John Mackenzie, 10–38. Manchester: Manchester University Press, 1992.
Marshall, David B. "'Methodism Embattled': A Reconsideration of the Methodist Church and World War I." *Canadian Historical Review* 46 (1985) 48–64.
———. *Secularizing the Faith: Canadian Protestant Clergy and the Crisis of Belief, 1850–1940*. Toronto: University of Toronto Press, 1992.
McNaught, Kenneth. *A Prophet in Politics: A Biography of J. S. Woodsworth*. Toronto: University of Toronto Press, 1959.
Morton, Desmond, and Glenn Wright. *Winning the Second Battle: Canadian Veterans and the Return to Civilian Life, 1915–1930*. Toronto: University of Toronto Press, 1987.
Moss, Mark. *Manliness and Militarism: Educating Young Boys in Ontario for War*. Toronto: Oxford University Press, 2001.
Mott, Morris. "British Protestant Pioneers and the Establishment of Manly Sports in Manitoba, 1870–86." *Journal of Sport History* 7 (1980) 25–36.
Prang, Margaret. *N. W. Rowell: Ontario Nationalist*. Toronto: University of Toronto Press, 1975.
Putney, Clifford. *Muscular Christianity: Manhood and Sports in Protestant America, 1880–1920*. Cambridge, MA: Harvard University Press, 2001.
Robbins, Keith. *England, Ireland, Scotland, Wales: The Christian Church, 1900–2000*. Oxford: Oxford University Press, 2008.
Schweitzer, Richard. *The Cross and the Trenches: Religious Faith and Doubt among British and American Great War Soldiers*. London: Praeger, 2003.
Semple, Neil. *The Lord's Dominion: The History of Canadian Methodism*. Montreal and Kingston: McGill-Queen's University Press, 1996.
Snape, Michael. *God and the British Soldier: Religion and the British Army in the First and Second World War*. New York: Routledge, 2005.
Socknat, Thomas. *Witness against War: Pacifism in Canada, 1900–1945*. Toronto: University of Toronto Press, 1987.
Vance, Jonathan. *Death So Noble: Memory, Meaning, and the First World War*. Vancouver: University of British Columbia Press, 1997.
Van Die, Marguerite. *An Evangelical Mind: Nathanael Burwash and the Methodist Tradition in Canada, 1839–1918*. Montreal and Kingston: McGill-Queen's University Press, 1989.
Vipond, Mary. "Canadian National Consciousness and the Formation of the United Church of Canada." In *Prophets, Priests and Prodigals: Readings in Canadian Religious History, 1608 to Present*, edited by Mark McGowan and David Marshall, 167–87. Toronto: McGraw-Hill Ryerson, 1992.

Watson, Alexander, and Patrick Porter. "Bereaved and Aggrieved: Combat Motivation and the Ideology of Sacrifice in the First World War." *Historical Research* 83 (2010) 146–64.

Wood, James. *Militia Myths: Ideas of the Canadian Citizen Soldier, 1896–1921*. Vancouver: University of British Columbia Press, 2010.

Wright, Robert. *A World Mission: Canadian Protestantism and the Quest for a New International Order*. Montreal and Kingston: McGill-Queen's University Press, 1991.

5

For Empire and God

Canadian Presbyterians and the Great War

Stuart Macdonald

ON THE LAST DAY of its annual General Assembly, 10 June 1914, the Presbyterian Church in Canada entertained two pieces of correspondence dealing with international peace. A great deal had happened over the previous ten days, including the reception of the report of the church union committee and a minority report on union. Earlier in the day the Assembly had sent a loyal address to the King assuring him "of our loyal devotion to Your Majesty's person and throne" and offering prayers "that by the mercy of God, the blessings of peace and prosperity may be maintained, and Your Majesty reign long over a happy and united people" throughout the Empire.[1] The Assembly showed considerable enthusiasm for a request from the General Assembly of the Presbyterian Church in New Zealand that they work together "in the interests of international peace." A motion was put forward strongly agreeing with their New Zealand co-religionists, requesting that "Peace Sunday be observed by our congregations in February, 1915" and suggesting presbyteries bring ideas to next year's Assembly that would help the Church establish "a permanent line of action in the direction of securing World Peace."[2] The motion carried and the Assembly turned to the next items

---

1. *A&P 1914*, 59.
2. Ibid., 91.

of business before adjourning with the traditional declaration: "In the name of the Lord Jesus Christ, only King and Head of the Church."[3]

The best-laid plans of Canadian Presbyterians were overtaken by events. By the time General Assembly met the next June, Canada was in its eleventh month of war and resolutions on international peace were no longer a major consideration. Presbyterians then and since have struggled to comprehend the experience. The understanding of the Christian churches in the Great War, including the Presbyterian Church in Canada, and of the impact that the Great War has had on the denominations has deepened over the last thirty years.[4] Studies of the South African War and the role that Canadian churches played in that conflict have challenged earlier understandings that saw developments and rhetoric used in the 1914–1918 conflict as original, when in reality they often had already been used during the war in South Africa.[5] Researchers have also benefited from regional studies, intense examinations of particular sources, and projects that have included discussions of the Great War. Given the appalling casualties of the Great War, historians have interpreted the war as creating fundamental change, either theologically or in terms of support for the church (including worship attendance) within broader society. Scholars have also understood the Great War in relation to the other wars that have occurred since the war to end all wars. Historian Michael Snape has noted that, in the themes and historiography that have developed related to the Christian churches' response to the Great War, much "harsh and self-righteous criticism" has been leveled at the "churches' wartime attitudes and activities."[6] To quote him directly: "the historiography of Christianity during the war years has been heavily focused on the churches and their leadership and has been strongly influenced by the pacifism of the inter-war and Cold War eras."[7] Snape goes on to recognize that while there is "plenty of scope for moralizing and recrimination" these themes have confused the understanding of these years: "what they have obscured is the fundamental fact that the churches interpreted the war and their role within

---

3. Ibid., 94.

4. For a discussion of the historiography of the Canadian Presbyterian Church in the Great War, see Macdonald, "Myth."

5. Heath, *Silver Lining*, 50, 126, 141; Miller, "Framing."

6. Snape, "Great War," 131–32.

7. Ibid., 131.

it in the light of their nineteenth-century experiences and outlook, not in the more chastened spirit of the later decades of the twentieth."[8] As difficult as this may be, historians do need to try to understand how Canadian Presbyterians interpreted the Great War within the light of their own values and circumstances. The Presbyterian tradition had no tradition of pacifism prior to the Great War, nor did it develop one during that conflict.[9] At the same time, the tradition affirmed an independence from the state, indeed the belief that God was always above the monarch and that the head of the church was ultimately Christ.

That tradition was proclaimed architecturally on the eve of the war. In September 1914, as war raged in Europe, theological students and professors at Toronto's Knox College began their classes in an unfinished building. Some time in those early months, a flag was carved into the fireplace in the Boardroom. The flag is a Covenanter flag, containing the words: "For Religion, Covenants, Crovn end Kingdoms." The choice of that flag, in a building with few internal carvings, suggests that one of the features of Canadian Presbyterianism on the eve of the Great War was an identification with the covenanting tradition. This identification may have been more romantic than real, but Canadian Presbyterians saw themselves as part of a tradition that had fought for freedom, religious as well as personal, against the monarchy. The College also had a copy of the National Covenant, signed in 1638, which was donated to the College by one of its graduates, C. W. Gordon (the novelist known as Ralph Connor). There was thus a variety of symbols that reminded Canadian Presbyterians of a time when they defied the government based upon religious principles. The covenanting tradition was one of the myths that shaped their understanding of their own history.[10] This was

8. Ibid., 132.

9. Klempa, "Puritan Thought," 86; McKim, "Calvin's Theology," 64. Thomas Socknat has given a very clear definition of what he meant by pacifism: "Since its initial appearance shortly before the Great War, 'pacifism' has often referred both to the belief that war is absolutely and always wrong, and the belief that war, although sometimes necessary, is always inhumane and irrational and should be prevented" (Socknat, *Witness*, 7). As he notes, the first understanding was limited to smaller traditions—"sectarians"—such as Quakers, those in the historic peace churches, and groups such as the Jehovah's Witnesses. But, is the second position, one that Socknat identifies with "liberal-progressive pacifists," a helpful category? It would seem that this "liberal-progressive" position was simply one articulation of just war principles. War was to be avoided whenever possible, but was still permissible for Christians.

10. Cowan, "Covenanting Tradition."

one of the distinctive features that would have differentiated Canadian Presbyterians from many of their Protestant colleagues. The question remains: how did this influence the Canadian Presbyterian response to the events that unfolded during the war?

Canadian Presbyterians showed strong support for the Empire throughout the war. This was reflected during the annual national gathering of Presbyterians, the General Assembly. Support for the war was evident in 1915 when the Assembly passed a resolution that, after calling for national confession and humility, then declared:

> We consider that the provocation of this conflict has been a crime against humanity and that the force which is arrayed against us, in ruthless and savage warfare, threatens the progress of Christianity and the very existence of civilization. We appreciate the noble response already made by our Canadian people, in common with the rest of the Empire and with our Allies, to contend against this aggression upon the sacred rights of the nations. We gratefully recognize the heroism and self-sacrifice of our soldiers who have maintained in battle the best traditions of our race.[11]

The resolution continued by appealing to members of the Church and all Canadians to be willing to sacrifice in order to achieve victory, called on God's protection for all who were in danger "on our behalf," and prayed that victory might be swift, "that He who makes the wrath of men to praise Him may overrule this most destructive conflict for the advancement of His Kingdom," and that peace might be restored.[12] Mounting casualties and the length of the war did not alter this conviction.[13] The Great War was a just war; Presbyterians did not waver in this conviction.

As a major force within society, Canadian Presbyterianism showed support for the war in various ways. Yearly, the Assembly assured the King of the loyalty of his Presbyterian subjects, and their willingness to stand with him in the midst of this conflict. In 1915, the Assembly

---

11. *A&P 1915*, 30.

12. Ibid., 30.

13. The only possible challenge to this unwavering support was an overture that appeared at the 1915 Assembly. The overture did not condemn Christian participation in war but used more general condemnations of war itself and called for the "prevention of war," not an end to participation in this war. This overture was not supported by the presbytery of Victoria, but merely passed on "simpliciter" or without comment. The Assembly took no action on this motion. See *A&P 1915*, 378–79.

pledged its special allegiance during the crisis: "Humbling ourselves before Almighty God, Who has permitted the scourge of desolating war to come upon us, we also declare before Him our absolute conviction of the righteousness of the cause for which Your Majesty's forces and their allies are so valiantly and self-sacrificingly contending."[14] At moments of military difficulty, the Assembly voiced its concerns and strong support for the continuation of the war until victory was achieved. The 1916 Assembly received a telegram from a member of the Church asking them, in light of the death of Earl Kitchener and the serious casualties from the Battle of Jutland, to call the Assembly to a special time of intercessory prayer. The request was granted and a statement was issued to the press:

> In humble confidence in the grace and power of Almighty God, to whom the issues of all events belong, the Assembly hereby calls upon the whole Church, more and more to abound in earnest daily intercession that, as a people, we may abide strong and steadfast in the great struggle for righteousness and human liberty in which, in common with the whole Empire and our faithful Allies, we are now engaged; that our trust in God may never fail, and that, through His favour upon us, our cause may triumph and abiding peace be speedily established.[15]

This same Assembly passed a patriotic resolution that supported the registration of individuals for military service and suggested that the best way to aid in this "sacred cause of freedom and righteousness" was by working with others to make sure that all of the necessary "men, materials, and money" were provided for the war effort. Ministers and members were instructed to "aid to their utmost in securing recruits for the Canadian Expeditionary Forces."[16] While meeting in Montreal the next year (1917) the Assembly voiced its support for "selective conscription" for military service and "universal conscription" of resources in Canada in order to win the war. In its support for mobilizing these resources, the Assembly's resolution voiced even stronger convictions as to the nature of this war, as it expressed "its approval of every legitimate effort to rouse the laggards among the youth of Canada to a conscious-

---

14. Ibid., 56.
15. A&P 1916, 30, 31.
16. Ibid., 63.

ness of duty and to enrol those who are available as soldiers in a great crusade for the world's freedom."[17]

One of the major ways in which the denomination supported the war effort was through the provision of chaplains.[18] Presbyterians supplied 98 chaplains for overseas service (22 percent of the overseas contingent) and 116 in total.[19] The national Church also voiced its support for chaplains, as well as dealing with some of the challenges posed by having ministers of congregations serving overseas. In 1915, the Assembly sent greetings to ministers serving as chaplains noting "the spirit of loyalty and self-sacrifice," hoping for their safe return, and anticipating that they would do "their duties with Christian courage and tenderness."[20] In 1916, the General Assembly not only expressed their greetings to the chaplains, but created a Military Service Board to coordinate the work of chaplaincy, both within the Church and with other agencies.[21] Individual chaplains addressed the Assembly and telegrams were received from chaplains.[22] At the end of the war, the General Assembly set aside an evening to hear reports from various returned chaplains.[23]

Support for the grieving, suggestions on prayer,[24] and calls for national days of prayer were also features of the denomination's response to the war. The main support for those whose sons, husbands, or fathers had died in the war would have been provided by individual congregations and their ministers. At the same time, the national Church also expressed its sympathy. The concluding section of the Patriotic Resolution passed in 1916 noted that "the Assembly expresses its sympathy with those of our Church who have lost dear ones, and commend the depen-

---

17. *A&P 1917*, 37.

18. For chaplains in the Great War, see Crerar, *Padres*. For a study of Canadian Presbyterian chaplains, see Anger, "Presbyterian Chaplaincy."

19. Anger, "Presbyterian Chaplaincy," 17. The total includes those serving in Canada.

20. *A&P 1915*, 59.

21. *A&P 1916*, 100.

22. One example would be Principal Oliver, then a Captain, who addressed Assembly in 1916 in the midst of a discussion on support for the war. See *A&P 1916*, 63; *A&P 1917*, 44; *A&P 1918*, 71.

23. *A&P 1919*, 45.

24. A small pamphlet "Prayer: A Call from God for This Hour," was published in 1918 by the National Service Commission of the Presbyterian Church in Canada. See PCA, National Service Commission Fonds, 1994–1022.

dents of our soldiers to the care and generosity of the members and adherents of the Church."[25] Calls for national days of prayer were heard at various times during the war. In 1916, the Assembly supported a request from the Anglican Archbishop of Toronto for a day of "national supplication and humiliation."[26] Again in 1918, the Assembly supported a call from the Secretary of State for a national day of prayer, only adding that "the recognition of the duty for praying for enemies be kept before the mind of the Church."[27] At the same time, the choice of day did raise some concerns. Presbyterians were strict sabbatarians and it was expected that, given that all Christians should be in worship on Sunday, this day of national prayer should be a day other than Sunday. Assembly supported an overture received in 1919 asking that this be the case in the future.[28]

The war had an impact on the Church. The most obvious—and serious—was in terms of the numbers of casualties. Other effects of the war were more institutional, and the Church was able, through its existing structures or through the creation of new bodies such as the Military Service Board, to deal with the challenges. Those challenges included the reality of providing pastoral care in situations where the minister was serving overseas and of dealing with the issues related to theology students serving abroad. Other issues were less easily resolved. The denominational Colleges faced challenges of declining enrolment, financial stress, buildings appropriated by the military, and significant casualties among their students.[29] For Hungarian Presbyterians on the prairies, the war raised serious questions about their loyalty.[30] Issues in the life of the denomination continued, despite the conflict, and needed to be dealt with. In 1916, the Assembly suspended negotiations relating to church union for the duration of the war.[31] The national crisis was one that called for working together and the debate on moving into the United

25. *A&P 1916*, 63.

26. Ibid., 45.

27. *A&P 1918*, 96–97.

28. *A&P 1919*, 30, 55. Among the claims of the overture was that the government establishing a special day of prayer on a Sunday was "an infringement of the rights and privileges of the Church." See *A&P 1919*, Appendices, 286.

29. *A&P, 1918*. College Reports in the Appendices, 148–85.

30. Bush, *Western Challenge*, 135.

31. See Moir, *Enduring Witness*, 211; *A&P 1916*, 45, 57; *A&P 1917*, 53.

Church only worked against unity. In 1918, the challenge of rail travel and the increased costs led to the calling of an Emergency Committee, which seriously considered not having the General Assembly meet that year.[32]

As the war dragged on and casualties mounted, Canadian Presbyterians tried to find a meaning in this war. A Commission was established by the General Assembly in 1917 to look at the issues that had arisen as a result of the war. The resultant pamphlet, "The War and the Christian Church," nowhere challenged the idea that the Great War was a just war, nor did it call for a radical change of direction in terms of theology or ethics. The pamphlet began by talking about the war as "an unparalleled opportunity," as a time when the Church could reach out and bring comfort and meaning to individuals. Despite some finger-pointing at weakness in the Canadian Church in terms of faith, "moral feebleness," inadequate preaching, and ineffective ministry, the cause of the war was ultimately seen to be sin: "we look upon the war, with its manifold losses, and indescribable sorrows, as the consequence, the exposure and the judgment of human sin."[33] While there was certainly enough sin to go around, the sin of Germany was specifically noted: "The *sin of Germany* is plain—'For a nation to repudiate national morality, as Germany has done in word and deed, is to take up arms against the Kingdom of God; it is to organize civilization in the service of the Kingdom of Evil; it is to sin the sin against mankind, which God has given mankind the office to arrest and judge, if there be international duty at all.'"[34] It was up to Germany's fellow humans "to arrest and judge" the culprit. The next section, outlining the general sins of modern civilization, as incriminating as it may be for Canadian Presbyterians, did not make them as guilty as those already named. It may be true that they had "sinned as a people" but that guilt was of a different, more generic, kind. While they lived "under the system which the war [was] judging" and all of them had "profited by it" and must therefore repent, the special note of Germany's faults still bears mention: "We confess our faith in Christ, the Historic Jesus, the Christ of Calvary, the living and exalted Lord, as the Saviour, even of such a world as this, the Redeemer of men who have so fearfully lost their way, the Hope of the German

---

32. *A&P 1918*, 26, Appendices, 543–44.
33. Kilpatrick, *War*, 3, 4, 5.
34. Ibid., 6, quoting P. T. Forsyth. Emphasis in the original.

race, which has sinned so grievously and has been so awfully afflicted."[35] In case the reader had not quite got the message that while all sinners are guilty some are more guilty than others, a later reference noted that God, would "not allow Satan, or Kaiser, to overthrow His Kingdom."[36] This definition of the war as a fight for the Kingdom against an evil opponent, personified not only in the Kaiser but in the German people, is noteworthy. This report indicated no major shift of direction for the Canadian Presbyterian Church. If anything, the war, with all of the heroism, courage, and self-sacrifice of the soldiers, had provided an example of what everyone must do. What the post-war world needed was what the pre-war world needed, only in the future it needed to be done more effectively. The report called for "Consecrated Self-sacrificing Service," for more effective evangelism, better preaching, and religious revival.[37] The Great War did not alter but merely affirmed the goals and direction in which the Church had already been heading.

Equally important as official doctrinal statements and reports in shaping Canadian Presbyterian attitudes and understandings were the news, opinions, and reports printed in the various denominational papers. The Presbyterian Church in Canada had four major publications during the years of the Great War.[38] The denominational publications displayed attitudes towards the war similar to those expressed by the General Assembly. In an editorial in the *Presbyterian Record* from October 1914 entitled "Fight and Pray," Ephraim Scott made his position clear:

> War is never wrong when it is war against wrong. It is not the type of weapon or of warfare that makes it right or wrong. A war of selfish spite or vengeance or for aggression or gain is always wrong; but a war in defence of weakness against strength, a war for truth and plighted pledge, for freedom against oppression, is God's war wherever waged, and with whatever weapons, whether tongue or pen or sword.[39]

---

35. Ibid., 7.
36. Ibid., 10.
37. Ibid., 12–13.
38. These publications have been major sources used by historians. For instance, see Christie, "Public Affairs"; Fowler, "Keeping the Faith"; Fowler, "Death."
39. *Presbyterian Record*, October 1914, 433.

In answer to those who wondered about "the horror and awfulness and sin of war," Scott proclaimed, "War is not itself a sin. There are times when it is a sin not to war."[40] Similar sentiments were expressed the next month in an editorial in the *Presbyterian Witness*, which called the conflict a holy war, and suggested the forces of German militarism were "the very embodiment of antichrist."[41] Presbyterian denominational publications supported recruitment, conscription, and all efforts to win the war.[42] The publications would also attack any efforts or attitudes they saw as potential contributors to the loss of the war. The *Record* spoke out against conscientious objectors and pacifists in a 1918 editorial, arguing that those who did not stand up and fight against evil were as guilty as those who were doing the evil: "In 'pacifism' we become sharers with Germany in her guilt. Such pacifism is a crime against humanity and against God."[43] Attacks were made on the American President Woodrow Wilson's call for a negotiated peace.[44] Indeed, the various Presbyterian publications all argued against any efforts at negotiation in the latter years of the war,[45] despite the enormous casualties that had already resulted. This was a just struggle that needed to be continued, and war weariness or negotiations that would merely put an end to the carnage were not acceptable options. The conviction that it was a just war, and the view that it was a "struggle between the forces of truth and right on one side, and the powers of falsehood, tyranny and ambition on the other,"[46] was consistent throughout the Great War.

One of the most important ways in which Canadian Presbyterians would have understood the war would be through the preaching that occurred Sunday by Sunday. While it would be helpful to know what was said week by week in every pulpit across Canada, the question of the survival of notes and texts from sermons as well as the scope of such a project make it unrealistic. The manuscript sermons of the Rev. Dr. Thomas Eakin, minister of St. Andrews Presbyterian Church, King St.,

40. Ibid., 435.
41. *Presbyterian Witness*, 14 November 1914, 4. Quoted in Christie, "Public Affairs," 125–26.
42. Christie, "Public Affairs," 129–34.
43. *Presbyterian Record*, June 1918, 161. Quoted in Christie, "Public Affairs," 134.
44. Christie, "Public Affairs," 136.
45. Fowler, "Keeping the Faith," 81–84.
46. *Presbyterian Witness*, March 1918, 4; Fowler, "Keeping the Faith," 81.

Toronto, provide a glimpse into the preaching from one Presbyterian pulpit during the Great War.[47] In his sermons were many of the themes seen at the national level, including a strong support for the war, an understanding of the war as a just war, and the use of the pulpit in encouraging recruitment. The war was also described as a crusade.

From the onset of conflict, Eakin preached that the war was a just war. He blamed the war on the Kaiser, whom he described as a man who "tears up treaties, makes war on a peaceful neighbour, his legions shooting citizens of another country who have done him no wrong, making a desolation of a fair and fruitful country to gratify an insane ambition to be another Napoleon."[48] Eakin rejected pacifism before the war and again in a 1916 sermon the week before Christmas: "But would any sane person accept literally the doctrine of non-resistance to a calculating and ruthless foe, to the most dastardly, inhuman and villainous barbarism that any age ancient or modern has witnessed?"[49] The events of the early days when the German army invaded the neutral country of Belgium were referred to not only in the early months of the war but also throughout his sermons. Language referring to the enemy as "barbarians" was not uncommon, and the war was referred to as a war for civilization against "all the forces of savagery."[50]

Eakin not only defined the war as a just war; he also chose images and phrases that pushed this understanding until the war was portrayed as a crusade. Eakin preached a series of sermons in February 1917 on the beatitudes. When he came to the text "Blessed are the peacemakers" he was clear in affirming his understanding that "Our soldiers are among the peacemakers today,"[51] and later that month he elaborated on this idea: "hence we say to those who contend with all the engines of warfare against the most hellish spirit of all time—Blessed are ye armed, booted, equipped for slaughter, we say it because we must, blessed are ye peacemakers."[52] In a sermon in May 1917 with members of the Princess Patricia Light Infantry present, Eakin described the war as a crusade

---

47. Ninety-three sermons can be identified as having been written during the Great War. See Macdonald, "Eakin."

48. PCA-KC, Eakin Sermon, August 1914. 207/0709.

49. Ibid., Eakin Sermon, 17 December 1916. 207/0687.

50. Ibid., Eakin Sermon, 9 April 1916, 207/0704; March 11, 1917, 207/0824.

51. Ibid., Eakin Sermon, 11 February 1917, 207/0706.

52. Ibid., Eakin Sermon, February 1917, 207/0707.

and those fighting against the Germans as crusaders. He again referred to German brutality, but the language then moved on to define it in apocalyptic terms: "This war which is convulsing the world today is a war against Anti-Christ, savage, bestial, loathsome, foul, unrestrained, in which there is no attempt to be governed by the principles of morality much less Christianity." If this was how Eakin defined the conflict, it is not surprising that he would define those fighting against such a foe, those who had acted out of a sense of "duty, the stern daughter of the voice of God," in equally strong terms: "Therefore they went out as the old crusaders went, Knight errants for God to uphold the cause of country, the cause of humanity, the cause of God."[53] The congregation was given a clear message as to the meaning of the war; how they should respond was also clear. On the day prior to the election in 1917, for which the issue of conscription was central, Eakin preached a powerful sermon twice, first in the morning at St. Andrews and then in the evening at Bloor Street Presbyterian Church, in which he argued passionately that a government must be elected who would prosecute the war until victory was achieved:

> It is along with Britain and all the other free nations for an imperiled civilization, it is to prevent the clock being thrust back 1,000 years. It is to prevent a nation of murderers and pillagers from working their diabolical will in the world. . . . To-morrow we exercise a sacred trusteeship. We either indicate our desire that this war should be prosecuted until this world is a safe and decent place in which to live or we indicate our desire to retire from this sacred crusade.[54]

The correct answer was not hard to guess. Canadians needed to continue to fight on the side of God in this crusade.

Individual Presbyterians, famous as well as ordinary, served in the war. Among the famous was Charles W. Gordon, who under his pen name Ralph Connor was one of the most popular novelists in North America prior to the war. Although 54 years old, Gordon served overseas as a chaplain with the 79th Cameron Highlanders. In his autobiography *Postscript to Adventure* he later reflected on the cause and meaning of the war. While expressions of universal human evil are present in his reflections, the dominant theme was of the British Empire "fighting for

53. Ibid., Eakin Sermon, 8 May 1917, 207/0713.
54. Ibid., Eakin Sermon, 16 December 1917, 207/0734.

world justice and world freedom"[55] against German militarism. While generally sympathetic to the German people, noting of the enemy soldiers that "the fellows responsible for this hell are not the fellows getting it," he went on to place the ultimate responsibility squarely on one side: "And that was the terrible pity of it. We all as a people must share our responsibility for our national attitudes. We have the governments we deserve; therefore, peoples must suffer for the sins of the governments they tolerate."[56] During his speaking tour in the United States, Gordon preached in many pulpits in order to persuade Americans to enter the war on the side of the British Empire. He later wrote, "And why not? To me the cause of the Allies was then a sacred cause, in complete harmony as I felt with the tenets and principles of the religion I professed. It was the cause of human freedom and justice toward weak and defenseless people against the tyranny of grasping national ambition and military aggression."[57] His opinion did not change significantly after the war.[58] Another Canadian who became famous was Col. John McCrae from Guelph, Ontario. McCrae's poem, "In Flanders Fields," contains images of sacrifice, as well as a call in the last stanza for renewed effort in order to triumph over the enemy.[59] One less famous Presbyterian was Toronto's Lance Corporal Frederick Spratlin, a tile setter and member of Emmanuel Presbyterian Church, who died at the Battle of Amiens. Spratlin's Bible noted some key passages, including Matthew 10 (in which Jesus sends out the disciples), which he annotated with the term "Marching Orders."[60] Another ordinary Presbyterian, D. F. MacKenzie, wrote back to his colleagues at Knox College, thanking them for sending a gift parcel and speaking of their common task: "What we are fighting here is merely a local phase of the world wide struggle against evil and injustice which you are training to enter. While we are trying to let daylight into the powers of darkness over here, you are helping to spread the

---

55. Mack, "Modernity," 305.

56. Gordon, *Postscript*, 253.

57. Ibid., 313.

58. *Postscript* was published twenty years after the war. Gordon notes that his opinions had not changed. See *Postscript*, 313. Barry Mack argues Gordon became more "ambivalent about his role in the war," something evident in his personal correspondence, although not as evident in *Postscript*. See Mack, "Ralph Connor," 63–68.

59. Dietrich, "John McCrae."

60. Fowler, "Frederick Spratlin," 45–46, 48.

Word which gives light."⁶¹ MacKenzie died later in the war. His reflections on why he fought were not untypical.

Historians have generally seen the war as having a major impact on Presbyterians, regardless of the denomination (whether the continuing Presbyterian Church in Canada or the United Church of Canada after 1925) in which they later found themselves.⁶² Yet, a re-examination of the evidence gives one pause. Michael Snape has creatively and appropriately brought to bear recent findings challenging the process of secularization and how this narrative has affected historians' understanding of the churches in the two world wars.⁶³ Historians are therefore left with the questions: what impact did the Great War have on Canadian Presbyterians? Did their theological approach to war change as a result of the experience in Flanders?

At the personal level, the impact on individuals and individual congregations was dramatic and extreme. The casualties of the Great War are still shocking. Even victories such as Vimy Ridge came at a tremendous cost (3,598 dead, 7,004 wounded),⁶⁴ as did the grinding assaults of the last hundred days. It is not surprising, therefore, that congregations invested after the war in memorials to the fallen. As Jonathan Vance has noted, these memorials tell a great deal about how the sacrifice was understood.⁶⁵ Rolls of honor, memorial plaques, memorial windows, and memorial organs were installed in churches at great cost. The inscriptions on these plaques speak of sacrifice for a larger good. The chapel at Knox College has a very simple memorial plaque, listing the sixteen who died during the conflict, with the single phrase "These All Died in Faith" at the bottom. In 1921, Knox Presbyterian Church in Calgary dedicated a memorial window to those killed in the war, in which a resurrected Christ was surrounded by medieval knights with various Canadian soldiers below.⁶⁶ Sacrifice was remembered. There are few indications

---

61. PCA-KC, Letter of D. F. MacKenzie to the Knox College Theological and Literary Society, Jan. 17, 1916, 601/0004.

62. Fraser, *Uplifters*; Bliss, "Methodist Church"; Marshall, "Methodism Embattled"; Macdonald, "Myth."

63. Snape, *British Soldier*, 3–4. The work of Callum Brown and others cited by Snape suggests that the major change in the place of Christianity in society did not take place until the 1960s.

64. Morton and Granatstein, *Marching*, 143.

65. Vance, *Death*.

66. Described in Vance, "Sacrifice," 20.

to suggest that this sacrifice was viewed as anything other than noble; rather, the memorials suggest that indeed a better world might come out of this sacrifice, which exemplified the Christian duty of those who died. A study of Presbyterian memorials from the Great War would be a worthwhile project.

Canadian Presbyterians remained committed theologically to the principle of the just war. In times of peace, some might call for the kind of evangelical outlawing of war that had previously succeeded in achieving the abolition of slavery,[67] but there was no move away from the position that war might be just. This was the understanding of the Presbyterian Church in Canada before, during, and after the Great War, and indeed significant challenges to this idea were not heard until after the Second World War.[68] The world that Canadian Presbyterians envisaged after the Great War was not markedly different from the world they had longed for prior to August 1914. The Church continued to call for the redeeming and saving of individuals, for transforming them with the saving knowledge of Christ, and then empowering them to transform society by abolishing alcohol, social vice (white slavery or prostitution), observing the Christian sabbath, and creating a more equitable economic system. The sacrifice of so many in war only emboldened Presbyterians to believe that God might profit their venture even more, if only they could improve preaching and evangelism. This understanding runs counter to the understanding of the Great War as a watershed, as a moment of fundamental change either in terms of theology or active participation.[69] Given the incredible casualties of the Great War, what better opportunity could there be for massive change? Yet, it is important to avoid generalizing too readily from particular individuals or misconstruing ecclesiastical rhetoric. Sin is always rising. The youth are always leaving. These are phrases designed to spur people to greater effort but are not necessarily descriptions of reality; as such, caution must be exercised when reading such statements.

67. *A&P 1924*, 60, Appendices, 522, 524.

68. No published study exists of the response to the Vietnam War, but the *Acts and Proceedings* demonstrates divided opinions. See *A&P 1966*, 28–29, 39, 81. For just war theory applied to Afghanistan, see Klempa, "Presbyterians and War."

69. Bliss, "Methodist Church"; Marshall, "Methodism Embattled"; Gauvreau, "Religious Certainty"; Moir, *Enduring Witness*, 241; Macdonald, "Eakin." See also the discussion in Macdonald, "Myth."

What remains striking when reading the pronouncements of the General Assembly, or the editorials of the *Presbyterian Record*, or the sermons of Thomas Eakin, or other documents of this period, is how foreign they sound. Today's Christians expect that the Church should have used more moderate rhetoric. Even in 1955 Edward Christie voiced his discomfort, wondering that these statements came from a Christian church.[70] Historians do need to hear these documents in their own time, not with the different values of today, nor with the knowledge that the ripples from the Great War led not only to another world conflagration but continue to echo down to today. Presbyterianism was not a tradition that had ever held to a strict pacifist understanding, but rather, it acted out of just war principles.

Although historians and others should not question the Church in terms of current values, one can ask whether the Church followed its own values. As already noted, one of those values was a tradition that remembered the Covenanters, that celebrated the separation of the church from the state, and that saw the state as in some way under the judgment of the values of the church. The denomination reminded itself of this when it ended each year's General Assembly by stating that the only King and Head was Jesus Christ. Given this, it is fair to question whether or not the Presbyterian Church—in practice if not in theory— abandoned this principle during the Great War. What is striking is how quickly, thoroughly, and completely Presbyterians identified with the British Empire's cause. There was little if any distance between the Empire's requirements and what the Church saw as God's call. The actions of the German nation in invading neutral Belgium, and the brutal acts done in conquering that country, were known to Canadians. Such acts, as well as the later use of poison gas and the sinking of ships full of civilians, such as the Lusitania, might be understood as creating the conditions for a just war. At the same time, did the Church ever wonder if any actions by the Empire might be similarly morally suspect? During the South African War, when the Empire had created concentration camps, criticism from the churches was muted.[71] What we see in each of these conflicts was an identification with the British Empire that was inconsistent with the Church's professed independence from that Empire.

---

70. Christie, "Public Affairs," 130, 140.
71. Heath, *Silver Lining*, 44–45.

Yet we should not conclude from this that Presbyterians were incapable of challenging the Empire or its government. Presbyterians were able to express their discomfort about specific issues when they felt the need. Throughout the Great War, various overtures raised concerns about venereal disease and soldiers being able to access alcohol, as well as the already mentioned concern that national days of prayer not be held on Sunday.[72] Thus, Presbyterians were able to raise issues, but never challenged the core issue of the war itself. Despite their yearly declarations of independence, Canadian Presbyterians made little distinction between their loyalty to King Jesus (to use the Covenanter phrase) and to their loyalty to the King of Great Britain and the Empire.

The move from seeing the conflict as a just war to seeing it as a holy war or crusade is equally striking to anyone today who reads these sources. This was not a political or economic contest, it was not a scramble for colonies or empire, but an apocalyptic struggle between good and evil. Interestingly, similar ideas were held by many in the German Church, who also saw the war as being fought for noble causes.[73] The use of religion in this way is striking and continued into the next conflict. In 1916, Thomas Eakin preached a sermon on the book of Daniel in which he compared the Kaiser to the ancient tyrant, Antiochus Epiphanes. During the Second World War he preached the same basic sermon, replacing "Kaiser" with "Hitler."[74] While the latter may be far more accurate than the former, what is noteworthy is that same sermon was used. The question, "What did the Great War change for Canadian Presbyterians?" remains an open one.

---

72. *A&P 1917*, Appendices, 275 overture 17; 282 overture 26; *A&P 1918*, Appendices, 270, overture on venereal disease. For an excellent overview of the differences between the churches and the reality of trench warfare, see Cook, "Demon Rum." Michael Snape argues that the key reality for many soldiers was not a loss of faith, but did involve a change in understandings of morality. See Snape, *British Soldier*, 194–200.

73. Snape, "Great War," 141.

74. PCA-KC, Eakin Sermon, March 1916; 19 September 1943, 207/0602.

BIBLIOGRAPHY

Primary Sources

ARCHIVES
PCA – Presbyterian Church in Canada Archives
PCA-KC – Presbyterian Church in Canada Archives, Knox College Collection

NEWSPAPERS
Presbyterian Record
Presbyterian Witness

OTHER
Acts and Proceedings of the General Assembly (A&P)
Kilpatrick, T. B. *The War and the Christian Church*. Toronto: Presbyterian Church in Canada, 1917.

Secondary Sources

Anger, Bob. "Presbyterian Chaplaincy during the First World War." *Canadian Society of Presbyterian History Papers* (2002) 15–31.

Bliss, J. M. "The Methodist Church and World War I." *Canadian Historical Review* 49 (1968) 213–33.

Bush, Peter. *Western Challenge: The Presbyterian Church in Canada's Mission on the Prairies and North, 1885–1925*. Winnipeg: Watson & Dwyer, 2000.

Christie, Edward A. "The Presbyterian Church in Canada and Its Official Attitude towards Public Affairs and Social Problems 1875–1925." MA thesis, University of Toronto, 1955.

Cook, Tim. "'More a Medicine than a Beverage': 'Demon Rum' and the Canadian Trench Soldier of the First World War." *Canadian Military History* 9 (2000) 6–22.

Cowan, Edward J. "The Covenanting Tradition in Scottish History." In *Scottish History: The Power of the Past*, edited by Edward J. Cowan and Richard J. Finlay, 121–45. Edinburgh: Edinburgh University Press, 2002.

Crerar, Duff. *Padres in No Man's Land: Canadian Chaplains and the Great War*. Montreal and Kingston: McGill-Queen's University Press, 1995.

Dietrich, Bev. "Colonel John McCrae: From Guelph, Ontario to Flanders Fields." *Canadian Military History* 5 (1996) 37–43.

Fowler, Michelle. "'Death Is Not the Worst Thing': The Presbyterian Press in Canada, 1913–1919." *War and Society* 25 (2006) 23–38.

———. "Faith, Hope and Love: The Wartime Motivations of Lance Corporal Frederick Spratlin, MM and Bar, 3rd Battalion, CEF." *Canadian Military History* 15 (2006) 45–50.

———. "Keeping the Faith: The Presbyterian Press in Peace and War 1913–1919." MA Thesis: Wilfrid Laurier University, 2005.

Fraser, Brian J. *The Social Uplifters: Presbyterian Progressives and the Social Gospel in Canada, 1875–1915*. Waterloo: Wilfrid Laurier University Press, 1988.

Gauvreau, Michael. "War, Culture and the Problem of Religious Certainty: Methodist and Presbyterian Church Colleges, 1914–1930." *Journal of the Canadian Church Historical Society* 29 (1987) 12–31.

Gordon, Charles W. *Postscript to Adventure: The Autobiography of Charles W. Gordon.* New York: Farrar & Rinehart, 1938.

Heath, Gordon L. *A War with a Silver Lining: Canadian Protestant Churches and the South African War, 1899–1902.* Montreal and Kingston: McGill-Queen's University Press, 2009.

Klempa, William J. "Presbyterians and War." *Presbyterian Record* (2002) 18–20.

———. "War and Peace in Puritan Thought." In *Peace, War and God's Justice*, edited by Thomas D. Parker and Brian J. Fraser, 81–103. Toronto: United Church Publishing, 1989.

Macdonald, Stuart. "Myth Meets Reality: Canadian Presbyterians and the Great War." *Canadian Society of Church History Papers* (2012) 103–20.

———. "The War-Time Sermons of the Rev. Thomas Eakin." *Canadian Society of Church History Papers* (1985) 58–78.

Mack, D. Barry. "Modernity without Tears: The Mythic World of Ralph Connor." In *The Burning Bush and a Few Acres of Snow: The Presbyterian Contribution to Canadian Life and Culture*, edited by William J. Klempa, 139–57. Ottawa: Carleton University Press, 1994.

———. "Ralph Connor and the Progressive Vision." MA thesis: Carleton University, 1986.

Marshall, David. "Methodism Embattled: A Reconsideration of the Methodist Church and World War I." *Canadian Historical Review* 66 (1985) 48–64.

McKim, Donald K. "War and Peace in Calvin's Theology." In *Peace, War and God's Justice*, edited by Thomas D. Parker and Brian J. Fraser, 53–69. Toronto: United Church Publishing, 1989.

Miller, Carman. "Framing Canada's Great War: A Case for Including the Boer War." *Journal of Transatlantic Studies* 6 (2008) 3–21.

Moir, John S. *Enduring Witness: A History of the Presbyterian Church in Canada.* 3rd ed. Burlington: Eagle, 2004.

Morton, Desmond, and J. L. Granatstein. *Marching to Armageddon: Canadians and the Great War 1914–1919.* Toronto: Lester & Orpen Dennys, 1989.

Snape, Michael. *God and the British Soldier: Religion and the British Army in the First and Second World Wars.* London: Routledge, 2005.

———. "The Great War." In *World Christianities c.1914–c.2000*, edited by Hugh McLeod, 131–50. Cambridge: Cambridge University Press, 2008.

Socknat, Thomas P. *Witness against War: Pacifism in Canada, 1900–1945.* Toronto: University of Toronto Press, 1987.

Vance, Jonathan F. *Death So Noble: Memory, Meaning and the First World War.* Vancouver: University of British Columbia Press, 1997.

———. "Sacrifice in Stained Glass: Memorial Windows of the Great War." *Canadian Military History* 5 (1996) 16–24.

6

The Anglican Church and the Great War

MELISSA DAVIDSON

THE FIRST WORLD WAR—THE Great War to contemporaries—is largely absent in histories of Canadian Anglicanism from the parish level up to the institutional level. Unless a mortgage was paid off, a new building consecrated, or a new rector arrived, a large number of parish histories are silent on the war years. This silence on the period of the war and its immediate aftermath persists in institutional histories. Philip Carrington, himself a former primate, devotes a single sentence in his *The Anglican Church in Canada* to the actions of the Church during the war, writing: "To use the wording of the old Catechism, both clergy and laity did their duty in whatever state of life it pleased the Lord to call them to."[1] Given the impact of the Great War on all aspects of Canadian life and its consistent presence in secular histories of the twentieth century, the war's absence in Anglican histories is striking. The absence of discussions of the war can, however, be at least partly explained by the consistent focus of most Anglican histories on the institutional church and its development. The Anglican war effort was not centrally directed—although bishops did occasionally organize diocesan days of prayer—and individual parishes largely organized their own efforts in collaboration with external groups, including the Red Cross, the Canadian Patriotic Fund, and various Belgian relief agencies. With many parishioners and parish priests occupied with war service, with other demands on scarce

---

1. Carrington, *Anglican Church*, 252.

funds, and with the flow of support from England essentially stopped, the institutional church was forced to pause its expansion work during the war and largely focus on maintenance. It is this maintenance-only period that appears as a gap in the historiography. This historiographical silence, however, does not mean that the war failed to have an impact on Anglicans as individuals, parishes, or as an institutional church.

In the fall of 1916, when the Canadian government released a report detailing the religious affiliations of recruits in the CEF, Anglicans made up roughly 40 percent of the CEF with 165,145 men in uniform.[2] With a total declared population of just over one million—about 15 percent of the overall Canadian population—Canadian Anglicans were clearly enlisting in numbers disproportionate to their overall population.[3] Given their pre-war population, as much as 12 to 16 percent of all Canadian Anglicans were in uniform by the fall of 1916. It is impossible to judge the enormous impact this must have had on the Church as a whole. On a personal level, regardless of the factors driving this phenomenon, it also meant that the emotional and economic hardships associated with men serving overseas were felt more broadly amongst Anglican families. On a parish or diocesan level, as the Archbishop of Algoma, George Thorneloe, told readers of the *Canadian Churchman* in July 1916,

> In almost every parish and mission our work has more or less languished through the loss of some of our best workers. And there is hardly a centre of Church life which is not to some extent straitened in circumstances in consequence of the unceasing demands upon the country on behalf of Patriotic and Red Cross funds.[4]

The theological colleges and seminaries had been largely emptied, with many of those remaining candidates either discharged soldiers or those who were unable to pass the military medical exams. In the fall of 1916, the Bishops of Calgary, Edmonton, Saskatchewan, Kingston, and Kootenay, the Archbishop of Rupert's Land, and the Missionary Society

---

2. "The Church of England in Canada's Army," *Montreal Churchman*, July 1916, 15. See also Bliss, "Methodist Church," 218. In round figures, there were more than 325,000 men enlisted in the CEF in the fall of 1916.

3. In its Historical Statistics of Canada (Section A: Population and Migration), Statistics Canada gives information from the 1911 census. See the figures on the first page of the Introduction to this volume.

4. George Thorneloe, as quoted in "The Church at Home," *Canadian Churchman*, 8 June 1916, 362.

all also expressed difficulties caused by a lack of workers and/or funds.[5] Although they could not have known it at the time, it must be remembered that at this point there were another two years of war remaining.

Recruiting statistics are one of the few readily available ways to quantify the denominational support of Canadian Anglicans for the First World War, but these statistics reflect neither the full extent of the Canadian participation in the war effort nor the deep support for the war expressed by those remaining on the home front. Monetary support to the Canadian Patriotic Fund, the Red Cross, Victory Loan campaigns, or any of the other local and national associations raising money for war-related causes is difficult to break down according to denomination.[6] It is clear, however, that Canadian Anglicans were offering their time and money to these causes. When Archdeacon H. J. Cody of Toronto's St. Paul's Church organized a fundraising drive for Belgian relief in January 1915, in only a month the congregation was able to send 2,382 bags of flour to the starving Belgians.[7] In the spring of 1915, when it was rumored that Canadian units were under-gunned, Anglican churches were among the organizations that almost immediately began raising money with the aim of providing the necessary machine guns. Across the country and for the duration of the war, Anglican women's groups gathered to roll bandages, knit socks, prepare care packages, sew bed jackets, and perform numberless additional tasks for the support of the overseas troops and the wounded in hospitals. Anecdotal evidence like this only suggests the level of popular support from the population as a whole. How did this support take shape for Canadian Anglicans?

---

5. *Canadian Churchman*, 3 August 1916, 495; "The Church at Home," *Canadian Churchman*, 8 June 1916, 362; "The Church at Home," *Canadian Churchman*, 15 June 1916, 378; "Diocese of Saskatchewan," *Canadian Churchman*, 13 July 1916, 443, 447; Edward J. Bidwell, "Address to Synod," *Canadian Churchman*, 6 July 1916, 427; "Diocese of Kootenay," *Canadian Churchman*, 20 July 1916, 460, 465; "Diocese of Rupert's Land," *Canadian Churchman*, 6 July 1916, 426, 431; "M.S.C.C. Finances," *Canadian Churchman*, 31 August 1916, 551.

6. For a treatment of the monetary side of the war effort, see Morton, *Fight*.

7. H. J. Cody, as quoted in "From Din of War to Day of Prayer," *Toronto Globe*, 4 January 1915, 7. On January 3 itself, $4785.79 was collected or pledged (equivalent to 957 barrels of flour or 2117 bags). An additional $1195.86 was collected or pledged the following Sunday, along with $100 for the Red Cross. The final totals are as given above, plus an additional $367 (115 bags of flour) for school children and a remaining $258.26 for additional supplies. Diary entries, 3–24 January 1915, H. J. Cody's diary, Cody Papers, F980, Series B-1, Box MU4980, Book 1915, Archives of Ontario.

When war broke out in the late summer of 1914, the Canadian government prepared a modest contribution to the Empire's war effort and clerics almost immediately took up the topic of the war to explain why it was necessary for Britain—and therefore its empire—to fight a European war. Treaty obligations to defend Belgian sovereignty, an alliance with France, and fears about German militarism were rhetorically transformed into questions of honor and duty, the need to defend liberty against despotism, and the philosophical divide between British civilization and the German "will to power." Most importantly for Canada's Anglican clergymen and their congregations, the war was a righteous war, one that was not only right to fight but necessary. As John Cragg Farthing, Bishop of Montreal, wrote a few weeks after the war began,

> The Empire risks its all, its very existence; by going into this war, we stand to lose everything: we stood to lose our honor and to break our obligations had we kept out of it. . . . Horrible as war is, to break our pledged word, and to see a weak nation wronged would be more horrible. At such a time, we must remember that Righteousness, not peace, is the ideal of Christ.[8]

With the *Book of Common Prayer*—whose words Farthing was echoing—providing a shared language of prayer and worship throughout the Empire, Canadian Anglicans had a shared vocabulary with which to understand and discuss the war in spite of divisions between Evangelicals and High Churchmen. Overwhelmingly, Anglican clerics made use of this shared vocabulary to declare the Great War a righteous war.

Using righteousness as a justification for an imperial war was not an innovation but had historical precedent in Canada stretching back beyond the Boer War[9] to the Napoleonic Wars of the early nineteenth century.[10] Justifying the war in this way evoked a civilizing national and imperial mission and, by making the Empire a defender of Christian values, clergymen were invoking a relationship that was both political and religious. In this context, patriotism was more than merely waving flags or making speeches, but was rather the building up and maintaining of a nation of ideals. This nation could then act as a force for good in

---

8. John Cragg Farthing, "A Message on the War," *Montreal Churchman*, September 1914, 3.

9. Miller, "Loyalty"; Heath, *Silver Lining*.

10. Wise, "Sermon Literature," 131; Wise, "Peculiar Peoples," 35

the world—in other words, it could perform God's work. This expanded sense of patriotism gave strength to the justifications of the Great War as a righteous war. In turn, the justification of the war as a righteous one would underlie the calls to prayer, patriotic sermons, encouragement, and memorialization offered for the four long years of war that separated the declaration of war in August 1914 from the Armistice in November 1918. Because of the influence that these early justifications had on the way that Canada's Anglican clergymen interpreted the unfolding war, it is important to understand that the war for them was neither a "just war" fought for political reasons nor a "holy war" fought because God had ordained it, but a righteous war fought in defence of Christian values and civilization understood as part of Britain's imperial mission.[11] The meaning with which the Great War had been imbued since its early days, in large part through the efforts of the clergy, played an important role in sustaining the morale and determination of Canadian Anglicans throughout the long conflict.

Although there seems to have been broad agreement among practicing Anglicans about both the necessity and the interpretation of the war, the 1915 General Synod meeting in Toronto revealed that there was disagreement within the Church about forms of patriotic expression and how war prayers should be offered. Special prayers for the safety of the troops, for guidance for the government, and for victory were rapidly authorized by the bishops at the outbreak of war and there are records of intercessory services being organized in many areas in the early months of the war. Although attendance at these services quickly dropped off, clergymen continued to call their parishioners to prayer throughout the war and in many parishes these prayers were part of the ordinary Sunday services. The discussion about prayer at the 1915 General Synod was not about whether prayers should be offered, but what form they should take. The focal point of discussion was the second verse of the National Anthem (God Save the King). Following from the familiar first verse, the second verse made direct reference to the Empire's enemies and it had been left out of the *Book of Common Praise*, the Canadian Anglican hymnal, in a pre-war revision.[12] Some of the delegates in the

11. For an outline of the differences between just war and holy war in historical clerical rhetoric, see Endy, "Just War."

12. The full text of the verse runs:

O Lord our God arise,

Lower House felt that the verse was a "Hymn of Hate" and believed its sentiments were un-Christian; others held that the circumstances justified the singing of the verse and that its sentiments perhaps did not go far enough. The result of the heated discussion was two motions requesting the authorization of the verse. Both were defeated.[13] A few days later, however, when the bishops sitting in the Upper House unanimously authorized the singing of the verse, the delegates in the Lower House responded to the news by enthusiastically singing all three verses of the National Anthem.[14] Although little evidence remains to completely reconstruct the arguments from either side, it would seem that those who objected to the verse did so because they did not feel that God should be asked to intervene against the Empire's enemies.[15] As the Rev. W. J. Boyd of Edmonton stated, the German people were not responsible for the "knavish tricks" of the army: "They had nothing to do with the awful atrocities and why should we ask God to confound them?" Toronto's Canon H. P. Plumptre felt that the war prayers authorized at the beginning of the war should provide the example for Christian patriotism because they were free from vindictiveness.[16] Even after the bishops authorized the use of the verse there were some delegates who

> Scatter his enemies
> And make them fall;
> Confound their politics,
> Frustrate their knavish tricks,
> On Thee our hopes we fix,
> God save us all!

13. At General Synod meetings, the bishops met as the Upper House and a variety of clergy and lay delegates sat as the Lower House. The first motion in the Lower House, a motion that the General Synod authorize the printing of the verse in the *Book of Common Praise* and its use be authorized throughout the Church, was defeated 72 to 89. The amendment to that motion, that the bishops authorize the use of the second verse during the war, was defeated 61 to 100. See *Proceedings of the General Synod*, 7th Session, Church of England in Canada, 1915, 38.

14. The message to the Lower House read, in part: "That in the judgment of the Upper House, 'in the time of war and tumult' the second verse of the National Anthem (beginning 'O Lord, our God, Arise') may be sung in our churches with perfect propriety." Message 10, *Proceedings of the General Synod*, 7th Session, 49. See also "The Seventh Session of the General Synod," *Canadian Churchman*, 23 September 1915, 605.

15. See also Nor'wester, "Sidelights on the General Synod," *Canadian Churchman*, 23 September 1915, 603; "The National Anthem," *Canadian Churchman*, 30 September 1915, 615.

16. W. J. Boyd and H. P. Plumptre, as quoted in "General Synod Spurns Empire's 'Hate' Verse," *Toronto Globe*, 17 September 1915, 7.

remained in their seats while it was sung. Archdeacon J. Paterson Smyth of Montreal's St. George's Church stood for the first verse but resumed his seat when the line "Confound their politics" was reached.[17] For those on the other side, including Archdeacon Cody, whose congregation had been using all three verses since the beginning of the war, there was no reason that the second verse should not be used to pray for victory and for the defeat of the enemy unless going to war had itself been wrong in the sight of God.[18] Calling the verse un-Christian was to misinterpret the true meaning of the words.[19] Others, including Canon Robert Ker of St. Catharines, Ontario, pointed out the similarities between the verse and the Prayer in Time of War and Tumults,[20] a collect from the 1662 *Book of Common Prayer* that had been returned without opposition to the working draft of the Canadian revision.[21] The prayer would have been used weekly in many Anglican churches and, as Archdeacon W. J. Armitage of Halifax explained, it "was too expressive of national need to be relegated to oblivion."[22]

This incident is worth noting despite the fragmentary evidence and its early date because it illustrates two key elements of the Anglican ex-

17. "Temperance Favoured, with Some Dissent," *Toronto Globe*, 20 September 1915, 7.

18. "Anthem's Verse of 'Hate' Defended by Dr. Cody," *Toronto Globe*, 20 September 1915, 6.

19. See H. J. Cody, "The History and Significance of the National Anthem," Speech delivered to the Empire Club of Canada (Toronto), 21 December 1916, for a complete explanation of his view. The full text of the speech is available in pamphlet form at the General Synod Archives or in the Cody Papers, Provincial Archive of Ontario. Also available online at http://speeches.empireclub.org/62030/data?n=1.

20. First used in the 1552 *Book of Common Prayer*, the collect known as "The Prayer in Time of War and Tumults" is appropriate for general use during times of war. It was, however, also one of the prayers specifically authorized by the bishops for intercessory use during the Great War. The text of the prayer from the 1662 *Book of Common Prayer* runs in full: "O Almighty God, King of all kings, and Governor of all things, whose power no creature is able to resist, to whom it belongeth justly to punish sinners, and to be merciful to those who truly repent; Save and deliver us, we humbly beseech thee, from the hands of our enemies; abate their pride, assuage their malice, and confound their devices; that we, being armed with thy defence, may be preserved evermore from all perils, to glorify thee, who art the only giver of all victory; through the merits of thy Son, Jesus Christ our Lord."

21. "Compromise on Creed: No Divorcees' Weddings," *Toronto Globe*, 23 September 1915, 6.

22. Armitage, *Revision*, 228.

perience of the war. First, the imperial ideology that shaped the Anglican war experience was rooted in religious language and understanding. Patriotic expression had a clear place in Anglican churches, perhaps especially during times of war, but the forms that expression took were shaped by the heritage of the *Book of Common Prayer*, even where particular interpretations differed. Second, far from there being a wholesale jingoistic embracing of war rhetoric, there were disagreements within the Church about the forms that support for the war should take. While support for the war within the Anglican Church seems to have been nearly universal, there clearly was variation in attitudes just as there was variation in people's actions. It is often difficult, however, to gauge the extent of these disagreements because of the autonomy granted to individuals on such questions. In this case, although the bishops and many of the delegates in the Lower House felt that it was acceptable to use the second verse, those clergymen who did object to either the sentiment or the wording could simply choose not to make use of the optional verse, an action that generally leaves no record.[23] Disagreements about the form that patriotic expression should take within the Church could, and did, take place among those who were committed to fighting a righteous war but, in many cases, such disagreements are extremely difficult to reconstruct.

As the war progressed, the official Canadian contribution grew and Canadian casualties mounted. The early justifications offered for the Empire's participation in the war served to provide both comfort for the sorrowing and a source of collective determination. For those who mourned and those separated from loved ones serving overseas, it would have been comforting to hear that their individual sorrows and sacrifices were bound up in a righteous cause. In this context, it should not be forgotten that clergymen speaking of the war were not only calling to action but were also attempting to comfort and console. Clergymen were aware of the problems and concerns of their congregations and their sermons would have taken these into account. By choosing to emphasize the righteousness of the cause—the need to defend Christian civiliza-

---

23. Even those who did not disagree with the sentiment of the verse may have substituted verses. A bulletin from a military service at Christ Church Cathedral, Montreal, held on 11 April 1915, leaves out the second verse. An optional third verse to the Dominion of Canada is, however, included. See 11 April 1915 (bulletin inserted), Service Book, Christ Church Cathedral (Montreal), Montreal Diocesan Archive (Anglican).

tion—Anglican clergymen not only addressed a pastoral need, but they also stiffened the resolve of their congregants. Although the end of the war and the return of peace was tempting, the objectives of defending liberty and democracy, defeating German militarism, and providing security for the world had not been achieved. When Germany suggested a compromise peace on 12 December 1916, the offer was summarily rejected by the Entente nations; it was not just the governments that rejected peace negotiations but the public, with grim determination, did so as well.[24] From the point of view of Anglican clergymen, this ongoing overseas struggle for civilization called for two things from those at home—prayer and the need to confront the moral problems facing Canada itself. As Archdeacon Cody wrote shortly before Easter 1916:

> A world is in arms; civilization is being threatened; our Empire and all the ideals for which it stands are in the balance . . . As certainly as Christ arose . . . so from the toil and struggle of time shall goodness, truth, purity, love, come forth victorious by the same power by which Christ rose from the dead. . . . We pray, as perhaps we have never prayed before, that through this awful crucible of war there may come forth a nation and a Church purified and strengthened. . . . This visitation of nations cannot be in vain, unless we deliberately refuse its call to repentance and hope.[25]

The balance between these two calls—the call to prayer and the call to action—varied depending on the time, place, and theological inclinations of the speaker, and it is difficult to judge the extent to which they were taken to heart by all listeners.[26] What is clear, however, is that as the war went on Anglican rhetoric was transformed, and the early justifications of righteousness did not become merely a "crusade" against German militarism or brutality, but a recognition of a responsibility to uphold the Empire's civilizing imperial mission and a desire to render

---

24. Fest, "British War Aims," 289–90, 308; Brunauer, "Peace Proposals 1917," 555–58, 561–63, 565, 567–68; Gregory, *Last Great War*, 149–50; Miller, *Our Glory*, 58–60.

25. H. J. Cody, "The Living One," *Canadian Churchman*, 20 April 1915, 245.

26. One marker of this focus is the formation of the Council for Social Service at the 1915 General Synod, which provided an institutional reaction to Canadian social problems. Both clergymen and the laity were involved with the Council for Social Service, but there were also local efforts outside the Church, including the movement towards Prohibition.

the nation worthy of the victory being purchased by the blood-sacrifice of Canada's soldiers.

By early 1917, the spirit of voluntarism which had driven the war effort for the first two years was beginning to reach its limits. The institution of National Registration in January 1917 was followed by the imposition of conscription that summer. Canadian Anglicans had been among those calling for government intervention before the passage of the Military Service Act in July 1917. These demands for the government to step in and manage manpower were accompanied by an increasing nationalization of the conflict. Although Canadians were still being urged to uphold their responsibility to defend the Empire and its civilizing mission, now they were also fighting for the freedom and future of Canada. John Richardson, Bishop of Fredericton, put the question in frank terms before a February 1917 meeting of his synod:

> Are we fighting for the Motherland? Or are we fighting for ourselves? That is the crucial question, for if we are, indeed, fighting for ourselves, if it is our own hearths and homes that are in danger—nay, more than that, if on the battlefields of stricken Europe, the eternal principles of youth, honour and justice are being defended against the unscrupulous attacks of moral anarchy, if the Allies are enlisted in the sacred service of humanity itself, then, I submit we have not done enough, and we shall not have done enough until the last man has been enrolled and the last dollar paid. . . . We know that we are fighting for ourselves, and in defence of those fundamental principles.[27]

The need to resort to conscription was regretted by Anglican clergymen, but it was a step they nonetheless supported, believing it necessary to sustain the Canadian war effort. This belief led many prominent Anglican clergy to voice openly their support for the Union Government from the pulpit during the December 1917 election campaign. For many who normally would have been leery of making direct political statements from the pulpit, the issues involved led them to speak out. For David Williams, Bishop of Huron, one of the determining factors was the high number of Anglicans already in uniform. In a letter to the clergy of his diocese—a letter that was reprinted in the *Canadian Churchman* just days before the vote—he wrote,

27. John Richardson, "Canada's Share in the War," *Canadian Churchman*, 22 February 1917, 116–17.

> I believe it to be the duty of everyone at this time to do his utmost to uphold what is the only honourable course . . . It is unthinkable for us [as Anglicans] to withdraw now, and so desert not only the high cause which we championed . . . but also our own flesh and blood. . . . Loyalty to our brave fellow Churchmen, as well as loyalty to the British Empire and Christian civilization . . . leaves us no option but . . . Union Government.[28]

The strong public statements of support for Unionists from the bishops and other clergymen may not have translated into the wholehearted support of the entire Anglican Church, either during the campaign or on election day, but on 18 December 1917, when the civil returns were issued—the military returns would take almost three months to sort out—it was a clear Union victory. Looking at the results on a riding-by-riding basis, it is clear that the majority of the Union support came from Canada's Anglophone population, a population which would have included Anglicans.[29]

Despite the victory achieved by the Canadian Corps at Vimy Ridge on Easter Monday, 7 April 1917,[30] and the ideologically cheering capture of Jerusalem on 9 December 1917,[31] the third full year of war had been a difficult one. Casualties had been heavy, both at Vimy and later at Passchendaele, and the question of conscription threatened to divide the

---

28. David Williams, "From a Letter from the Bishop of Huron to His Clergy," *Canadian Churchman*, 13 December 1917, 802.

29. For more detailed treatments of the Union election, see Granatstein and Hitsman, *Broken Promises*, 76–78; Miller, *Our Glory*, 139, 142, 158–60; Rutherdale, *Hometown Horizons*, 163–80, 190–91; Nicholson, *Official History*, 346–47; Thompson, *Harvests of War*, 122–46. Voter turnout has been estimated at 75 percent, the highest of the period—see Elections Canada, "Voter Turnout at Federal Elections and Referendums," online http://www.elections.ca/content.aspx?section=ele&dir=turn&document=index&lang=e. For a riding-by-riding breakdown of the election results, use Parliament of Canada, "History of Federal Ridings Since 1867," online http://www.parl.gc.ca/About/Parliament/FederalRidingsHistory/HFER.asp.

30. For the most important comprehensive works on the story of the CEF in France, see Nicholson, *Official History* and the more recent two volumes, Cook, *Sharp End* and *Shock Troops*. There are, of course, many others. For a discussion of how Vimy Ridge entered the Canadian cultural imagination, see Vance, "Battle Verse."

31. For a contemporary discussion of the significance of the capture of Jerusalem, see Gould, "Imperial Significance." Gould notes, "We must remember that though Jerusalem is the centre of our hearts' affection from any directions yet . . . it is not a strategic centre. . . . The Imperial significance of the capture of Jerusalem rests largely upon the fact that it is one of the three pedestals of the religious world."

country.³² Shortages of fuel and calls for voluntary controls of food were becoming more common. At home, too, there was hardship and devastation—the port of Halifax had been destroyed by a massive explosion on 7 December 1917 that had killed some 2000 people, wounded 9000, destroyed some 13,500 buildings, and left thousands homeless.³³ On top of the more domestic concerns, the Russian Revolution was an undeniable blow to the Allied war effort. To mark the beginning of a new year, on Epiphany Sunday, 9 January 1918, Canadian Anglicans joined the British Empire in a united day of intercession. This was not the first day of prayer to be held in relation to the war, but it was the first time that King George V had set aside an empire-wide day of prayer. In Toronto's St. James's Cathedral, Canon H. P. Plumptre took the occasion to offer encouragement to his congregation, saying,

> Now we are passing through a critical period, the outcome of which is still unsettled, for among other things the failure of Russia has upset all our calculations. The next few months will be extremely critical in the issue of the war, and if there ever was a time when the call of our king to prayer was opportune it is now, and the best prayer is the turning away of those sins within ourselves. The great need of the hour is, are we worthy of victory?—and our first desire should be to come to God with a clean hand and a pure heart. If we can do that, then I believe victory will soon be ours.³⁴

With war-weariness becoming apparent, Canadian Anglicans who gathered on this Sunday used both special prayers and the familiar words of the *Book of Common Prayer* to offer intercessions for the nation, the Empire, for those serving at the front, and for all those who suffered. They prayed not only for victory, but for a righteous and timely peace, asking, "Cleanse both us and our enemies from all hatred and covetous-

---

32. For a full treatment of conscription and conscientious objectors, see Granatstein and Hitsman, *Broken Promises*; Shaw, *Conscience*. The tensions over conscription resulted in minor riots in Montreal in the summer of 1917, but would boil over again with serious consequences with riots in Quebec City in the spring of 1918. For a full treatment of the Quebec riots and the government reaction, see Auger, "Brink"; Armstrong, *Crisis of Quebec*, 227–37.

33. For the impact on Halifax Anglicans in particular, see "Wrecked Churches in Halifax," *Canadian Churchman*, 20 December 1917, 815; Miller, *Our Glory*, 156; Prince, *Catastrophe*, 71; Kitz, *Shattered City*, 69; Robertson, "After the Storm," 219–27.

34. H. P. Plumptre, as quoted in *Canadian Churchman*, 10 January 1918, 28–29.

ness, and so strengthen and guide us that neither may any weakness or weariness in us bring this war to an unrighteous end, nor a righteous peace be delayed by our blindness or self-seeking."[35]

Prayer was not only called for by the government, but it was also the response of the Church to the German Spring Offensive, news of which broke to Canadians on Friday, 22 March 1918, just before Holy Week. As the Church marked the days leading up to the Crucifixion, German armies advanced further in places than they had in 1914, shelling Paris and threatening to drive the Allied armies apart. On Passion Sunday, at St. John's Church in Port Hope, Ontario, Bishop James Fielding Sweeny of Toronto told parishioners that the sad and terrible coincidence of this great crisis in the war with Holy Week, when the church was day by day tracing the footprints of the Son of God along the way of sorrow, was not accidental, but was "Divinely ordered." The flood of anxiety and sorrow unleashed as a result of the German offensive in France would drive men and women to the foot of the Cross of Christ, where alone they could find healing, strength, and comfort. Church people should, with the greatest intensity and earnestness, pray for the success of the Allied armies and a righteous and abiding peace.[36] In Ottawa, Christ Church Cathedral was the site of a united service of intercession on the Monday of Holy Week.[37] Maundy Thursday was a day of continuous intercession at Christ Church Cathedral in Montreal.[38] On Easter Sunday, churches in Ottawa, Toronto, Montreal, and other towns and cities across Canada were full, sometimes to capacity, not only for the Easter celebrations but as a response to the military situation in Europe. In Toronto, on the Wednesday following Easter the bells of St. James' Cathedral rang out at noon for fifteen minutes "call[ing] men of every denomination to that edifice for a special service of prayer for the success of the allied armies in France."[39] Archdeacon Cody addressed the service, telling petitioners,

> It is surely right and proper that at such a time as the present we should meet together for prayer for victory in our cause.

35. "Prayers for War-Time," *Canadian Churchman*, 3 January 1918, 8.
36. *Canadian Churchman*, 4 April 1918, 222. "Divinely ordered" is capitalized as it appears in the original report.
37. 28 March 1918 entry, Service Book, St. Bartholomew's (Ottawa), 601 S5 2 (1917–1925), Anglican Diocese of Ottawa Archives.
38. *Canadian Churchman*, 4 April 1918, 224.
39. "Chimes Will Call Toronto to Prayer," *Toronto Globe*, 3 April 1918, 8.

> Yet prayer was not a wild cry of panic. God does not need to be moved to do his duty. It is we who are called to fit ourselves for the doing of His will. There never was a time when the call to do the will of God was more important than at the present hour.... We can bring our cause to the very throne of God. It is bound up with the very cause of civilization.[40]

Although the war clearly did not cause a religious revival in Canada, the availability of traditional Anglican forms of prayer and intercession provided comfort and a sense of purpose for those at home when it seemed the Allies might be facing defeat. These services, organized rapidly in response to an evolving military situation overseas, as well as more formally organized services—like the empire-wide day of intercession and the anniversary services held each year in early August—were well-attended. And when the tide finally started to turn against the Germans in the late summer of 1918, there were those who attributed the successes to the fervent prayer the German offensive had provoked. The Rev. C. E. Luce of Birchcliffe, Ontario wrote, "Of course, it is always dangerous to take God's name lightly on our lips. But is it not equally dangerous to be blind to His working? ... On August 4th, King George and the Parliament for the first time knelt together to throw our cause humbly before the Feet of God. And this great appeal to the Throne was instantly heard.... We have asked ... and He has put forth His power."[41] In a pastoral letter, William R. Clark, Bishop of Niagara, wrote, "While the Government called for more men, more munitions, more money, they hesitated to ask for prayer and look to God. However, on the 4th August last, the nation in its corporate capacity bowed for the first time ... and from that moment we have been marvellously successful."[42]

On 11 November 1918, the churches were a part of celebrating the signing of the Armistice, their bells helping to announce the news. The service book of St. Bartholomew's Church in Ottawa contains the following notation for Monday, 11 November 1918: "On Monday morning at 3:10 am the Church bells were rung by Mr. Hughes and Sergt. Brooks to help announce the news that the Armistice had been signed; fighting on every front ceased at 11 am. There was a celebration of the Holy

---

40. H. J. Cody, as quoted in "Prayer Spirit Grips Toronto," *Toronto Globe*, 4 April 1918, 7.

41. C. E. Luce, *Canadian Churchman*, 31 October 1918, 700 (emphasis original).

42. W. R. Clark, as quoted in *Canadian Churchman*, 14 November 1918, 736.

Communion at 8 am at which 25 were present. In the evening at 7 pm the Church was packed for a Thanksgiving Service."[43] In Toronto, while "the city was in a wild uproar, the bells of the Church of the Epiphany, in Parkdale, rang joyously for an hour, and at two o'clock a fine congregation came into the church for a service of praise and thanksgiving."[44] In Halifax, "when the noon-day gun boomed announcing the hour set by Royal Proclamation for public thanksgiving, the doxology of praise rang forth in Old St. Paul's from a chorus of two thousand tongues. None will ever forget the moment."[45] On Armistice Day, with the guns in Europe silent, Montreal's the Rev. J. A. Osborne was one of many clergymen conducting thanksgiving services. He told the congregation of St. Columba's Church,

> Do let us remember that God has been very good and gracious to us and to our allies. He has given us far more than either we desire or deserve ... All that we deserve is only mercy for our sins, and yet God is pouring into our hands almost more than we are able to receive. Let us make no mistake about it, the victory over materialism and self-worship has been won, "not by might and not by power," but by that Spirit which can be evoked only by prayer, and used only by those who are faithful to the end ... If we love our God, our King, our Empire, and our Dominion, can there be any other answer save that of the beautiful prayer of our Eucharist, "Here we offer and present unto Thee, O Lord, ourselves, our souls and our bodies."[46]

The experience of the Great War changed Canada forever. For Canadian Anglicans, their experience of the war was shaped by their environment and thus the experience of a Toronto clerk would have been very different from the experience of a Saskatchewan farmer, despite the fact that they were members of the same church. On the other hand, bound together by the shared worship and language of the *Book of Common Prayer*, both rural and urban Canadian Anglicans would have viewed the great overseas struggle through a common religious worldview. Although they were members of a Protestant denomina-

---

43. 11 November 1918 entry, Service Book, St. Bartholomew's (Ottawa), 601 S5 2 (1917–1925), Anglican Diocese of Ottawa Archives.

44. *Canadian Churchman*, 14 November 1918, 734.

45. Ibid., 21 November 1918, 751.

46. J. A. Osborne, "The Voice of the City," *Montreal Churchman*, December 1918, 10.

tion, there was a strong emphasis on prayer as a necessary contribution from those who remained at home, and the sacrifices made necessary by the war were given additional meaning by their relationship to the righteousness of the cause. Through the ties of the *Book of Common Prayer*, Canadian Anglicans were bound up with other Anglicans in Britain and throughout the Empire, and this perception helped shape their experience of the war. Canadian Anglicans, however, also experienced the war as Canadians. The war changed the lives of millions, and it fundamentally changed the relationship between the people and their nation. The intensity of the shared experience of the war and its sacrifices brought Canadians together and, in noting the growing Canadian identity in their sermons and at memorial services, Anglican clerics were among those who helped to strengthen and shape this identity. On Armistice Day, Canadians—Canadian Anglicans among them—were no less proud to be citizens of the British Empire than they had been on 4 August 1914, but they had discovered a new pride and a new sense of responsibility as Canadians.

BIBLIOGRAPHY

Primary Sources

ARCHIVES

Parish Records, located at Anglican Diocese of Ottawa Archives and Montreal Diocesan Archives

Cody Papers, located at Archives of Ontario.

NEWSPAPERS

Canadian Churchman
Montreal Churchman
Toronto Globe

OTHER

Proceedings of the General Synod, 7th Session, Church of England in Canada. 1915.

Gould, Sydney. "The Imperial Significance of the Capture of Jerusalem." (Speech, The Empire Club of Canada Addresses, Toronto, Canada, 20 Dec 1917). Online: http://speeches.empireclub.org/62527/data?n=1.

Secondary Sources

Armitage, W. J. *The Story of the Canadian Revision of the Prayer Book*. Toronto: Stewart & McClelland, 1922.

Armstrong, Elizabeth H. *The Crisis of Quebec, 1914–1918*. Toronto: McClelland & Stewart, 1974.

Auger, Martin. "On the Brink of Civil War: The Canadian Government and the Suppression of the 1918 Quebec Easter Riots." *Canadian Historical Review* 89 (2008) 503–40. doi: 10.3138/chr.89.4.503.

Basavarajappa, K. G., and Bali Ram. *Historical Statistics of Canada, Section A: Population and Migration*. Statistics Canada. Online: http://www.statcan.gc.ca/pub/11-516-x/sectiona/4147436-eng.htm.

Bliss, J. M. "The Methodist Church and the First World War." *Canadian Historical Review* 49 (1968) 213–33. doi: 10.3138/CHR-049-03-01.

Brunauer, Esther Caukin. "The Peace Proposals of December 1916–January 1917." *The Journal of Modern History* 4 (1932) 544–71. Online: http://www.jstor.org/stable/1899360.

Carrington, Philip. *The Anglican Church in Canada: A History*. Toronto: Collins, 1963.

Cook, Tim. *At the Sharp End: Canadians Fighting the Great War 1914–1916*. Toronto: Viking, 2007.

———. *Shock Troops: Canadians Fighting the Great War 1917–1918*. Toronto: Viking, 2008.

Endy, M. B., Jr. "Just War, Holy War, and Millennialism in Revolutionary America." *The William and Mary Quarterly* 42 (1985) 3–25. Online: http://www.jstor.org/stable/1919608.

Fest, W. B. "British War Aims and German Peace Feelers during the First World War (December 1916–November 1918)." *The Historical Journal* 15 (1972) 285–308. doi: 10.1017/S0018246X00002570.

Granatstein, J. L., and J. M. Hitsman. *Broken Promises: The Story of Conscription in Canada*. Toronto: Oxford University Press, 1977.

Gregory, Adrian. *The Last Great War: British Society and the First World War*. New York: Cambridge University Press, 2008.

Heath, Gordon. *A War with a Silver Lining: Canadian Protestant Churches and the South African War, 1899–1902*. Montreal and Kingston: McGill-Queen's University Press, 2009.

Kitz, Janet. *Shattered City: The Halifax Explosion and the Road to Recovery*. 3rd ed. Halifax: Nimbus, 2008.

Miller, Carman. "Loyalty, Patriotism, and Resistance: Canada's Response to the Anglo-Boer War, 1899–1902." *South African Historical Journal* 41 (1999) 312–23. doi: 10.1080/02582479908671896.

Miller, I. H. M. *Our Glory and Our Grief: Torontonians and the Great War*. Toronto: University of Toronto Press, 2002.

Morton, Desmond. *Fight or Pay: Soldiers' Families in the Great War*. Vancouver: UBC Press, 2004.

Nicholson, G. W. L. *Official History of the Canadian Army in the First World War: Canadian Expeditionary Force 1914–1919*. Ottawa: Queen's Printer and Controller of Stationary, 1962. Online: http://cefresearch.com/matrix/Nicholson/.

Prince, S. H. *Catastrophe and Social Change*. New York: Columbia University, 1920.

Robertson, Allan B. "After the Storm: The Church and Synagogue Response." In *Ground Zero: A Reassessment of the 1917 Explosion in Halifax Harbour*, edited by Alan Ruffman and Colin Howell, 219–27. Halifax: Nimbus, 1994.

Rutherdale, Robert. *Hometown Horizons: Local Responses to Canada's Great War*. Vancouver: UBC Press, 2004.

Shaw, Amy J. *Crisis of Conscience: Conscientious Objection in Canada during the First World War*. Vancouver: UBC Press, 2009.

Thompson, John Herd. *The Harvests of War: The Prairie West, 1914–1918*. Toronto: McLelland & Stuart, 1978.

Vance, Jonathan. "Battle Verse: Poetry and Nationalism after Vimy Ridge." In *Vimy Ridge: A Canadian Reassessment*, edited by Geoffrey Hayes, Andrew Iarocci, and Mike Bechthold, 265–77. Waterloo: Wilfrid Laurier University Press, 2007.

Wise, S. F. "God's Peculiar Peoples." In *God's Peculiar Peoples: Essays on Political Culture in Nineteenth Century Canada*, edited by A. B. McKillop and Paul Romney, 20–43. Ottawa: Carleton University Press, 1993.

———. "Sermon Literature and Canadian Intellectual History." In *God's Peculiar Peoples: Essays on Political Culture in Nineteenth Century Canada*, edited by A. B. McKillop and Paul Romney, 3–17. Ottawa: Carleton University Press, 1993.

7

"O God of Battles"

The Canadian Baptist Experience of the Great War

MICHAEL A. G. HAYKIN AND IAN HUGH CLARY

AS ONE ENTERS THE auditorium of the neo-Gothic building of Jarvis Street Baptist Church in Toronto from its north-eastern access, almost immediately one comes across a brass plaque on the building's northern wall that lists forty-one names of "our brave young men who nobly died for the cause of righteousness in the War of 1914–1918." Those who erected this plaque appear to have been confident that the Canadians who fought in the First World War were engaged in a struggle for "righteousness." Contrary to the way the war has sometimes come to be remembered and described by historians in more recent days, this early reflection on the meaning of the war was that it was a noble and just war fought against an enemy who was definitely in the wrong and who was, by implication, ignoble. Of the forty-one names, all but one of them are clearly British surnames, another clue as to why the cause was a righteous one: it involved the defense of Great Britain, the motherland at the heart of the empire of which Canada was then a part. Finally, underneath the list of names there is a portion of a Scripture verse that invites the viewer to compare the sacrifice of these young lives to that of Jesus Christ: "Greater love hath no man than this" (John 15:13a, KJV). This verse—often with the second part of the verse included, "that a man lay down his life for his friends"—was a favorite one for war memorials, as it told the viewer that the deaths of the slain were rich with meaning and purpose even as Christ's violent death had been. This plaque's reflections about the Great War serve as a guide to this chapter, along with two issues that were germane to the Canadian context—conscription and its challenge to the Baptist love of freedom, and the question of when America would enter the war.[1]

The Great War plaque at Jarvis Street Baptist Church, Toronto.
Photo by Chisso Wang.

---

1. Most of the evidence that we have assembled to discuss the Canadian Baptist experience of the war is from Ontario. However, we have every reason to believe that Baptists in other areas of the country would not substantially differ in any of the areas we have examined.

"THE CAUSE OF RIGHTEOUSNESS": WHY CANADIAN BAPTISTS WENT TO WAR

When Britain declared war on 4 August 1914, Canada was also at war—as a Dominion of the Empire it had no choice.[2] Among Baptists in Canada, the response to the declaration was mixed. In the *Canadian Baptist*, the denominational magazine of the Baptist Convention of Ontario and Quebec (BCOQ), an editorial was published on 6 August—oddly, two days after the British declaration—asking "Is It to Be War for Canada?"[3] The editors spoke not only for Baptists but for their fellow citizens in general when they said, "All Canadian hearts are perturbed at the war situation of Europe, and which in all probability will involve Great Britain and the Empire." If Britain was to enter (which it had), then Canada must be expected to "do her duty." They continued: "We are not lovers of war, but if necessity thrusts Canada into it we are glad to know that her loyal sons will not shirk any responsibility."[4]

Baptists were indeed not "lovers of war." Although in the seventeenth century they owed much of their growth to their involvement in Oliver Cromwell's New Model Army, Baptists often eschewed militarism and publically expressed a distaste for war.[5] For instance, on 14 August 1803, the English Baptist theologian Andrew Fuller (1754–1815) gave an address in Kettering during the so-called "invasion scare" when it was feared that the hated Napoleon Bonaparte would invade England.[6] In his sermon *Christian Patriotism*, he recognized the sometime necessity of war—for the case at hand, Fuller saw conflict as a matter of national defense—and made the comment: "You know, my brethren, I have always deprecated war, as one of the greatest calamities."[7] More pointedly, the Victorian Baptist Charles Haddon Spurgeon (1834–1892) preached the

---

2. Cook, *Sharp End*, 22.
3. "Is It to Be War for Canada?" *Canadian Baptist*, 6 August 1914, 1.
4. Ibid.
5. For an overview of early Baptist views on war, see Cross, "Baptists on Peace and War." William Brackney says that "the presence of Baptists in the New Model Army is a vivid illustration of the progress which Baptists had made." He also comments: "One of the marked distinctions between Baptists and the true Anabaptists was the willingness of the Baptists to bear arms." See Brackney, *Baptists*, 8.
6. Cf. Lloyd, *French Are Coming*.
7. Fuller, "Patriotism," 1:205.

following on Christmas Eve 1871, a few months after the conclusion of the Franco-Prussian War:

> A nation's joy can never lie in the misery of others. Killing is not the path to prosperity; huge armaments are a curse to the nation itself as well as to its neighbors. The joy of a nation is a golden sand over which no stream of blood has ever rippled. It is only found in that river, the streams whereof make glad the city of God.[8]

Following in this general anti-war perspective, British Baptists were working towards peace during the summer that the Archduke Franz Ferdinand was assassinated. Keith W. Clements describes their overall perspective thus: "On the eve of war . . . leading Baptist opinion was deeply committed to internationalism, opposed to militarism, and even prepared to defend German policy in the face of English accusations."[9]

Baptists in pre-war Canada shared similar sentiments with their British counterparts, and late-Victorian Canadian Baptists had shared with other English Protestants the heightened imperial fervor associated with imperial conflicts, especially the war in South Africa. However, as Gordon Heath has shown, support for Empire and Canada's role in it did not mean *carte blanche* support for any and every conflict; war was lamented and only to be fought as a last resort for righteous ends.[10] In 1909, a Canadian Defense League had been formed in response to Germany's growing military might. The League called for universal cadet training for students in peacetime but, as Charles M. Johnston explains, "only the Baptists, of all the denominations called upon, refused to support its aims." When in 1911 McMaster University, a Baptist institution in Toronto, was asked to take part in militia work, "it responded by tabling the proposal out of respect for the feelings of the denomination." Part of this was due to their hope that in the peaceful society they inhabited, war would prove to be impossible.[11] When war was thus declared, initially

---

8. Spurgeon, "Joy Born," 17:706. We owe this reference to Mark Nenadov of Essex, Ontario.

9. Clements, "Baptists," 82.

10. For an examination of Canadian Baptist attitudes to war and empire in the late nineteenth century, see Heath, *Silver Lining*; Heath, "Traitor, Half-Breeds"; Heath, "Missionaries"; Heath, "Nile Expedition."

11. Johnston, *McMaster*, 129. For the spread of military drill and imperialism among Canadian Methodists and Presbyterians, see Heath, "Prepared to Do."

Canadian Baptists were hesitant in their support of it. Nearly ten days after the onset of the war, the *Canadian Baptist* ran an editorial urging its readers not to allow the emotions that surround war make them lose sight of the demands of the kingdom of God. A month later an editorial comment stated, "We have tried not to forget that we are followers of the Prince of Peace," but concluded nonetheless that this was a just war.[12] So, when the Ontario and Quebec Baptists held their convention on 14–19 October 1914, a "patriotic resolution" was adopted, and the need for prayer was urged. However, it was concluded that more than prayer was needed; the denomination was urged to "do everything in our power to support the cause of Great Britain in the present terrible and deplorable war."[13] Similarly, the Maritime Baptists, who held their convention in Fredericton, New Brunswick, on 17–20 October 1914, devoted time to considering what was now called the "righteous war."

Thus, it was not long before general Baptist sentiment warmed to the war, with leaders becoming more and more outspoken in their support of it. A. L. McCrimmon (1865–1935), Chancellor of McMaster University, thought it wholly consistent to be a Baptist and to be in support of the war. At the McMaster commencement for 1915–1916 he stated that the school was true to the historic position of Baptists in the giving of its students to the war. For McCrimmon, the war was a stand against oppression and the "outrageous theology" that one nation is the vice-regent of God charged with the task of "crucifying" lesser breeds to his greater glory.[14]

Britain had declared war because Germany invaded Belgium. Three German armies totalling some 600,000 men had swept into the small country and conquered it with savagery. When Belgians responded to the occupation by retaliating against their occupiers, the Germans began executing civilians and "enacted a brutal policy of oppression."[15] When

12. "Editorial Comment," *Canadian Baptist*, 13 August 1914, 1; "The Negotiations before the War," *Canadian Baptist*, 24 September 1914, 8.

13. "The Patriotic Resolution," *Canadian Baptist*, 5 November 1914, 8.

14. "McMaster University Commencement Exercises 1915–1916," *Canadian Baptist*, 18 May 1916, 3. McCrimmon's reference to "crucifying" may refer to the rumor that the Germans had crucified a Canadian, although post-war historians give little credence to whether this really happened. See Fussell, *Great War*, 117–18. Thanks to Eugene McNamara of Windsor, Ontario, for this reference.

15. Cook, *Sharp End*, 60.

German brutality became known, the rest of the world reacted with indignation and shock. After compiling a report on the atrocities committed, Britain entered a war that her people saw as "a crusade to save Belgium."[16] This was how the Canadian Baptists justified their eventual support. A news bulletin in the *Canadian Baptist* declared, "The Goths have burned Louvain. The dark ages have come again."[17] In an issue of the *McMaster University Monthly*, an undergraduate student, Bernard Trotter (1890–1917), published a poem entitled "To the Students of Liège" in which he expressed his support for the Belgians: "When Right and Freedom called in their distress—/Not vain your sacrifice nor lost your work:/The World's free heart beats high because of you!"[18] In a later poem, Trotter spoke of the "ravishing Hun."[19] O. C. S. Wallace (1856–1947), pastoring in Westmount, Quebec, wrote an editorial comment in January 1915 saying that there is a sense in which "no war is justifiable," but in this war Britain was justified "in coming to the defense of Belgium." He added: "I abhor war with all my soul. I support Britain in the present war with all my heart."[20] After the war, George G. Nasmith (1877–1965), who had served with the Canadian Army Medical Corps for the entirety of the war, wrote a substantial overview of Canada's role in the hostilities. He did not hesitate to depict the culture of the German Empire as one of "insolence, which knew no pity and felt no love" and which, consumed by "lust of conquest," had led to the onset of war. As Nasmith thought about German actions during the war, it seemed to him that the German military had been directed by "the reincarnated rude and savage gods of their German ancestors."[21]

16. Ibid.

17. "War News in Brief," *Canadian Baptist*, 3 September 1914, 9. In a later issue practical steps towards helping Belgium were outlined in C. E. MacLeod and James Ryrie, "Help Little Belgium," *Canadian Baptist*, 7 January 1915, 1.

18. Trotter, "Students of Liège," *McMaster University Monthly*, October 1914, 1, cited in Johnston, *McMaster*, 130. Bernard Trotter was the son of Thomas Trotter, professor of homiletics and pastoral theology at McMaster. He was killed on the Western Front on 7 May 1917; see "McMaster and the War," *Canadian Baptist*, 14 June 1917, 2.

19. Trotter, "A Kiss," 36. This poem can also be found in the anthology edited by Busby, *Flanders Fields*, 113–15.

20. "Editorial Comment," *Canadian Baptist*, 28 January 1915, 1. He went on to say that he found it difficult to count a man "a proper Christian who declines to enter the fray when the interests of King and country and home are at stake and when the Kingdom of Christ and all its gracious principles are threatened. . . . The sword of the true Christian is sometimes stained with blood."

21. Nasmith, *Canada's Sons*, 286–87.

It was not only for this beleaguered European nation that the Baptists justified their support; they clearly saw themselves as part of the British Empire and so sided with their "motherland," as many Baptists called Britain.[22] One of the most vocal advocates of Canadian entrance onto the fields of France and Flanders was T. T. Shields (1873–1955), the pastor of Jarvis Street Baptist Church in Toronto. Shields was a powerful preacher and a key leader in the later Fundamentalist-Modernist controversy that was fought as regards to McMaster University in the 1920s. Born in Bristol, England, Shields had emigrated to Canada with his family as a child and went on to pastor a number of churches in Ontario before accepting a call to one of Canada's most famous pulpits.[23] When war was declared, he was vacationing at a lake north of Toronto, typical of the scene described by author Stephen Leacock who said of Canada's first hearing of the war: "For Canada it came out of a clear sky—the clear sky of vacation time, of the glory of the Canadian summer, of summer cottages and bush camps."[24] In his first sermon after returning from vacation Shields preached on Exodus 15:3, "The Lord is a Man of War."[25] In it he spoke of how Germany "nursed national robbery and murder" in her heart, and how the Germans had sinned not only against Belgium, France, or Britain, but against the "whole moral order" and against a "higher government," namely God's.[26]

Shields clearly identified himself as a citizen of the Empire, as Mark Parent says: "For T. T. Shields his 'Britishness' was particularly intense. Throughout his life he identified himself as a British citizen. For him, Britain stood for all that was good and worthwhile within human civilization."[27] In a sermon on Psalm 76:7–10, preached on 13

22. Cf. a sermon by John MacNeill, pastor of Walmer Road Baptist in Toronto, which he preached at City Temple in London, England on 8 September 1914, reprinted in *Canadian Baptist*, 10 September 1914, 3. See also Thomas Trotter, "Educational Lessons from the War," *Canadian Baptist*, 8 July 1915, 3; H. H. Bingham, "The Ideal Empire," *Canadian Baptist*, 1 July 1917, 2.

23. A largely uncritical biography of Shields is Tarr, *Shields of Canada*. For a more critical interpretation of the split with McMaster, see Rawlyk, "Christian Education." For a study of Shields and the war, though needing more detail and a more nuanced interpretation, see Parent, "Shields and the First World War." See also Adams, "Call to Arms."

24. Cited in Cook, *Sharp End*, 21.

25. Shields, "Man of War."

26. Ibid., 9–10.

27. Parent, "Shields and the First World War," 46.

September 1914, Shields compared British and German views of "justifiable war." Britain was a completely righteous combatant, whereas German militarism was criminal: "The difference between British & German armaments is the difference between a policeman's baton & a burglar's slingshot."[28] This Canadian hatred of many things German persisted to the war's end. George T. Webb, editor of the *Western Baptist*, wrote a piece in December 1918 saying that the epithet "Hun" should not be used to describe Germans because, according to him, Germans were worse than the ancient "Huns." He writes: "Nothing would please the German rulers more than to be able to hide their own blackened reputation behind the word 'Hun.' Let the 'German' carry its own story to the future and bear its own burden of suggestion to all the generations yet to come. The name 'German,' not 'Hun,' shall in all coming years be the symbol of all that is superlatively despicable and fiendishly diabolical."[29]

Shields's ardent Anglophilia was not unique amongst Canadian Baptists.[30] Arthur Hale of Rockland in the Ottawa Association published a piece entitled "The Call of the King To-day," in which he referred to the British Empire as "the most truly Christian Empire which ever existed."[31] John MacNeill of Walmer Road Baptist in Toronto, who would go overseas to conduct evangelism campaigns for the soldiers, wrote that "the British Empire has a righteous cause." He qualified this statement by noting that it could be the case that "England needs this baptism of blood" as, in the quest for gain and pleasure, "we have been forgetting God." Yet, MacNeill continued, God would use such a crisis to produce good as he had done in the past. The Toronto pastor cited a number of historical examples to support this point, including sixteenth-century England's war against Spain, after which there dawned the "Golden Age" of English literature.[32] This pro-British sentiment is well expressed in verse by Thomas Watson, writing from Ridgetown, Ontario in 1917:

28. Shields, "Sermon #1101," 13. In another sermon he said that the principles that dominate Germany are "the devils of autocracy and predacious militarism"; see T. T. Shields, "To-day, and To-morrow, and the Day Following," *Canadian Baptist*, 10 October 1914, 3.

29. George T. Webb, "Hun or German," *Western Baptist*, December 1918, 2.

30. Cf. Clarke, "English-Speaking Canada," 335.

31. "The Call of the King To-day," *Canadian Baptist*, 13 July 1916, 3.

32. "The Duties of the Hour," *Canadian Baptist*, 10 September 1914, 2.

> The British Empire names Thee
> As Truth's unfailing spring;
> Each Allied nation claims Thee
> As righteous Lord and King.
> On land and air and ocean
> May it be clearly shown
> That all the world's commotion
> Is ruled by Thee alone.[33]

However, not all Baptists were so enthusiastic about the war. While there is no evidence of outright pacifism, there were voices raised against the enthusiasm for war. I. J. Ransom, the Baptist minister in Maxville, Ontario, wrote to the *Canadian Baptist* just after the 1st Canadian Division joined the fighting in Europe, saying that Satan was stirring up great wars, and that a pro-war stance should be rejected by Baptists because of the words of Jesus in John 18:36: "My kingdom is not of this world." He further asked why the Church could not be true to "her hitherto professed peace-principles." Interestingly, the editors inserted a response after the letter stating that they "differ[ed] radically" from the views expressed and that his words breathed "unqualified opposition to Christian patriotism."[34]

By 1917, Canadians had been in active combat for nearly two horrible years. The ravages of war had taken their toll and the initial romanticism about the war had begun to fade for many. "Militarism has lost its glamour," as a Canadian pastor living in England put it.[35] Baptists were beginning to consider the future: when would the war to end all wars end? What would the world look like after it ended? Their perspective was not always bright. A. D. Carpenter—a McMaster graduate and one-time pastor in Blenheim, Ontario, just before the war—wrote a letter from Newton College in the United States about the role Canadian Baptists should play after the end of hostilities.[36] He argued that postbellum churches would never be the same, and that Baptists had to be prepared theologically and ethically for change. They needed to regain a

33. Thomas Watson, "Three Years of War," *Canadian Baptist*, 2 August 1917, 1.

34. "Correspondence: Mr. Ransom Protests," *Canadian Baptist*, 18 February 1915, 2. I. J. Ransom resigned from the Maxville church on 9 May 1915, after only nineteen months. See *Canadian Baptist*, 20 May 1915, 9.

35. Cited in Johnston, *McMaster*, 135.

36. A. D. Carpenter, "Canadian Baptists and the New Age," *Canadian Baptist*, 18 January 1917, 2–3.

personal view of God that had been lost in the pre-war years, and which would in turn shape their moral outlook. Baptists had to reconsider their relationship with war, rethink their view of church and state, and work through what it meant for members of Christ's body to go to war against one another and on behalf of the state.[37] "The war," wrote Carpenter, "hangs like a pall over the earth, with its harvest of mangled bodies; broken homes, burdened generations to come; and hate, and hell."[38] He argued that if the church had held a firmer grip on the world, the war would not have happened.

"A VOTE FOR THE KAISER": THE DEBATE ABOUT CONSCRIPTION AND BAPTIST PRINCIPLES

Carpenter also asked the question of conscription: "Is compulsory military service justifiable under any conditions in a free state?" Canadian Baptists struggled with this very question in the summer of 1917 when Prime Minister Robert Borden's (1854–1937) Union Government voted to implement compulsory military service. Some Baptists saw this as striking at the heart of the principles of liberty and democracy; state-enforced military service had been traditionally opposed. Baptists in Great Britain, along with most Nonconformists, had often sided with the Liberal or Whig political philosophies that tended against such infringements on personal liberty.[39] A similar political alignment was also found in Canada. It is telling that at McMaster's commencement service in the spring of 1917 the address was given by Newton Rowell (1867–1941), the leader of the Opposition Liberals in Ontario. Rowell argued that the war was about democracy, which he said is the essence of the Baptist view of church and state, and that it was a struggle against autocracy. Canadians must see to it that the crime of war was not possible again.[40] In federal politics, the Liberal leader was the former Prime Minister Sir Wilfrid Laurier (1841–1919). Laurier refused to join Borden

---

37. Ibid.

38. Ibid.

39. In Britain the Baptists had been largely supportive of the Liberal Prime Minister William Ewart Gladstone (1809–1898); see Bebbington, "Gladstone and the Baptists," 224–39.

40. "The Progress of Democracy during the War," *Canadian Baptist*, 10 May 1917, 4.

in the Union Government, and likewise refused to advocate conscription. How would Baptists respond?[41]

For Canadians in general, though many opposed it for reasons including religious convictions, conscription was a necessary evil.[42] The war had taken a terrible toll on morale among troops, especially after the horrors of Verdun and the Somme. The earlier sense of adventure that the war seemed to foster had largely disappeared, and it was difficult to find a ready-and-willing body of men to enlist. Not long after Borden returned from Britain in May 1917, he announced the need for conscription. This in turn led to a political battle that summer and the signing of the Military Service Act on 29 August, which was enforced on 1 January 1918. But, as Gordon Heath observes, "Conscription threatened to divide the nation along ethnic and religious lines."[43] This was due to the fact that French Roman Catholics had stood largely aloof from the war. When conscription was brought in, many Quebecois felt alienated, and in turn, many English-speaking Canadians were critical of their French countrymen. Four thousand troops, for example, were brought into Quebec City to quell a conscription riot during Easter 1918.

Conscription was a conundrum for Baptists, who in principle should have opposed it; as Amy J. Shaw writes, "the roots of the Baptist denomination lay in individual dissent."[44] Reflecting this sentiment, one preacher who had called for mobilization reasoned, "Christ is today calling for volunteers. We will draft no soldiers." Thus, when the question "Is there to be conscription?" was asked in 1915, the answer was, "With all our heart we hope not."[45]

Yet, by 1917 things had changed. The *Canadian Baptist* ran an editorial in May of that year supporting "the force of sweet compulsion" and

---

41. A detailed account of Protestant responses to conscription in Canada is Heath, "Protestant Denominational Press." It should be noted that McMaster conferred an LLD on Borden at their 1915–1916 commencement; see "McMaster University Commencement Exercises 1915–1916," *Canadian Baptist*, 18 May 1916, 3.

42. Cf. Shaw, *Crisis of Conscience*, which explores the role of pacifism during conscription.

43. Heath, "Protestant Denominational Press," 28.

44. Shaw, *Crisis of Conscience*, 115.

45. L. Brown, "Mobilizing for Active Service—the Soldier's Oath," *Canadian Baptist*, 24 September 1914, 3; "Is There to Be Conscription?" *Canadian Baptist*, 18 November 1915, 1.

said "'amen' to the government decision."[46] Two months later another editorial supported a "selective draft," which, it was argued, could be justified in some cases, even though it was often used by "despots." This was so because all citizens were under obligation to defend their country.[47] In somewhat threatening tones, a column entitled "Baptists and the War" ran in the same publication, maintaining: "It would not be difficult to name churches and communities in Ontario, as well as Quebec, from which relatively few have enlisted. We are not going to say that we rejoice at the prospect of conscription, but we shall not be grieved if many of those who are quite eligible to join the colors, but who so far have been 'slackers,' should be forced by conviction or by The Militia Act, to do their duty to State and humanity."[48]

It is not surprising that T. T. Shields in Toronto strongly supported conscription. Early in the war he was using his pulpit to enlist men for the war effort.[49] As John Stackhouse notes, for Shields, conscription was "especially justified . . . in the defence of his beloved England. He vehemently championed it and denounced the Roman Catholic Church in Quebec for its reluctance to support the Allied cause."[50] An example of this is the fifteen-minute talk Shields gave before the 10 June 1917 evening sermon at Jarvis Street that he entitled "Should We Have Conscription?"[51] Shields argued that Canada had come to a critical moment in its history and Canadians must not doubt the righteousness of their cause. The Germans were a menace to democracy, and Allied resistance was urgent—there could be no neutral stance on the war. Appealing for a final victory in honor of the fallen soldiers, he said, "We owe it to those who have already fallen to fight on to a successful conclusion, they died in the faith of our doing so." Likewise, Canadians owed it to those who were at the Western Front, who needed as much support as possible. "Conscription," Shields argued, "is the only equitable plan."

46. *Canadian Baptist*, 24 May 1917, 1. See also "Conscription and National Service," *Maritime Baptist*, 23 May 1917, 4; "Canada and Conscription," *Maritime Baptist*, 27 June 1917, 4; and "Conscription and National Service," *Maritime Baptist*, 25 July 1917, 4.

47. *Canadian Baptist*, 12 July 1917, 1.

48. "Baptists and the War," *Canadian Baptist*, 21 June 1917, 1.

49. Parent cites a sermon from 24 October 1915 in which Shields sought to enlist his hearers: "Shields and the First World War," 50.

50. Stackhouse, *Canadian Evangelicalism*, 25.

51. Shields, "Sermon #1280."

Moreover, it was the state's right to enlist able-bodied men, even by compulsion. Adding a personal twist, Shields put his own name on the line. If he were asked to join, how would he respond? "Personally," replied Shields, "I would welcome the opportunity. . . . Every man should be made legally a potential soldier." It is noteworthy that in the entire talk, no mention was made of the infringements conscription would have on Baptist principles of freedom. Later he would publish a piece saying that a "vote against our men who are crying out for reinforcements [is] therefore a vote for the Kaiser."[52]

A number of students at McMaster, on the other hand, were opposed to conscription. In the *McMaster University Monthly*, one contributor argued that conscription would do violence both to Baptist principles and to the British people, namely their idea of "individual right." It was argued that "personal freedom is the great fundamental principle which underlies all our institutions."[53] As Johnston notes, the students who sided against conscription were not necessarily against enlistment; rather, they did not want to abandon traditional liberal principles by enforcing compulsory military service.[54]

Some Baptist disagreements with the war led to imprisonment for conscientious objection. George Henry VanLoon, of Brantford, Ontario, was called into service at the age of twenty. He put in a claim of exemption, only to have it rejected and exchanged for a ten-year prison sentence at the Kingston Penitentiary. Another, Nicholas Shuttleworth of Brandon, Manitoba, was court-marshalled in England after he converted to the International Bible Students Association, a Russellite group that regularly sought exemption status.[55]

The ethnic and religious factors that Heath highlights had a part to play in the changing attitudes of many Baptist leaders. For those who struggled to reconcile their Baptist beliefs with the idea of uniting with Conservatives and bringing in conscription, the issue turned more on a concern over the Catholic and French Canadian responses to the war.[56] McCrimmon concluded that French Canadians were not "doing

52. Cited in Johnston, *McMaster*, 143.

53. *McMaster University Monthly*, November 1916, 51, cited in Johnston, *McMaster*, 141.

54. Johnston, *McMaster*, 143.

55. Shaw, *Crisis of Conscience*, 115.

56. The editors of the *Canadian Baptist* put out a call to vote for a union gov-

their bit," as they failed to match English Canada's contribution.⁵⁷ For some, this failure made them as culpable as Germany.⁵⁸ As Johnston explains, conscription "would for all its faults have the one great merit of ending supposed inequities and forcing ungrateful French Canadians to accept their responsibilities as Christian citizens living in a civilized community."⁵⁹ Many who voted in favor of conscription primarily saw themselves as voting against French Canadians.

By the conclusion of the war Canada had conscripted 125,000 men, though only 25,000 of them had actually gone to the front. But conscription left Canada divided. Baptists saw the problem clearly. As the *Maritime Baptist* put it: "In this we find one of the gravest problems which confronts our nation. It is almost inevitable that the gap which now divides the two races in Canada will be further widened as an outcome of war. . . . Where shall we look for its solution?"⁶⁰

"WILSON'S IMPERTINENCE": BAPTIST CONCERN ABOUT THE ENTRY OF AMERICA INTO THE WAR

While the conscription crisis of 1917 was a problem specific to Canadians, that same year saw an external problem answered—at least in the eyes of Allied supporters. When war was first declared, the United States opted for a position of neutrality, wanting, in the words of its president Woodrow Wilson, to remain a "great nation at peace." For the first three years of the war the supporters of the Entente Powers yearned for American involvement. Such was the case with Canadian Baptists, who regularly expressed their desire to see the Americans join the battle. Editorials in Baptist presses bemoaned America's lack of involvement, decrying the country south of its border for being "aloof to the greatest

---

ernment in the August election, which meant a joining of Liberals and Conservatives under Borden's leadership. See *Canadian Baptist*, 2 August 1917, 1.

57. The 22nd Battalion, often referred to as the Van Doos, was a French-Canadian Battalion that served with distinction in the war. See Ferland, "Patriotism and Allegiances."

58. Johnston, *McMaster*, 141–42.

59. Ibid., 142.

60. "Our National Problem," *Maritime Baptist*, 21 March 1917, 4, cited in Heath, "Protestant Denominational Press," 40. Another ethnic problem faced by Canadian Baptists was the question of what to do with the German Baptists who had nearly twenty-five churches in Alberta and southwestern Saskatchewan. See Priestly, "Baptist 'Home Mission.'"

moral issue of the day" and expressing distrust of Americans in general.[61] Even after the infamous sinking of the RMS Lusitania on 7 May 1915 by German U-boats, in which a number of American passengers died, the United States did not come into the war. This became a cause for great frustration.[62] Two days after the ship was torpedoed, Shields preached a sermon entitled, "Sinking of the Lusitania," in which he made the naval tragedy the high-water mark of German atrocity—higher even than the invasion of Belgium and the use of gas warfare as at Ypres in 1915.[63] Citing the loss of over one hundred American citizens, he asked of the United States: "What will they do?" Certainly a democratic nation like the United States would not accept dictation from Imperial Germany. According to Shields, they had to face the outrage: "American prestige will not recover from the blow for generations."[64] There would later be an added personal element for Shields in the sinking of this ship. On 9 July 1917, he sailed on its cousin, the *Aurania (2)*, to England to take in the Canadian war effort and visit soldiers in France. This was his fourth of five such voyages across the Atlantic during the war. He kept a diary of his trip that lasted much of the summer and saw him preach regularly for his friend A. C. Dixon (1824–1925) at Spurgeon's Metropolitan Tabernacle in London. In the journal he recorded some harrowing experiences once his ship entered the war zone. For instance, on July 19 the escort destroyers engaged in a fire-fight on the horizon. That night Shields slept in his clothing and, according to his journal, "divided [his] sermons into 4 packages, & put them in the pockets of [his] overcoat & pinned them in with safety pins."[65] Surely the Lusitania must have been on his mind as he traveled from New York to Liverpool.

In early March 1917 Wilson discovered that the Germans had sought to enlist Mexico as an ally through the "Zimmermann Telegram"—written by Arthur Zimmermann, Germany's foreign secretary—and as a

---

61. See *Canadian Baptist*, 15 February 1917, 7.

62. It was also proof of German wickedness: the report of the Lusitania "makes clear the worst that was said about German atrocities in Belgium is only too true. All this makes clearer than ever the nature of the Prussian tyrants against whom we are struggling." See *Canadian Baptist*, 5 May 1915, 8.

63. Shields, "Sermon #1147."

64. Ibid., 9. For another sermon in which Shields again expressed consternation with the United States, see Shields, "Sermon #1246."

65. Shields, "1917 Letters," 20. For his thoughts on London in the war years, see Shields, "England in War Time."

result, the U.S. approved entrance into the war on 6 April 1917.[66] Six days later an editorial in the *Canadian Baptist* breathed a sigh of relief, saying that "the world is now a unit in a new sense" and expressed hope that the war would soon come to an end.[67] American troops first landed in France in June 1917, although the American Expeditionary Force would not arrive until that November. A year later the war was over, and President Wilson was working towards the idea of a League of Nations.

Henry A. Porter, originally from Nova Scotia but at the time serving in Atlanta, Georgia, expressed relief for the military cause of his homeland after his adopted home finally entered the theatre of war. Seeing brightness on the horizon, Porter believed that the world was on the precipice of a new age—the "Turkish crescent" was a waning moon, and the sun sought by the Kaiser was going into eclipse. Not only the church, but Christian schools like McMaster, his Alma Mater, must be part of "reconstruction." They must stress democracy over autocracy, by which he meant, "The rule of the people would mean not only the end of autocracy in government, but the end of priestcraft and state churches." These were to "make way for the absolute and solitary lordship of Jesus Christ!"[68]

"OUR BRAVE YOUNG MEN": BEREAVEMENT AND THE WAR'S COST

Though the Allies were victorious over the Central Powers when Armistice was declared on 11 November 1918, the losses suffered by both sides were grim. Of the over 600,000 Canadians who had served in the military, more than 56,000 had died; 141,418 returned wounded.[69] Due to the constant shelling, the hail of machinegun fire that the soldiers were forced to march into, the sickness and disease, and the gas warfare, it is amazing that more were not killed or maimed. As one Canadian soldier, Thomas Hannah, put it: "This is not war, it is simply murder. . . . What I have seen would turn men's hair white."[70]

---

66. Cf. Boghardt, *Zimmermann Telegram*.
67. *Canadian Baptist*, 12 April 1917, 8.
68. Henry Alford Porter, "Facing the Future," *Canadian Baptist*, 24 May 1917, 3.
69. Statistics Canada, "Number of Casualties."
70. Thomas Hannah, Letter, 9 July 1915, cited in Cook, *Sharp End*, 188–89.

In 1917, the *Canadian Baptist* printed a column written by a William Farquharson who witnessed the return of many of the soldiers. Of them, the wounded and unfit for service were the highest proportion. He described in gruesome detail the wounded: those whose bodies had been shot through, who had pierced lungs, and missing or destroyed limbs. He spoke of others with broken skulls, those who had been poisoned with gas, and others who had suffered shell shock or were stricken with disease. Of them Farquharson commented: "The marvel is that so many come back as from the gates of hell with heart still fresh and spirit unbroken." These were soldiers of various religious or denominational backgrounds—Church of England, Presbyterians, Roman Catholics, Baptists, Salvation Army, Latter Day Saints, Buddhists, Confucians, Jews, even atheists—and of them he said, "We feel a certain brotherhood towards them all." This last statement he clarified by quoting William Shakespeare's *Henry V*, "For he to-day that sheds his blood with me/ Shall be my brother."[71]

How did the carnage of the war psychologically affect those Baptists who served? For many, it was a sobering confrontation with the reality of human evil, and yet their belief in God and his goodness remained. For others, it was a time of tremendous spiritual struggle. One example of how the war negatively affected Baptist soldiers is that of Cyril Martin of Edmonton, Alberta. Martin was raised a Baptist but during the butchery in France lost his belief in the goodness of God. He said that children with missing limbs "really got me. I thought, if God is all-powerful, why doesn't he stop this war? And it was quite a while afterwards before I got it back." After coming home he came to see that the war had signaled a revolt against Christianity in society and that it was the product of an unbiblical power-struggle between countries. Eventually his faith in God returned, which he credited to time spent meditating on Psalm 46:10: "Be still and know that I am God." He said that this verse "got [him] thinking. Be still and you will know; use your brain. War is one of the evil things we do when we are not doing what God wants." Violence, he said, is sometimes "forced on you," and the good must fight. In 1929 he was ordained as a minister in the United Church of Canada and later served in the Second World War as a chaplain.[72]

71. William Farquharson, "The Mission of the Church to the Returning Soldiers," *Canadian Baptist*, 7 June 1917, 4.

72. For the story of Cyril Martin, see "Forgotten Heroes of a Fearful War," *Western Reporter*, 11 November 1996, 28–33.

What was the actual response of churches both to the war and to the soldiers upon their return? During the war, Canadian Baptists offered support to the country's war effort in numerous ways. For instance, they sent chaplains to Canadian and British bases, sent letters and gifts to the soldiers in Europe, and supported families at home. Primarily, however, support came from those churches that sent men and women overseas to serve. In early June 1917, the *Canadian Baptist* sent a circular letter asking churches to provide statistics of those from their number who were in active service, highlighting the fallen or those who had won honors for heroism. This was toward collecting and "worthily recording" exact statistics concerning "the share we Baptists have had in the war." It was also their desire to honor the "brave Baptist lads."[73] Within one issue after the letter was sent, churches were responding—and they continued to respond, so much so that the magazine made a policy of the publication of regular statistics. Churches provided their total membership, named their members and adherents who were serving and in what capacity. They also gave numbers of the wounded and killed in action. Occasionally churches published letters from soldiers. In some cases, the numbers were as would be expected, but in others, they were alarming. While the church in Forest, Ontario, pastored by H. Elmer Green, sent six members and fifteen adherents—which is a fairly average number—Jarvis Street in Toronto recorded that by June 1917 they had sent 226 of its people to the war, 88 of whom were members and 138 adherents. Of this number, 26 were officers, 31 NCOs, and 169 privates. At the time of their sending in statistics, the church had suffered fifteen casualties, another fifteen wounded, and five prisoners of war. T. T. Shields was proud of his church's contribution: "In our denominational activities the Jarvis Street Church has always been 'at the front,' and now in patriotic endeavour it has sustained its reputation for enlightened leadership."[74] Shields may have spoken more than he knew, as one of the officers from Jarvis Street was Col. George G. Nasmith, one of the first to confirm that the gas used by the Germans at Ypres was chlorine and to suggest the use of masks. Nasmith was awarded the Companion of the Order of St. Michael and St. George by the King.[75]

73. "Baptists and the War," *Canadian Baptist*, 7 June 1917, 7.
74. Ibid.
75. For Nasmith discovering that the gas was chlorine, see Cassar, *Hell in Flanders Fields*, 108–10. For Nasmith on the war, see Nasmith, *On the Fringe*.

British Columbia Baptist Churches were drastically impacted by the war and also by a recession that, in the words of Gordon H. Pousett, resulted in a "crisis of leadership." Many left the province either to serve overseas, or to look for work, leaving the churches without pastors. "Though few pastors had enlisted," says Pousett, "the number serving churches dropped from thirty-six in 1914 to twenty-six in 1916. The smaller churches, and those in the interior, were particularly hit by the loss of leadership, and a number of them had lost twenty-five to thirty percent of their members."[76] In 1916, "the ebb tide began to turn" as wartime shipbuilding had begun in port towns like Vancouver, Victoria, and Prince Rupert. Due to an organized mission effort to get pastors and leaders in churches, the 1918 convention saw the number of pastor-less churches reduced to seven.[77]

In a summer 1917 issue of the *Canadian Baptist*, William Farquharson had an essay titled, "Mission of the Church to the Returning Soldiers," in which he discussed the moral effect of the war on the men and what the churches should do about it.[78] He wrote of the nobility of the toil and sacrifice on the part of the soldiers, what he called "moral elevation." Yet he acknowledged that even among soldiers there was evil: "The profanity of the soldier is proverbial." For example, there were drinking and women; physicians warned of the diseases that the soldier would spread. But the men, said Farquharson, would pass through the struggles, albeit with scars.[79] Their failures were not defeats; rather they were "triumph's evidence for the fullness of days." He reassured readers that many would come back morally and spiritually stronger than before they left. In light of such observations, Farquharson suggested three ways that churches could minister to returning soldiers. First, churches needed to have sympathetic attitudes toward them in light of financial losses accrued during the war. Many soldiers gave up jobs in order to serve, and returned to find those positions filled by others.

---

76. Pousett, "History of the Convention," 100.

77. Ibid., 101.

78. William Farquharson, "Mission of the Church to the Returning Soldiers," *Canadian Baptist*, 14 June 1917, 4.

79. A letter from one McMaster student, Aaron P. Wilson, indicated the temptations the soldiers experienced: "In the midst of such fierce temptations as one meets with here this task is not easy, but it is not impossible." Cited in "McMaster and the War," *Canadian Baptist*, 14 June 1917, 3, col.1. Wilson would return to Canada to pastor Mount Pleasant Road Baptist Church in Toronto; see Haykin and Clary, *O Lord*, 14–17.

Second, churches should not be self-righteous with the soldiers, but instead should recognize their own moral frailty. Third, churches were to remember the presence of God and the power of his grace; they should not forget the power of repentance.

T. F. Matthews, addressing the Peterborough Baptist Association of which he was the moderator, gave similar advice. In his talk he asked two questions: What are churches doing for soldiers at the front and how will they receive them? What will be done to preserve the churches after the war? With regard to the first question, Matthews judged that Canadian Baptist churches were doing splendidly. Their first duty had been to those returning soldiers who were wounded. In regard to them, it had to be remembered that "the trenches are in some features the rivals of the churches" and they "produce a more genuine religion" because they bring forth men's superior attributes. Sociologically the churches had to be prepared for problems, including the higher rate of women to men in Canadian society. As well, there would be more boys than men available to work, and many of the men who could work would be physically unfit for the task. This is not to mention the millions who would need employment but who would have a hard time finding it—they would need to get accustomed to lesser wages.[80] In response to the second question about how to preserve the church, Matthews had "no satisfactory answer." What was certain was that churches would have to respond to the ensuing skepticism, and "all the church's batteries will have to be brought into action to combat so deadly an argument." On a related apologetics front, Matthews foresaw the rise of magic and paganism, and warned the church to be ready for that challenge as well.[81]

While the advice of Farquharson and Matthews may not be too surprising or controversial, there were others who expressed views more reflective of the liberal Protestantism that stressed the universal Fatherhood of God and brotherhood of man that had been common in certain pre-war circles. A well-known Canadian Baptist who expressed theological liberalism was Henry S. Mullowney, who held a bachelor of divinity from McMaster and had been ordained to ministry in 1910. On 2 October 1915, Mullowney received his commission to serve as a chaplain with the Canadian Expeditionary Force and in July, 1917, he began service with the Forestry Corps. After the war he left ministry to pursue

80. T. F. Matthews, "The War and Our Work," *Canadian Baptist*, 21 June 1917, 5.
81. Ibid.

a legal career, and in 1923 ran a losing campaign as a Liberal in Ontario politics. Duff Crerar explains that Mullowney "challenged fellow Baptists to embrace the social gospel before the war" and he stirred up conservatives at home with his criticisms of "Baptist dogmatism, pessimism, and the traditional Baptist view of conversion."[82] He was also critical of denominationalism—what he called ecclesiastical "hot air"—and wrote, "We must put the Empire of Jesus Christ in our minds, our hearts and actions.... It seems to me that the present crisis has prepared the people of Canada for a large programme in Constructive Statesmanship within in the Churches."[83] In late August 1917 Mullowney wrote a letter to the *Canadian Baptist* from Shorncliffe Camp in England, sharing his experiences.[84] In spite of the havoc he had witnessed, Mullowney remained hopeful regarding the post-war condition of the world. He wrote that the war had forced the world into a new epoch, and as a result, "We shall be more brotherly and therefore more divine." The war would make Christians more practical and thus more God-like, so long as they lived by principles and not rules. Of the religious condition of the soldiers, Mullowney said that their new creed is "The Fatherhood of God and the brotherhood of man."[85]

In a vein similar to that of Mullowney was an article written by S. G. Cole of Quebec City. During the war Cole was a ministerial licentiate, and a student at McMaster. While in Quebec he conducted evangelism services with Percy G. Buck for soldiers training in Valcartier.[86] In his article entitled "The Religion of the Returned Soldier," Cole made statements about the status of the soldier's soul that would make conservative evangelicals uneasy and eventually provoke responses. While he served the troops, Cole conducted interviews with those who had been in battle. He claimed that 600 men returned weekly to the port in Quebec, later to head west to their homes throughout Canada. A key observation that he made of these soldiers was that few professed any creed. "What is

---

82. Crerar, *No Man's Land*, 174.

83. Cited in ibid.

84. H. S. Mullowney, "Letter from Chaplain Mullowney," *Canadian Baptist*, 23 August 1917, 4.

85. Ibid.

86. Cf. Percy G. Buck, "Valcartier Camp," *Canadian Baptist*, 13 September 1917, 3. Buck noted that "the only men that have done any extensive work at Valcartier Camp were Baptists."

far better," Cole asked, "they have worked out for themselves their own salvation in the war-racking crucible in Europe." In the entire article, Cole never once mentioned the express need for faith in Christ—a hallmark of conservative Baptist convictions regarding salvation. Rather, the "God of battles, who fights for the right always, has been at work with them and in them." The soldiers did not need to indicate their religious conceptions in biblical language, but due to their noble conduct, they embodied "religious truths of primary significance." Cole argued that the troops revealed their spiritual convictions in their "course of action. Their religion was not theoretical, but intensely practical."[87] As if his language were not controversial enough, Cole went on to liken the battlefield to Golgotha, saying that there was emerging "on the field of the skull in France, a regeneration of men; vital principles of Christ are finding expression in manly conduct that will assist immensely in saving the world from the paucity of her religious practices today."[88]

It did not take long for a response to Cole to be published. Jonathan McIntosh, who had a bachelor of theology from McMaster and pastored in Toronto, wrote the "Returned Soldier's Religion." Cole's piece, according to McIntosh, "is so far from revelation as to necessitate some protest." It differed from Scripture on the doctrine of salvation by the blood of Christ, justification, and the new birth. McIntosh argued that character alone did not make someone a Christian: "If a soldier is not born again, he cannot by any manner or means be classed as a man of God." However, an editorial comment was inserted after McIntosh's piece, stressing that "suffering in a common cause cements souls into a genuine brotherhood. Until we have learned to sympathize, which means to suffer with any one, we have failed to discover the strongest bond that binds our hearts in Christian love."[89]

McIntosh reflected a perspective already expressed in the first year of the war by T. T. Shields. On 12 December 1915, Shields preached "Does 'Killed in Action' Mean 'Gone to Heaven?'" Based on John 3:14–15, the sermon argued that the salvation of a sinner is by the grace of God alone. Due to the universal depravity of all people—including soldiers—the

---

87. R. G. Cole, "The Religion of the Returned Soldier," *Canadian Baptist*, 2 August 1917, 8.

88. Ibid.

89. Jonathan McIntosh, "Returned Soldiers' Religion," *Canadian Baptist*, 16 August 1917, 4.

only means of salvation is the regeneration of the entire person who has put his or her faith in Christ. Shields pointed out, "All our sins are put away by the death of Christ. What can any man add to that infinite price? If the death of Christ does not satisfy the claims of justice, what can?" Because there is no merit in faith, and because salvation is by grace alone, it is impossible for a soldier who does not put his faith in Christ to go to heaven merely due to his service or death in battle, no matter how meritorious these might be. Only Jesus, the one who died victoriously in battle, the battle of Golgotha, is the means whereby one may have victory over sin and share in the hope of heaven. "One thing is clear—only the sacrifice of Christ can save."[90] In light of the clarity of these words, it is curious that Shields would later invite the famous author Ralph Connor—the pen name of Charles William Gordon (1860–1937), a Presbyterian minister from Winnipeg—to preach at Jarvis Street. On 25 November 1917, Connor preached a sermon whose theme was the salvation of the soldier through armed sacrifice. At one point in the sermon Connor expressed confidence that a soldier who died fighting for his country would be saved. When he was finished, Shields stood up before the congregation and disavowed everything Connor said, and quickly called for an evangelistic hymn about salvation through Christ's blood atonement to be sung![91] The words of Mullowney, Cole, and Connor on the one hand, and McIntosh and Shields on the other, were a pre-cursor of the coming battle between theological liberals and conservatives that would eventually tear the Baptist denomination in Canada apart.

A POEM—A CODA

This chapter began with mention of a brass memorial to forty-one Toronto Baptists who died in the Great War. It concludes with a poem. The First World War gave rise to some of the most remarkable poets of the twentieth century, men like Rupert Brooke, Wilfred Owen, Edward Thomas, and Siegfried Sassoon.[92] Some consider that the Canadian Baptist, Bernard Trotter, referred to above, wrote well enough to be

---

90. Shields, "Sermon #1180." This sermon was preached again on 24 September 1916.

91. Tarr, *Shields of Canada*, 61, cited in Parent, "Shields and the First World War," 52.

92. For an analysis of Canadian war poetry from a previous conflict, see Heath, "Passion for Empire."

ranked among these soldier poets.⁹³ A good source for Canadian Baptist poetry written during the war years is the *Canadian Baptist*; it regularly published poems that helped express the emotions its readers on the home front were experiencing. A lot of it is mawkish stuff, but now and then, there is a poem that is reasonably good. Such is a poem written by Ernest Garside Black, who fought at the Somme in 1916, and whose poem appeared in the 22 February 1917 issue of the *Canadian Baptist*. It was entitled "The Soldier's Prayer (written as the trenches were approached)" and provides a helpful summary of the themes examined in this chapter.⁹⁴

Right from the opening address, "O God of Battles," the poem assumes the justification of war. Few Canadian Baptists at the time seem to have doubted the righteousness and nobility of their cause. Then, in the line, "I do not ask to put the cup away," there is an implicit comparison of the experience of what the soldier was facing to what Christ had faced in Gethsemane, which gave meaning to his sufferings. Black emphasizes the role of duty to the Empire in his use of the expressions "to serve and do my part" and "play the man." Interestingly enough the latter was used by James Moffatt to translate the Greek term *andrizesthe* from 1 Corinthians 16:13 in his translation of the New Testament that first appeared in 1913. And finally, the cost of war is evident in the body's fear, wounds, and the real possibility of death. While mere words will never capture the anguish felt by those who served and those who suffered the loss and maiming of loved ones, this chapter, like this poem, has sought to capture something of the Canadian Baptist experience of the Great War.

---

93. See the selection of his poetry in Busby, *Flanders Fields*, 111–19. On the jacket of the second edition of his poems, *A Canadian Twilight*, he was described as the "Canadian Rupert Brooke."

94. For his personal account as a gunner in the war, see Black, *One Volunteer*. *Canadian Baptist*, 22 February 1917, 2.

BIBLIOGRAPHY

Primary Sources

ARCHIVES
PTTS – Jarvis Street Baptist Church Archives, Toronto, Ontario. Papers of T. T. Shields.

NEWSPAPERS
Canadian Baptist
Maritime Baptist
Western Baptist
Western Reporter

OTHER

Fuller, Andrew. "Christian Patriotism." In *The Complete Works of the Rev. Andrew Fuller*, edited by Joseph Belcher, 1:202–9. 1845. 3 vols. Reprint, Harrisonburg, Virginia: Sprinkle Publications, 1988.

Nasmith, George G. *Canada's Sons and Great Britain in the World War*. Toronto: John C. Winston, 1919.

———. *On the Fringe of the Great Fight*. Toronto: McClelland, Goodchild & Stewart, 1917.

Shields, T. T. "England in War Time." *The Canadian Magazine of Politics, Science, Art and Literature* 52 (November 1918–April 1919) 546–52.

———. "Sermon #1101: The War and Its Compensations." PTTS; twenty-one page unpublished ms., preached 13 September 1914.

———. "Sermon #1147: Sinking of Lusitania." PTTS; nine-page unpublished ms., preached 9 May 1915.

———. "Sermon #1180: Does 'Killed in Action' Mean 'Gone to Heaven?'" PTTS; seventeen-page unpublished ms., preached 12 December 1915.

———. "Sermon #1246: President Wilson's Impertinence." PTTS; eighteen-page unpublished ms., preached 24 December 1916.

———. "Sermon #1280: Should We Have Conscription?" PTTS; nine-page unpublished ms., preached 10 June 1917.

———. "Shields 1917 Letters." Jarvis Street Baptist Church Archives, Toronto, Ontario; thirty-five page ms., 1917.

———. "The Lord Is a Man of War." PTTS; twenty-two page unpublished ms, preached 5 September 1914.

Spurgeon, Charles. "Joy Born at Bethlehem." In *The Metropolitan Tabernacle Pulpit*. 17:697–708. 63 vols. London: Passmore & Alabaster, 1872.

Statistics Canada. "Number of Casualties in the First World War, 1914 to 1918, and the Second World War, 1939 to 1945." No pages. Online: http://www65.statcan.gc.ca/acyb02/1947/acyb02_19471126002-eng.htm.

Trotter, Bernard. "A Kiss." In *A Canadian Twilight and Other Poems of War and of Peace*, edited by Bernard Trotter, 36–37. 2nd ed. Toronto: McClelland, Goodchild, & Stewart, 1917.

Secondary Sources

Adams, Doug. "The Call to Arms: Reverend Thomas Todhunter Shields, World War One and the Shaping of a Militant Fundamentalist." In *Baptists and War*, edited by Gordon L. Heath and Michael A .G. Haykin, forthcoming.

Bebbington, David. "Gladstone and the Baptists." *The Baptist Quarterly* 26 (1975–1976) 224–39.

Black, Ernest Garside. *I Want One Volunteer*. Toronto: Ryerson Press, 1965.

Boghardt, Thomas. *The Zimmermann Telegram: Intelligence, Diplomacy, and America's Entry into World War I*. Annapolis, MD: Naval Institute Press, 2012.

Brackney, William H. *The Baptists*. Westport, CT: Praeger, 1994.

Busby, Brian, ed. *In Flanders Fields and Other Poems of the First World War*. London: Arcturus, 2008.

Cassar, George H. *Hell in Flanders Fields: Canadians at the Second Battle of Ypres*. Toronto: Dundurn, 2010.

Clarke, Brian. "English-Speaking Canada from 1854." In *A Concise History of Christianity in Canada*, edited by Terence Murphy and Roberto Perin, 261–369. Toronto: Oxford University Press, 1996.

Clements, Keith W. "Baptists and the Outbreak of the First World War." *The Baptist Quarterly* 26 (1975–1976) 74–92.

Cook, Tim. *At the Sharp End: Canadians Fighting the Great War 1914-1916*. Toronto: Penguin, 2007.

Crerar, Duff. *Padres in No Man's Land: Canadian Chaplains and the Great War*. Montreal and Kingston: McGill-Queen's University Press, 1995.

Cross, Anthony R. "Baptists on Peace and War: The Seventeenth-Century British Foundations." In *Baptists and War*, edited by Gordon L. Heath and Michael A. G. Haykin, forthcoming.

Ferland, Raphael Dallaire. "Patriotism and Allegiances of the 22nd (French Canadian) Battalion, 1914–1918." *Canadian Military Journal* 13 (2012) 51–60.

Fussell, Paul. *The Great War and Modern Memory*. 25th Anniversary Edition. Oxford: Oxford University Press, 2000.

Haykin, Michael A. G., and Ian Hugh Clary. *"O Lord, Thy Word is Settled in Heaven": A Celebration of the History of Mount Pleasant Road Baptist Church, 1920-2013*. Toronto: Mount Pleasant Road Baptist Church, 2013.

Heath, Gordon L. "The Nile Expedition: New Imperialism and Canadian Baptists, 1884–1885." *Baptist Quarterly* 44 (2011) 171–86.

———. "Passion for Empire: War Poetry Published in the Canadian English Protestant Press during the South African War, 1899–1902." *Literature and Theology* 16 (2002) 127–47.

———. "'Prepared to do, prepared to die': Evangelicals, Imperialism, and Late-Victorian Canadian Children's Publications." *Perichoresis* 9 (2011) 3–27.

———. "The Protestant Denominational Press and the Conscription Crisis in Canada, 1917–1918." *Historical Studies* 78 (2012) 27–46.

———. "Traitor, Half-Breeds, Savages, and Heroes: Canadian Baptist Newspapers and Constructions of Riel and the Events of 1885." In *Baptists and Public Life in Canada*, edited by Gordon L. Heath and Paul Wilson, 198–217. Eugene, OR: Pickwick, 2012.

———. *A War with a Silver Lining: Canadian Protestant Churches and the South African War, 1899–1902*. Montreal: McGill-Queen's University Press, 2009.

———. "When Missionaries Were Hated: An Examination of the Canadian Baptist Defense of Imperialism and Missions during the Boxer Rebellion, 1900." In *Baptists and Mission*, edited by Ian M. Randall and Anthony R. Cross, 261–76. Milton Keynes: Paternoster, 2007.

Johnston, Charles M. *McMaster University.* Vol.1, *The Toronto Years.* Toronto: University of Toronto Press, 1976.

Lloyd, Peter A. *The French Are Coming: The Invasion Scare of 1803–5.* Tunbridge Wells: Spellmount, 1991.

Parent, Mark. "T. T. Shields and the First World War." *McMaster Journal of Theology* 2 (1991) 42–57.

Pousett, Gordon Harold. "A History of the Convention Baptist Churches of British Columbia." MTh thesis, Vancouver School of Theology, 1982.

Priestly, David T. "The Effect of Baptist 'Home Mission' among Alberta's German Immigrants." In *Memory and Hope: Strands of Canadian Baptist History*, edited by David T. Priestly, 55–68. Waterloo, ON: Canadian Corporation for Studies in Religion, 1996.

Rawlyk, George A. "Christian Education and McMaster University." In *Reckoning with the Past: Historical Essays on American Evangelicalism from the Institute for the Study of American Evangelicals*, edited by D. G. Hart, 322–53. Grand Rapids: Baker, 1995.

Shaw, Amy J. *Crisis of Conscience: Conscientious Objection in Canada during the First World War.* Vancouver: University of British Columbia Press, 2008.

Stackhouse, John. *Canadian Evangelicalism in the Twentieth Century: An Introduction to Its Character.* Toronto: University of Toronto Press, 1993.

Tarr, Leslie K. *Shields of Canada: T. T. Shields, 1873–1955.* Grand Rapids: Baker, 1967.

8

Canadian Lutherans and the First World War

Norm Threinen

IN MANY RESPECTS, IT is difficult to talk about a Lutheran Church in Canada in 1914. Like other Christian churches, the Lutheran Church was largely an immigrant church; however, more than many other churches, it was not a homogeneous body when the First World War began. Because they or their ancestors had come from various countries where Lutheran state churches predominated, most Lutherans in Canada were a part of ethnic churches that were self-consciously German, Icelandic, Norwegian, Swedish, Finnish, or Danish. The use of European languages in worship and community life tended to attracted immigrants to Canada who were at home in these languages and who chose to associate with people of like interests in the new land.

To be sure, there were pockets of Lutherans in Canada where English had replaced the original European languages, especially in the areas that had developed earlier: Nova Scotia, the Loyalist townships on the St. Lawrence River, and Toronto. In a number of other urban communities in southern Ontario, a shift into English had also taken place to accommodate the younger generation for whom the European languages of their parents were becoming more and more foreign. However, the general picture of Lutheranism in Canada in 1914 was that of a multilingual church divided along ethnic lines, whose members were often very European in their attitudes and loyalties.

Most of these ethnic churches were further divided in 1914 on the basis of theological orientation. Some of these divisions went back to the immigrants' European country of origin, but most of them can be traced to the experiences of the Lutheran churches in the United States from which missionaries had come to organize the church in Canada. Such missionary activity had resulted in the Lutheran Church in Canada being, in almost all cases, an extension of Lutheranism south of the border. As such, the Lutheran Church in Canada tended to look for financial support and theological leadership to the larger and more developed Lutheran churches in the United States, and the church structures in Canada were all synods, districts, or conferences of the American church bodies that produced them.[1] Most of the pastors who served the Lutherans in Canada had also been trained in the United States, and this further solidified the American connection of Canadian Lutheranism.

Since they were integral parts of the American churches in 1914, it may be surprising to many that, while the earliest Lutherans in Canada had German roots, they were actually pro-British. Some had originated in German Lutheran *diaspora* congregations in England. Others had been indentured troops that German princes had provided to the British to fight in the Revolutionary War against the break-away American colonies.[2] Still others were United Empire Loyalists who wanted to remain loyal to the British King. Subsequently, ethnic Lutherans came to Canada as part of the American moving frontier, which helped populate first Ontario, and then western Canada. Some also came from the Lutheran countries of Europe.

By 1914, most Lutherans in Ontario had lived in Canada for several generations. Even those with more recent roots in Western Europe had often lived in Canada for a long time. While they tenaciously clung to the language and culture of their ancestors, they generally had little relationship to, or sympathy with, the German imperialism of Kaiser Wilhelm II. In western Canada, where immigration occurred later, the picture of the Lutherans was even more complex. Many Lutherans were Scandinavians who had been members of ethnic Lutheran churches in the mid-west United States. Others were Germans who had been artisans and farmers in the eastern provinces of the Austro-Hungarian Empire or

---

1. The terms for the regional organization of the general bodies varied with the different Lutheran bodies. See Threinen, *Mosaic*, 88–99.

2. Wilhelmy, *Mercenaries*, 55–56, 74.

in Russia for generations; there they had constituted "Germanic islands in a Slavic sea"[3] and since 1867 had been under a Polish administration.[4]

No matter where in Canada they lived or at what point in time they had come to Canada, Germans before the Great War had generally been "exempted from the hostile nativism directed at non-English-speaking immigrants."[5] They were generally known to be thrifty, intelligent, and industrious—characteristics that their English-speaking neighbors recognized as important for the prosperity of the country.[6] Not all Germans were Lutherans, but most were, and a good number of them had been gathered into Lutheran churches by German-speaking missionary-pastors. Although they continued to appreciate their German heritage, by 1914 most of them regarded themselves as Canadians.[7] In Ontario, they participated actively in the public life of the country, in some cases even holding elected political positions.[8] On the controversial conscription issue in 1917, for example, the two political leaders from Waterloo who teed off against each other were both Lutheran. Member of Parliament W. G. Weigel sided with Prime Minister Borden's Union government, which supported conscription. Berlin Mayor William D. Euler ran as an independent and was endorsed by Sir Wilfrid Laurier, who opposed conscription. The Union party won the election, but Euler was successful in unseating his fellow Lutheran.[9] Euler then served for the next twenty-three years until he was elevated to the Senate in 1940.

In western Canada, where the immigrants were more recent arrivals, the participation of German Lutherans in the politics and public life of their new homeland was much less obvious; most of them were too busy getting established, building churches, and attempting to develop a healthy congregational life. Having left behind areas of potential conflict in the Old World, they were by-and-large simply grateful to be

3. Cobb, "Prairie Provinces," 194.
4. Ibid., 188.
5. Thompson, *Harvests*, 74.
6. Comments of Lord Dufferin in 1874, quoted by Heick, "Waterloo County," 23.
7. This was particularly true of German Lutherans who tended to emphasize obedience to legally constituted authority in contrast to Germans with an Anabaptist heritage who were more tentative in their relation to the state.
8. William D. Euler was the Mayor of Berlin (later named Kitchener) and W. G. Weigel was the Member of Parliament for North Waterloo in 1914.
9. Heick, "Waterloo County," 23.

living in peace as subjects of the British crown. Although not yet actively involved in the politics of their new homeland, they exercised their responsibilities as good citizens by paying their taxes, exercising the vote, obeying the laws, and praying for the authorities in their recently adopted country. Their identification with, and love for, the British crown is evidenced by the fact that some parents named their children after the ruling British monarch of the day,[10] and that a number of rural congregations gratefully accepted as a gift from the Queen forty acres of land in their communities for a church, parsonage, and cemetery.[11]

In May 1914, the Governor General of Canada was still praising Germans for their "thoroughness," "tenacity," and "loyalty."[12] Even when war began, Canadian leaders were not prepared to give up these preconceptions of Germans; Prime Minister Borden stated publicly that Canada had "absolutely no quarrel with the German people."[13] However, as the war progressed, there was a complete reversal of how the government viewed Germans, and the general population in Canada also began to look with suspicion upon Germans on account of their German heritage. Some Germans changed their names to hide their German identity for business reasons; census reports of 1911 and 1921, which indicate place of birth, show that many Germans informally became Swedes, Norwegians, or Dutch.[14] For those who openly identified with a German Lutheran congregation rather than simply being "census" Lutherans, it was not as easy.

The drastic change in attitude toward the Germans when war was proclaimed resulted, at least to an extent, from actions taken by the Canadian government. "Both the German and Austrian Empires had traditionally conscripted able-bodied young men for military training followed by long-term reserve service," and when war was declared, the German and Austrian authorities called upon these reservists "to honour commitments many had long since abandoned."[15] For those who

---

10. My father, for example, was named "Edward" since Edward VII was on the British throne when he was born in 1906. When his brother was born in 1908, he was named "George" after George V who was then on the throne.

11. Threinen, *Seventy-five Years*, 9.

12. Quoted by Heick, "Waterloo County," 23.

13. Quoted by Thompson, *Harvests*, 75.

14. Ibid., 77.

15. Boudreau, "Interning," 16.

were willing to return to Europe, these authorities made arrangements for them to travel to the United States as a first step toward their return; however, many of the reservists had been naturalized in Canada and had no desire to return. Concerned that immigrants from Germany or Austria could turn out to be the enemy within the borders of Canada, the Canadian government declared them to be "enemy aliens." As enemy aliens under the terms of the War Measures Act, all natives of the Austro-Hungarian Empire and Germany in Canada were required to carry identification with them at all times. To enforce this, and to identify potential enemy agents, the Mounted Police made routine checks of Germans and Austrians.[16] They were also forbidden to possess firearms, leave the country without permission, or publish or read anything in a language other than English or French. Internment camps were set up in various places across the country, and among those interned were members of the Lutheran Church.[17] The government passed orders in council protecting the rights of enemy aliens "so long as they quietly pursued their ordinary avocations."[18] However, by depicting them as "enemy aliens" they raised questions among the general population about the loyalty of all Germans and, by extension, of all Lutherans.

Germans in Canada were distressed by "the suddenness with which the tenor of the times changed," especially because of "the utter lack of reason behind it."[19] One Lutheran historian of German ancestry blamed this change in attitude on "the chauvinistic English-Canadian element of society which, in its fervor to defeat the Kaiser and his Prussian militarism across the Atlantic, turned on anything which smacked of being German at home."[20] Another less judgmental explanation was that "Canadians with limited knowledge of European history or geography tended to brand any central or eastern European as an 'enemy alien.'"[21]

The anti-German sentiment was particularly strong in areas where there was a high concentration of Germans, such as Berlin, Ontario (renamed Kitchener later in the war). The Mennonites, who constituted

16. Jelly, *Mounted Police*, 146.
17. Conversation, 13 November 2011, with Dr. Ralph Mayan who grew up in the Lutheran Church in Vernon.
18. Wilson, *Ontario*, xx.
19. Heick, "Waterloo County," 24.
20. Ibid., 24.
21. Boudreau, *Interning*, 17.

a large proportion of the population in the area, were conscientious objectors and declined to participate in the war effort at all. German Lutherans volunteered for war service but they generally lacked the great enthusiasm of the British, and they responded to the war effort more out of a sense of duty than patriotism. The combination of these two large people-groups, both of whom spoke German, provided a special challenge for recruitment into the armed forces, further fueling anti-German sentiment.[22]

The sentiment against the Germans took on tangible form less than a month after the war began. On 22 August 1914, someone threw the bust of Kaiser Wilhelm I, which had been erected in Berlin's Victoria Park, into a nearby lake. Individuals who occupied leadership positions in the German community were soon personally attacked. Lutheran pastors were particularly vulnerable to accusations of siding with the enemy since many of them had personal contacts in Germany. A pastor serving a German Lutheran congregation in Pembroke had chosen June 1914 to make a four month visit to Germany and was prevented by the outbreak of the war from returning.[23] A German-born Lutheran pastor, H. A. Sperling, was accused of accepting money from individuals to send to Germany and some extremists tried to have him interned.[24]

C. R. Tappert, another Lutheran pastor, was accused of using the public prayers in a Sunday worship service to pray for the success of the German army. In trying to defend himself, Tappert only made matters worse when he wrote a letter to the editor of the Berlin newspaper in which he said, "I am not ashamed to confess that I still love the land of my fathers—Germany." In reaction to this statement, a gang of soldiers got him out of bed one night, roughed him up, and paraded him through the streets of Berlin with a black eye and a cut on the back of his head.[25] The public pressure against him forced him to resign his parish.

Other Lutheran pastors besides Sperling and Tappert also experienced this anti-German sentiment because they conducted their ministry in German. Prominent among them were the pastors who had received their seminary training in Kropp, Germany, in the years before the war. When the military buildup began in Germany, the army

22. Wilson, *Ontario*, lxxiv.
23. Eyland, *Lutherans*, 117.
24. Heick, "Waterloo County," 25.
25. Wilson, *Ontario*, lxxiii.

had compelled them to do military service prior to coming to Canada.²⁶ They had then been specifically brought to Canada to minister in the German language, and most had not mastered the English language sufficiently to preach comfortably in English.²⁷

Among other things that helped inflame the situation in Canada were anti-British comments such as those made by Theodore Schmauk, the German-American president of the General Council to which many Lutheran congregations in southern Ontario belonged. In 1914, he wrote, "This war is the result of the British plan of destroying Germany's foreign commerce and relations, and of doing away . . . with a rival."²⁸ The publication of such views by American Lutheran churchmen in support of the German cause made the lot of Canadian Lutherans even more difficult. Three years later, when the United States entered the war on the side of Great Britain, the support of American churchmen for the German cause ceased, but by then the anti-German sentiment in Canada had taken on a life of its own.

The anti-German sentiment among the general population in Canada increased significantly after May 1915 when the British Ocean liner *RMS Lusitania* was attacked by a German U-boat off the coast of Ireland and sunk by a German torpedo. Even newspapers that had taken a moderate stance in regard to the Germans because they felt that "the British estimate of Germany must be heavily biased" began to take a harder line and say that "Germany has proved herself an outlaw."²⁹ Many Canadians lost their lives in this early casualty of the war and allegations abounded that pro-German organizations in Canada, such as German-language Lutheran churches, had celebrated the sinking of this ship. As a result of such allegations from the general public, some Lutheran churches felt constrained to close their doors.³⁰ As one observer commented in 1916, "The Canadian government keeps a watchful eye on German [Lutheran] pastors and congregations who must be careful not to reflect a pro-German or anti-British stance. The populace and the press are openly anti-German."³¹

26. Kraemer, "Mission," 290.
27. Heick, "Waterloo County," 29.
28. Quoted in Gritsch, *Lutheranism*, 213.
29. Quoted in Thompson, *Harvests*, 76.
30. Threinen, *Mosaic*, 106.
31. *Siloah*, June 1916.

The anti-German sentiment was also fanned by comments in Canada of a small but vocal minority among the recent arrivals who openly or covertly expressed sympathy with the enemy countries, the land of their birth or ancestry. Two German newspapers on the Canadian prairies, which were not official church papers but were published by Lutherans,[32] took strong pro-German stances at the beginning of the war.[33] Since only newspapers published outside Canada had been prohibited, they were subject only to the censorship imposed on the entire press. However, loss of advertising revenue forced both of them to suspend operations in 1915.[34]

In rural communities on the prairies where German Lutherans constituted virtually the entire population, there was little anti-German sentiment and Lutherans had no difficulty in maintaining an active worship life in a German context; in fact, many people moved from the cities, where the anti-German sentiment had caused them to lose their jobs, to rural communities where they could take out homesteads.[35] As homesteaders, the farmers provided most of the labor required and their sons did not usually enlist in the army, nor were they normally conscripted for military service.[36] The conservatism of the German immigrant farmers in crop selection resulted in comparatively greater prosperity than that of their English neighbors. This in turn led to additional hostility against the Germans among English-Canadians during 1917 and 1918, as well as demands for conscription of enemy aliens for farm labor at remuneration equal to the men in the armed forces.[37] Lutherans of Scandinavian origin did not suffer discrimination to the same degree as did the Germans, but many patriotic Canadians also regarded them as guilty by association because of the German origins of Lutheranism.

Lutheran pastors and influential lay leaders tried to provide a balance by speaking out publically on behalf of the Germans in Canada. Mayor William D. Euler wrote to the Berlin newspaper: "With few ex-

---

32. Paul Bredt had founded the *Saskatchewan Courier* in 1907 and Gustav Koermann founded the *Alberta Herald* in 1903. Both were prominent laymen in the Lutheran Church.

33. Archer, *Saskatchewan*, 169; MacGregor, *Alberta*, 231.

34. Thompson, *Harvests*, 79.

35. Threinen, *They Called Him Red*, 11.

36. Thompson, *Harvests*, 85–86.

37. Ibid., 86–87.

ceptions, the German population are British in their sympathies during the present war, and have appreciated the freedom and liberty they enjoy under the British flag."[38] Member of Parliament W. G. Weichel addressed the Canadian House of Commons early in 1915 and pointed out that German-Canadians were not supporters of the Prussian militarism of Germany against which war was being waged. They did appreciate the contributions of Germany and were justifiably proud of them—the advances in science, art, music, literature, philosophy, and chemistry; the literary works of Schiller and Goethe; and the compositions of Mendelssohn, Mozart, Hayden, Bach, Liszt, and Wagner.[39] The Lutheran churches also affirmed their loyalty in a corporate way. In June 1915, the Central Canada Synod passed a resolution that said, "We commend the hearty loyalty of our people to our beloved British Empire in the present war crisis. Our loyalty as Lutherans to the flag of the country whose protection we enjoy is historic."[40]

Although German Lutherans did not share the patriotic fervor of their English compatriots, they quickly became involved in various ways on the home front as the war continued. Under the leadership of Lutheran political leaders such as W. G. Weichel and George Clare, they responded to the call to support the war through financial contributions to various patriotic and relief fund drives. A Toronto magazine complimented these efforts by saying, "It is a unique tribute to British institutions that the town [of Waterloo, Ontario], which has made the most generous showing [in the Patriotic Fund drive] yet recorded in Canada should be the most characteristically German municipality in Canada."[41] As the gravity of the war situation grew, German Lutherans were also among the volunteers in the army. Eighty percent of the soldiers in the 118th Battalion from Waterloo County that went overseas in January 1917 were of German descent, most of them Lutherans.

In western Canada, the long-established Icelanders, many of whom were Lutherans, accepted the war with enthusiasm. Over one thousand enlisted in the Canadian Expeditionary Force. One observer commented that "they were very loyal to our cause during the war and made

---

38. Quoted by Heick, "Waterloo County," 24.
39. Canada House of Commons, *Official Report of Debates* (1915), 8–9.
40. Quoted by Heick, "Waterloo County," 26.
41. Quoted in ibid., 30.

great sacrifices."⁴² In the more recently established Scandinavian communities, members of the Lutheran churches were initially skeptical of the need for the British Empire to be at war and favored a peace policy; however, as the war continued, many of them also showed their loyalty by enlisting in military service. As a result, a Scandinavian battalion was formed.⁴³ In Saskatchewan, where many Scandinavian Lutherans had settled, one historian noted there was "an evident spirit of sacrifice—an urge to fight for democracy" particularly among the Scandinavian element.⁴⁴ Thus, the Canada Conference of the Swedish Augustana Synod heard a report in 1917 that "a large number of Augustana Lutheran men were at the front in Europe and many perished on the battlefield."⁴⁵

In spite of these acts of loyalty on the part of German and other Lutherans, there continued to be elements among the non-Germanic part of the population who constantly watched for any use of the German language and who picked up rumors of unpatriotic leanings. Homes were marked and people were molested if there were doubts about their political leanings. Troops checked houses that were reported to have pictures of the German Emperor hanging on the wall.⁴⁶ Although the unfair accusations that others brought against them were undoubtedly resented, there is no record of strong German Lutheran reaction. Instead, prominent churchmen continued to emphasize the loyalty of German-Canadians who were Lutheran. Thus, a Canadian-born Lutheran pastor, Nils Willison, told soldiers in Toronto in June 1916 that the Lutheran Church had always stood for liberty, the cause for which the Allies were fighting.⁴⁷

The Great War Veterans Association, which was established in 1917 to promote the rights of returning armed forces personnel, lobbied strongly against all things German in Canada. It called for the suppression of "enemy alien" newspapers, compulsory badges for foreigners, and forced labor for Austrian and German men in Canada. This affected German Lutherans in particular since many of them had been

42. Quoted by Thompson, *Harvests*, 82.
43. Palmer, *Alberta*, 169.
44. Archer, *Saskatchewan*, 167.
45. Baglo, *Augustana Lutherans*, 40.
46. Heick, "Waterloo County," 26.
47. Ibid., 27. See also Nils Willison, "The Lutheran Church and the War," *Canadian Lutheran*, June 1916, 14.

accustomed to reading the German magazines published by their parent church bodies in the United States, as well as organs of their regional body in Canada. Partly as a result of such pressure, the Canadian government proclaimed through the War Time Elections Act passed on 20 September 1917 that all Germans in Canada who had been naturalized after 31 March 1902 were "enemy aliens" and stripped them of their right to vote. This was followed up with an order-in-council on 2 October 1918 in which the government prohibited publication of any newspaper in German.[48] Included were German church papers published by the Lutheran bodies in the United States.

To counter the increased hatred against the Germans that the war was promoting, Lutheran pastors responded to the attacks being made in the public press. In April 1918, John Herzer of Calgary responded to a scathing attack by a representative of the Great War Veterans Association in the *Canadian* saying, "When you lay a blanket charge against Lutheran preachers, presumably because they use the German language as a medium . . . it is an unjust charge and tends to stimulate persecution against a church which . . . is loyal to the State against anarchy, rebellion, and sedition." In response to the criticism that the residents of Riverdale (Calgary) had lived in Canada and the United States long enough to become familiar with the English language, Herzer responded that "two-thirds of them could not derive benefit from a service held in English."[49]

Lutheran pastors resisted the government's efforts to use their worship services and to influence the content of their sermons in order to promote the war effort directly. As the war continued, however, editors of church papers began to advise that "theologically . . . Lutherans were free to make any adjustment, put up with any inconvenience, yield to any of the needs of government and society so long as the Word of God or the free preaching of the Law and the Gospel and the administration of the sacraments were not violated."[50] This also opened the way for the Lutheran bodies to affirm their loyalty to their country very explicitly by passing "Loyalty Resolutions" at their conventions. One such resolution in 1918 in Ontario stated:

---

48. Kalbfleisch, *German-Language Press*, 144–45.
49. Quoted by Threinen, *Like a Leaven*, 11.
50. Nelson, *Lutherans*, 399–400.

> We solemnly reaffirm our loyalty to our Government in this present crisis of the empire and pledge our energetic and unswerving support to the limit of our capacity and ability; and we encourage our membership to render full and loyal service in those tasks which the Government has asked of them, and may still ask of them, as citizens and organizations of citizens, for the successful prosecution of the war, ever mindful of the divine injunction to "render unto Caesar the things that are Caesar's" and finally, we pray Almighty God to give counsel to all such as are in authority, to grant . . . success to our forces, and to those of our Allies, on land and sea.[51]

When hostilities came to an end in November 1918, Lutheran churches continued to feel the effects of anti-German propaganda as returning veterans bitterly complained that "enemy aliens" had taken their jobs. The *Vernon News* of 6 February 1919 reported that the Great War veterans were urging "the deportation of undesirable aliens, the examination into the loyalty of those suspected of enemy sympathies, and the curtailment of certain rights of such as may be permitted to remain in the country."[52] A week later the same newspaper wrote that the Vancouver City Council had unanimously passed a resolution calling for the expulsion of all enemy aliens from Canada. "Returned soldiers will not tolerate members of the nationalities against whom they have been fighting so bitterly to occupy civilian jobs which should be theirs by right," wrote the *News*.[53] Such sentiments prompted Lutheran clergy such as Alfred Rehwinkel, a German-American pastor in Edmonton, to launch a vigorous campaign for fair and equitable treatment of all citizens. To accomplish this, he helped organize the German-Canadian Association and conducted mass meetings in different locations to discuss the problem. He urged Germans to become more involved in politics and public office.[54] He met with government officials to secure their cooperation. He contributed articles to the German press and carried out extensive correspondence with people throughout western Canada. He even translated "O Canada" into German for use in public meetings.[55]

---

51. Quoted by Threinen, *Like a Mustard Seed*, 67.
52. *Vernon News*, 6 February 1919.
53. Quoted in the *Vernon News*, undated clipping in the Vernon City Archives.
54. Grams, "Rehwinkel," 22.
55. Threinen, *Built on the Rock*, 17.

The anti-German sentiments and the measures enacted by the government during the war had significant adverse effects on the German Lutheran churches. In his 1915 presidential address to the Canada District of the Missouri Synod, William C. Boese reported, "In some localities our work is pretty well in ruins because of the war and because we are Germans."[56] A missionary-pastor in Ontario reported, "In the wake of the war, we are losing ground everywhere."[57] Even congregations that had been started with English as their language of worship were adversely affected because they were Lutheran. Thus, only three years after First English Lutheran Church in Calgary began services as an English mission in 1913, the pastor had to relocate to another congregation.

In western Canada, the government's war-time restrictions on immigration from Germany or the Austro-Hungarian Empire deprived Lutheran congregations of growth that might have occurred through the arrival of new immigrants; in the decade before the war, the extent of such growth through immigration is indicated by the fact that the German Lutherans in western Canada affiliated with the three German Lutheran bodies had tripled.[58] The normal pattern of activities in city congregations was also disrupted by members having to accept lower-paying jobs or lose their jobs entirely.[59] The war also ended large-scale American immigration to the Canadian West as many Americans showed reluctance to leave their peaceful home for a country they felt was in the midst of a war.[60] Since this pre-war immigration had brought many Scandinavian Lutherans into western Canada in the previous two decades, this end to the flow of immigrants also stunted the growth of Lutheran congregations that used a Scandinavian language in their worship life.

Another indirect adverse effect of the war on the German Lutheran churches in western Canada was the closing of all of the Lutheran parochial schools. For the German Lutherans from the Austro-Hungarian Empire and from Russia, who had been a minority among the Slavic population of their earlier adoptive homelands for more than a century, their "church community and place community was generally

56. Quoted by Threinen, *Like a Mustard Seed*, 67.
57. Quoted in ibid., 67.
58. Cobb, "Prairie Provinces," 328.
59. Threinen, *Like a Leaven*, 42.
60. Thompson, *Harvests*, 85.

conterminous."[61] In that situation, the church school was essential to the health of the community inasmuch as it was the means by which the Lutheran faith as well as the German culture and language had been perpetuated. It had enabled the minority German Lutheran population to survive and avoid assimilation by the huge Slavic majority in Eastern Europe and Russia. A prime motivation for the immigration of Lutherans from these areas to Canada in the early years had, in fact, been the serious difficulties that these schools were experiencing. When these German immigrants came to Canada, they sought to duplicate the experience that had been so successful in Eastern Europe; they opened schools wherever they could as part of their community. These church schools were intended to fulfill the same function as they had in Eastern Europe and Russia; as they perpetuated German culture and language and prevented assimilation into the Slavic culture of Eastern Europe, so the immigrants hoped they would prevent assimilation into the English culture in Canada.

Assimilation of the immigrants into the English culture, however, was precisely what the governments in Canada felt essential for the good of the country. Proponents of assimilation recognized that the immigrant generation would only adapt superficially; their only hope of having the immigrants ultimately adapt was in the education of the second generation. Thus, German church schools were closed and new school legislation was introduced in the various Prairie Provinces around 1916 that required attendance in public schools. Only in Stony Plain, Alberta, where a German-Lutheran pastor was available who had become certified as a provincially trained teacher and where political pressure could be exerted on a newly-elected provincial government, was it possible to reopen a church school that had been closed during the war, years after hostilities had ceased.[62]

The ostensible reason for compulsory attendance at public schools was so that all students might learn the skills needed to take their place in Canadian society. But compulsory attendance was also used to inculcate patriotic sentiments and foster Canadian nationalism. Thus, the public school was a natural outgrowth of public opinion engendered by the war. The requirement that all children attend the English public school hastened the transition of the German immigrant population to

61. Cobb, "Prairie Provinces," 173.
62. Threinen, *Like a Leaven*, 53.

functioning more and more in English, not only in public but also in the home and church. Even a Lutheran church body that stated that German was its official language in 1911 permitted both German and English to be used in their conventions and eventually used English exclusively.[63]

It could be argued that the change in the educational systems of the Prairie Provinces occurred during the war, not because of it. However, the comments made by Lutheran clergy who lived at the time showed that they accepted the closure of the church schools as one of the conditions of wartime. Aside from the legal requirement of compulsory attendance at a public school, in almost all cases the Lutheran church schools, which were still in the frontier stage of development, could not compete with the government-funded public schools. Thus, the churches had to resort to teaching the German language and culture that were previously taught in the church schools as a once-a-week add-on activity on Saturdays and in an annual two-week summer school.

The closure of church schools during the Great War was a severe blow to German Lutheran communities in terms of their identity; however, the impact was not entirely negative. The small size of most German Lutheran communities usually meant that these schools were conducted by the pastor who often had to be absent on account of other duties. The school buildings and equipment were usually inadequate in many respects. The curriculum focused on German history, culture, and language to the detriment of English, mathematics, history, and geography. Three fundamental texts of German Lutheran literature: Luther's translation of the Bible, Luther's Small Catechism, and the Hymnal, took precedence as teaching tools. While these were important for the faith and life of those who professed Lutheranism, they did not do a great deal to enable the upcoming generation to prepare for a life of responsible citizenship, especially since this education only had an eighth grade equivalent as its goal.[64] By the requirement of the various provincial governments that all children attend public schools, the process of Canadianization among the German Lutherans, which had already advanced to a considerable degree in Ontario, also occurred among their co-religionists in the Prairie Provinces.

As indicated, the leadership of most of the German and Scandinavian Lutheran bodies in the United States tended to support

63. Hedlin, "Language Transition," 23.
64. Cobb, "Prairie Provinces," 339.

Germany against Great Britain prior to American involvement in the conflict. The same was true of Lutheran leaders in Sweden, which, like the United States until 1917, was formally neutral in the conflict.[65] As a result, Canadian Lutheran leaders felt the need to distance themselves from the views of these Lutheran leaders in their neutral countries of origin. Thus, the Canadian leadership of the German Lutheran bodies was led publicly to state that they had no connection whatsoever with the Lutheran Church in Germany.[66] The need for churches to make statements that disagreed with the leadership of their parent bodies led Canadian Lutherans to become aware that they were not merely a northern branch of North American Lutheranism; they had an identity that was uniquely Canadian.

This awareness that Lutherans in Canada had a unique role to play among the North American Lutheran church bodies also surfaced as Canadians addressed the issue of the training of pastors. By 1914, seminaries were in place in Waterloo, Ontario and in Saskatoon, Saskatchewan. Two other German Lutheran bodies in western Canada that were sending their prospective seminarians to seminaries in the mid-western United States were in the process of establishing preparatory schools in Canada for these seminarians. This development came about largely due to the war-time regulations of the United States on the basis of which German Lutheran students from Canada were routinely denied visas to pursue their seminary studies south of the border. Some students tried unsuccessfully to gain entry for several years and were drafted after conscription was introduced in Canada in 1917.[67] Others gave up and remained on the family farm.[68] Still others turned to the seminaries in Canada and changed churches to pursue a Canadian route to pastoral training.

The First World War also played a direct role in leading the Lutheran bodies in Canada to cooperate in support of certain vital ministries and in the process raised their awareness of their Canadian identity. Chief among these ministries was the need to provide spiritual care to Lutheran servicemen. There is no record of any spiritual care being given to those Lutherans who volunteered for action in Canada during the first three

---

65. Wadensjo, *Communion*, 50.
66. *Canada Lutheran*, 1915, 13.
67. Threinen, *Mosaic*, 109.
68. Ohlinger, *Thoughts*, 5.

years of the war; spiritual care was likely given by Lutheran pastors whose parishes were in close proximity to military installations. With entry of the United States into the conflict and the adoption of conscription in Canada, however, this changed in both countries. Thousands of young men in the military needed spiritual care and governments in both Canada and the United States refused to recognize the various Lutheran denominations individually. This led to a meeting of national leaders of seven Lutheran bodies in the United States in October 1917 to organize one central board for Lutheran war-service, known as the National Lutheran Commission for Soldiers' and Sailors' Welfare.[69] In Canada, a corresponding agency to serve Lutheran servicemen was formed on 22 May 1918. Called the Canadian Lutheran Commission for Soldiers' and Sailors' Welfare, it was brought into being at a meeting of the presidents of the various regional units of the Lutheran churches in Canada in Ottawa. The executive of this new Canadian Commission consisted of Bjorn B. Jonson, president of the Icelandic Synod, as chairman; John R. Lavik, president of the Canada District of the Norwegian Lutheran Church, as secretary; and C. N. Sandager, a Norwegian Lutheran pastor, as executive secretary. Hjalmar O. Gronlid, principal of the Norwegian college in Outlook, Saskatchewan, was appointed as the first Lutheran chaplain in the Canadian armed forces. A likely indicator that a disproportionate number of Canadian Lutheran servicemen were Scandinavians is the fact that the president was Icelandic and that there were no Germans on the executive. The war was over soon after the Canadian Commission was organized, but the chaplain's appointment continued until April 1919.[70]

Efforts among Lutherans to express their Canadian identity had already occurred prior to the formation of this Commission in connection with movements to unify Lutheran bodies in North America. However, these efforts had only occurred among bodies of the same ethnic background. One such effort involved the unification of three Norwegian Lutheran bodies in North America as part of the celebration the four-hundredth anniversary of the sixteenth-century Lutheran Reformation. Because of the war, the celebration in North America concentrated on "the content of the Reformation message rather than on its place of ori-

---

69. Nelson, *Lutherans*, 100–101.
70. Threinen, *Mosaic*, 108–9.

gin or the language it helped to shape."⁷¹ In the context of this union and of the war, Norwegian Lutherans in Canada were prompted to reflect on their need to express their identity as Canadians. The answer came in the provision that the merged church made for a Canada District in western Canada, which was subsequently incorporated as the Norwegian Lutheran Church of Canada.⁷²

A similar effort to develop structure that would enable the church to assert its Canadian identity was shown by the German Synod of Ohio and other States, when it incorporated the Board of Management of its Canada District in 1914. With its head office in Melville, Saskatchewan, this board served "the purposes of administering in Canada the property, business and other temporal affairs" of the Synod in Canada.⁷³

In addition to these structural provisions that the church bodies provided for expressing their Canadian identity, some Lutheran congregations in Canada celebrated the four-hundredth anniversary of the Reformation jointly with the fiftieth anniversary of Canada's Confederation. An example of such an occasion was one held in the German community of Peace Hills, Alberta on 8 July 1917. Spearheaded by a young American-born Lutheran pastor, Albert Schwermann, it drew a crowd of 800 people. A procession, headed up by the Canadian flag followed by a bearer of a 5x3 foot Reformation banner made by the pastor's wife, preceded the worship service that day in a celebration that also saw the attendance of three other Lutheran pastors from the area.⁷⁴

The cooperation that the churches experienced in serving military personnel led directly into cooperation in other areas in the post-war period. For five years after the armistice was declared, the Canadian government did not permit any immigration of Germans to Canada. However, when German immigrants were again allowed to enter Canada in 1923, an organization emerged that channeled the new German immigrants into existing German Lutheran communities. This cooperative organization, which involved the presidents or mission directors of the three German Lutheran bodies in Canada, was called the Lutheran Immigration Board. Chief architect of this organization was an American-born former Lutheran pastor by the name of Traugott

71. Nelson, *Lutherans*, 395.
72. Threinen, *Mosaic*, 96–97.
73. 1914 Proceedings of the Minnesota District of the Lutheran Missouri Synod, 8.
74. Threinen, *They Called Him Red*, 17.

Herzer, who had entered the employ of the Canadian Pacific Railway immediately after the war.[75]

An even more important outgrowth of Lutheran war-time cooperation came in the form of the National Lutheran Council. Following the war, the leadership of the Lutheran bodies based in the United States recognized that service to military servicemen was not the only need that had to be met cooperatively. While no Canadian agency was formed at that time, the Lutheran Church in Canada was an integral part of the larger North American churches and was a beneficiary of the new impulses of cooperation that had begun in the context of the challenges of the war but was to characterize Lutherans in the decades ahead.

In summary, one cannot help but repeat the words of one Canadian Lutheran historian of German ancestry, "For the German [Lutheran] Canadians, the First World War was a period of awakening out of their dream world and a coming to grips with the realities of life. It was also a period of clarification, for themselves as well as the non-German element."[76] What was true of German Lutherans in Canada was true of all Canadian Lutherans.

---

75. Threinen, *Convergence*, 8–10.
76. Heick, "Waterloo County," 23.

BIBLIOGRAPHY

Primary Sources

NEWSPAPERS

Canada Lutheran (official publication of the Evangelical Lutheran Synod of Central Canada).
Siloah (a German publication of the General Council produced in Philadelphia).
Vernon News (clippings in the Vernon City Archives).

Secondary Sources

Archer, John Hall. *Saskatchewan: A History*. Saskatoon: Western Producer Prairie Books, 1980.
Baglo, Ferdy E. *Augustana Lutherans in Canada*. Canada Conference of the Augustana Lutheran Church, 1962.
Boudreau, Joseph. "Interning Canada's 'Enemy Aliens' 1914–1918." *Canada: An Historical Magazine*, 1974, 15–28.
Cobb, John M. "German Lutherans in the Prairie Provinces before the First World War." PhD diss., University of Manitoba, 1991.
Eyland, Waldimar J. *Lutherans in Canada*. Winnipeg: The Icelandic Evangelical Lutheran Synod in Canada, 1945.
Grams, Grant W. "A. M. Rehwinkel: Advocate of the German-Canadian Culture in Alberta." *Alberta History* (2006) 21–26.
Gritsch, Eric W. *A History of Lutheranism*. Minneapolis: Fortress, 2010.
Hedlin, Edward. "The Language Transition of the Canada District, ALC." STM thesis, University of Chicago, 1963.
Heick, Welf H. "The Lutherans of Waterloo County, Ontario, 1810–1959: A Historical Study." MA thesis, Queen's University, Kingston, 1959.
Jelly, William, and Nora Jelly. *The Royal Canadian Mounted Police: A Centennial History*. Edmonton: Hurtig, 1973.
Kalbfleisch, Herbert K. *The History of the Pioneer German-Language Press in Ontario*. Toronto: University of Toronto Press, 1968.
Kraemer, Richard. "The Mission and Ministry of German-Speaking Lutherans in Western Canada, 1870–1914." ThD diss., Concordia Seminary, St. Louis, 1995.
MacGregor, James Grierson. *A History of Alberta*. Edmonton: Hurtig, 1972.
Nelson, E. Clifford, ed. *The Lutherans in North America*. Philadelphia: Fortress, 1980.
Ohlinger, John. *Thoughts of the Past*. Self published, n.d.
Palmer, Howard, and Tamara Jeppson Palmer. *Alberta: A New History*. Edmonton: Hurtig, 1990.
Thompson, John Herd. *The Harvests of War, 1914–1918*. Toronto: McClelland & Stewart, 1978.
Threinen, Norman J. *Built on the Rock: A Centennial Sketch of St. Peter's Historic Lutheran Church, Edmonton, Alberta, 1904–2004*. Edmonton: St. Peter's Lutheran Church, 2004.
———. *Fifty Years of Lutheran Convergence: The Canadian Case Study*. Dubuque, IA: Lutheran Historical Conference, 1983.

———. *Immanuel Ev. Lutheran Church, Landestreu, Saskatchewan: Seventy-five Years of Grace 1895–1970*. Landestreu, SK: Immanuel Evangelical Lutheran Church, 1970.

———. *Like a Leaven: A History of the Alberta-British Columbia District of Lutheran Church—Canada*. Edmonton: Alberta-British Columbia District, 1996.

———. *Like a Mustard Seed: A Centennial History of the Ontario District of Lutheran Church—Canada (Missouri Synod)*. Kitchener: Ontario District, 1989.

———. *A Religious-Cultural Mosaic*. Vulcan, AB: Today's Reformation Press, 2006.

———. *They Called Him Red: The Life and Times of Albert Schwermann*. Vulcan, AB: Today's Reformation Press, 2008.

Wadensjo, Bergt. *Toward a World Lutheran Communion: Developments in Lutheran Cooperation up to 1929*. Uppsala: Universitetet, 1970.

Wilhelmy, Jean-Pierre. *German Mercenaries in Canada*. Translated by Honey Thomas. Beloeil, QC: Maison des Mots, 1984.

Wilson, Barbara M., ed. *Ontario and the First World War, 1914–1918*. Toronto: University of Toronto Press, 1977.

9

Quakers and Mennonites and the Great War

ROBYNNE ROGERS HEALEY

Quakers and Mennonites are traditionally associated with pacifism based on faith-based opposition to war and the taking of human life. Despite the clear peace testimonies currently articulated by both groups, neither Quakers nor Mennonites have had consistent and clearly-defined pacifist strategies for dealing with war. Consider the Quaker Peace Testimony, which began as an anti-war, not pro-peace, position. In 1660, early in the sect's organization, leaders of the Religious Society of Friends declared to King Charles II of England: "We, as to our own particulars, do utterly deny; with all outward wars and strife, and fightings with outward weapons, for any end or under any pretence whatsoever; this is our testimony to the whole world."[1] The Quakers' anti-war standpoint was clarified through the many experiences of the eighteenth century, a century in which the English were frequently embroiled in armed conflict. By the time of the French Revolution, the epistles of the London Yearly Meeting—the parent body of Quakerism at the time—were clear: do not engage in activities associated with war; do not talk about war; pray.[2] Even though Quakers practiced what Peter Brock has referred to as "integrational pacifism," as opposed to the "separa-

---

1. "A Declaration from the harmless and innocent people of God, called Quakers, against all sedition, plotters and fighters in the world," in *Journal or Historical Account*, 354.
2. London Yearly Meeting, *Epistles*, 373–74.

tional pacifism" of the Mennonites,[3] the traditional Quaker response to war until the early twentieth century was to maintain as much distance from it as possible.

The years preceding the First World War and the war itself were a turning point for the Religious Society of Friends' interpretation and practice of the peace testimony. Canadian Quakers, alongside Quakers around the world, began to take an active position for peace and against war, seeking to understand and ameliorate the underlying causes of armed conflict. Putting some of their own schismatic differences behind them, Quakers combined religious pacifism and social activism[4] and refashioned the peace testimony into one that actively worked to prevent war.[5] Quakers had already become well integrated into mainstream Canadian society in the nineteenth century.[6] In the twentieth century they became peace activists and played a leading role alongside other pacifists, religious and secular, in the emerging peace movement, advocating for a just world without war.

The war was also pivotal for Canadian Mennonites. While they remained committed to the separation of their communities from mainstream Canadian society in this period, the war brought disparate Mennonite groups together in cooperation.[7] In 1918, representatives from a number of Mennonite groups joined together to establish the Non-Resistant Relief Organization (NRRO)[8] to raise a donation to the government in appreciation for their exemption from the 1917 Military Service Act.[9] Later, it was Mennonites who had been influenced by their experience in the First World War who spearheaded the founding

---

3. Brock, *Pacifism in Europe*, 474–75.

4. Brock, *Pioneers*, 353–58; Dorland, *Quakers*, 327–35; Socknat, *Witness*, 60–89.

5. Socknat argues that "the full impact of Quaker leadership [in the peace movement] was not felt in Canada until after the First World War when the three separate branches of the Society of Friends began to co-operate with one another" (*Witness*, 21).

6. See Healey, *From Quaker to Upper Canadian* for an examination of the process in the Canadian context. Hamm, *Transformation*, explores this process in the American context.

7. Socknat, *Witness*, 119.

8. Mennonites from the Ontario Mennonite Conference, Old Order Mennonites, Mennonite Brethren in Christ, Brethren in Christ, and Amish Mennonites were represented in the NRRO.

9. Burkholder, *Brief History of the Mennonites*, 174–73; Epp, *Mennonites in Canada*, 376–77.

of the Conference of Historic Peace Churches in 1940.[10] Despite the similar impact of the war on each group, ethnic identity separated the war experience of Quakers and Mennonites in Canada. Unlike Mennonites, whose German language and heritage made them targets of nativist sentiment, Quakers, with their Anglo-Celtic heritage, aroused less suspicion from the broader Canadian public. Amidst the rhetoric of patriotism, ethnic nationalism, and anti-Germanism of the First World War, pacifist Mennonites were considered dirty shirkers, potential spies, and unfit as "true" Canadians.[11] Quakers, on the other hand, were respected as "honest conscientious objector[s]" and even extolled as examples of conscientious objectors with "informed conscience[s]."[12]

The Quaker or Mennonite response to the First World War in Canada has received relatively little attention from scholars. The two standard surveys on each "sect," Arthur Dorland's *The Quakers in Canada* and Frank Epp's *Mennonites in Canada*, only touch on responses to the war and conscription.[13] Peter Brock's monumental contribution to the understanding of pacifism in general provides a broad contextual history of pacifism in Europe and the United States.[14] Canadian Quakers and Mennonites are touched on indirectly in some of Brock's work inasmuch as they shared experiences with Quakers and Mennonites in other parts of the world.[15] Most of this work, however, stops before the Great War or begins after the war, leaving aside the experience of the war itself.[16]

---

10. Harder-Gissing, "Companions," 5–7; Shaw, *Crisis of Conscience*, 58–59; Socknat, *Witness*, 227–36. CHPC played a decisive role in ensuring alternative service options for conscientious objectors in the Second World War.

11. Epp, *Mennonites in Canada*, 391–410; Neufeldt, "Tolerant Exclusion," 213–15; Shaw, *Crisis of Conscience*, 7–8, 68–70.

12. William Lacey Amy's wartime diatribe against COs mentions "the honest conscientious objector, like the Quaker." In an article for the *North Atlantic Review*, British reformer and economist Sidney Webb assessed Quakers' position as against war as "informed." Both are quoted in Shaw, *Crisis of Conscience*, 135.

13. Dorland's survey (*Quakers*) was originally published in 1927 and reprinted in 1968. It commits a single chapter to the Quakers and "the struggle for peace"; the Boer War and the First World War are covered in eight pages (327–34). Epp's 1974 survey (*Mennonites in Canada*) dedicates two chapters to the First World War (365–414).

14. For instance, see Brock, *Pioneers*; Brock, *Colonial Era*; Brock, *Pacifism in Europe*; Brock, *Freedom from War*.

15. For instance, Brock's *Pioneers* reflects on American peace efforts in which Canadian Friends participated, such as the 1901 American Friends Peace Conference.

16. Brock, *Pioneers*; Brock, *Quaker Peace Testimony*; Brock and Socknat, eds.,

Thomas Socknat's and Amy Shaw's scholarship is at the forefront of understanding pacifism and conscientious objection in Canada; Shaw's work remains one of the few studies of conscientious objection in First World War Canada.[17] Work on American and British peace history is much more developed and demonstrates that Quakers and Mennonites did not always interpret their respective peace testimonies consistently.[18] This chapter is an opportunity to examine how the war and conscription legislation compelled both sects to act on their pacifism.

PRELUDE TO WAR

As a result of nineteenth-century schisms, pre-war Canadian Quakers were divided into three groups.[19] Additionally, Quakers were not numerous, although their influence has always exceeded their numbers in

---

Challenge to Mars. The exception to this is Brock's edited anthology of memoirs of conscientious objectors, *These Strange Criminals,* which includes Mennonite and Quaker WWI COs from the United States and Britain. The only Canadian CO memoir in the collection is that of John Evans, a Christadelphian. Brock's *Twentieth-Century Pacifism* does dedicate a chapter to the First World War but, with the exception of four pages dedicated to "conscientious objection outside Great Britain and the United States" (60–63), the focus remains on European and American experiences.

17. Socknat, *Witness*; Brock and Socknat, eds., *Challenge to Mars*; Shaw, *Crisis of Conscience*. There are a few articles that explore Canadian Mennonites in the First World War. Friesen's "Stirrings of Conscience" is a fictionalized autobiography, or "docu-poem," of Victor Paul Snyder's experience as a Mennonite pacifist during the war. Bergen's "World Wars and Education" examines the impact of the wars on Canadian Mennonite schools, but its focus is largely the Second World War.

18. On Mennonites in the American context, see Driedger and Kraybill, *Peacemaking*; Funk, "Divided Loyalties"; Horman, "Military Justice"; Horman, *Great War*; Huxman, "Mennonite Rhetoric"; Juhnke, "Ambivalent Civil Religion"; Mock, *Writing Peace*; Neufeldt, "Tolerant Exclusion"; Strege, "Demise"; and Teichroew, "Mennonite Migration." On Quakers in the American context, see Curry, "Devolution"; Frost, "Our Deeds"; Hamm et al., "Decline"; Howlett, "Quaker Conscience"; Keim and Stolzfus, *Politics of Conscience*; Kohrman, "Respectable Pacifists"; Manousos, "North Carolina"; and Miller, "Times of War." For Quakers in the British context, see Den Boggende, "Reluctant Absolutist"; Den Boggende, "Fellowship"; Gatrell, "Refugees"; Greenwood, *Friends and Relief*; and Waugh, "League of Nations."

19. The three branches of Canadian Quakers were represented by the Canada Yearly Meeting (Orthodox), the Canada Yearly Meeting (Conservative), and the Genesee Yearly Meeting (Hicksite). The Hicksites were part of a Yearly Meeting that encompassed both Canadian and American congregations.

Canadian society,[20] and they were spread across the country.[21] Even so, Quakers, like Mennonites, had well-established agreements with the Canadian government about military service. These had been determined prior to either group's immigration and were revisited when it was felt necessary. In 1806, Quakers reminded Lieutenant-Governor Gore of their refusal to take up arms and assured him of their loyalty.[22] The first Canada Yearly Meeting of Friends reiterated this position in 1867 in an address to Canada's first Governor General and Prime Minister.[23] Canadian Quakers had experienced the pain of internal schisms in the nineteenth century. Unlike their American brethren, however, after the War of 1812 they had not come face to face with armed conflict on their own soil.

Generations of living in a peaceful country—if not a peaceful religious society—had affected the way many Quakers viewed the peace testimony. While it persisted as a mark of Quaker distinctiveness, it retreated into the background as a primary facet of Quaker identity.[24] Scholars have suggested that this decline of pacifist commitment can be attributed to a number of factors. Principal were the holiness revivals of the 1870s and 1880s that affected Quakers in Indiana, Kansas, Ohio, and Oregon.[25] Some evangelical Friends, who absorbed converts from other denominations, even came to consider the peace testimony as superfluous—a quaint, but unnecessary aspect of membership in the Society.[26]

Canadian Friends were aware of, and in some cases involved in, these debates; nevertheless, the official position of the three Yearly Meetings of Canadian Quakers was pacifist.[27] This perspective is evi-

---

20. The *Fifth Census of Canada, 1911*, 2–3, enumerates 4,027 Quakers. Compare this with the 44,611 Mennonites recorded in the same census.

21. The majority of Quakers were in Ontario but, at the time, there were also meetings in Hartney, Manitoba; Swarthmore, Saskatchewan, near Battleford; in Calgary, Alberta; and Victoria and Vancouver, British Columbia. See Dorland, *Quakers*, 271–72.

22. Healey, *From Quaker to Upper Canadian*, 44–45.

23. Dorland, *Quakers*, 325.

24. Brock, *Pioneers*, 350.

25. Ibid., 350–52.

26. Curry, "Devolution"; Frost, "Our Deeds"; and Hamm et al., "Decline."

27. It is important to remember that Quakers, like members of other religions, vary in their dedication to their faith. Some Quakers were devout. Some were barely adherent, "Quaker" only by birthright affiliation. There are examples of individual Canadian Quakers denying their pacifist roots (see Dorland, *Quakers*, 331, and Shaw,

dent in all three groups' interactions with government. Beginning in 1869, Orthodox Friends expressed misgivings about the martial spirit of the textbooks used in Canadian Common Schools. Their meeting with Egerton Ryerson, Chief Superintendent of Common Schools, resulted in assurances that Quakers' concerns would be considered when the books were revised.[28] Quakers maintained vigilant oversight of school texts and curricula, especially as war loomed, considering it "one of our first duties to correct the present tendency towards militarism in our Canadian schools, and to substitute, for the lure of military display, intelligent teaching as to the terrible results of war economically and morally to a nation."[29] In 1896 Prime Minister Wilfrid Laurier favorably received Hicksite Friends who traveled to Ottawa to restate the Quaker position on "The Responsibilities of Public Men, Militarism, Temperance, Judicial Oaths, and Capital Punishment."[30]

In addition to petitioning their own government, Canadian Friends joined with American Quakers in peace efforts. Beginning in 1894, Albert Smiley began hosting an Annual Conference on International Arbitration at his Lake Mohonk resort in New York State.[31] Canadian Friends attended these conferences, which shaped opinion favoring arbitration as a way of settling international disputes.[32] When the South African War broke out in 1899, Canadian Friends passed stern resolutions condemning the bellicose spirit in Canada.[33] At the same time, the Peace Association of Friends in America remarked on mounting international aggression and invited Canadian Friends to appoint two members to their Advisory Board.[34] Threats to global peace were definitely on the minds of many Quakers, although the Peace Committee at the 1899 Yearly Meeting of Orthodox Friends expressed "regret there is not more interest on the part of our members generally in this im-

---

Crisis of Conscience, Table 2, 191–95), but this was not the official position of the Religious Society of Friends in Canada.

28. Dorland, *Quakers*, 325–26.
29. *Minutes of the Canada Yearly Meeting, 1913* (Orthodox), 25.
30. *Minutes of the Genesee Yearly Meeting, 1897*, 13.
31. Barbour et al., *Quaker Crosscurrents*, 241–44.
32. Dorland, *Quakers*, 326–27. Attendance at these conferences was not exclusive to Quakers; non-Quakers also attended. See Socknat, *Witness*, 28–30.
33. Dorland, *Quakers*, 327.
34. *Minutes of Canada Yearly Meeting, 1899* (Orthodox), 22, 56–57.

portant subject."[35] Despite the lack of "general" interest in peace, there was certainly a sustained concern from some engaged Quakers. At the end of the South African War, a group of Hicksite Friends organized Canada's first peace organization, "The Peace and Arbitration Society," a nondenominational group that counted a number of prominent civic, business, and religious leaders among its members.[36]

Quakers did unite in an important turn-of-the-century initiative to renew the peace testimony. For three days at the end of 1901, North American Quakers representing all branches of the Society of Friends gathered in Philadelphia to discuss issues of war and peace. The conference invitation demonstrates both the desire for unity among Quakers and the renewal of approaches to peace itself: "Do we not owe it to ourselves, to our history, to our profession before the church and the world . . . to declare ourselves anew today—and in a united way, as we have never done before—on the great and pressing question of the peace of the world, of the rescue of mankind from the awful iniquities and crushing burdens of modern militarism?"[37] Organizers were true to their commitment to representation from all divisions; the four Canadian representatives on the General Organizing Committee accounted for all three branches of Canadian Friends and included a woman.[38] The conference sustained a grueling pace: forty-three papers were presented in eight sessions over the course of three twelve-hour days. Topics ranged from biblical exegesis on issues of war and peace to historical analysis and theoretical papers on topics like "internationalism" and "militarism."[39] Peter Brock has observed that "the conference had little to say about the economic causation of war or about the clash of rival imperialisms and the search of finance capitalism for overseas markets," to which socialist and labor movements of the day were pointing as the causes of interna-

---

35. Ibid., 22.

36. Dorland, *Quakers*, 327–28; Socknat, *Witness*, 28–31; Shaw, *Crisis of Conscience*, 13.

37. *American Friends' Peace Conference*, 4.

38. The four Canadian representatives on the organizing committee were William Greenwood Brown, Sarah Ann Dale, Elias H. Rogers, and Samuel P. Zavitz. See *American Friends' Peace Conference*, 5–6.

39. The publication of the conference proceedings (*American Friends' Peace Conference*) included all of the papers along with verbatim commentary and discussion, amounting to 236 pages of text, not including the index.

tional conflict.⁴⁰ It did, however, mark a shift in Quaker approaches to war and their efforts to be activist peacemakers. Isaac Sharpless' closing comments are suggestive of this shift in tone and approach:

> Friends have not been very active propagandists. The very feeling of their own complete rightness has made many of them slow to take the stump and proclaim the arguments for the good cause. But this is changing. . . . Shall we lose this historic character as we part with the aloofness from the world which perhaps produced it . . . ? Not so, I think, if he [a Quaker] comes under the spirit of George Fox; if he is a peace man not because he believes war to be wasteful, and productive of suffering, or contrary to some pet theory of morals, but because down in his heart he feels the warm spirit of divine love and power that takes away the occasion and the desire and the possibility of war and revenge and hatred. Pile up your other arguments as you will, such a man . . . will be efficient and practical, and at the same time graceful and moderate, generous in his sympathies, and kindly in his criticisms—an undaunted advocate, a charitable opponent.⁴¹

Significant initiatives like the 1901 Peace Conference helped Friends to renew their peace testimony so that it included addressing the causes of war. As integrational pacifists, seeking to adapt Christian pacifism to the realities of a global arms race and increased militarism, they were able to exert considerable influence on the liberal reform peace movement.⁴² They also questioned the Canadian government's priorities: "Is it not strange," they asked in 1913, "that the so-called practical man and the practical Government should see no better way out of this nightmare of war preparation than to increase the armament and thereby build still higher the walls that keep alive and active the mutual distrust now separating the great civilized peoples into hostile camps?"⁴³ Canadians' resources would be much better invested, they suggested, on "peace propaganda under the care of a strong National Peace Commission or Department."⁴⁴

---

40. Brock, *Pioneers*, 358.
41. *American Friends' Peace Conference*, 232.
42. Socknat, *Witness*, 41.
43. "Memorial of the Religious Society of Friends to the Government and People of Canada," *Minutes of Canada Yearly Meeting, 1913* (Orthodox), 24.
44. Ibid., 25.

As much as they might agree with secular liberal pacifists on the consequences of war and cooperate with them on peace initiatives, Quakers were mindful that their faith was at the heart of their pacifism.[45] Consider the way Arthur Dorland's comments on militarism in the 1913 *Canadian Friend* echo Isaac Sharpless' remarks of a decade earlier. Liberal pacifists might decry the outcome of war, but their reason for doing so differed from that of Quakers. Quakers would never believe that "many wars are under certain circumstances justifiable and right." Whether passively anti-war or actively pro-peace, by the time of the Great War, Quakers asserted that their faith commitment dictated that war was always immoral and never right.[46]

Mennonites' pre-war pacifism was predominantly defined by what Brock has called separational pacifism—nonviolence characterized by the separation of the sect from mainstream society "so as to shape their lives according to a higher righteousness than the one accepted by the unredeemed."[47] Their immigration to Upper Canada had been premised on the same right to exemption from militia duties that Quakers had claimed, although Mennonites were willing to pay fines in lieu of service, something Quakers refused.[48] After Confederation, an 1873 Order in Council directed at migrating Russian Mennonites granted "an entire exemption from any military service . . . to the denomination of Christians called Mennonites." The Militia Act of 1906 was not quite as clear-cut. It did not name the sects exempted from military service, but it did exempt individuals who "from doctrines of their religion, are averse to bearing arms or rendering personal military service."[49]

The pre-war Mennonite experience was not only characterized by its isolation from Canadian society, it was also typified by division between Mennonite groups. One journalist reported that there were sixteen separate branches of Mennonites in Canada at the time of the Great War.[50] Divided from one another and separated from mainstream so-

---

45. This position was clarified increasingly throughout the twentieth century. For instance, see Healey, "Thirty-One Hours"; Healey, "Wrestling"; and Healey, "Reconciling."

46. Dorland, "Militarism"; *Canadian Friend*, July 1913, 14.

47. Brock, *Pacifism in Europe*, 474.

48. Socknat, *Witness*, 13–14; Healey, *From Quaker to Upper Canadian*, 45; Shaw, *Crisis of Conscience*, 45–46.

49. Epp, *Mennonites in Canada*, 367.

50. Ibid., 366.

ciety, Mennonites were, Epp concludes, "ill-prepared for the onslaught of federal legislation, administrative regulations and adverse public opinion" that was thrust upon them when the war began. Until directly confronted with the War Measures Act (1914), the Wartime Elections Act (1917) and the Military Service Act (1917), they remained silent on the war.[51]

Mennonites' segregation did allow them to preserve aspects of their German culture, including their language, which acted as a buffer between the sect and mainstream society. Before the war, these ethnic markers had been considered desirable. Canadians of German ancestry had been lauded as being "thrifty, intelligent, industrious, sober, thorough, loyal, good citizens."[52] All that changed in 1914. Mennonites, who had been considered "good Canadians," became targets of anti-German, nativist sentiment. They were viewed as potential spies and threatened with disenfranchisement, confiscation of their land, and lower wages.[53] As Neufeldt concludes, this behavior "illuminates the ethnic connotations associated with being 'American' and 'Canadian'. Key markers of national belonging were the use of English and an Anglo-Saxon heritage."[54] Mennonite expressions of loyalty to the state and even the Anglicization of family and place names—for instance the renaming of Berlin, Ontario to Kitchener—did little to combat the feeling of many Canadians that the country was playing host to potential enemies.[55]

THE WAR

Despite their thoughtful renewal of their peace testimony and their petitions to government opposing military training in schools and munitions expenditures, Canadian Quakers remained relatively silent in their opposition to the war once it began. In 1913, the London Yearly Meeting

---

51. Socknat, *Witness*, 53. Shaw contends that this separational stance accounts for the absence of conscientious objection in the larger narrative of Canada's Great War. Mennonites' experience with tribunals convinced them that their separation from society was indeed appropriate. They were more likely to return quietly to their farms than to record their experiences for public consumption or become activists. Shaw, *Crisis of Conscience*, 13.

52. Epp, *Mennonites in Canada*, 368.

53. Neufeldt, "Tolerant Exclusion," 213.

54. Ibid., 215.

55. Epp, *Mennonites in Canada*, 367–69; 391–418; Shaw, *Crisis of Conscience*, 130–31; Neufeldt, "Tolerant Exclusion," 213–15.

Epistle warned Friends everywhere that "the time may not be distant when we too shall be called upon to defend our principles at heavy cost."[56] Canadian Friends did maintain public pressure. Just one month before war erupted, they sent a sternly-worded communiqué to the Premier of Ontario, the Minister of Education for Ontario, and the press:

> Whereas militarists, though few in number in comparison with the population of our country, are actively attempting to secure the general adoption of military training among the boys of our schools, we respectfully desire to call attention of the educational authorities, and of the general public, to this military propaganda, which we believe is seeking to take an unfair advantage, not only of the youth in our schools, but of the great majority of parents, by utilizing the school connections to instil in the young minds the military spirit and a false and pugnacious ideal of patriotism. We believe that the best interests of our young people and of the future of our country demands that the teaching in our schools should provide an enlightened knowledge of the horrors of actual warfare rather than the glamour of militarism, and should instil the higher patriotism of social service and of international brotherhood, which will make all war between civilized peoples impossible.[57]

Compared to this level of engagement, the 1915 and 1916 minutes seem curiously silent on the issue of war. Certainly, Friends continued to encourage pacifist efforts, but the reminder that "no opportunity should be lost by individuals to testify that all war is contrary to Christ's teaching" seems oddly subdued in contrast to earlier peace activities.[58]

It was not until debate on the 1917 Military Service Act, which introduced conscription, that Quakers composed a response on "the subject of peace in connection with the Society of Friends in Canada." The Society declared its support for "those who, though not members of our Society, nevertheless hold genuine religious objections to war." Two recommendations were directed at the MSA. One approved the collaboration of the Peace Committee and the Genesee Yearly Meeting's Legislative Committee to study the proposed legislation; the second authorized issuing certificates of membership should they be required by the tribunals. Friends were also reminded that "while during the

---

56. *Minutes of Canada Yearly Meeting, 1913* (Orthodox), 28–29.
57. *Minutes of Canada Yearly Meeting, 1914* (Orthodox), 22.
58. *Minutes of Canada Yearly Meeting, 1916* (Orthodox), 18.

present crisis we should endeavor consistently to observe our traditional attitude as Friends against active participation in war, it is therefore our especial duty to exert ourselves as individuals and as a Society along these lines of work in which we can consistently engage so that we shall render to our country and to those who have suffered because of the war some equivalent service and even sacrifice." In this vein, the example of Pickering College being loaned as a convalescent hospital was offered as evidence of Quakers' practical service to the country.[59]

Quakers did call on Borden to broaden the exemption clause to include "anyone whose conscience forbade them to carry arms regardless of their membership in any particular church or society."[60] In these efforts, though, Canadian Quakers were not nearly as outspoken in their opposition to conscription as their British brethren.[61] They were undemanding in their requests. In 1917, when Charles A. Zavitz, clerk of the Genesee Yearly Meeting, sought clarification from Borden on the position of COs, he "sincerely ask[ed] if there is to be compulsory military enlistment in Canada those religious denominations be exempt whose doctrines are opposed to war." There would be no ultimatums by Canadian Friends equivalent to those British Quakers sent to the Home Office in 1916: "Should [conscription] become law, the opposition of our Society to it will in no sense be modified or withdrawn. . . . [And] if any such measure should become law the support and cooperation of Members of the Society will be available for those outside their own body whose conscientious objection is based upon the same grounds as their own."[62] Shaw suggests a number of reasons for Friends' reluctance to protest the MSA: there were far fewer Quakers in Canada than in the United Kingdom; there did not seem to be many Quaker males of service age; and Canadian Quakers, like Quakers everywhere, poured their energies into relief work instead of demonstrations.[63]

Relief work was one of the main ways Quakers responded to the horrors of the Great War. Immediately, British Quakers organized the War Victims Relief Committee and the Friends' Ambulance Unit. Faced with conscription themselves in 1917, American Quakers formed the

---

59. *Minutes of Canada Yearly Meeting, 1917* (Orthodox), 23–24.
60. As quoted in Shaw, *Crisis of Conscience*, 49.
61. Shaw, *Crisis of Conscience*, 49.
62. As quoted in ibid., 51.
63. Shaw, *Crisis of Conscience*, 49.

American Friends Service Committee (AFSC) to organize alternative service work during the war.⁶⁴ Canadian Quakers served in these units as well as other alternative service or non-combatant corps, some affiliated with the army.⁶⁵ Because they undertook this work, Quakers appeared as patriotic Canadians; it also helped that they shared a British heritage with Anglo-Canadians. As a result, they were criticized less than other conscientious objectors, especially those who were German-speaking.⁶⁶ It is difficult to know how many Canadian Quakers supported the war effort. Work on American Quakers shows a fairly high level of support for the allied effort to destroy German "barbarism."⁶⁷ We know that some Canadian Quakers joined the military. Dorland claims these were "nominal members"⁶⁸ and this is entirely plausible. Unfortunately, because the Canadian tribunal records were destroyed,⁶⁹ it is impossible to identify the extent of individual Canadian Quakers' support for the war.

Indeed, corporately the Yearly Meetings seemed reluctant to do anything that would jeopardize their respectable position in Canadian society. When deliberating on the possible impact of the Military Service Act and the Wartime Elections Act, which disenfranchised COs, Orthodox and Hicksite Friends "decided that any protest to the Government in this would be inadvisable as well as futile."⁷⁰ Albert S. Rogers, head of the Peace Committee from 1917–1918, responded to an inquiry about Quaker chaplains visiting imprisoned Friends with the same cautious tone: "There has been so much indifference and even a

---

64. M. Jones, *Ploughshares*; R. Jones, *Love in Wartime*; Greenwood, *Friends and Relief*; and Frost, "Our Deeds."

65. "Report of the Joint Legislative and Peace Committees," *Minutes of Canada Yearly Meeting, 1918* (Orthodox), 22–24.

66. Frost, "Our Deeds," 11; Shaw, *Crisis of Conscience*, 135–36.

67. Thatcher, "Attitude," 238–39; Frost, "Our Deeds," 4–5. Kohrman concludes that, despite opportunities for alternative service provided by the AFSC, at least two-thirds of American Quakers subject to conscription accepted combat duty. This is suggestive of the level of support for the war in the United States ("Respectable Pacifists"). Similarly, British Quakers showed individual support for the war despite the strong corporate opposition of the London Yearly Meeting. Waugh shows that one-third of Quaker men joined the armed forces; at the same time, many British Quakers were imprisoned for their refusal to serve (Waugh, "League of Nations," 60–61).

68. Dorland, *Quakers*, 329.

69. Shaw, *Crisis of Conscience*, 15.

70. "Report of the Joint Legislative and Peace Committees,"*Minutes of Canada Yearly Meeting, 1918* (Orthodox), 22.

tendency to pro-Germanism in some quarters that we feel that Friends should be exceedingly careful not to compromise their own reputation for sincerity by giving any sort of encouragement to any conscientious objectors whose previous life has not demonstrated a truly religious aspect."[71] The Society's caution may have been a response to the nationalist rhetoric circulating in Canada's religious press.[72] Prior to the war, Quakers had countered this rhetoric and chastised those who encouraged it. During the war they retreated from this malicious rhetorical combat. Arthur Dorland recalled its tenor: "[Justification for the war] was backed by press and pulpit in every country, and later by an organized system of propaganda which, while purporting to keep up the war morale, blasted the very souls of men with all the indecencies of hate."[73] Quakers decided to focus their efforts on relief for victims of war or understanding war's causes.[74]

When war broke out, Mennonites were immediately affected by federal legislation and altered attitudes towards Canadians of German heritage. The War Measures Act gave sweeping powers to the government to censor publications and to arrest and detain those considered to be enemy aliens. Immediately, German-language publications originating in the United States came under the watchful eye of censors. Many were identified as containing pro-German sentiments or "objectionable material," and were banned from circulation in Canada; in one six-month period, sixty-seven German-language papers, were barred from entering Canada.[75] German-language papers published in Canada were also viewed suspiciously. Anything outside a narrowly-defined "religious character" was strictly prohibited and no religious publications could have "the character of a newspaper." A number of Canadian Mennonite publications were suspended under these regulations.[76]

71. Albert Rogers to David Priestman, Letter, 23 September 1918, Military Service Act Folder, CYMA.

72. Socknat, *Witness*, 49.

73. Dorland, *Quakers*, 329.

74. As early as 1917, Quakers began to examine the implications of their peace testimony in areas such as the connection between capitalism and war. *Minutes of the Genesee Yearly Meeting of Friends, 1917*, 59; *Minutes of Canada Yearly Meeting, 1917* (Orthodox), 25.

75. Epp, *Mennonites in Canada*, 393.

76. Both *Der Mitarbeiter*, the monthly newsletter of the Conference of Mennonites in Canada, and the *Steinbach Post*, a community paper from the East Reserve, were suspended during the war. See ibid., 394.

Beyond having their publications suppressed, Mennonites became anxious when they were included in the directive for the January 1917 inventory of all Canadian males between the ages of sixteen and sixty-five.[77] Mennonites' exemption from military service had been clearly established by a series of nineteenth-century statutes. How were they to respond? There was no united reaction. Bishops from at least two orders dispatched letters to Borden assuring him of Mennonites' loyalty, but refusing to complete the National Service Cards. A delegation representing western Mennonites delivered the same message when they traveled to Ottawa to meet with National Service officials.[78] Bennett vowed to respect Mennonites' position under the 1873 Order in Council; he did ask that the cards be completed to provide an inventory of potential agricultural labor. Mennonites could, he advised, write "Mennonite" across the face of the card, identifying them for exceptional treatment.[79] Questions about National Service registration foreshadowed the legislative problems Mennonites faced with the 1917 Military Service Act. These were compounded by discriminatory attitudes that painted German-speakers as potential threats to national security.[80] Most Anglo-Canadians took a dim view of Canadians who spoke German and refused to take up arms to protect king and country. War-time migrations of American Mennonites and Hutterites to Canada heightened nativist fears and exaggerated figures of German-speaking immigrants "flooding" to the prairies circulated in the media and the House of Commons.[81] Many questioned if these "Canadians" could be considered Canadian at all.[82]

Sensitive about their position in Canadian society, Mennonites faced greater misunderstanding with the passage of the Wartime Elections Act and the Military Service Act in 1917. The Wartime Elections Act

77. Ibid., 369.

78. Ibid., 369–70.

79. Ibid., 370–71.

80. Ibid., 392–94; Neufeldt, "Tolerant Exclusion," 213–15; and Shaw, *Crisis of Conscience*, 130.

81. On the migrations themselves, see Teichroew, "Mennonite Migration"; Armishaw, "Hutterites' Story." Ministers of Parliament bandied about highly-inflated immigration figures that ranged between 30,000 and 60,000. The Minister of Colonization and Immigration assured the House that no more than 500–600 Mennonites and 1,000 Hutterites entered Canada in 1918, the year the migration was highest. As quoted in Epp, *Mennonites in Canada*, 395.

82. See Neufeldt, "Tolerant Exclusion," for an analysis of the effect of ethnic nationalism on views of Mennonites in Canada and the U.S. during both world wars.

disenfranchised conscientious objectors; at the same time, it deprived them of the right to claim CO status if they did vote. Conflicting interpretations of the act in the election that year caused great confusion for Mennonite voters and did little to help Mennonites who then faced debates about whether they were excluded or exempted from conscription.[83] Epp suggests that discussions about conscription may have precipitated the articulation of a statement on Mennonites' position on war.[84] Representatives of the Mennonite General Conference convened at Goshen, Indiana to this end. While Mennonites were appreciative of "the consideration given our religious convictions," the statement was absolutely clear: "We cannot participate in war in any form; that is, to aid or abet war, whether in a combatant or non-combatant capacity." Aware that this might be interpreted as either "disloyalty or cowardice," the statement reiterated that the only position acceptable to Mennonites was to "hold aloof from every form of military service."[85] Interestingly, the statement was issued the same day the Military Service Act received royal assent.

Mennonites' unwillingness to perform any military service—combatant or non-combatant—complicated the question of exception from or exemption under the Military Service Act. Epp argues that the MSA had no intention of undoing nineteenth-century statutes granting Mennonites exception to military service. The problem was that exemptions under the MSA applied only to combatant service. Armed with their 1917 statement on military service, the Mennonite Conference of Canada and Amish Mennonites sent a delegation to Ottawa seeking clarification on their position. Rather than appealing for exception from the Act, they claimed the right to exemption under the Act. While they had no way of knowing the impact of this decision, Epp contends that it created a number of challenges for Mennonites and the tribunals that would process their claims.[86] The claim to exemption on religious grounds was problematic for Mennonites who, unlike Quakers, practiced the sacrament of baptism as central to their faith. Baptism signaled the moment when one's name was entered into the church register as a fully-fledged member; for most Mennonites this occurred about age

---

83. Epp, *Mennonites in Canada*, 372–77; Shaw, *Crisis of Conscience*, 32–33.
84. Epp, *Mennonites in Canada*, 373–74.
85. *Mennonites on Military Service*.
86. Epp, *Mennonites in Canada*, 373–84.

twenty-one, well after the eligible age for conscription. Could a non-baptized Mennonite be considered a Mennonite? Seeing tribunals "splitting hairs," S. F. Coffman, bishop in the Mennonite Conference of Ontario, appealed to common sense: "No one ever intimated to me, nor tried to make me believe, that a young man whose father was a Mennonite all his life and belonged to the Mennonite church was not also considered a Mennonite."[87] Beyond appeals to government, Mennonites also dealt with the issue by lowering the baptismal age or certifying young men as Mennonites whether they were baptized or not.[88] These methods did not go unchallenged as investigators were dispatched to confirm rumors of this behavior.

Misunderstandings between Mennonites and other Canadians were not improved by the belief that Mennonites were German sympathizers shirking their patriotic duty. Feeling harassed from all corners, Saskatchewan Mennonites gathered in 1918 and drafted a powerful appeal to the Governor General:

> We are accused of fraud. We are referred to by leaders of our fellow citizens from public platforms as outlawed parasites. . . . Parasites we are not. We are earning our bread by honest labour, and if we mistake not, our labour has assisted materially in advancing the material welfare of our country. We do not depend for our living on sustenance or efforts of others excepting as we give and take. We do not require any one to shed his blood for us. We would rather die ourselves or languish in prison or leave our home and again settle in some wilderness, the same as our forefathers have done, than to require a sacrifice of any kind by any one on our behalf. Everyone knew at the time of the last Dominion elections who were Mennonites and who were not. Neither the registrar not the tribunal nor the public seem to know now.[89]

Confrontations with government officials over who was, and who was not, a Mennonite were settled by the middle of 1918.[90] This was the same year that Mennonite and Hutterite immigration from the United States reached its apex. The influx of more German-speaking "draft dodgers" from the United States, where Mennonites were viewed even more intol-

---

87. As quoted in ibid., 380.
88. Epp, *Mennonites in Canada*, 380–81.
89. As quoted in Epp, *Mennonites in Canada*, 381.
90. Epp, *Mennonites in Canada*, 384; Socknat, *Witness*, 76.

erantly than in Canada, did little to improve Canadian sentiment about Mennonite pacifists. The fullest expression of this negative attitude was reached in 1919 when the government issued an Order in Council prohibiting their immigration.[91]

In addition to collaborating on the statement on military service, Mennonites cooperated in other areas as well. Government assurances that the Mennonite position on military service would be respected were met with a decision to raise a gift to express appreciation.[92] Nineteenth-century schisms had divided Swiss Mennonites in Ontario; the decision to form the Non-Resistant Relief Organization to "raise a generous fund . . . as a memorial of appreciation for religious liberty"[93] brought these disparate factions together in a common initiative. Epp maintains that the formation of the NRRO was "a big step for Ontario Mennonites."[94] In the wake of a clear ruling from the Justice Department, fundraising commenced immediately, and roughly $80,000 was eventually disbursed.[95] However, as public opinion influenced interpretation of the Act, Mennonites became hesitant and the work of the NRRO was "sidetracked by the uncertainties of the Mennonite position under the law."[96] The work may have been unfocused, but collaboration in the NRRO did sow the seeds for cooperative efforts among Canadian Mennonites. Mennonite women formed the Ontario Branch of the Mennonite Women's Missionary Society and contributed clothing for relief of war victims and those affected by the Halifax explosion. And, while the NRRO went dormant after the war, it was reactivated and placed under the administration of the Conference of Historic Peace Churches when it was established in 1940.[97] The formation, in 1920, of the Mennonite Central Committee (MCC) by North American Mennonites to assist Russian Mennonites affected by war and famine is another example of the joint efforts of Mennonites that grew out of their wartime experience.[98]

91. Epp, *Mennonites in Canada*, 405–8.
92. Ibid., 371, 376–77.
93. As quoted in Burkholder, *Brief History of the Mennonites*, 274.
94. Epp, *Mennonites in Canada*, 377.
95. Burkholder, claims that $75,000 was raised by the NRRO (*Brief History of the Mennonites*, 275); Epp provides the figure of $80,000 (*Mennonites in Canada*, 377).
96. Epp, *Mennonites in Canada*, 377.
97. Harder-Gissing, "Companions," 5.
98. Ibid., 5.

CONCLUSION

Although their experiences differed, Quakers and Mennonites were profoundly affected by the events of the Great War. Quakers had begun to revisit their peace testimony at the end of the nineteenth century, but until the conflagration of this global conflict, their approach to war remained quite distant. Initial forays into reassessing the Quakers' relation to a peaceful world focussed on advocating arbitration to solve international disputes. It is little wonder that Canadian Quakers greeted the establishment of the League of Nations so thankfully.[99] Not all Quakers were pleased with the police powers endowed in the League, but many considered it the best alternative under the circumstances.[100] The intensity of slaughter and emotion in the First World War caused Quakers to think beyond the value of arbitration. Alternative or non-combatant service could relieve some miseries of armed conflict, and reconstruction work such as that of the Quaker International Centres could address some of the immediate effects of war.[101] But how could war be prevented? What were its causes and how could the Religious Society of Friends be part of the solution to the problems of international conflict? How could the world be made more just? These were the questions to which Quakers turned their attention at the end of the war. Having worked cooperatively throughout the war, Canadian Quakers discovered that the differences that divided them were not as great as the concerns they shared.[102] Noticeable during this period was a change in conviction to active pacifism. Quakers in the post-war years focused their efforts on reforming the political and economic order within and among nations.[103] Canadian Mennonites were occupied with meeting the needs of their Russian brethren who faced war and famine in the post-war Soviet Union. The activist stage of their peace work would not

---

99. *Minutes of the Canada Yearly Meeting, 1919* (Orthodox), 20–21.

100. Waugh, "League of Nations."

101. In 1919, British Quakers formed the Council of International Service to carry the peace message to Europe and overseas. Through this initiative, Quaker Embassies, later renamed Quaker International Centres, were established in most major European cities: by 1923 they were located in Paris, Berlin, Frankfurt, Nurnberg, Geneva, Warsaw, Vienna, and Moscow. See Waugh, "League of Nations," 63.

102. In 1931, Quakers from all three branches were instrumental in establishing the Canadian Friends Service Committee that tackles social justice issues nationally and internationally.

103. Socknat, *Witness*, 115.

begin until later in the century,[104] but their experience in the First World War drew them into cooperation with one another and heightened "a new awareness of themselves, their unique position within Canadian society, and their possible future role in non-violent constructive action in this world."[105]

---

104. Driedger and Kraybill, *Peacemaking*; Regher, *Mennonites 1939–1970*
105. Socknat, *Witness*, 78.

BIBLIOGRAPHY

Primary Sources

Archives

CYMA – Canadian Yearly Meeting Archives, Newmarket, Ontario
The Canadian Friend, 1910–1920. Accessed in CYMA.
Military Service Act Folder. In CYMA.
Minutes of the Canada Yearly Meeting of the Society of Friends (Conservative), 1898–1920. In CYMA.
Minutes of the Canada Yearly Meeting of the Society of Friends (Orthodox), 1898–1920. In CYMA.
Minutes of the Genesee Yearly Meeting of Friends, 1898–1920. In CYMA.

Publications

The American Friends' Peace Conference Held at Philadelphia, Twelfth Month 12th, 13th and 14th 1901. Philadelphia: Published by the Conference, 1902.
Fifth Census of Canada, 1911. Ottawa: C. H. Parmlee, 1913.
A Journal or Historical Account of the Life, Travels, Sufferings, Christian Experiences, and Labour of Love, in the Work of that Ancient, Eminent, and Faithful Servant of Jesus Christ, George Fox; Who Departed This Life in Great Peace with the Lord, the 13th of the 11th Month, 1690. 6th ed. Leeds: Printed by Anthony Picard, 1836.
London Yearly Meeting. *A Collection of the Epistles from the Yearly Meeting of Friends in London, to the Quarterly & Monthly Meetings in Great Britain, Ireland, and Elsewhere, from 1675 to 1820; Being from the First Establishment of That Meeting to the Present Time*. New York: Samuel Wood & Sons, 1821. Accessed in CYMA.
Mennonites on Military Service: A Statement of our Position on Military Service, as adopted by the Mennonite General Conference, 29 August 1917. http://www.gameo.org/encyclopedia/contents/statement_of_our_position_on_military_service_mennonite_church_1917.
Thatcher, Albert G. "The Quakers' Attitude toward War." *The Advocate of Peace* 79, no. 8 (1917) 238–39.

Secondary Sources

Armishaw, Bradley. "The Hutterites' Story of War-Time Migration from South Dakota to Manitoba and Alberta." *Journal of Mennonite Studies* 28 (2010) 225–46.
Barbour, Hugh, Christopher Densmore, Elizabeth H. Moger, Nancy C. Sorel, Alson D. Van Wagner, and Arthur J. Worrall. *Quaker Crosscurrents: Three Hundred Years of Friends in the New York Yearly Meetings*. Syracuse, NY: Syracuse University Press, 1995.
Bergen, John J. "The World Wars and Education among Mennonites in Canada." *Journal of Mennonite Studies* 8 (1990) 156–72.
Brock, Peter. *Freedom from War: Non-Sectarian Pacifism, 1814–1914*. Toronto: University of Toronto Press, 1991.
———. *Pacifism in Europe to 1914*. Princeton, NJ: Princeton University Press, 1972.

———. *Pacifism in the United States from the Colonial Era to the First World War.* Princeton, NJ: Princeton University Press, 1968.
———. *Pioneers of the Peaceable Kingdom: The Quaker Peace Testimony from the Colonial Era to the First World War.* Princeton, NJ: Princeton University Press, 1968.
———. *The Quaker Peace Testimony 1660 to 1914.* York: William Sessions, 1990.
———. *Twentieth-Century Pacifism.* New York: Van Nostrand Reinhold, 1970.
Brock, Peter, and Thomas Paul Socknat, eds. *Challenge to Mars: Essays on Pacifism from 1918 to 1945.* Toronto: University of Toronto Press, 1999.
Brock, Peter, ed. *"These Strange Criminals": An Anthology of Prison Memoirs by Conscientious Objectors from the Great War to the Cold War.* Toronto: University of Toronto Press, 2004.
Burkholder, Lewis J. *A Brief History of the Mennonites in Ontario.* Toronto: Mennonite Conference of Ontario, 1935.
Curry, Cecil B. "The Devolution of Quaker Pacifism: A Kansas Case Study, 1860–1955." *Kansas History* 6 (1983) 120–33.
Den Boggende, Bert. "Reluctant Absolutist: Malcolm Sparkes' Conscientious Objections to World War I." *Quaker Studies* 10 (2005) 67–86.
———. "The Fellowship of Reconciliation's Propaganda and Theodora Wilson Wilson's Literary Contribution." *Quaker Studies* 12 (2007) 107–28.
Dorland, Arthur G. *The Quakers in Canada: A History.* Toronto: Ryerson, 1968.
Driedger, Leo, and Donald B. Kraybill. *Mennonite Peacemaking: From Quietism to Activism.* Scottsdale, PA: Herald, 1994.
Epp, Frank H. *Mennonites in Canada, 1786–1920: The History of a Separate People.* Toronto: Macmillan, 1974.
Friesen, Jennifer D. "Stirrings of Conscience: Dreams of a Soldier of Peace." *Journal of Mennonite Studies* 8 (1990) 115–30.
Frost, J. William. "'Our Deeds Carry Our Message': The Early History of the American Friends Service Committee." *Quaker History* 81 (1992) 1–51.
Funk, Merle J. F. "Divided Loyalties: Mennonite and Hutterite Responses to the United States at War, Hutchinson County, South Dakota, 1917–1918." *Mennonite Life* 52 (1997) 24–32.
Gatrell, Peter. "Refugees and Forced Migrants during the First World War." *Immigrants & Minorities* 26 (2008) 82–110.
Greenwood, John Ormerod. *Friends and Relief.* Vol. 1 of *Quaker Encounters.* York: William Sessions, 1975.
Hamm, Thomas D. *The Transformation of American Quakerism: Orthodox Friends, 1800–1907.* Bloomington, IN: Indiana University Press, 1988.
Hamm, Thomas D., Margaret Marconi, Gretchen Kleinhen Salinas, and Benjamin Whitman. "The Decline of Quaker Pacifism in the Twentieth Century: Indiana Yearly Meeting of Friends as a Case Study." *Indiana Magazine of History* 96 (2000) 45–71.
Harder-Gissing, Laureen. "Companions on the 'Lonely Path': The Conference of Historic Peace Churches, 1940–1964." *Canadian Journal of Quaker History* 76 (2011) 1–16.
Healey, Robynne Rogers. *From Quaker to Upper Canadian: Faith and Community among Yonge Street Friends, 1801–1850.* Montreal and Kingston: McGill-Queen's University Press, 2006.
———. "Reconciling Approaches to Non-Violence and Apartheid: Pacifist Conflict between Southern African Quakers and the AFSC in the 1970s and 1980s."

Paper presented at the Eighteenth Biennial Conference of Quaker Historians and Archivists, Pickering College, Newmarket, Ontario, 22 June 2012.

———. "Thirty-One Hours on Grindstone Island: The Canadian and American Friends Service Committees' Experiment in Civil Defence." *Canadian Quaker History Journal* 71 (2006) 22–32.

———. "Wrestling with the Lesser Evil: Quakers and the Sons of Freedom in Mid-Twentieth Century British Columbia." In *Historical Papers 2006: Canadian Society of Church History*, edited by Brian Gobbett, Bruce L. Guenther, and Robynne Rogers Healey, 55–70.

Horman, Gerlof D. *American Mennonites and the Great War, 1914–1918*. Scottsdale, PA: Herald, 1994.

———. "Mennonites and Military Justice in World War I." *Mennonite Quarterly Review* 66 (1992) 365–75.

Howlett, Charles F. "Quaker Conscience in the Classroom: The Mary S. McDowell Case." *Quaker History* 83 (1994) 99–115.

Huxman, Susan Schultz. "Mennonite Rhetoric in World War I: Lobbying the Government for Freedom of Conscience." *Mennonite Quarterly Review* 67 (1993) 283–303.

Jones, Mary Hoxie. *Swords into Ploughshares: An Account of the American Friends Service Committee, 1917–1932*. New York: Macmillan, 1937.

Jones, Rufus. *A Service of Love in Wartime: American Friends' Relief Work in Europe, 1917–1919*. New York: Macmillan, 1920.

Juhnke, James C. "Mennonites and Ambivalent Civil Religion in World War I." *Mennonite Quarterly Review* 65 (1991) 160–68.

Keim, Albert N., and Grant M. Stolzfus. *The Politics of Conscience: The Historic Peace Churches and America at War, 1917–1955*. Scottsdale, PA: Herald, 1988.

Kohrman, Allan. "Respectable Pacifists: Quaker Response to World War I." *Quaker History* 75 (1986) 35–53.

Manousos, Anthony. "Guilford College, North Carolina Friends and the First World War." *Southern Friend* 25 (2003) 27–38.

Miller, Andrew T. "A Quaker Community in Times of War: Friends in Salem, New Jersey." *New Jersey Folklife* 15 (1990) 37–49.

Mock, Melanie Springer. *Writing Peace: The Unheard Voices of Great War Mennonite Objectors*. Telford, PA: Pandora, 2003.

Neufeldt, Reina C. "Tolerant Exclusion: Expanding Constricted Narratives of Wartime Ethnic and Civic Nationalism." *Nations and Nationalism* 15 (2009) 206–26.

Regher, T. D. *Mennonites in Canada, 1939–1970: A People Transformed*. Toronto: University of Toronto Press, 1996.

Shaw, Amy. *Crisis of Conscience: Conscientious Objection in Canada during the First World War*. Vancouver: University of British Columbia Press, 2009.

Socknat, Thomas P. *Witness against War: Pacifism in Canada, 1900–1945*. Toronto: University of Toronto Press, 1987.

Strege, Merle D. "The Demise of a Peace Church: The Church of God (Anderson), Pacifism and Civil Religion." *Mennonite Quarterly Review* 65 (1991) 128–40.

Teichroew, Allan. "World War I and the Mennonite Migration to Canada to Avoid the Draft." *Mennonite Quarterly Review* 45 (1971) 219–49.

Waugh, Maureen. "Quakers, Peace and the League of Nations: The Role of Bertram Pickard." *Quaker Studies* 6 (2001) 59–79.

10

Dismissed

Military Chaplains and Canadian Great War History

Duff Crerar

Many Canadian Great War chaplains came home from their war with high hopes for a church-led revolution in public life, one in which they would play a leading role. Their story had been one of progress from maladministration to professionalism, from the rear area to the front line, from baggage and handymen to agents of God as the soldier's comrade. They had outlasted what they felt was a corrupt Minister of Militia and his chaplain cronies and reformed the service from within. Over 450 had served in Canadian uniform, and many others in the Allied forces of France, Great Britain, and the United States.[1] In the field, they had overcome regulations and attitudes that almost kept them cloistered from the men at the front. Canadian chaplains led the way among the British and Dominion troops and paid the cost in wounds, death, and disablement. They had been energized by closer and more intimate relationships with the rough, tough, and ruthlessly

---

1. This number is based on actual personal files kept in LAC, RG9, Militia and Defence, Series IIIC15, CEF records, Canadian Chaplain Service, Vols. 4615–75. Since 1995, David Love has done more than any Canadian scholar to reconstruct an exact chaplain count. His conclusions raise the number, despite a task complicated by chaplains that claimed Canadian origin, yet served in other contingents, or CEF chaplains born elsewhere, such as missionaries to Canada, who demobilized as immigrants and served in Canadian churches after the war. See Love, *A Call to Arms*.

democratic Canadian soldiers who had accepted them into their fellowship, and they believed this would be a tremendous asset in bringing these men back to tired and class-ridden churches in order to create a new Christian Canada. Yet the victory did not bring vindication. One by one, the government, their denominations, some of their beloved soldiers, and most Canadian historians dismissed them. For a nation once self-styled and institutionalized as one of the most Christian nations on earth, where clergy occupied positions of pride and influence in private and public life, and where the social passion and Christian involvement in Canadian public life continued on for generations after the war, the phenomenon of the Great War military chaplaincy offers a challenge for both those examining Canadian faith and those examining the fighting spirit of the troops overseas. Joining up as individuals, they served together in a mighty national entity, the Canadian Expeditionary Force, where their branch gave meaning and purpose to the brutality, chaos, and pain of war. Coming home, they found themselves alone again, individuals left by the tides of demobilization, serving congregations alienated, divided, and often unwilling to take on the postwar mission the chaplains envisioned overseas.

Almost every chaplain went to war with the endorsement of his denomination, though after a year or so some spouses, bishops, and local parishes regretted their departure. As Gordon Heath has demonstrated, the Canadian churches during the South African war also pioneered the discourse and expectations of the churches in the next war, based on an entirely optimistic view of providence. By 1914, Canadians had been told for generations that God used war to make, break, and edify the nations. In the optimistic and ambitious era of competing Canadian nationalisms before and during the war, the proper responses of a nation, ranging from repentance to militant idealism, were interpreted by many public leaders—and often by the clergy—as signs of the progress of the Kingdom of God. Missionary movements were furthered by and depended on the military service of Christian soldiers. Even humiliating setbacks and disasters, such as those in the Crimean and South African Wars, could be integrated into the optimistic matrix of beliefs as the Bible provided ample stories of sin, defeat, and humiliation leading to national repentance and vindication.[2] Nor, initially, did most Canadians have doubts about the righteousness of the war. Reading the

---

2. Heath, *Silver Lining*, 63–70, 87–108, 128–38; Heath, "Sin in the Camp."

papers and digesting news from the old countries, it seemed indisputable that Germany's aggression had guaranteed a general war in Europe after Sarajevo. Reports of the firing of Dinant and Louvain in 1914, followed by the use of gas against Canadians, the Bryce report on alleged German atrocities, and the sinking of the passenger liner *Lusitania* in the spring of 1915, justified a war without limits.[3] There would be no place, even in the darkest and most disappointing hours of 1916, for sober reassessment of such commitments, and years later, grieving Canadians would fiercely deny that the war had been a waste.[4]

While Canadians at home endured, their soldiers grappled with glory, defeat, sacrifice, and loss. Within weeks of arriving in England, most realized that a gulf had opened between them and home that would never entirely be closed, even if they lived long enough to get back. Their truth, their experiences, their realities, could never be conveyed home, partly because there were no words to describe them. To pass into uniform and cross the seas was to enter a different world, where only fellow soldiers could understand and offer support and courage. Naïve enthusiasm fell away, replaced by black humor, ribaldry, and the culture of revolt, though few soldiers ever acted against the necessity of fighting it out to the end.[5] To keep up the will to engage the enemy required a special type of moral spirit, one conditioned to the pace and character of a tremendous siege. The unliveable had to be made purposeful. Religion thus had its place, both at home, and overseas, where Christian teaching, even if only residual, played an important role in soldier thinking.[6] Canadian troops were not heartless killers, but paradoxically were ferocious fighters who also turned over their own rations to needy civilians and refugees, tended enemy wounded and dying with rough tenderness, and prayed fiercely or worshipped devoutly when no one was watching, when the chips were down, and even when not ordered to do so. Church parades were resented and official religion rebuffed, but a deep and abiding creed of fairness, generosity, and devotion to others, an ethic not that different from what religious leaders called for, one that blended disdain for conventional sentimental religiosity and moralism with outspoken

3. Crerar, *Padres*, 29, 40–41, 163.
4. Vance, *Death So Noble*, 3, 12–18, 26, 32–24.
5. Cook, "Anti-heroes," 171–93. See also Cook, *Sharp End*, and Cook, *Shock Troops*.
6. It is hard to imagine how the load of grief every nation had to bear in the Great War could have been managed without its churches and other religious institutions.

practical democracy, loyalty, and service, characterized so many soldiers of the CEF, that at the front observers could easily think that the war had worked some kind of religious revival.

Into this matrix of hope and hell came the officers expected to ground the troops in the home truths of religion and right thinking. Like many in the CEF, most chaplains joined up as complete amateurs, with little military experience, training, culture, or discipline, and, like their brother officers and soldiers, by the end of 1916 most had become objects or victims of direct intervention and manipulation by their political master, Sir Sam Hughes. Though his personal, if erratic, oversight gave the chaplains more clout at the War Office over their organization and deployment than any other Dominion chaplaincy—even, at times, the British Army—his personally selected and sycophantic chaplaincy leaders gave the padres an increasingly bad reputation. His rough and ready, generally helpful advice to take castor oil instead of pistols, and orders to cheer the men on their way instead of treating them to religious "soft stuff," came from the distillation of his own South African war cavalry experience and the exploits of previous militia chaplains who had served in the 1885 Saskatchewan and South African contingents.[7] Yet Hughes knew how competitive the churches had always been over chaplaincy appointments. Denominations vied with each other to put their stamp on the nation's men and public consciousness in such times of crisis and glory, calculating that their success in achieving appointments and distinction in war would enhance their recognition as truly leading institutions of religion in the young nation.[8] Anglicans and Catholics, as the crises of 1870 and 1885 demonstrated, expected and often received preference in appointments, making the Methodist church outrageously jealous.[9] Similar jousting occurred in 1899, resulting in an Anglican priest being rushed up the gangplank just in time to sail with the Royal Canadian Regiment Special Service Force, which already boasted two other chaplains and a YMCA social worker. As in 1870, Methodists

---

7. Crerar, *Padres*, 21–23, 26–28, 31–33. Since 1914, characterizations of Hughes have ranged from genius to lunatic. Desmond Morton's astute assessment is found in *A Peculiar Kind*, 19–26, 99, 114–16.

8. Crerar, *Padres*, 22; Heath, *Silver Lining*, 73, 79–80.

9. Crerar, *Padres*, 15.

brought their objections to the floor of the House of Commons while Anglicans seethed in the religious press.[10]

To Hughes, this legacy provided both political dangers and opportunities. He already had curried the favor and trust of fellow Methodists—and Canadian mothers—by banning drinking at militia camps and enlisting leading Methodists such as Fenian Raids chaplain and Methodist educator Nathaniel Burwash as spokesmen for the cadet training movement.[11] Hughes determined that CEF chaplains would be recruited his way, appointed his way, and managed his way, while an Orange Lodge crony, Major the Rev. R. H. Steacy, an Anglican, was instructed to manage the religious ministry to the troops as one involuntarily ecumenical service. Ostensibly the ecumenical scheme pleased the minister's sense of national unity and equality, but also ensured that no special favors would be granted Roman Catholics and that, on his own authority, special dispensations would grant chaplaincies to groups such as the Salvation Army. Both decisions outraged, in turn, Catholics and Anglicans. British army officials would also be treated to lectures by Steacy (backed by Hughes from afar) on the interchangeability of Presbyterians and Methodists, since Canadian church union was only being deferred by the war, and on the fact that Canadians had no obligation to abide by War Office limitations on their numbers.[12] As long as Sir Sam was in charge, Steacy and his erstwhile Catholic deputy A. E. Burke would do as they were told.[13] The chaplains did have a pre-existing right to communicate directly with their own authorities on religious matters, but Hughes counted on Burke and Steacy suppressing any troublemakers from the front.

The Canadian Chaplain Service was thus designed for mismanagement. Hughes's control over appointments at home kept Canadian denominations divided and uninvolved in chaplaincy affairs and gave chaplains at the front no influence on service matters. The Minister's prejudices played, oddly enough, against both Roman Catholics and his

10. Ibid., 13–22; Heath, *Silver Lining*, 74–80.
11. Wood, *Militia Myths*, 177–85.
12. Crerar, *Padres*, 38–39, 46–55.
13. In August 1915, Rev. A. E. Burke, the controversial—and former—head of the Catholic Extension Society in Canada, had wangled a chaplaincy and passed himself off to the Pope as specially empowered by Ottawa to supervise Roman Catholic padres for Steacy. On Burke's pre-chaplain days, see McGowan, *Waning of the Green*, 232–40, 246–47, 254, also 401 n. 84.

own Methodist Church. Methodists, since 1884 the largest Protestant denomination in Canada, never accepted the fact that their young men refused to obey the law of statistics and enlist in large numbers in order for their denomination to qualify for the most Protestant chaplains.[14] Methodist troops were embarrassed by the gap between their leaders' public outrage and their sometimes pitifully low numbers in the ranks. Though Methodists often pilloried French-Canadian Roman Catholics for not enlisting, their own young men seemed too tied up in home front matters, while Catholic Irish and Scots from Toronto and the Maritimes were making sacrifices proportionately as great as or greater than both.[15] Yet Hughes blithely kept sending Methodist and Presbyterian chaplains in large numbers with each battalion or battery arriving overseas, despite the obviously greater proportion of Anglicans and Roman Catholics in the CEF. When Steacy advised the Minister to appoint more Anglicans, Hughes's menacing telegrams quickly brought him back into line. Hughes joked that Steacy already had enough Anglican padres to form his own brigade, but overseas it was Presbyterians and Methodists who were seen in embarrassing numbers.[16]

Nothing, however, disturbed Hughes manipulations and miscalculations more than the growing fury of Roman Catholic chaplains overseas. Troubles ranged from a general shortage of priests (leading to complaints in the Catholic press by soldiers themselves of pals dying without their ministry), to units such as the 22nd Battalion's (the Van Doos) arrival disrupting the entire 5th Brigade religious ministry since it also included a Nova Scotian battalion that required a Gaelic-speaking priest. Although Hughes consistently backed and won for his chaplains any request for more chaplains per division, he quickly intimidated Steacy and Burke into never allowing any exception to the one priest per Brigade ratio.[17] To Hughes, this was the essence of fairness to all denominations, but was an outrage to Roman Catholics. After their complaints to Bishops Morrison and Gauthier became public, and Burke publicly backed Steacy's breezy dismissal of the charge in the Canadian press, the priests overseas were pushed towards mutiny. Catholic chaplains already resented being placed under Protestant senior

14. Heath, *Silver Lining*, 76–80; Crerar, *Padres*, 39–43, 51–55.
15. McGowan, *Waning of the Green*, 256–68.
16. Crerar, *Padres*, 47–48, 55–56.
17. Ibid., 48–49.

Chaplains, contrary to canon law. During the summer of 1916, led by J. J. O'Gorman, Catholic priests at the Canadian Corps refused to serve any longer under Protestant supervision, or to take any more orders from Steacy or Burke. Steacy predictably suppressed the petition before it got back to Cabinet.[18] The churches were helpless. Unless a chaplain could get direct access to the Cabinet and rally an influential minister with as much or even more clout than Hughes, the overseas chaplaincy would stagger on. Something like a divine intervention was needed to break the situation open.

In August, 1916, the Canadian First Division was fighting on the Somme. As usual, Canada's chaplains, having outlived a 1914 directive banning chaplains from visiting the trenches, were scattered across the First Divisional area including the front lines. Like the most intrepid of their British colleagues, the Canadian padres realized that their influence on the men was directly proportional to the risks they shared with them. Some padres had already been winged by shrapnel or suffered blast injuries, and one, W. F. Harris, later died in hospital of shrapnel wounds.[19] John J. O'Gorman, too, was shipped back home to Ottawa with a badly mutilated arm. The Germans had given a tremendous gift to the Catholics overseas, for O'Gorman was from the Ottawa Archdiocese, widely known for his pro-war and pro-empire sentiments, and well respected by the Minister of Justice, C. J. Doherty, spokesman for English-speaking Catholics in Robert Borden's Cabinet. O'Gorman soon presented another copy of the infamous mutiny petition, letters, reports, and his own observations to Doherty.[20] After hearing from Doherty, the Prime Minister was livid. It is highly unlikely that O'Gorman alone tipped the balance against Hughes, especially as he was already in enough trouble for deceiving Borden in other ways, but it must have helped.[21]

18. Ibid., 50–55.
19. Ibid., 110, 118.
20. On Doherty's pre-war views, see McGowan, *Waning of the Green*, 177.
21. Crerar, *Padres*, 59–62.

Canadian Chaplain presides at the burial of an Officer, Oct, 1916, at the Somme. It was while performing a funeral such as this that Chaplain W. H. F. Harris was hit by shrapnel in the spine. He died a few months later in England. Image Credit: Canada, Department of National Defence/Library and Archives Canada, copy negative PA-000652.

January 1917 brought decisive reforms to the Chaplain Service. Major the Rev. John Almond (a South African War padre who, since 1914, had won the support of both his Protestant and Catholic staff at the front), Arthur Currie, Julian Byng, and other senior officers at Corps HQ presented a lengthy report and copies of incriminating documents that soon sent Steacy packing.[22] Burke, owing to his ecclesiastical status (equivalent to that of a bishop) and his claim to appointment by the Pope, lingered until Borden heard from the Catholic hierarchy, but soon he was on his way back to Canada, where he eventually found an appointment to the military flying schools in Texas.[23] Almond, with the trusted and brilliant Catholic chaplain W. T. Workman at his side, moved to London and became Director. Since 1915 Almond had seen signs of a character

22. Morton, *A Peculiar Kind*, 114–16.
23. Crerar, *Padres*, 62.

change in the soldiers that he attributed to religious revival, reporting that "the men have got hold of religion."[24] This conviction drove his reforms, preparing both the padres and especially the home churches for what he believed might be the most decisive contribution the war could make to Canada: the return of over half a million men who had seen the contribution of Christianity and the churches to their country, the war, the army, and victory, and who would transform churches and nation when they returned to Canadian life. This conviction, shared with many chaplains during and even after the war, empowered his greatest contributions to the Canadian chaplaincy, and ultimately resulted in his own and his chaplains' greatest disappointments in the peace that followed.

While the Canadian Corps trained for Vimy Ridge, Almond had sick, inefficient, demoralized, and surplus chaplains quietly returned to Canada. Almond presented a blueprint of the new Chaplain Service, the first since 1914. Despite an unorthodox requirement for more chaplains with the fighting units than any other military force, Almond was able to justify to General R. E. W. Turner, commander of the Canadians overseas, a permanent establishment of chaplains, with the denominations of the chaplains in direct proportion to the number of members of their communions overseas. He established a small galaxy of talented representatives of every denomination in his staff, making Workman his Roman Catholic Deputy and withdrawing any Protestant interference in Catholic administration. Almond's denominational parallelism kept each denomination working within its own lines, yet all knew that they had a credible representative in his leadership circle. A similar structure was employed at the Corps, and later with troops on Line of Communication. He mended fences with the Fifth Brigade, and in every increase of establishment (by war's end Canadians led the way in Dominion and British forces in numbers of chaplains per division) Roman Catholics were included. Not all Catholics were mollified, and the earlier situation would be seen as a barrier to any future combined service in 1939, but the Catholic Chaplains could now get back to winning the war with a fair chance to serve their flocks.

Almond was not, however, content with getting the chaplaincy in proper order. Soon Almond was able to place padres in almost every Canadian unit, from Forestry to Railway troops in England or France, as well as the huge and usually crowded hospitals. He put a chaplains' team

24. Ibid., 58; Morton, *Number's Up*, 242–43.

on the streets of London to divert soldiers on leave to safe and secure accommodation, and steer them away from vice and disease. He supported the senior Salvation Army chaplain serving with the Canadian Corps, who created a Chaplains' Social Service department, putting the long-debated Canadian ideal of ministering to bodies as well as souls into practice. Concert parties, cinemas, canteens, sports programs, and especially the provision of coffee and tea in the forward areas during assaults put chaplains in highly visible positions with cups of coffee and recreational goods in their hands as well as Missals and Bibles. Chaplains who sometimes disregarded orders or got themselves into scrapes with military authorities received his discreet backing, so long as it was justified as an opportunity to improve support to the troops.[25]

There was little doubt that the new Director and his methods were welcomed by CEF leaders. Almond and Arthur Currie, the Canadian Corps commander, corresponded often during the later months of the war, which probably contributed to Currie's Easter 1918 confirmation as an Anglican at Corps HQ. By then Almond had arranged a visit by a Canadian Bishop from New Westminster, who travelled to several sites to confirm scores of soldiers as Anglicans.[26] Almond arranged for other denominational officials to visit the troops, meet with their chaplains, introduce their soldiers into membership in their churches, and support the Service when they got home. Through Workman and O'Gorman (who returned in 1918) he welcomed the arrival of the Knights of Columbus Catholic Army Huts, alleviating Catholic complaints that their men were being forced into Protestant YMCA huts and canteens. Finally, in 1918, he received authorisation to create a parallel Chaplain Service branch in Canada in order to recruit new chaplains for overseas and also minister to the large training and recruiting depots and hospitals in each Military District. During a visit to Canada to inspect the new arrangement, Almond met with the war service boards and other officials of the Protestant denominations and of the YMCA in order to quell feuds and catalyze interdenominational harmony to support the work of the chaplains.[27] The chaplains were leading the churches into full mobilization to support their work and employ them in the post-war world, a far cry from the isolated and stifling early years overseas.

25. Crerar, *Padres*, 64–70.
26. Ibid., 63–64, 128–30.
27. Ibid., 71–82.

A Canadian Chaplain visits with the wounded at a relay station behind the line. Image Credit: Canada, Department of National Defence/Library and Archives Canada, copy negative PA-001779.

It was clear that Almond had big plans for his padres, as did the Anglican hierarchy for their post-war chaplains in England.[28] His early conviction that the war was turning troops back to God, and that chaplains could lead a religious revolution with them when they came back to the churches, led him to create two lengthy papers for the guidance of the churches back home. He spent the late summer of 1918 dispatching questionnaires and surveys to chaplains under his leadership, subsequently putting together a compendium of lessons learned and recommendations for home church adaptations so that they might welcome and harness the soldiers of Canada in the national regeneration that was expected to flow from the war. The Roman Catholics politely declined to take part, but Almond sponsored two separate reports, one to the Canadian Anglican hierarchy and another to the general community of Protestant denominations back home.

Over sixty Anglicans worked on the briefing for their church, led by D. V. Warner, well-known social gospel advocate in the General

---

28. Madigan, *Faith under Fire*, 25–27, 33–34, 43–48.

Synod. Two-thirds of the Anglican padres overseas endorsed the final product, which Warner and many others hoped would help church leaders at home bring soldiers, many having never darkened a church door before, into their congregations as the backbone of a mighty national revival. Although not all chaplains replied, and a few vigorously disagreed with the preliminary findings, by war's end Almond and his Protestant leadership, including G. G. D. Kilpatrick, E. H. Oliver, and H. A. Kent, as well as other Baptist, Congregationalist, Anglican, and Methodist representatives, produced their own outspoken and profoundly ambitious document, entitled "The Chaplains' Message to the Canadian Churches." It proclaimed that overseas the troops had learned a gospel of comradeship and social engagement, truer and more vital than the old dogmatism and class divisions that made the home churches repugnant to the veterans, and it was these men who had seen the Kingdom of God in action that were most needed in the church. This was the vital moment to remove any impediment—from doctrine to social teaching—to their cooperation with and through the churches, giving them a leading role in making Canada His Dominion. And there were no better representatives of the churches to advise and even lead these men back home than their padres.[29]

The chaplains overseas came to the last days of the war and the Armistice exhausted but hopeful. In the last one hundred days of the fight, more chaplains had been in action, and were sometimes wounded, killed, or suffering shell shock, than in any previous part of the war. Those that preached the great thanksgiving services at Mons and CEF locations in November 1918 lost no chance to point out how the great causes were both vindicated and yet imperilled by the victory. Canadians overseas must make sure the world did not slip back into its old ways, or that Canada remained untouched by the virtues of the soldiers and the lesson of their achievements won by such sacrifice. Soldiers were invited to swear a new oath to serve Canada in peace as faithfully and devotedly as they had served her and all humanity in the war. Having won the war, it was time now to win the peace.[30]

To chaplains returning to Canada over the next six months, however, the prospects of realizing this vision dimmed quickly. The Militia and reserves for Navy and Air Force underwent revision and reform,

29. Crerar, *Padres*, 167–71.
30. Ibid., 171–72, 201–6.

thanks to Arthur Currie, but the Canadian government had no intention of sponsoring a permanent military chaplaincy. For chaplains expecting this, or paid employment with Veterans' Re-establishment hospitals, there was only disappointment. William Beattie, former Director of Almond's Canadian arm and now Almond's successor, fought long and hard to retain a chaplaincy to the Permanent Force, but civilian clergy who had lost their small garrison stipends to Beattie's padres (and their Bishops) combined with finance and militia authorities determined to cut costs, and this meant his pleas, even with strong backing from Cardinal Begin and J. C. Roper, Anglican Bishop of Ottawa, fell on deaf ears. Beattie persuaded the Adjutant General to request a handful of army chaplaincies and one or two naval chaplains in Halifax and Esquimalt for the sake of discipline and good order, but even his support had no effect.[31] When Beattie appealed for backing from the Protestant churches, the Federal Council of Churches stood silently by.[32] On 31 December 1920, Beattie closed his office, and, on 1 June 1921, the Service was placed in the Non-Permanent Active Militia; unsupported by the churches, the chaplaincy was dismissed from military service.

Many chaplains also discovered that they were not entirely welcome even in their own denominations, especially when they began sharing their new ideas with those who had kept the home fires burning. Roman Catholics perhaps received the most simple and sincere welcome back since they had no revolutionary message, but many seemed in later years to stand apart from the mainstream clergy. A few, like B. J. Murdoch, suffered such extreme post-combat stress, or dealt with such crippling wounds, that they were unable to carry on normal parish ministries.[33] Among the others, and unlike chaplain veterans of the next war, none of the Great War priests were elevated to Bishop's rank. A rumor spread that they had been made too ecumenical, cooperating perhaps too easily with other denominations in the combined service, and one was bundled off to New England under the cloud of being a Jansenist.[34] A

31. LAC, "S. C. Mewburn to Adjutant General, 22 November 1919," RG9 IIIC 15, Chaplain Service Records, Vol. 4657, "Permanent Force" file. See also LAC, Beattie-Adjutant General Correspondence, Jan–11 March, 1920" Vol. 4649, "DCS Canada" file; see also LAC, RG 24, DND Central Headquarters Registry, Vol. 6558, HQ 868-15-1AC.

32. DND, "Militia General Orders, 1921, 19–20; General Order # 161, 1 June 1921." HQ 203-1-98, PC 1709 of 25 May 1921.

33. Daley, "Joseph Murdoch."

34. Telephone interview with nephew, name withheld, 26 August 1999.

few, such as Michael Gillis and Miles Thompkins, threw themselves into the Antigonish Movement. Others turned to foreign missions.[35]

Anglicans returned to a more openly ambivalent welcome. Beginning in the summer of 1918, editors and columnists in the Anglican press commented sourly that chaplains full of advice needed to settle down, get over their war, and get on with the normal work of the church. Wars did not turn men into saints; the bishops and parishes had suffered enough without their clergy off having adventures that had little or no relation to the real Kingdom work still needing to be done on mission fields and in the cities.[36] A communion already unsettled by the early seeds of the social gospel, now fully alarmed by what revolutionary socialism was doing in Russia, was likely to be hostile ground for sowing by wide-eyed padres just back from the war. If this was discouraging, even more bewildering and yet decisive in the eyes of Anglican chaplains was the absolute non-endorsement of their cause by the hierarchy. Rather than debate and propose implementations of the report publicly, the Anglican hierarchy suppressed the report and refused to pass it on to diocese and clergy. Next, the bishops vetoed the proposal to send it out through the War Service Commission of the General Synod, which endorsed this decision.[37] The chaplains to over half the Expeditionary Force had been dismissed by their church. Something much the same would occur in the other non-Catholic communions.

A similar series of disappointments met the authors of "The Chaplains' Message to the Canadian Churches." Beattie sent copies off to the Presbyterian Church and every non-Catholic Seminary in Canada, but there was no ringing endorsement afterwards.[38] Churches were encouraged to reach out to returned men, but there was no plan made to employ them as agents of reform. After making encouraging noises, all denominations rushed to demobilize their war service commissions. It seemed the churches were eager to forget the war, not undertake extensive reform or change priorities because of it. Methodists endorsed

35. Crerar, *Padres*, 132, 196; Cameron, *For the People*, 214–16, 315–18, 156, 166.

36. *Canadian Churchman*, 21 February 1918; 2 May 1918, 283; 27 March 1919, 200.

37. CACGSA, "Council for Social Service Papers, Box 8 War Service Commission Reports, 1918–1922," WSC meeting 29 April 1919; *Canadian Churchman*, 19 June 1919, 396; 11 September 1919, 585.

38. Presbyterian Church, *Acts and Proceedings, 1919*, 45, 266–67; *Presbyterian and Westminster*, 23 June 1919, 9; 3 July, 1919, 10.

an abbreviated version published in the *Christian Guardian*, but their War Service Commission undermined it, after its delegation returned from Europe, by stating that the men were happy with the church at home and willing to accept prohibition.[39] The Commission believed that probationers and theological students were eager to resume their progress in the ministry, and predicted that reform in the Methodist church would flow almost automatically into their church and national life. While these comments convinced a few Methodist chaplains that the leadership of their church was more out of touch with veterans than they realized, Baptist chaplains also divided into two factions over the "Message," a hint of the deeper schism in their ranks to come.[40] It was especially galling to Methodist chaplain dissenters with long service overseas, such as Chaplain E. E. Graham, that the General Superintendents' responses to their letters blended incomprehension with offers of recall, assuming they had been burned out, not enlightened, by long arduous service. The chaplains, optimists and realists alike, had been dismissed by the churches.

Some still hoped the returned men from overseas would stand by them in the battle for His Dominion, though alarming news from Winnipeg soon even turned chaplain against chaplain. Canon Scott slipped away from medical recuperation to join his boys at the General Strike, but as he was still in uniform, military authorities soon bundled him onto the next train back to Quebec.[41] Across the nation, veterans calling for social justice and a fair chance at jobs found chaplains divided for and against them, those in uniform showing little sympathy, and others in mufti speaking out against any manifestation of Bolshevism. Few seemed to have reflected on the image this dissension left of broken promises of postwar brotherhood. Some veterans resentfully returned to this theme in the United Church magazine, *New Outlook*, in 1936, calling chaplains back to their original compassion and advocacy for the soldiers.[42] Though many had talked spiritual radicalism overseas, in the face of secular radicalism most padres had proven to be moderates on the side of wealth, authority, and order.

39. *Christian Guardian*, 11 June 1919, 29–30; 12 March 1919, 2.

40. *Canadian Baptist*, 10 July 1919, 2; 17 July 1919, 2; 25 November 1920, 2. Crerar, *Padres*, 174–78, 207–8.

41. LAC, RG9 IIIC 15, Vol. 4641, F. G. Scott file; Crerar, *Padres*, 209–10.

42. Crerar, *Padres*, 210–11, 226.

In spite of the disappointments, one movement's success attracted prominent chaplains and seemed in line with the hopes of 1918. Presbyterian, Methodist, and Congregationalist ex-padres played leading roles in Church Union, founding the United Church of Canada. Their long-awaited hopes to create a truly national Protestant church, however, ironically led to complete alienation from almost a third of Presbyterian padres, who chose to remain with the continuing Presbyterians.[43] The Presbyterian chaplains who had contributed to the Chaplains' Message had endorsed the Union plan, but some supported a minority view for a federation, not organic union. Their voices were smothered by others impatiently clamoring for organic union. Events proved that the wartime solidarity of the Presbyterian chaplains was broken. In the ugly and unedifying conflicts that arose—in parishes, in the courts, and even in Parliament—chaplains found themselves gathered in opposing factions. While the new United Church of Canada, led by prominent ex-chaplains such as E. H. Oliver and Charles Gordon, embarked on the crusade for His Dominion, perhaps the greatest enterprise of Christian modernism in Canadian history left behind a battle-scarred and resentful remnant, dug in to preserve the past glories of Presbyterianism.[44]

As the 1920s drew to a close, the dynamism and disappointments could be kept in perspective by ex-chaplains who drew on their personal relationships with veterans in the drill halls and vestries, but others experienced perhaps the hardest rebuff of all when, in published memoirs and novels, even soldiers dismissed the padres. Initially, soldier writers as well as regimental chroniclers had little bad to say, especially in the first decade after the war, although L. M. Gould, who had served in the ranks, lambasted church parades and padres who believed in them. W. B. Kerr, like many others, singled out the brave and dedicated chaplains, especially Canon F. G. Scott, whose intrepid sallies into the trenches and sincere affection for the troops gave him a unique status in the Corps during and after the war. Gould's commentary confirmed something that Scott had noted: soldiers denounced padres, but would defend their own unit chaplain as different from the rest. Angry veterans, however, did not respect such nuances.[45] The publication of Charles Yale Harrison's *Generals Die in Bed* triggered a reply from Will Bird, a

43. LAC, RG9 IIIC 15, Vol. 5633, Questionnaire file; Crerar, *Padres*, 213–16.
44. Clifford, *Resistance*, 71–72, 106, 131–57, 170–71.
45. Scott, *Great War*, 99, 115–16; Crerar, *Padres*, 333 n. 21.

Maritime soldier repelled by Harrison's negative portrait of Canadian soldiers. Unfortunately for the padres, Bird's *And We Go On* (later republished as *Ghosts Have Warm Hands*) denounced his own chaplain as a consort of a widely-hated medical officer and who, though brave enough, was "for officers only."[46] To Bird, the more crusading the talk of a padre, the less he was in touch with the real soldier, and the more repellent his preaching. First published in the anti-war 1930s and re-released in the similar climate of the 1960s, Bird's account set the new conventional image of the Canadian chaplain, chiming in with similar caricatures produced by British writers such as Robert Graves and C. E. Montague. From the Depression era onwards, the literature on Canada's Great War padres followed divergent paths: the quietly courageous but war-wise padre, who recognized that his men often practised a purer form of comradeship than ever could be experienced in civilian life, or, on the other hand, the loud and unconvincing preacher, who without irony or insight preached the crusade and then ran for cover.[47]

Evidently Almond, and many of his padres, had misread the religious temper of the CEF. Embedded in many soldiers was a type of rage directed at crusading rhetoric and millennial idealism, which Will Bird's protagonist, Tommy, vented towards the conclusion of *And We Go On*. Tommy had only one word for padres, manifestly unfair to most chaplains, but one that rings throughout the pages of Canadian literature in the presence of clergy: "hypocrite." The chaplains, betrayed by their own education and by their own bonding with the troops overseas, had been blind to how much of the soldier's ethic was created by the struggle to survive in total war, and how great the gulf between wartime comradeship and home front incomprehension had become.

The preaching of the social gospel provided a providential vision for officers and men with similar education and religious upbringing, and the constant encounters with shell-shattered roadside crucifixes blended with the chaplains' preaching and the solidarity they promoted between suffering soldiers and the Savior at Calvary.[48] Soldiers wrestling with fear and injustice could readily see in Jesus a saviour who was not like the red-tabbed staff officers and ruthless military planners

---

46. Crerar, "Where's the Padre?" 151–54; Bird, *Go On*, 3–6, 279–81, 297–300, 337; Bird, *Communication Trench*; Bird, *Ghosts*, 139.

47. Noyes, *Stretcher Bearers*, 89–90, 168–69.

48. Crerar, *Padres*, 180–83.

who commanded them to die without sharing the hell of the trenches.[49] Yet the manly Jesus of the trenches offered many soldiers a model and a standard for Christianity to which they could compare their own padres or home churches, and not always with approval. Throughout the war, chaplains had been baffled by the tiny numbers of soldiers who took communion. Try as they might, Protestant padres seemed unable to coax many men forward, and often they turned envious eyes to the Catholic chaplains, whose men frequently and devoutly came to sacraments of reconciliation and renewal.[50] But most soldiers would not take communion in such a profane world, where their life and deeds included killing on command. Killing and killing again in the mouth of Hell for the Kingdom of God seemed a massive, even damnable, act of hypocrisy.[51] It was this intolerance of hypocrisy that made many ex-soldiers, from critics like Will Bird to thousands of silent—or absent—veterans in church circles after the war, disappointed and disillusioned, alienated from crusading preaching, churches, and parsons. For many veterans, God had been profoundly silent, even absent, from the Western Front, though his chaplains had filled the silence and absence with their words and deeds. But, as returned Baptist chaplain H. R. Nobles mused in front of the cenotaph in Regina at midnight, 11 November 1929, they had returned to something that was even more corrosive than war, the dismissal of the uncomprehending and ungrateful.[52]

Dismissed as a movement, the padres carried on as individuals. In the churches and the Legion halls most veterans greeted the padres, especially those they had known overseas, those whose attitude revealed they had not lost their ability to see each man as a worthy individual, in or out of uniform. Other chaplains went out to the drill halls and armories, experiencing the satisfaction of working with young and active men who held their service ribbons and grey hairs in awe, but who also demanded ministers and priests who were able to give practical help as well as sermons. These padres gave dignity to the work of military chaplaincy in such a way that when war broke out in 1939, their example inspired dozens of clerics to serve overseas, keeping the memory of the padres

---

49. See also Vance, *Death So Noble*, chap. 2.

50. Crerar, *Padres*, 149.

51. These doubts and difficulties are reflected throughout artillery veteran Philip Child's novel, *God's Sparrows*; see 146, 276–82.

52. H. R. Nobles's poem provided by Anita Nobles, 1983.

green among militia leaders. Perhaps more could be accomplished by their mere presence and kindness when veterans sidled up at the Legion, quietly turned up at the back door of the parsonage, nodded a greeting at a cenotaph, or shyly shook hands at the church door and used the old army line: "Padre, do you remember me?"

Though the Second World War temporarily renewed chaplain credibility, the debate among scholars and critics continues. To generations raised by veterans struggling with their own memories of the Second World War and disillusioned by the savage decolonization wars in Africa and Asia, it was inconceivable that clergymen would unprotestingly support the troops in the bloodbath of the trenches unless they were ridiculous buffoons or cynical hypocrites. The rehabilitation of padres by Canadian religious historians in the 1980s, however, made room for a more nuanced reassessment. Scholars, beginning with Carl Berger,[53] Michael Bliss,[54] and Richard Allen[55] and continuing through the works of Marguerite Van Die, Mark McGowan, Neil Clifford, Michael Gauvreau, Gordon Heath, and many others, have brought to life a period when Canadian religious teachers and leaders, and the young clerics destined to be chaplains, were already in preparation for a Great War, without knowing that their spiritual crises and critical studies were forearming them with the theological and militant idealism necessary for a physical as well as a moral and spiritual crusade.[56] Even the ancient Roman Catholic church, seemingly aloof from such passions, had its own view of the encroachments of modernism and secularization that were preparing the world for something like an eschatological judgment, a view that seemed already vindicated by the constant conflict of mutually exclusive nationalisms in Canada and abroad.[57] Given the coming of a war so brutal, so all-encompassing, and so revolutionary, few Canadians could resist the temptation to see the war as the work of Providence that must turn visions into millennial reality.[58]

53. Berger, *Sense of Power*.
54. Bliss, "Methodist Church and World War I."
55. Allen, *Social Passion*.
56. Van Die, *Evangelical Mind*. The key works of the historians listed here can be found in the Bibliography.
57. Murdoch, *Red Vineyard*, 169–71.
58. Grant, *Canadian Era*, 115; Crerar, *Padres*, 188–93.

Echoes of the negative stereotype continue today in the scholarship of military historians such as Desmond Morton and the secularization studies by David Marshall.[59] To Michael Gauvreau, though, the new religious temper of chastened "Christian Realism" and anti-ecclesiastical mysticism from the trenches prepared neo-orthodox or pragmatic evangelicals for the leadership of Canadian believers since the wars.[60] Jonathan Vance rehabilitated accounts of the interwar years from anachronistic stereotypes, demonstrating how the profound antiwar writing of the elite soldier writers did not represent the views of most Canadians, who, though often in grief and anger, recalled the war as just, the soldiers worthy, and the Christian interpretation of the war acceptable.[61] His work showed that writers such as Bird and Harrison found their largest audiences not in the interwar period, but in the anti-war 1950s and 1960s, where their agnostic and often bitter diatribes were eagerly snapped up by those who hated war, imperialism, and militarism of any kind. It was impossible for them to reach back over the intellectual watershed of the 1930s, much less the 1960s, as Gauvreau, Marshall, and Vance had. It is this inability to reach past—or, having reached past and grasped, to refrain from judgment—that seems continually to put our chaplains back into the photo albums, with the old uniforms and the bits of kit lying in attics across the nation.

However, recent wars, declared and undeclared, have brought the Canadian Forces, and especially the wellbeing of their soldiers and families, to the center of public life, and so media and pundits have given sympathetic attention to the labors of contemporary chaplains. Historical anecdotes and recollections have also reminded Canadians that soldiers continue to face ultimate issues, and that those who are trained in and conversant with meaning-making and regeneration of emotion and spirit still have an important role to play.

---

59. Morton, *Number's Up*, 241–43; Marshall, *Secularizing the Faith*, 163–75, 183.
60. Gauvreau, *Evangelical Century*, 260–65.
61. Vance, *Death So Noble*, 262–66.

BIBLIOGRAPHY

Primary Sources

ARCHIVES

CACGSA – Canadian Anglican Church General Synod Archives
DND – Department of National Defence
LAC – Library and Archives Canada
Presbyterian Church in Canada, *Acts and Proceedings, 1919.*

NEWSPAPERS

Canadian Baptist
Canadian Churchman
Christian Guardian
Presbyterian and Westminster

OTHER

Bird, Will R. *And We Go On*. Toronto: Hunter Rose, 1930.
———. *The Communication Trench*. Toronto: Briggs, 1933.
———. *Ghosts Have Warm Hands*. Toronto: Clarke, Irwin, 1968.
Child, Philip. *God's Sparrows*. Toronto: McClelland & Stewart, 1975 [1937].
Murdoch, B. J. *The Red Vineyard*. Cedar Rapids: Torch, 1923.
Noyes, Frederick. *Stretcher Bearers . . . At the Double!* Toronto: Hunter Rose, 1937.
Scott, F. G. *The Great War as I Saw It*. Toronto: McClelland & Goodchild, 1922.

Secondary Sources

Allen, A. R. *The Social Passion: Religion and Reform in Canada, 1914–1928*. Toronto: University of Toronto Press, 1972.
Berger, Carl. *The Sense of Power: Studies in the Ideas of Canadian Imperialism, 1867–1914*. Toronto: University of Toronto Press, 1970.
Bliss, Michael. "The Methodist Church and World War I." *Canadian Historical Review* 49 (1968) 213–33.
Cameron, James D. *For the People: A History of St Francis Xavier University*. Montreal and Kingston: McGill-Queen's University Press, 1996.
Clifford, Neil Keith. *The Resistance to Church Union in Canada, 1904–1939*. Vancouver: University of British Columbia Press, 1985.
Cook, Tim. "Anti-heroes of the Canadian Expeditionary Force." *Journal of the Canadian Historical Association* 19 (2008) 171–93.
———. *At the Sharp End: Canadians Fighting the Great War 1914–1916*. Toronto: Viking, 2007.
———. *Shock Troops: Canadians Fighting the Great War, 1917–1918*. Toronto: Viking, 2008.
Crerar, Duff. *Padres in No Man's Land: Canadian Chaplains and the Great War*. Montreal and Kingston: McGill-Queen's University Press, 1995.

———. "'Where's the Padre?': Canadian Memory and the Great War Chaplains." In *The Sword of the Lord: Military Chaplains from the First to the Twenty-first Centuries*, edited by Doris L. Bergen, 141–64. South Bend: Notre Dame University Press, 2004.

Daley, Chris. "Benedict Joseph Murdoch." New Brunswick Literary Encyclopedia. Online: http://w3.stu.ca/stu/sites/nble/.htm.

Gauvreau, Michael. *The Evangelical Century: College and Creed in English Canada from the Great Revival to the Great Depression*. Montreal and Kingston: McGill-Queen's University Press, 1991.

Grant, John Webster. *The Church in the Canadian Era*. Toronto: McGraw-Hill Ryerson, 1972.

Heath, Gordon. "Sin in the Camp: The Day of Humble Supplication in the Anglican Church in Canada in the Early Months of the South African War." *Journal of the Canadian Church Historical Society* 44 (2002) 207–26.

———. *A War with a Silver Lining: Canadian Protestant Churches and the South African War, 1899–1902*. Montreal and Kingston: McGill-Queen's University Press, 2009.

Love, David. *A Call to Arms: The Organization and Administration of Canada's Military in World War One*. Winnipeg: Bunker to Bunker Books, 1999.

Madigan, Edward. *Faith under Fire: Anglican Army Chaplains and the Great War*. New York: Palgrave McMillan, 2011.

Marshall, David. *Secularizing the Faith: Canadian Protestant Ministers and the Crisis of Belief, 1850–1940*. Toronto: University of Toronto Press, 1992.

McGowan, Mark. *The Waning of the Green: Catholics, the Irish and Identity in Toronto: 1887–1922*. Montreal and Kingston: McGill-Queen's University Press, 1999.

Morton, Desmond. *When Your Number's Up*. Toronto: Random, 1993.

———. *A Peculiar Kind of Politics: Canada's Overseas Ministry in the First World War*. Toronto: University of Toronto Press, 1982.

Wood, James. *Militia Myths: Ideas of the Canadian Citizen Soldier, 1896–1921*. Vancouver: University of British Columbia Press, 2010.

Vance, Jonathan. *Death So Noble: Memory, Meaning, and the First World War*. Vancouver, University of British Columbia Press, 1997.

Van Die, Marguerite. *An Evangelical Mind: Nathanael Burwash and the Methodist Tradition in Canada, 1839–1918*. Montreal and Kingston: McGill-Queen's University Press, 1989.

11

Paying "the price of war"

Canadian Women and the Churches on the Home Front

LUCILLE MARR

A WOMEN'S MARCH, REPORTED the 12 September 1918 *Canadian Churchman*, had been staged recently at the Toronto Exhibition to highlight the significant roles that women had been playing on the home front during the Great War's long, cruel years. The mobilization of civilians as volunteers in the Red Cross, along with a myriad of other organizations devoted to supporting enlisted men and their families, such as workers in industry, including munitions and farm labor, had created the concept of a "home front" during that war.[1] As Suzanne Evans has shown, far from the battlefield, "relying on censored letters from the trenches" and newspapers for their experience of the actual front, the experience of bereaved mothers was deeply poignant.[2] "Mother" brought up the rear of the parade, as the article put it, with "her hands full of gifts, her heart full of prayers, her gaze set overseas . . . ever ready with cheer and counsel and practical help for the girl-workers at home."[3]

---

1. Grayzel, *Women and the First World War*, 3; Elshtain, *Women and War*, 107, 111, 186; Prentice et al., *Canadian Women*, 144–46, 231; Francis et al., *Destinies*, 234; Heyman, *Daily Life*, 154–74; Whiteley, *Methodist Women*, 215.

2. Evans, *Mothers of Heroes*, 129. See also Vance, *Death So Noble*, 14; Lougheed, *Letters*.

3. "Women's Work," *Canadian Churchman*, 12 September 1918, 586.

Represented in that parade were what political theorist Jean Bethke Elshtain has named "civic cheerleaders" and "official mourners." The former signifies women who urged "men to behave like men, praising the heroes and condemning the cowardly." Meanwhile the latter—ironically often the same women—"lamented the destruction of the war" with its "most horrendous possibility . . . not so much of the deaths of particular individuals"—even "their own husbands and sons"—but of the British Empire's defeat by the Germans.[4] These "beautiful souls," Elshtain has argued, willingly paid the price of war from the home front.[5]

While much has been made of women's significant roles in support of the war effort, little has been written on the "Canadian war mother"[6] or the "pacifist few," as Elshtain has dubbed the wives and mothers of conscientious objectors.[7] Indeed, the latter were notably absent from the Canadian Exhibition parade. Although families of conscientious objectors did follow closely the tragic developments as war unfolded, supporting the suffering in quiet ways, and some even losing sons in battle, they also frequently experienced the xenophobia that emerged on the home front.[8] Further, as historian Marlene Epp has argued, Mennonite women carried the "nonconformity banner" that designated them as a people whose ethic of "love and nonresistance" separated them from the mainstream.[9]

The focus of this chapter is on the essential role played by the churches in supporting and shaping women's contributions to the war effort from the home front, and how women's involvement in religion gave them space to fulfill and expand their roles.[10] It has been well established that women were actively involved in the churches, and that they provided the majority of members.[11] As Marguerite Van

---

4. Elshtain, *Women and War*, 121; McClung, *In Times like These*, 15.

5. Elshtain, *Women and War*, 164–65.

6. Evans, *Mothers of Heroes*, 4–5.

7. Elshtain, *Women and War*, 202.

8. Burkholder, "Valley of the Shadow," *Gospel Herald*, 3 May 1917; *Diaries of Susannah Cressman*, 45, 54, 60–61; Epp, *Mennonite Women*, 204; Elshtain, *Women and War*, 115, and Heyman, *Daily Life*, 155.

9. Epp, "Nonconformity and Nonresistance," 62.

10. Allen has noted the significant role played by the churches in recruiting, organizing sewing and knitting circles, and inviting soldiers who were far from home to participate in recreational activities. See Allen, *Social Passion*, 35.

11. See Prentice et al., *Canadian Women*, 126; Christie, *Households of Faith*, 13–14.

Die has noted, the domestic sphere actually nurtured women's public expression of religion, with the churches providing a bridge between the private and the public.[12] For the purposes of this discussion, two religious communities—Canadian Anglicans[13] and Ontario Swiss or Old Mennonites[14]—will serve as case studies to illustrate the extremes in Canadian church women's experiences on the home front. As "civic cheerleaders" and "official mourners" on the one hand, and as carriers of the "banner of nonconformity" for the "pacifist few" on the other, Anglican and Mennonite women provided stability in their respective faith communities. Readers will discover how at times they offered parallel contributions, while at other times they came into conflict as they fostered the "values, beliefs and customs" of their particular affiliation.[15]

For Canadians, Britain's decision in the fall of 1914 to take sides in the conflict that had been brewing for some time on the continent would greatly disrupt the long peace and prosperity of a century.[16] In early September, Anglican Women's Association president Caroline Hall wrote from her home in Westmount, Quebec, naming the anxiety that had set in as tens of thousands of men—the majority from her own denomination—responded by enlisting:[17] "It seems difficult to settle

---

12. Van Die, "Revisiting," 236. As her title suggests, Billson has concluded that women from a variety of ethnic groups were "keepers of the culture." See Billson, *Keepers*, 3.

13. It is ironic that despite Anglican self-identification as "the best possible citizens" who demonstrated their willingness "to die for the Commonwealth" by supplying a much greater percentage of soldiers than any other denomination, there is a remarkable paucity of literature on Canadian Anglicans and war. The first Canadian contingent was 62 percent Anglican, and in 1918 the Bishop of Quebec told his synod that 45 percent of Canadian soldiers overseas were from the denomination. See Friesen, "Citizenship," 115; Knowles, "Many Messengers," 182.

14. Mennonites have countered their perceived irrelevance as pacifists in the historical record by thoroughly documenting their belief in separation of church and state, as is reflected in a lifestyle characterized by difference from the broader culture including nonresistance to violence and war. In boundless writings, they have expounded their "condemnation of war and killing as contrary to Christ's ethic of love." See Socknat, *Witness*, 12. Indeed, according to Heath, the "attention paid" to the small number of Canadian Mennonites and war is "unmatched." See Heath, "Churches and War," 64.

15. Billson, *Keepers*, 2–4. See also Vance, *Death So Noble*, 150.

16. Socknat, *Witness*, 43; Denison, "War and Women," 249.

17. Francis et al., *Destinies*, 227–28; Friesen, "Citizenship," 115. In a letter home shortly after he signed up, William Kedey alluded to his mother's attempts to convince

down to our ordinary routine when our thoughts and sympathies are with those whose husbands, sons and brothers are going to the front in answer to the call of the Empire."[18] Although Mennonites, with their stance of separation from the world, felt the impact of the war less immediately, they certainly were aware of the potential of this crisis. Already on New Year's Eve 1915, Susannah Cressman, an active member of the Berlin, Ontario (later Kitchener) Mennonite Ladies' Aid, recorded in her diary: "This has been the most remarkable year in history, the year of the greatest war the world has ever seen."[19]

Initially some mothers and wives, along with liberal pacifists and reformers, protested, echoing Methodist spokeswoman Nellie McClung and others who proclaimed loudly that "women . . . had nothing to say . . . except" to "pay the price."[20] They believed, as Olive Schreiner declared in the Anglican *Canadian Churchman* in the fall of 1915:

> The day when woman takes her place beside the man in the governance and arrangements of the external affairs of her race will also be the day that heralds the death of war as a means of arranging human differences. . . . [It] is because, on one point and on this point almost alone, the knowledge of woman, simply as woman, is superior to that of man; she knows the history of human flesh; she knows its cost, he does not.[21]

With the close association of faith identity and citizenship, belief in the war as a righteous cause and their role as citizens quickly overrode

---

him to stay at home (Lougheed, *Letters*, 8-9).

18. *Letter Leaflet*, October 1914, 391, MDA.

19. *Diaries of Susannah Cressman*, 54. See also Marr, *Transforming Power*, 28-30.

20. "Editorial," *Canadian Churchman*, 27 August 1914, 551. Prentice et al. have insisted that "Canada's involvement in the war . . . presented the greatest challenge to female reformers" with their "strong condemnation of violence, associated with men and male power." In what the former have described as "one of the most eloquent condemnations of all forms of war," Canadian suffragist McClung protested eloquently that war was a male enterprise. See Prentice et al., *Canadian Women*, 233. See also McClung, *In Times like These*, 15-18; Denison, "War and Women," 250. For further discussion, see Socknat, *Witness*, 4, 34, 50-51; Grayzel, *Women and the First World War*, 10.

21. "War and Woman," *Canadian Churchman*, 7 October 1915, 635. See also "Home Life," *Canadian Churchman*, 28 October 1915, 680. Denison also noted that "women paid the first great price." See Denison, "War and Women," 251. Socknat notes the irony that "women who helped popularize the idea that women would react to war differently from men because of their moral superiority were the very ones who contributed substantially to the disintegration of this myth through their various wartime endeavours." See Socknat, *Witness*, 48.

the reticence of most Canadian church women.²² Even Nellie McClung, with "a good deal of serious soul-searching" in Thomas Socknat's words, moved from pacifism to "a passionate desire for victory."²³ Though they had yet to gain the franchise, Canadian church women would, with the exception of a "pacifist few," come to support the Great War in all of the ways that demonstrated good citizenship.²⁴ Ironically, as Elshtain has emphasized, "mother and mother's milk serve[d] as a foundation for civic-spiritedness."²⁵ At the Divine Service held at the 1915 annual meeting of the Diocesan Women's Auxiliary, for instance, the Bishop of Montreal reminded those sitting in the pews of Christ Church Cathedral that "Motherhood" is "the greatest glory of women." He urged "all Mothers to seek the highest things for their sons and bring them to Christ's feet as workers for Him, remembering that it is in Christ and His Kingdom alone that the life of man can find its truest and fullest satisfaction."²⁶

With women long "considered the more pious of the sexes," as war mounted both Anglican and Mennonite church officials, along with families, counted on women's spirituality to provide stability.²⁷ In a world in chaos, home was lifted up as a place of "permanence" and "security" where children could be nurtured spiritually. For Anglicans, it was held up as a haven where men could return to receive comfort and restoration once the war was won.²⁸ As one soldier put it in a letter from the front:

> You angels at home are like the Spiritual Army Service Corps. Love and comfort flow out from you to us, and keep up the morale, without which an army is more useless than without its food. My mother is perfectly wonderful . . . she inspires one

---

22. A small core of radical feminists did maintain their pacifist stance throughout the war. See Socknat, *Witness*, 55–58; Chown, *Stairway*, 296.

23. Socknat, *Witness*, 51. See also Shaw, *Crisis of Conscience*, 8; Allen, *Social Passion*, 39.

24. Elshtain, *Women and War*, 111, 148–49; "Women in the Church," *Canadian Churchman*, 1 March 1917, 131; Knowles, "Many Messengers," 181; Allen, *Social Passion*, 42.

25. Elshtain, *Women and War*, 68.

26. 29th Annual Meeting of the Montreal Diocesan Branch Women's Auxiliary (23–26 February 1915), Minute Book, 93–94, MDA.

27. Van Die, "Revisiting," 238.

28. J. D. Masterman, "The Children and the War," *Canadian Churchman*, 7 October 1915, 635; "Home Life," *Canadian Churchman*, 28 October 1915, 680.

with confidence—always cheerful letters, and therefore she must always be deliberately banishing gloomy thoughts.[29]

Mennonite leaders, too, emphasized the home's influence on the church. With threats of conscription looming, mothers' prayers became a bedrock of security. On the same page as an article affirming historic conscientious objection privileges, for instance, the editor of the denominational publication *Gospel Herald* cited the following anonymous quotation: "The older I get the more thankful I am that I had a praying mother."[30] Pieces such as Orie Yoder's appeared, affirming the home's influence on the church, with some explicitly detailing women's prayer lives.[31] Women's support was essential to congregational prayer meetings as diarist Susannah Cressman suggested in the fall of 1917: "Sunday went to church in forenoon. . . . Service again in the afternoon, special prayer being offered in behalf of the boys who may after all have to go to war."[32]

The twin roles of mother and prayer warrior were also foundational to the divine service Anglican churchmen promoted for women. While challenging their congregations "to do their duty for God, king and country,"[33] they urged women to "pray . . . as you have never prayed before."[34] Calls for prayer appeared regularly in the *Churchman* and the Women's Auxiliary's *Letter Leaflet*. With the prayers provided, women were able to organize vigils in their "drawing rooms" and "chains of intercession" with "continuous prayer for our men on the front."[35]

Evidence abounds of Anglican women supporting the troops through devotional practices.[36] A letter from an anonymous mother

---

29. "Soldiers and Their Mothers' Influence," *Canadian Churchman*, 22 July 1915, 464.

30. J. C. G., "Military Service Act," *Gospel Herald*, 25 October 1917, 556.

31. Orie D. Yoder, "The Influence of the Home upon the Church," *Gospel Herald*, 18 July 1917, 278; "Mother's Easy Chair," *Gospel Herald*, 24 September 1914, 414.

32. *Diaries of Susannah Cressman*, 77.

33. Knowles, "Many Messengers," 182.

34. A. F. Winnington-Ingram, *Canadian Churchman*, 3 September 1914, 570. See also E. J. Hardy, "Divine Service," *Canadian Churchman*, 4 November 1915, 698.

35. See *Letter Leaflet*, October 1914, 363; "The Church Woman," *Canadian Churchman*, 8 July 1915, 428.

36. "The War and Devotion," *Canadian Churchman*, 22 April 1915, 248.

published in the *Churchman* spoke of heart-wrenching anguish in her call for women's prayers:

> The war is upon us; an awful war to which our men have responded nobly, and immediately. And our women have given them gladly, at the cost of suffering, privation and aching hearts. They follow them with hospital aid, money and care for their loved ones left behind, all of which call for untold time and strength. But another message would go to them through a sister-woman . . . that all women unite in prayer, earnest, believing prayer for peace. The peace God wants, and we want—and when our desire is one with His, the outcome is assured.[37]

A few months later Bessie Porter Head called for weekly prayer meetings in women's "drawing rooms." Naming "pleasure seeking" and the "great evil of increased drinking" as social ills to be overcome, she challenged *Churchman* readers: "We cannot go to the front to fight our country's battles, but we can go into the quiet room and "pray to our Father who seeth in secret."[38]

Moral decline also worried Mennonite leaders. They, too, emphasized temperance, but for them, as their young women began taking positions vacated by enlisting men, dress became the critical issue.[39] Obliquely reminiscent of Anglican mothers who were asked to release the sons they had borne, Mennonite officials insisted, in essence, that their women put their bodies on the line by providing a visible marker of what it meant to be a separate people. While Anglican clergy were encouraging women to do their duty for God, King and Country, Mennonite ministers were instructing female members to wear the cape dress (a vest of identical fabric over the bodice) and a prayer covering fashioned from white muslin or netting to demonstrate their faith. In May 1917, for instance, linking attitudes towards war and dress code, the *Gospel Herald* ran an article on "The Christian and War"; on the same page another promoted plain dress, reminding women of Saint Paul's admonitions to early Christians in 1 Timothy 2 and Romans 12:2, that

37. A Mother, "A Call to Prayer," *Canadian Churchman*, 3 September 1914, 575.

38. "Women and the War," *Canadian Churchman*, 1 April 1915, 198. Clergy viewed alcohol as an enemy equal to the Central Powers. See J. B. Funsten, "The Issues of the War," *Canadian Churchman*, 1 July 1915, 411. In 1915–1916, provincial governments from New Brunswick west, with the exception of Quebec, passed prohibition laws. See Allen, *Social Passion*, 39.

39. Epp, *Mennonite Women*, 185; *Diaries of Susannah Cressman*, 44.

women must dress modestly as an expression of their nonconformity to the world.[40] The head covering had taken on the significance of an ordinance, along with baptism, foot washing, and communion, based on their interpretation of 1 Corinthians 11, where Paul stated that women must cover their heads during worship to show their subordinate place.[41]

Controversy around the bonnet, designed to cover the prayer veiling in public spaces, would become a major issue during the war. Women began to protest this distinction designed to display their separation from "the militarism of society around them" because it rendered them vulnerable to xenophobia.[42] Indeed with their distinct apparel, Mennonite women "frequently felt public censure because their menfolk were perceived to be shirking their duty to the country."[43] Nowhere was this experienced more intensely than in Berlin, Ontario. (By the fall of 1916 Berlin city councilors would re-name the city Kitchener, after the famous commander Lord Kitchener.)[44]

In their history of that community, John English and Kenneth McLaughlin have described in detail "the dangers of the British-German war for people with roots shared by the enemy."[45] Although the first Berliner to fall was Elgin Eby, great-great-grandson of the city's Mennonite founder and well known among members of Berlin Mennonite Church, few German boys enlisted.[46] In her diary, Susannah Cressman detailed the riots and looting perpetrated by the largely British enlistees in the 118th Battalion, many of whom were from St. John's Anglican.[47] Indeed, the unit quickly gained what Laureen Harder

40. J. W. Smith, "Conformity to the World in Dress," *Gospel Herald*, 10 May 1917, 99–100. See also A. C. Good, "Dress," *Gospel Herald*, 24 May 1917, 130–31.

41. Epp, "Nonconformity and Nonresistance," 65; Epp, *Mennonite Women*, 181–84; R. J. Heatwole, "Ordinances," *Gospel Herald*, 24 September 1914, 411.

42. The bonnet question would develop into a source of deep tensions and ultimately cause a church split in Kitchener shortly after the war. For discussion of this issue, see Epp, *Mennonite Women*, 184, 188, 192, 204; "Nonconformity and Nonresistance," 55, 62; Harder, *Risk*, 33.

43. Epp, *Mennonite Women*, 204.

44. English and McLaughlin, *Kitchener*, 119; Epp, *Mennonite Women*, 220; *Diaries of Susannah Cressman*, 60.

45. English and McLaughlin, *Kitchener*, 113. For a full discussion on the xenophobia that developed during the war, see English and McLaughlin, *Kitchener*, 107–34; Heyman, *Daily Life*, 155.

46. Loewen, *Inside Out*, 257.

47. *Diaries of Susannah Cressman*, 37, 41, 57, 67. See also English and McLaughlin, *Kitchener*, 111; "Church News," *Canadian Churchman*, 30 March 1916, 202.

has described as "a loutish reputation." Soldiers harassed mercilessly "those who ... did not show enough enthusiasm for the war."[48] Learning to cherish "'public freedom' above 'private devotion,'" to use Elshtain's words, Anglican mothers supported their soldier sons in these activities, sometimes even expressing their gratitude for government compensation as families of enlistees by recruiting other mothers' sons; a St. John's mother demonstrated her enthusiasm by encouraging her daughter to volunteer as a dispatch messenger.[49] Meanwhile, Susannah Cressman's careful record of violent incidents and war hype suggests that Mennonite women felt forced to confront what carrying the nonconformity banner meant in a city that had become fraught with ethnic tension.[50]

Whatever stance they took, as wartime anxiety added strain to the strenuous duties already demanded in running the large households of the era, both Anglican and Mennonite women found comfort in their congregations and parishes. Anglican women had long brought the expertise gained from managing family budgets to supporting missions through the Women's Auxiliary and their congregations through Ladies' Guilds.[51] For instance, towards war's end the Arthur, Ontario, Women's Guild paid off a long-standing mortgage debt.[52] By all accounts, the Women's Auxiliary, launched fifty years earlier, also kept up a healthy momentum throughout the war years. In the fall of 1917, Anglican Women's Associations reported a membership of 35,000 women and girls; President Caroline Hall, who had recently returned from England where she had voyaged to nurse her wounded son, reported solid growth in the Women's Associations, despite war work "and the deep sorrow and anxiety brought by the war into the lives of many members."[53] Meanwhile, Mennonite women also expanded their mission. That same year, local sewing circles came together under the

---

48. Harder, *Risk*, 31.

49. Elshtain, *Women and War*, 93; Evans, *Mothers of Heroes*, 98; A Mother, "A Call to Prayer," *Canadian Churchman*, 3 September 1914, 575; "Editorial Notes," *Letter Leaflet*, October 1914, 386.

50. Harder, *Risk*, 33.

51. Fletcher, "Women's Separateness," 280; Prentice et al., *Canadian Women*, 233. In "The Church Woman," a regular column in the *Canadian Churchman*, the Anglican Women's Associations reported their activities. For instance, see *Canadian Churchman*, 5 March 1915, 136.

52. "The Church Woman," *Canadian Churchman*, 4 April 1918, 222.

53. "General Board of W. A.," *Canadian Churchman*, 18 October 1917, 667–68; "The Church Woman," *Canadian Churchman*, 4 April 1918, 222.

leadership of Kitchener Ladies' Aid member Mary Ann Cressman, with her election as president of the new Ontario branch of the Mennonite Woman's Missionary Society.[54]

These church-based organizations provided structures where women could draw consolation as they expanded their mission to knit bandages and socks for the Red Cross and prepare comfort packages to send to the front.[55] In July 1915, the *Churchman* carried a report of a "stirring paper" on "our Responsibilities during War Time" read at the Women's Association annual meeting held in Prince Albert, Alberta; it also itemized an impressive list of donations to the Red Cross from Toronto's St. David's parish: "156 handkerchiefs, 100 sheets, 28 pillow-slips, 11 towels, 88 bandages, 69 arm pads, 806 pads, 28 nightshirts, 42 pairs of socks, 4 pairs of wristlets, 21 Balaclava caps, 11 cholera belts, 1 pneumonia jacket, 9 surgical binders, 171 mouth wipes, 11 bags, 48 wash cloths, 1,598 pieces in all."[56]

In addition to their regular Auxiliary and Guild work, in 1917 the women from Toronto's St. Paul's reported contributions of an average of nine boxes per week, with a total of no less than 20,586 articles. Items requested from the front such as khaki flannel shirts, vermin resistant underwear, socks, pneumonia jackets, hot water bottle covers, pyjamas, amputation cases, face cloths, stretcher caps, surgical pads and compresses filled the boxes. Grieving and fearful hearts found ways to soften the harsh conditions in the trenches, tucking in Christmas stockings, baking, and other homemade treats.[57]

Meanwhile as the potential of conscription threatened their men, Mennonite women's pacifism, non-verbal as their required clothing illustrates, expanded to include "providing material relief ... to war sufferers overseas."[58] In March 1917, Susannah Cressman recorded in her diary: "Caller Red Cross lady to collect for whirlwind campaign to raise $150,000 for Patriotic purpose, gave $2.00"; "Sewing Circle met at M. C. Cressman's to make quilts for Red Cross Society."[59] The First Mennonite

54. Roth, *Willing Service*, 2–3; Harder, *Risk*, 32.

55. Grayzel, *Women and the First World War*, 3; Prentice et al., *Canadian Women*, 231–33; Whiteley, *Methodist Women*, 214; Francis et al., *Destinies*, 234.

56. "Church Woman," *Canadian Churchman*, 1 July 1915, 414.

57. Whiteley, *Methodist Women*, 216; "Church News," *Canadian Churchman*, 7 February 1918, 90; Lougheed, *Letters*, 33–34.

58. Epp, *Mennonite Women*, 205.

59. *Diaries of Susannah Cressman*, 69.

Ladies' Aid minutes confirm: "Made up 3 quilts and 4 doz bandages for Red Cross work." They also sent cash and clothing donations to Halifax for the survivors of the 1917 explosion. Regular meetings to knit and quilt would continue through war's end and after.[60]

It was through the churches that women were able to sustain, and reshape, ethnic and spiritual values threatened by war. Women in both groups were intentional about offering expressions of gratitude to those who enlisted, as they expanded their respective missions to offer succor through the Red Cross, the Canadian Patriotic Fund, and other organizations and initiatives that mushroomed during the war.[61] For both, their expressions of thankfulness were closely tied to their convictions. On their side, Mennonite women wished to demonstrate gratitude for the conscientious objection privileges offered their sons and brothers. As Epp has noted, Mennonite women's support of the Red Cross walked a "fine line . . . between patriotism and pacifism."[62] Despite the restrictions imposed on them, young Mennonite women were also counted among the "massive numbers" of Canadian women who joined the workforce as "the wartime economy moved into full gear."[63] Some even joined the Women's Institutes, closely affiliated with the Imperial Order of Daughters of the Empire.

Meanwhile, Anglican women responded to their obligation to support the Empire through the "strongly patriotic" IODE and a plethora of other organizations. "Encouraged to shame men into uniform," they were among Canada's chief recruiters, providing refreshments and entertainment for soldiers in parish halls, raising funds through social events and garden parties, creating spaces to care for injured soldiers, and even encouraging their children to raise funds.[64] Formed in 1902 with the mission of looking after the graves of soldiers who fell during the Boer War, the IODE played a significant educational role in Anglican

---

60. First Mennonite Ladies' Aid Minute Book, March 1917, MAO; Harder, *Risk*, 32.

61. Epp, *Mennonite Women*, 219; *Diaries of Susannah Cressman*, 42, 49; First Mennonite Ladies Aid Minute Book, 1916–23, MAO; "W. A. and Red Cross," *Canadian Churchman*, 21 June 1917, 400.

62. Epp, *Mennonite Women*, 212–13.

63. Prentice et al., *Canadian Women*, 143–44, 146.

64. Bucknal, *Witness*, 62, Morton and Wright, *Second Battle*, 191; "Church News," *Canadian Churchman*, 1 July 1915, 414; 8 July 1915, 434.

parishes.⁶⁵ Take for instance the Diocese of Columbia's Oak Bay St. Mary. In November 1915, the local chapter presented the Girl Guides with the Union Jack; clergyman G. H. Andres taught the meaning of the colors: "Purity, Truth, and Sacrifice," the cross denoting faith.⁶⁶

By 1917, with its strategic mobilization of women who, it was hoped, would teach their children to become informed members of the British Empire, the Daughters' zeal brought a membership increase of 10,000, with close to 100 new chapters. Fund-raising brought in more than 1.5 million dollars, and by war's end it was one of Canada's largest women's voluntary organizations.⁶⁷ Along with the IODE, Anglican women supported a variety of other organizations and created new ones: Soldiers' Comfort Leagues, Khaki Leagues, Queen Mary's Needlework Guilds, Sailors' Guilds, Suffragist War Auxiliaries, Daughters of the King clubs, YWCA Clubs, and Girls' Friendly Societies.⁶⁸

It is important to remember how much courage this civic cheerleading must have demanded, as women were forced to separate from the maternal ideal of protecting their children, to think larger than themselves towards a grand common purpose with its high price: supreme sacrifice.⁶⁹ Drawn into the larger political drama being played out on a European battlefield, Anglican women had no choice but to give up their sons and lovers.⁷⁰ In December 1917, for instance, the Anglican Young People's Association in the Hamilton diocese boasted to readers of the *Churchman* that every eligible young man had enlisted: "In spite of the loss they have sustained, those who are of necessity left behind, together with the assistance of the young ladies, are working to 'keep the home fires burning' till the boys come home."⁷¹

65. Prentice et al., *Canadian Women*, 232. See also English and McLaughlin, *Kitchener*, 111; Socknat, *Witness*, 49, 62; Evans, *Mothers of Heroes*, 79–80.

66. "Church News," *Canadian Churchman*, 25 November 1915, 751; Elshtain, *Women and War*, 107.

67. Prentice et al., *Canadian Women*, 114, 232. For the significant role women have taken in promoting nationalism during war, see Elshtain, *Women and War*, 118.

68. Prentice et al., *Canadian Women*, 231, 233; Evans, *Mothers of Heroes*, 98; Whiteley, *Methodist Women*, 214; "Church News," *Canadian Churchman*, 22 July 1915, 461; "Red Cross," *Canadian Churchman*, 14 October 1915, 654; *Canadian Churchman*, 18 November 1915, 732; 22 November 1914, 751; 7 February 1918, 90.

69. *Canadian Churchman*, 3 September 1914, 570.

70. Heyman, *Daily Life*, 243; Elshtain, *Women and War*, 75, 93.

71. "A. Y. P. A. Entertains Returned Soldiers," *Canadian Churchman*, 13 December 1917, 803.

For Mennonites, courage meant something quite different. Teaching nonresistance as the only way, the church overtly condemned combatants. In July 1917, the *Gospel Herald* reminded parents that their sons who had enlisted were "destroy[ing] men's lives—in the face of the edict, 'Thou shalt not kill.'" The editor opined: "The thing which ought to give to Christian parents having soldier boys the greatest concern" is not "what may happen to my body, but what am I doing to my fellow men and what will happen to my soul?"[72]

This hard hitting teaching presents a jarring contrast to the empathetic tone in the Anglican press with its stories revealing the suffering of countless young wives and mothers who had lost loved ones at the front."[73] People craved comfort, for the "good death" dictated by cultural norms and religious tradition, "in the family home with loving relatives gathered at the bedside," had been wrested away by the war machine. With some 60,000 young Canadian men dying violently far from home within a mere four years, in historian Neil Heyman's words, "often with their bodies unrecoverable if not completely destroyed," most Canadian families suffered deep psychological trauma.[74] Evidence of the grief and nervous strain resulting from these violent deaths permeates the pages of the *Churchman*. Poems, prayers, sermons, editorials, and children's stories were punctuated by advertisements with military imagery projecting relief for those who were willing to try Dr. Chase's nerve food: "Headaches, sleeplessness, and tired draggy feelings soon disappear when you restore vigour to the exhausted nerves by using Dr. Chase's Nerve Food," one ad promised.[75]

With its convictions, the Mennonite community was unable to provide public consolation to those suffering loss. While names of soldiers killed in action and records of military funerals appear in the privacy of Mennonite diaries, a heart-wrenching article published in *Gospel Herald* in the spring of 1917 stands out in its pathos.[76] Naming the silent grief

---

72. "The Serious Question," *Gospel Herald*, 5 July 1917, 257; J. R. Shank, "Lessons for Us from the Present World War," *Gospel Herald*, 15 November 1917, 610–11.

73. Stanley Clibey, "Fightin' for God," *Canadian Churchman*, 8 July 1915, 433; "Family," *Canadian Churchman*, 23 December 1915, 827; Jesmond Dean, "Women's Work," *Canadian Churchman*, 26 September 1918, 618.

74. Heyman, *Daily Life*, 239, 243.

75. *Canadian Churchman*, 19 August 1915, 531.

76. Loewen, *Inside Out*, 246, 249, 257; *Diaries of Susannah Cressman*, 77, 87–88; Epp, *Mennonite Women*, 212; Vance, *Death So Noble*, 118.

experienced by many, a young pastor, Oscar Burkholder, demonstrated unusual courage in attempting to make the issue public in the Mennonite community. Recently widowed himself, he confided: "I've watched my mother's face since two of her boys enlisted. The shadow is there—not sometimes, but continually." Underscoring his family's experience, he insisted, "We have the first family to meet that is not mourning because of the death of one on the battlefield, or in expectation of such a death. We are walking 'in the valley of the shadow of death.'"[77] Burkholder's piece suggests that although hardly a Mennonite family was unaffected by war's trauma, their nonresistant beliefs left little space to provide comfort for those who failed to conform.[78]

For Anglicans, the parish did provide a haven, bringing together the battlefield and sorrowing families, the "private sorrows of individuals" becoming "the common sorrow of the people."[79] Already in December 1915, for instance, the Deaconess House in Toronto solicited help for the escalating number of needy mothers who were losing husbands at the front.[80] Meanwhile the pages of the *Churchman* documented countless funerals and memorial services. Take for instance these parishes in the Huron Diocese. In July 1915, St. Paul's in Woodstock, Ontario, mourned the death of Lieutenant Cecil James and other members of the 22nd Oxford Rifles who had fallen by parading the Regiment "in full strength."[81] A military funeral at St. John's featured an organ solo of the "Dead March" in "Saul": "As the last strains of the organ died away, shrill and clear, from the back of the church came the sad bugle notes of the last post, long drawn out, as blown over a soldier's grave, working up into a

---

77. Burkholder, "Valley of the Shadow," *Gospel Herald*, 3 May 1917, 82; Bender, *Four Earthen Vessels*, 57–59, 63–64.

78. While there has been no close analysis of Mennonite soldiers during the First World War, studies of the Second World War have shown not only fairly large numbers of enlistees, but also how support for their families was withheld in their communities. See Regehr, "Lost Sons," 461–80.

79. "Canadian Losses," *Canadian Churchman*, 13 May 1915, 295. Grayzel has noted that "one way to characterize post-war Europe was as a world in mourning" (*Women and the First World War*, 111).

80. "Family," *Canadian Churchman*, 23 December 1915, 827. Anglican parishes contained as many as 50 percent of the 30,000 Canadian widows, children and parents bereft and dependent on "public bounty for their survival." See Morton and Wright, *Second Battle*, ix.

81. *Canadian Churchman*, 1 July 1915, 414.

volume of sound and finally dying away into silence."[82] Countless rituals marking the placing of brass plaques and stained glass windows, along with gifts including engraved offering plates, brought the battlefield and those who grieved together in the sacred space of the churches.[83]

Women often provided the funding and mothers were recognized in memorial services, as Canon Tucker of Carling's Heights' expression of sympathy for "the bereaved mother and other sorrowing ones" illustrates.[84] And yet as Suzanne Evans has pointed out, as official mourners, in order not to "damage the morale of others," mothers were required to accept their sons' deaths in quiet dignity.[85] The only memorials for the mothers who had sacrificed their sons were their broken hearts, the silence of their homes, and their sons' empty rooms. As a poem published in the *Churchman* poignantly put it, "a woman lowly kneeling . . . in her hand she holds a V.C. tightly . . . in her heart a grave in Flanders lies."[86]

Historians have stressed that rather than being given real opportunities to grieve, a mother became a symbol, "a bearer of memory for the community of her fallen son."[87] Reminiscent of the Mennonite woman's role as nonconformity bearer, Anglican mothers of fallen sons became Silver Cross mothers. Recipients of the Memorial Cross put out in December 1919 as a way of immortalizing the loss and sacrifice of mothers and widows by the Christian symbol of the cross, women bore the sign of their loved ones' graves.[88] As official mourner, in Evans words, she was not a "hysterical, wailing, hair-rending presence, but was stoical

---

82. "Church News," *Canadian Churchman*, 20 January 1916, 42.

83. "Church News," *Canadian Churchman*, 16 December 1915, 809; *Canadian Churchman*, 16 March 1916, 169; 19 April 1917, 253; 4 April 1918, 223; 18 April 1918, 254; "Personal and General," *Canadian Churchman*, 6 December 1917, 774.

84. *Canadian Churchman*, 22 July 1915, 414. See also "Church Woman," *Canadian Churchman*, 19 April 1917, 253.

85. Evans, *Mothers of Heroes*, 7–8. See also Vance, *Death So Noble*, 149.

86. "A Mother," *Canadian Churchman*, 23 March 1916, 183. See also Mrs. C. Cameron Waller, "Thoughts on the WA Devotional Portions," *Canadian Churchman*, 25 October 1917, 681; Lillie A. Brooks, "Canadian Mother," *Canadian Churchman*, 5 August 1915, 496; Elshtain, *Women and War*, 191; Heyman, *Daily Life*, 244.

87. Grayzel, *Women and the First World War*, 111; Evans, *Mothers of Heroes*, 4, 139; Vance, *Death So Noble*, 51.

88. Evans, *Mothers of Heroes*, 7, 101–2.

in her grief, a pillar of dignity, honouring her dead child and sanctifying the struggle by ensuring that we remember—but not too much."[89]

Canada honored bereaved mothers and widows with both "societal respect" and "material rewards" including political gains and pension plans, all with the stiff price of supreme sacrifice.[90] Robert Borden's union government, promoted from Anglican pulpits the Sunday before the election, had strategically planned to finally give women the franchise for which they had long been lobbying; however, it came with a price, in Evans words, "only to those who could reasonably be expected to vote for conscription."[91] Conscientious objection was "clearly anathema to most Canadians in 1917."[92] They and their families lost their right to participate in the political process. The Borden government's Military Voters Act and Wartime Elections Act bestowed the franchise only on the wives, widows, mothers, sisters, and daughters" of those, "alive or deceased, who had served or were serving in the Canadian or British military or naval forces." Drawing strong reactions among Quebecois, farmers, and pacifist groups, as feminist scholars have put it, the act "drew both praise and outrage from suffrage advocates."[93] The majority of Anglican women received this political reward for paying the ultimate price, while others, including Mennonite women, were deliberately excluded.

With their separate stance, this was unlikely to be an issue for most Mennonites;[94] for them, the problem was conscription.[95] In Socknat's words, Mennonites had "remained more or less silent on the war until they were threatened directly with conscription."[96] Women supported

89. Ibid., 157.

90. Ibid., 78; Francis et al., *Destinies*, 234, Prentice et al., *Canadian Women*, 234.

91. Evans, *Mothers of Heroes*, 97–98. See also Prentice et al., *Canadian Women*, 231; Francis et al., *Destinies*, 234; Heyman, *Daily Life*, 156.

92. Allen, *Social Passion*, 48.

93. Prentice et al., *Canadian Women*, 234. See also Shaw, *Crisis of Conscience*, 8; Evans, *Mothers of Heroes*, 96–97; Francis et al., *Destinies*, 234, 240–41. Kitchener Young People's Literary Society held a "large meeting" to debate women's suffrage already in 1915. See *Diaries of Susannah Cressman*, 180; Epp *Mennonite Women*, 216.

94. Epp, *Mennonite Women*, 216.

95. There is evidence that despite their separation from the world, Ontario Mennonites of the era did vote, at least in some elections. See "Diaries of Barbara (Bowman) Shuh," 59, cited in Epp, *Mennonite Women*, 216.

96. Socknat, *Witness*, 53.

their men's decision to provide a "'memorial gift for war relief'" as an expression of the historic "good will" that had allowed them conscientious objection privileges through Red Cross work from their settlement in Canada just over a century earlier. In 1918, twelve Ontario Mennonite sewing circles contributed 498 garments worth $214.81.[97]

In the roles of "nonconformity bearer," "civic cheerleader," and "official mourner," the First World War transformed Canadian womanhood. The price was high. Yet while mothers and lovers quietly mourned, the massive loss of young men opened up a new world, one that Elshtain and others have suggested the "new woman" had been waiting for.[98] Already by the summer of 1915, E. M. Knox, principal of Havergal College for women, had envisioned the potential: "Whilst the flower of our youth and manhood passes from us, the flower and youth of our womanhood remains," she told *Churchman* readers.[99] Two years later she optimistically confirmed: "Despite the tragedy on every side . . . the girls of today are in many respects brighter and more hopeful than the girls of past generations." They have suddenly awakened to a knowledge that they are intensely wanted. . . . A new world is opening at their feet."[100] Indeed history bears out that a result of the horrific devastation was the affirmation of "the propriety of women working for wages before marriage." By 1921, over 40 percent of all clerical workers were women and huge numbers of single women had developed professions.[101]

Meanwhile, with the high price symbolized by Silver Cross Mothers, official mourners provided for historical memory, a usable past that emphasized the nation's obligation to those who had fallen.[102] "Civic cheerleading" raised awareness of a variety of social issues including the adverse effects of alcohol, child labor, and conditions in mental hospitals

---

97. Epp, *Mennonites in Canada*, 376; cf. 365–66, 401; Marr, *Transforming Power*, 29, 31–33; First Mennonite Ladies' Aid Minute Book, 3 April 1918; WMSC Financial Records, Report of War Sufferers Relief Work for France and Belgium, 10 October 1918, MAO.

98. Elshtain, *Women and War*, 187; Francis et al., *Destinies*, 224; Grayzel, *Women and the First World War*, 62–64, 77; Prentice et al., *Canadian Women*, 146; Vance, *Death So Noble*, 51.

99. E. M. Knox, "An Answered Prayer," *Canadian Churchman*, 29 July 1915, 474.

100. E. M. Knox, "School Girl's War Outlook," *Canadian Churchman*, 5 July 1917, 427.

101. Prentice et al. *Canadian Women*, 145–46.

102. Vance, *Death So Noble*, 5, 9, 51.

and prisons, and ultimately gave Canadian women suffrage politically. On their part, Mennonite women turned their role as "nonconformity bearers" into expressions of gratitude as they contributed to the post-war relief that would became integral to the Mennonite mission of offering succor during future wars and conflicts.[103] Although both the Mennonite and Anglican churches were exasperatingly slow to recognize women in public roles, the conversation had begun.[104] Knox said it well, in these words penned with war's end in sight. "The heartbreak may remain, but 'high hope is ours.'" As she predicted, the dedication of women, with the support of the churches, would be highly significant in "the winning out of a new and spiritual future for a land bought back at a price."[105]

103. Marr, *Transforming Power*, 31–34.

104. Elizabeth Tilley, "Letter to the Editor," *Canadian Churchman*, 18 March 1915, 172; "Personal and General," *Canadian Churchman*, 24 June 1915, 401; Henry Macklin, "Women and Vestries," *Canadian Churchman*, 22 March 1917, 188; "Woman Movement and the Church," *Canadian Churchman*, 6 December 1917, 777; Prentice et al., *Canadian Women*, 231, 234; Francis et al., *Destinies*, 234; Socknat, *Witness*, 49.

105. E. M. Knox, "The Men Who Attain," *Canadian Churchman*, 12 September 1918, 587. Prentice et al. have argued that it is unlikely that the economic transformation Canada experienced post-war would have happened without women's support. See Prentice et al., *Canadian Women*, 113.

BIBLIOGRAPHY

Primary Sources

ARCHIVES
MAO – Mennonite Archives of Ontario.
MDA – Montreal Diocesan Archives (Anglican).

NEWSPAPERS
Canadian Churchman, 1914–18. Accessed in McLennan-Redpath Library, McGill University.
Gospel Herald, 1914–1918. Accessed in Conrad Grebel University Library.

OTHER
Diaries of Susannah Cressman, 1911–1946. Selected and prepared by Anne Eby Millar, and edited and annotated by D. Douglas Millar. Kitchener, ON, 1997. Accessed in MAO.
"Excerpts from Diaries of Barbara (Bowman) Shuh." In *Diaries of Pennsylvania German Ancestors, 1846–1925*, 45–70. Vol.15 of *Canadian-German Folklore*. Kitchener, ON: The Pennsylvania German Folklore Society of Ontario, 2002.
First Mennonite Ladies' Aid Minute Book, 1916–19. Accessed in MAO.
Letter Leaflet, October 1914–15. Women's Auxiliary papers. Accessed in MDA.
McClung, Nellie. *In Times like These*. Toronto: University of Toronto Press, 1972 [Reprint of 1915 edition].
Ontario Branch of the Mennonite Woman's Missionary Society Financial Records, 1918. Report of War. Accessed in MAO.
Sufferers Relief Work for France and Belgium. Accessed in MAO.
Women's Auxiliary Minute Book, 1914–1915. Women's Auxiliary papers. Accessed in MDA.

Secondary Sources

Allen, Richard. *The Social Passion: Religion and Social Reform in Canada, 1914–1928*. Toronto: University of Toronto Press, 1971.
Bender, Urie A. *Four Earthen Vessels: Biographical Profiles of Oscar Burkholder, Samuel F. Coffman, Clayton F. Derstine, and Jesse B. Martin*. Kitchener, ON: Herald, 1982.
Billson, Janet Mancini. *Keepers of the Culture: The Power of Tradition in Women's Lives*. New York: Lexington, 1995.
Christie, Nancy, ed. *Households of Faith: Family, Gender, and Community in Canada, 1760–1969*. Montreal: McGill-Queen's University Press, 2002.
Chown, Alice, with an introduction by Diana Chown. *The Stairway*. Toronto: University of Toronto Press, 1988.
Denison, Flora. "War and Women." In *The Proper Sphere: Woman's Place in Canadian Society*, edited by Ramsay Cook and Wendy Mitchinson, 249–52. Toronto: Oxford University Press, 1976.
Elshtain, Jean Bethke. *Women and War*. New York: Basic Books, 1987.

English, John, and Kenneth McLaughlin. *Kitchener: An Illustrated History.* Waterloo, ON: Wilfrid Laurier University Press, 1983.
Epp, Frank H. *Mennonites in Canada, 1786-1920: The History of a Separate People.* Toronto: Macmillan, 1974.
Epp, Marlene G. *Mennonite Women in Canada: A History.* Winnipeg: University of Manitoba Press, 2008.
———. "Nonconformity and Nonresistance: What Did It Mean to Mennonite Women?" In *Changing Roles of Women within the Christian Church in Canada*, edited by Elizabeth Gillan Muir and Marilyn Färdig Whiteley, 55-74. Toronto: University of Toronto Press, 1995.
Evans, Suzanne. *Mothers of Heroes, Mothers of Martyrs: World War I and the Politics of Grief.* Montreal: McGill-Queen's University Press, 2007.
Fletcher, Wendy. "The Garden of Women's Separateness: Women in Canadian Anglicanism Since 1945." In *Seeds Scattered and Sown: Studies in the History of Canadian Anglicanism*, edited by Norman Knowles, 280-320. Toronto: ABC, 2008.
Francis, R. Douglas, Richard Jones, and Donald B. Smith. *Destinies: Canadian History since Confederation.* Toronto and Montreal: Harcourt, 2000.
Friesen, Paul. "Citizenship, Worship, and Mission: Three Sources of Anglican Identity during the National Era." In *Seeds Scattered and Sown: Studies in the History of Canadian Anglicanism*, edited by Norman Knowles, 112-47. Toronto: ABC, 2008.
Grayzel, Susan R. *Women and the First World War.* London: Pearson, 2002.
Harder, Laureen. *Risk and Endurance: A History of Stirling Avenue Mennonite Church.* Waterloo, ON: Stirling Avenue Mennonite Church, 2003.
Heath, Gordon. "Canadian Churches and War: An Introductory Essay and Annotated Bibliography." *McMaster Journal of Theology and Ministry* 12 (2010-2011) 61-124.
Heyman, Neil M. *Daily Life during World War I.* Westport, CT: Greenwood, 2002.
Knowles, Norman. "'By the Mouth of Many Messengers': Mission and Social Service in Canadian Anglicanism (1867-1945)." In *Seeds Scattered and Sown: Studies in the History of Canadian Anglicanism*, edited by Norman Knowles, 148-200. Toronto: ABC, 2008.
Loewen, Royden. *From the Inside Out: The Rural Lives of Mennonite Diarists, 1863-1929.* Winnipeg: University of Manitoba Press, 1999.
Lougheed, Peter. *Letters from Flanders Fields: The Letters of Pvt. William Moses Kedey to His Parents Henam and Annie Kedey 1915-1916.* Ottawa: Printed by Author, 2001.
Marr, Lucille. *The Transforming Power of a Century: Mennonite Central Committee and Its Evolution in Ontario.* Waterloo, ON: Pandora, 2003.
Morton, Desmond, and G. Wright. *Winning the Second Battle: Canadian Veterans and the Return to Civilian Life, 1915-1930.* Toronto: University of Toronto Press, 1987.
Prentice, Alison, Paula Bourne, Gail Cuthburt Brandt, Beth Light, Wendy Michinson, and Naomi Black. *Canadian Women: A History.* Toronto: Harcourt Brace, 1996.
Regehr, T. D. "Lost Sons: The Canadian Mennonite Soldiers of World War II." *Mennonite Quarterly Review* 66 (1992) 461-80.
Roth, Lorraine. *Willing Service: Stories of Ontario Mennonite Women.* Waterloo, ON: Mennonite Historical Society of Ontario, 1992.
Shaw, Amy J. *Crisis of Conscience: Conscientious Objection in Canada during the First World War.* Vancouver: University of British Columbia Press, 2009.
Socknat, Thomas. *Witness against War: Pacifism in Canada 1900-1945.* Toronto: University of Toronto Press, 1987.

Vance, Jonathan. *Death So Noble: Memory, Meaning, and the First World War.* Vancouver: University of British Columbia Press, 1997.

Van Die, Marguerite. "Revisiting 'Separate Spheres': Women, Religion, and the Family in Mid-Victorian Brantford, Ontario." In *Households of Faith: Family, Gender, and Community in Canada 1760–1969*, edited by Nancy Christie, 234–63. Montreal: McGill-Queen's University Press, 2002.

Whiteley, Marilyn Fardig. *Canadian Methodist Women, 1766–1925: Marys, Marthas, Mothers in Israel.* Waterloo, ON: Wilfrid Laurier University Press, 2005.

Name Index

Aitken, Max (Lord Beaverbrook), 94
Almond, John, 9, 26, 248, 250–53, 257
Armitage, W. J., 158
Asquith, Herbert, 53
Asselin, Olivar, 85, 87, 90

Beattie, William, 253
Bégin, Louis-Nazaire, 6, 76, 79, 85, 90, 96, 253
Belcourt, Napoleon-Antoine, 79, 81
(Pope) Benedict XV, 17, 36, 43, 52–53, 245, 248
(Pope) Benedict XVI, 44
Bennett, R. B., 232
Bird, Will, 256–58, 260
Black, Ernest Garside, 193
Borden, Robert, 6–7, 75–76, 79, 81, 85–87, 91, 94, 115, 179, 199–200, 229, 232, 247–48, 278
Bourassa, Henri, 57–58, 79–80, 88, 92, 94, 96
Bourque, Thomas-Jean, 87–88
Boyd, W. J., 157
Brohman, George, 42
Brooke, Rupert, 192
Brown, F. G., 107
Bruchési, Paul, 7, 76, 79–80, 85, 91–93
Budka, Nykyta, 36, 52
Buck, Percy G., 190
Burke, Alfred E., 43, 49–50, 245–48

Burkholder, Oscar, 276
Burnett, H. W., 119–21
Burwash, Nathaniel, 245
Byng, Julian, 248

Carman, Albert, 105, 107
Carpenter, A. D., 178
Casey, Timothy, 39
Caswell, W. B., 116
Chadwick, Ethel, 44
Charlebois, Charles, 89
Chown, S. D., 103, 105–7, 109, 113–16, 118–19, 127–28
Church, Tommy, 63
Clare, George, 205
Clarke, William R., 165
Cody, H. J., 154, 158, 160, 164
Coffman, S. F., 234
Cole, S. G., 190, 192
Creighton, W. B., 105, 127
Cressman, Susannah, 266, 268, 270–72
Cromwell, Oliver, 172
Cummings, J. P., 42
Currie, Arthur, 248, 250, 253

D'Aigle, Louis-Cyriaque, 84
Descarries, J. A., 93
DesRosiers, Henri, 85
Dinnick, W. S., 62
Dixon, 184
Doherty, Charles J., 44, 59–61, 91, 247
Doherty, Marcus, 61

285

Name Index

Donovan, William, 43
Drummond, Lewis, 60

Eakin, Thomas, 142–43, 148–49
Eby, Elgin, 270
Emard, Joseph, 50
Euler, William D., 204

Fallis, George O., 108, 111
Fallon, Michael, 24, 39, 44, 49, 59–60, 90
Farrell, A. C., 123–24
Farquharson, William, 186, 188
Farthing, John Cragg, 155
Ferdinand, Franz, 3, 36, 52, 73
Fitzpatrick, Charles, 37, 44
Francoeur, Joseph-Napoléon, 96
Frost, Harry A., 109–11
Fuller, Andrew, 172

Gaudet, Jean V., 83
Gordon, C. W., (Ralph Conner), 135, 144–45, 192, 256
Gouin, Lomer, 81, 90, 96
Gould, L. M., 256
Graham, E. E., 115, 255
Graham, Hugh (Lord Atholstan), 95
Graves, Robert, 257
Green, H., Elmer, 187
Gronlid, Hjalmar O., 213
Groulx, Lionel, 7, 76, 91, 97

Hale, Arthur, 177
Hall, Caroline, 271
Harris, W. F., 247
Harrison, Charles Yale, 256, 260
Hart, E. I., 34, 60
Head, Bessie Porter, 269
Hertzer, John, 207
Herzer, Traugott, 215
Hingston, William, 61
Hitler, Adolf, 11, 149
Hobson, John A., 21

Hocken, Horatio, 52
Howland, Miles P., 41
Hughes, Sam, 48–49, 58, 82, 86–87, 244–46

James, Cecil, 276
Jonson, Bjorn B., 213

Kaiser Wilhelm II, 28, 141, 143, 149, 179, 182, 185, 198, 201–2
Kent, H. A., 252
Ker, Robert, 158
Kilpatrick, G. G. D., 252
King George, 165
King, William Lyon Mackenzie, 60
Kitchener, Earl, 137
Knox, E. M., 279–80

Laferté, Hector, 96
Landry, Pierre-Amand, 79
Laurier, Wilfrid, 19, 59, 79, 81, 94, 96, 179, 223
Lavell, A. E., 124
Lavergne, Armand, 90, 96
Lavik, John R., 213
LeBlanc, Édouard, 83, 88
Luce, C. E., 165

Macaulay, A. C., 61
MacDonald, Alexander, 39, 46
MacDonald, A. C., 59
MacKenzie, D. F., 145–46
MacNeill, John, 177
Matthews, T. F., 189
Maxwell, John, 54
McCarthy, Edward, 39
McClung, Nellie, 266–67
McCrae, John, 145
McCrimmon, A. L., 174, 182
McGee, D'Arcy, 55
McGivney, Michael J., 44
McIntosh, Jonathan, 191
McLaughlin, C. J., 55

Name Index

McNally, James T., 39
McNeil, Neil, 34, 39–41, 53, 60, 63, 90
Meighen, Arthur, 86
Mignault, Arthur, 81
Montague, C. E., 257
Moore, T., Albert, 109, 114, 126
Morrison, James, 39, 62, 246
Mullowney, Henry S., 189–90, 182
Murdoch, A. J., 253
Murphy, Charles, 60, 89
Murray, Joseph L., 62
Murray, Norman, 51

Napoleon, Bonaparte, 143, 172
Nasmith, George G., 175, 187
Nobles, H. R., 258

O'Brien, Cornelius, 37
O'Brien, Michael, 39
O'Gorman, John J., 49, 55, 61, 88, 247, 250
O'Leary, Arthur, 60
O'Leary, Peter, 26, 48
O'Leary, Louis, 39
O'Neill, A. B., 59
O'Neill, John, 63
Oliver, E. H., 252, 256
Osborne, R. J., 166
Owen, Wilfred, 192

Perley, George, 118
Perrier, Philippe, 7, 76
Plumptre, H. P., 157, 163
Poirier, Pascal, 79, 87–88
Porter, Henry A., 185
Power, Charles, 60
Power, Lawrence Geoffrey, 38

Redmond, John, 53–54
Rehwinkel, Alfred, 208
Richardson, John, 161
Riel, Louis, 81
Robb, A. D., 117–18, 122, 124

Robidoux, Ferdinand J., 87–88
Rogers, Albert S., 230
Roper, J. C., 253
Rowell, Newton Wesley, 52, 179
Ryan, Patrick, 39
Ryan, William J., 41
Ryerson, Egerton, 223
Sammut, A., 42
Sandager, C. N., 213
Sassoon, Siegfried, 192
Schwermann, Albert, 214
Scollard, Joseph, 90
Scott, Ephraim, 141–42
Scott, F. G., 23, 255–56
Sharpless, Isaac, 226
Shields, T. T., 8, 176, 181–82, 184, 187, 191–92
Shuttleworth, Nicholas, 182
Sinnott, Alfred, 39
Smyth, J. Paterson, 158
Smiley, Albert, 223
Sperling, H. A., 202
Spratlin, Frederick, 145
Spratt, Michael J., 39–40
Spurgeon, Charles Haddon, 172, 184
Steacy, R. H., 48–50, 245, 247
Sullivan, William W., 38
Sweeny, James Fielding, 164

Tappert, C. R., 202
Thomas, Edward, 192
Thomas, H. E., 117
Thorneloe, George, 153
Trotter, Bernard, 175, 192
Turner, R. E. W., 249
Turpin, George, 122, 129

VanLoon, George Henry, 182

Wallace, O. C. S., 175
Warner, D. V., 251–52
Warren, J. R. H., 28
Watson, Thomas, 177

Watterson, C. T., 126–27
Webb, George T, 177
Weigel, W. G., 199, 205
Whelan, Matthew, 60, 63, 88
Williams, David, 161
Willison, Nils, 206
Wilson, T. A., 125
Woodsworth, J. S., 115
Workman, Wolston, 61, 248, 250

Yoder, Orie, 268

Zavitz, Charles A., 229

Subject Index

Acadians, 7, 78, 87, 95, 97
Act of Union, 79
American Expeditionary Force, 47
American Friend's Service
   Committee, 230
Ancient Order of Hibernians, 45,
   54–55
Anglican Women Association, 265
Annual Conference of International
   Arbitration, 223
Arbitration, 2, 236
Armenian Genocide, 4, 11, 28
Armistice, 156, 165–67, 252
Attendance (postwar church),
   127–29
Atrocity Accounts, 27, 175–76, 184,
   230, 243
Atheists, 186
Austria-Hungary, 3, 198, 201, 206,
   209

Battles
   Amiens, 126, 145
   Flers-Courcelette, 83
   Jutland, 137
   Lens, 126
   Mons, 252
   Passchendaele, 4, 126
   Somme, 3, 114, 118, 126, 180,
      247
   Verdun, 180
   Vimy, 3, 83, 118, 126, 146, 162,
      249
   Ypres, 3, 110, 118, 126, 184, 187

Belgium, 3, 8, 43, 56, 79, 143, 148,
   174–75
Belgium Relief Fund, 40, 44, 152,
   154
Berlin (Ontario). *See* Kitchener, ON
Boers, 27
Boy Scouts, 108
British Expeditionary Force, 54
Buddhists, 186
Bulgaria, 3

Cadet Movement, 108, 173
Canadian Army Medical Corps,
   126, 175
Canadian Defense League, 173
Canadian Lutheran Commission
   for Soldier's and Sailor's
   Welfare, 213
Canadian Patriotic Fund, 152, 154,
   273
Canadianization, 1, 10, 166–67,
   200, 210–11, 215
Catholic Army Huts, 56, 61–62, 250
Catholic Church Extension Society,
   52
Catholic Order of Foresters, 45
Catholic Mutual Benefit
   Association, 59
Catholic Truth Society, 59
CEF, 2, 3, 8, 35, 40, 44–45, 47–50,
   56, 61, 77, 104, 111, 113, 126,
   128, 153, 162, 189, 205, 241,
   250, 252

Central Canada Synod (Lutheran), 205
Chaplain Service, 245, 249–50
Chaplain's Social Service Report, 250
Chaplaincy, 25, 44, 49, 55, 61, 102, 109, 116–18, 138, 186, 189, 241–62
Church Parade, 120, 123
Church Schools (closure of), 9
Church Union, 1
Confederation, 1
Conference of Historic Peace Churches, 9, 220, 235,
Confucians, 186
Congrès de la langue française, 97
Conscientious Objectors, 10, 202, 233, 273, 278
Conscription, 7, 9, 28–29, 35, 54, 57–60, 85, 88, 91–95, 114–15, 161–62, 179–82, 199, 228–29, 233–35, 242, 244–45, 272, 278
Conscription (Australian), 58
Convention Assembly (Baptist), 174
Covenanter Flag, 135
Covenanters, 148–49
Crisis of Faith (of soldiers), 128
Crusade, 27, 111, 143, 160, 175

Daughters of the King, 274
Days of Humiliation/Humble Supplication/Repentance, 24, 137–39, 160, 163, 165
Deaconess House, 276
Department of Evangelism and Social Reform, 109
Department of Militia and Defense, 58, 113–14
Diocesan Women's Auxiliary, 267–68, 271

Easter Monday (1916), 54
Eastern Orthodoxy, 5

Enemy Aliens (in Canada), 201–12, 220, 231–32, 234, 264, 270
episcopus castrensis, 50
Ethnic Minority Groups
  Aboriginal, 35, 37, 42
  Danish, 8, 197
  Finnish, 8, 197
  German, 8, 37, 42, 183, 197
  Hungarian, 139
  Icelandic, 8, 197, 205
  Irish, 34–74
  Italians, 37
  Norwegian, 8, 197, 213–14
  Polish, 37
  Scottish, 35, 36
  Swedish, 8, 197, 206, 235
  Ukranians, 37, 52
Evangelism (of soldiers), 119–22, 177, 188, 190–91

Fathers of Confederation, 97
Federal Council of Churches, 253
Fédération nationale Saint-Jean-Baptiste, 93
Fenians, 54
Forward Movements, 11
France, 3
Franco-Ontarians, 7, 95
Friend's Ambulance Unit, 229
Fundamentalism (or Modernism), 176, 191–92, 259

General Assembly (Presbyterian), 133–34, 136–41, 148
General Strike, 255
General Synod (Anglican), 156–57
Girl Guides, 274
Girl's Friendly Societies, 274
Great War Veterans Association, 62, 206–7

Hague Conference
  First (1899), 2
  Second (1907), 2

Halifax Explosion, 163
Havergal College, 279
Home Mission Work, 1
Home Rule (Irish), 53–54, 56

Imperial Navy (German), 47
Imperial Order of the Daughters of the Empire, 273–74
Imperialism, 15, 18–19, 21, 43, 260
Internment Camps, 201
Interwar Period, 11
Italian National Club of Toronto, 45
Italy, 3

Jesuits, 42, 61
Jews, 186

Khaki Leagues, 274
Kitchener (Berlin, ON), 9, 201, 224, 266, 270
Kitchener Ladies' Aid, 272
Kiwanis, 62
Knights of Columbus, 44–45, 56, 61, 250
Knox College, 135, 145–46

Latter Day Saints, 186
League of Nations, 11, 236
London Yearly Meeting (Quaker), 218, 227
Lower House (Anglican), 157, 159
Lusitania, 148, 184, 203, 243

Masons, 62
Memorial Cross, 277
Memorials, 146–47, 170–71
Mennonite Central Committee, 235
Mennonite Conference of Canada, 233
Mennonite General Conference, 233
Mennonite Ladies Aid, 266
Methodist Army and Navy Board, 24, 104, 114, 118, 125–26
Methodist Code of Discipline, 119

Métis, 81
Militarism, 145, 155, 172–73, 177, 201, 205, 224, 226, 260, 270
Military Cross (for valor), 49
Military Service Act (1917), 28–29, 59, 61, 92, 161, 219, 227–30, 232–33
Military Service Board (Presbyterian), 139
Military Voters Act, 278
Militia Act of 1906, 226
Missouri Synod (Canada District—Lutheran), 209
Moral Issues, 147, 160, 188–89, 279
   Sexual Diseases/Immorality, 7, 104, 117–19
   Alcohol/Prohibition/Temperance, 7, 104, 109–10, 116–19
   Card Playing, 117–18
Muscular Christianity, 108, 258

Nation-building Churches, 17, 18
National Covenant, 135
National Lutheran Council, 215
National Register, 7, 76, 161
National Service Cards, 232
National Service Registration, 232
Non-Resistant Relief Organization (Quaker), 9, 218, 227

Orange Order, 52–53, 87–88, 245
Ordre de Jacques Cartier, 97
Ottoman Turks, 3

Pacifism, 106, 113, 115, 142, 178, 218–19, 222, 226, 273
Papacy, 52
Pastoral Care, 10, 11
Patriotic Fund, 22, 40–41, 44–45, 80, 205
(The) Peace and Arbitration Society (Quakers), 224
Peace Association of Friends, 223
Peace Committee, 230

Peace Conference (1901), 225
Pentecostals, 5
Poland, 56
Postwar, 124–27, 178–79
Prohibition, 126
Providence, 242
Prussian Militarism, 39–40

Quebec Act of 1774, 80
Queen Mary's Needlework Guilds, 274
Quiet Revolution, 77

Recruitment by Clergy, 24, 40–41, 44, 112, 114
Red Cross, 40–41, 44, 152, 154, 263, 272–73
Reformation, 214
Regulation 17, 89–91, 97
Religious Tensions
    Protestant-Catholic, 2, 18–19, 29–30, 34, 75, 87–98, 182–83
    Catholic-Catholic, 18, 75, 87–98
    Protestant-Protestant. Over Chaplaincy Issues, 25, 252
Returned Soldiers (condition of), 124–27, 187
Revival, 123, 249, 251
Riots
    Montreal, 29
    Quebec City, 59, 95–96, 180
Rotary, 62
Russia, 3, 199, 209–10, 236, 254

Sabbath, 116
Sailor's Guilds, 274
Saint Stanislaus Novitiate of the Society of Jesus, 61
Salvation Army, 5, 186, 245
Salvation Through Sacrifice, 122
Schools (closure of German), 210–11
Silver Cross, 277, 279

Social Gospel, 20–21, 147, 189–90, 251, 257
Société Saint-Jean-Baptiste, 93
Soldiering (idealized), 26
Soldier's Comfort Leagues, 274
Spanish Influenza, 4
Spring (German) Offensive, 164
Statistics
    Denominational Percentages in Canada, 1
    War Casualties, 3, 4, 16, 185
    Canadian Troop Enlistment, 3, 36, 45–48, 50–51, 57, 77, 82–87, 113–14, 153, 183, 245–46
    Canada's Irish Catholic Recruits by Birth, 64
    Recruitment by Denomination, 65
    Social Analysis of Recruitments, 66–67
    Catholics in the Ottawa Valley, 68–69
    Irish Catholic Canadian Nurses, 70
Suffragist War Auxiliaries, 274
Swedish Augustana Synod, 206

Treaty of Brest-Litovsk, 3
Treaty of Versailles, 11

Ukrainian Catholic, 39, 52
Union Government, 29, 58–60, 161–62, 179, 199
United Church of Canada, 146
United Empire Loyalist, 198
United States, 145, 171, 183–84, 198, 203, 213, 229, 234
Universities/Colleges
    McMaster, 173–74, 176, 178–79, 182, 185, 189
    St. Francis Xavier University, 45
    St. Joseph's (New Brunswick), 59
Upper House (Anglican), 157

Valcartier Camp, 109
Victory Loan, 154
Vote (women's), 267, 278, 280

War Measures Act, 201, 227, 231
War Service Commission of the General Synod (Anglican), 254
War Victim's Relief Committee, 229
Wars
    American War of Independence, 38
    Napoleonic War, 155, 218
    War of 1812, 39, 222
    Crimean War, 26
    Franco-Prussian War, 173
    South African War (Boer War), 2, 6, 15–33, 38, 48, 62, 79, 82, 115, 133, 148, 155, 223–24, 244, 248
    Second World War, 4, 11, 15, 37, 259
    Cold War, 4, 134

Wartime Elections Act, 207, 227, 232, 278
Weariness of War, 163
Woman's Guild, 271

YMCA, 108, 244, 250, 274

Zimmermann Telegram, 184

Scripture Index

Exodus
15:3 — 176

Psalm
46:10 — 186
76:7–10 — 176

John
3:14–15 — 191
15:13 — 170

Romans
12:2 — 269

1 Corinthians
11 — 270
16:13 — 193

1 Timothy
2 — 269

www.ingramcontent.com/pod-product-compliance
Lightning Source LLC
Chambersburg PA
CBHW061430300426
44114CB00014B/1627